The Critical Response to
Saul Bellow

Recent Titles in
Critical Responses in Arts and Letters

The Critical Response to
Saul Bellow

Edited by
Gerhard Bach

Critical Responses in Arts and Letters, Number 20
Cameron Northouse, Series Adviser

GREENWOOD PRESS
Westport, Connecticut • London

Library of Congress Cataloging-in-Publication Data

The critical response to Saul Bellow / edited by Gerhard Bach.
        p.   cm.—(Critical responses in arts and letters, ISSN
  1057–0993 ; no. 20)
      Includes bibliographical references and index.
      ISBN 0–313–28370–2 (alk. paper)
      1. Bellow, Saul—Criticism and interpretation.   I. Bach, Gerhard,
  1943–   . II. Series.
  PS3503.E4488Z618   1995
  813'.52—dc20   95–22756

British Library Cataloguing in Publication Data is available.

Library of Congress Catalog Card Number: 95–22756
ISBN: 0–313–28370–2
ISSN: 1057–0993

First published in 1995

Greenwood Press, 88 Post Road West, Westport, CT 06881
An imprint of Greenwood Publishing Group, Inc.

Printed in the United States of America

The paper used in this book complies with the
Permanent Paper Standard issued by the National
Information Standards Organization (Z39.48–1984).

10 9 8 7 6 5 4 3 2 1

Copyright Acknowledgments

Contents

Short Fiction: *Mosby's Memoirs and Other Stories* (1968);
  Him with His Foot in His Mouth and Other Stories (1984)

More Die of Heartbreak (1987)

A Theft (1989)

The Bellarosa Connection (1989)

"Something to Remember Me By" (1990)

Series Foreword

Critical Responses in Arts and Letters is designed to present a documentary history of highlights in the critical reception to the body of work of writers and artists and to individual works that are generally considered to be of major importance. The focus of each volume in the series is basically historical. The introductions to each volume are themselves brief histories of the critical response an author, artist, or individual work has received. This response is then further illustrated by reprinting a strong representation of the major critical reviews and articles which collectively have produced the author's, artist's, or work's critical reputation.

The scope of *Critical Responses in Arts and Letters* knows no chronological or geographical boundaries. Volumes under preparation include studies of individuals from around the world and in both contemporary and historical periods.

Each volume is the work of an individual author, who surveys the entire body of criticism on a single author, artist, or work. The editor then selects the best material to depict the critical response received by an author or artist over his/her entire career. Documents produced by the author or artist may also be included when the editor finds that they are necessary to a full understanding of the materials at hand. In circumstances where previous, isolated volumes of criticism on a particular individual or work exist, the editor carefully selects material that better reflects the nature and directions of the critical response over time.

In addition to the introduction and the documentary section, the editor of each volume is free to solicit new essays on areas that may not have been adequately dealt with in previous criticism. Also, for volumes on living writers and artists, new interviews may be included, again at the discretion of the volume's editor. The volumes also provide a supplementary bibliography and are fully indexed.

While each volume in *Critical Responses in Arts and Letters* is unique, it is also hoped that in combination they form a useful documentary history of the critical response to the arts, and one that can be easily and profitably employed by students and scholars.

Cameron Northouse

Acknowledgments

The editor wishes to acknowledge the substantial support of the following: the contributors, journal editors, and publishers who granted permission to reprint the essays and reviews collected here; the publishers of the works by Saul Bellow for permission to reprint excerpts from his works; Gloria Cronin and Blaine Hall for permission to access the Saul Bellow archives at Brigham Young University; Kody Partridge for her assiduous compilation of the index and careful manuscript-editing; Mark Christiansen and Carol Lee Duffin for their editorial assistance; the College of Humanities at Brigham Young University for generous research support; Cameron Northouse for his guidance; and, particularly, Maureen Melino and Jane C. Lerner for their editorial support and valuable suggestions. Special thanks go to Gloria Cronin, Peter Hyland, and Brigitte Scheer-Schaezler for their contributions on the more recent works by Bellow. Their essays are printed here for the first time.

Chronology

1915	Born June 10 (officially recorded as July 10) in Lachine, Quebec, a suburb of Montreal, the youngest of the four children of Abraham Bellow and Liza Gordon Bellow, immigrants from St. Petersburg, Russia, in 1913.
1924	Bellow family moves to Chicago.
1933	Graduates from Tuley High School and enrolls at University of Chicago.
1935	Transfers to Northwestern University.
1937	Graduates from Northwestern with B. A. in anthropology and sociology.
1938	Returns to Chicago; joins WPA Writers' Project. Teaches at Pestalozzi-Froebel Teachers College until 1942.
1941	"Two Morning Monologues," first publication.
1942	"The Mexican General"; joins the editorial department of the Encyclopedia Britannica to work on M. J. Adler's "Great Book" series (until 1946).
1944	*Dangling Man*, first novel.
1946-48	Teaches English at the University of Minnesota.
1947	*The Victim*.
1948	Guggenheim Fellowship; travels to Paris and Rome; begins work on *The Adventures of Augie March*, segments of which are published between 1948 and 1950 in various magazines.
1949	"Sermon by Dr. Pep."
1950	Returns to live in New York; teaches at New York University; writes book reviews and articles for *Partisan Review*, *Commentary*, and other journals.
1951	"Looking for Mr. Green"; "By the Rock Wall"; "Address by Gooley MacDowell to the Hasbeens Club of Chicago."
1952	National Institute of Arts and Letters Award; joins faculty of Princeton as Creative Writing Fellow.

1953	*The Adventures of Augie March* (National Book Award); translates I. B. Singer's "Gimpel the Fool" from the Yiddish; joins faculty of Bard College.
1954	"The Gonzaga Manuscripts"; "The Wrecker" (one-act play).
1955	"A Father-to-be"; Guggenheim Fellowship; travels in Nevada and California.
1956	*Seize the Day*.
1958	"Leaving the Yellow House"; Ford Foundation grant.
1959	*Henderson the Rain King*.
1960-62	Co-editor of *The Noble Savage*; Friends of Literature Fiction Award.
1962	Moves to Chicago; Honorary Doctor of Letters, Northwestern University; joins Committee on Social Thought at the University of Chicago.
1963	Honorary Doctor of Letters, Bard College; edits *Great Jewish Short Stories*.
1964	*Herzog* (National Book Award, Fomentor Award, Prix International de Littérature); *The Last Analysis* premieres at the Belasco Theatre in New York City in October.
1965	"Out from Under," Orange Soufflé," "A Wen" (three one-act plays produced in 1966 as *Under the Weather* in London, Spoleto, and New York).
1967	"The Old System"; covers the Six-Day War for *Newsday*.
1968	*Mosby's Memoirs and Other Stories*; Jewish Heritage Award (B'nai B'rith); Croix de Chevalier des Arts et Lettres (France).
1970	*Mr. Sammler's Planet* (National Book Award).
1974	"Zetland: By a Character Witness."
1975	*Humboldt's Gift* (Pulitzer Prize).
1976	*To Jerusalem and Back: A Personal Account*; Nobel Prize for Literature; Neil Gunn Fellow (Scottish Arts Council).
1977	Gold Medal for the Novel (American Academy and Institute of Arts and Letters); Jefferson Lecture for the National Endowment for the Humanities.
1978	"A Silver Dish"; National Arts Club Gold Medal of Honor; New York premiere of Leon Kirchner's *Lily* (opera adaptation of *Henderson the Rain King*).
1982	*The Dean's December*.
1984	*Him with His Foot in His Mouth and Other Stories*; Commander of the Legion of Honor (France).
1985	Lachine Public Library renamed "Bibliothèque Municipale Saul Bellow."

1986   Film adaptation of *Seize the Day* produced for PBS by
           Robert Geller (producer) and Fielder Cook (director), with
           Robin Williams in the role of Tommy Wilhelm.
1987   *More Die of Heartbreak*.
1988   National Medal of Arts.
1989   *A Theft*; *The Bellarosa Connection*.
1990   "Something to Remember Me By"; republished in 1991
           together with the two novellas of the previous year as
           Something to Remember Me By: Three Tales.
1991   "A Half Life: An Autobiography in Ideas" (*Bostonia*).
1992   "Memoirs of a Bootlegger's Son" (from a 1954 manu-
           script).
1994   *It All Adds Up: From the Dim Past to the Uncertain
           Future* (nonfiction collection of previously published
           essays).
1995   "By the St. Lawrence" (story).

Introduction

"The artist labors in dreams."
Saul Bellow (1974)

The relationship between Saul Bellow and America has always been an ambiguous one. While he is respected as one of the finest writers of the twentieth century, he has neither enjoyed the status of fame of his Nobel predecessors Faulkner, Hemingway, and Steinbeck, nor has he become one of America's cult figures like Norman Mailer, with whom he is often compared in contrast. It seems as if Bellow has always resented the kind of publicity by which images are cultivated into icons, as though a too-close relationship with America, its political culture and intellectual milieu, would have imprisoning consequences. He disdains categorization, such as "Jewish-American" or "humanist." He has never cared to be a likable public figure; his public appearances have been rare, and when asked to address matters of public concerns he has invariably cut to the core of social adversities and needs. Thus, for five decades now, Saul Bellow has been a most persevering chronicler of America's restless search for a definable self, articulating more prominently and more consistently than any of his contemporaries the common needs and ills of American society at large. Each of his novels feels the pulse of its decade, exposing the social and intellectual issues at hand. None of his works allow for easy identification or rejection; as a consequence, none have gone uncontended — the controversies they address seem to beckon our response.

The numerous honors that have been bestowed upon Bellow suggest that, for many readers around the world, he is America's finest and most consistent writer of the present. Such prominence, again, has not come undisputed. Not in a single case has the critical response to Bellow's oeuvre been unanimous. Not even *Herzog*, which is generally considered his worthiest achievement, has gone unchallenged. While some have claimed in Bellow America's greatest writer of the twentieth century, others have discounted him as discouragingly redundant, tell-

ing the same story over and over again. While over the past decade
revisions in critical theory have expanded the scope of Bellow criticism, as in new historicist or feminist approaches, many of the "old"
questions persist: Is Bellow an "affirmativist" or a "negativist" writer?
Which tradition is the more prominent for this "hyphenated American"
— the Jewish or the American? To what extent is Bellow's voice identical with that of his narrators? Indeed, are their views of the contemporary world shared by their author? To these and other questions
and challenges, when directed at his art, the author himself has
generally responded with the same disinterestedness, mockery, and
occasional disdain that make his characters so distinctive. However,
when directed at the issues themselves — whether social, philosophical, ethical, or otherwise — Bellow has never been diffident to the
public's response. Thus, to see Bellow engaged, since the 1950s, in an
ongoing exchange of ideas with his readers, reviewers, and critics
reveals to us a continuous narrative containing the author's views of
America and his position on its most pressing concerns in the twentieth
century. While Bellow has professed the convenience of self-protection
in having his characters speak his mind, this protective veil has become
transparent with time, so much so that what we "know" about Saul
Bellow today is simultaneously fed from the two sources of fact and
fiction. It is a condition Bellow himself appears to favor, as he usually
refuses to respond to questions pertaining to personal convictions,
saying in effect that there is nothing worth knowing about him that he
hasn't already addressed in his books.

The glimpses of himself that Bellow has offered, through his fiction, essays, interviews, and public addresses, do reveal consistent patterns and specific recurring concerns. In summary, they disclose an artist highly sensitive to the erosion of the individual's *contrat social* in
the twentieth century. Here is a writer and intellectual whose primary
business has been to reveal, in fiction as well as in fact, the artist's
struggle with the world's overvaluation of the material, and to champion the survival of art in an age that worships the dehumanizing
forces of technology. As a result of such an ongoing dialogue with the
public,[1] the Bellow-image that has developed is composed of facets
partly created and partly self-created, and a relationship of artist and
audience has emerged which befits Melville's observation about the
interchange of reader and writer, when he claims:

> No man can read a fine author, and relish him to his very bones, while he
> reads, without subsequently fancying to himself some ideal image of the
> man and his mind. And if you rightly look for it, you will almost always
> find that the author himself has somewhere furnished you with his own
> picture.[2]

These observations on the writer as artist *and* public figure provide, in part, a referential frame for the present collection of Bellow
criticism. Individually, the reviews and essays will connect the reader

to the source of Bellow's own voice and the diverse modes of his artistic expression. Collectively, they serve a double purpose. On the one hand, they present a critical kaleidoscope of the prominent themes issuing from Bellow's art. On the other hand, they vividly reflect the changes in the field of criticism itself — its purpose, its responsibility to the author as well as to the reader, its perception of art and the artist, its function as an agent for social change, to name only a few. Criticism, as the diverse examples in this collection show, is as much a reader's self-definition and self-assertion as it is a critiquing of the authorial or narrative stance projecting from an individual work. In this panoramic view, the present collection also illustrates that, over time, Bellow's reviewers and critics have come to respond not only to Bellow but also to each other. Speaking to each other across the boundaries of critical theories, historical differences, and cultural diversifications, the community of Bellow readers, scholars, and critics continues to generate new questions and responses to Bellow's oeuvre. In many cases they keep returning to earlier fictions with questions provoked by the author's more recent work.

Bellow himself has his own way of dealing with the critics and scholars. His opinion of the critical profession at large has been consistently unfavorable. In *Humboldt's Gift*, the would-be artist Von Humboldt Fleisher expresses, in his usual venomous distrust of the world, what he thinks about the "educated": "For them the whole purpose of art is to suggest and inspire ideas and discourse. [They] are a thinking rabble at the stage of what Marx called primitive accumulation. Their business is to reduce masterpieces to discourse."[3] While Bellow typically keeps a safe distance by putting this verdict into the mouth of an artist who utterly fails in his professed art, it reverberates the author's personal exasperation with the academic world and its propensity for self-adoration. To be sure, Bellow himself has always been part of the academic establishment, most prominently so in his lasting association with the Committee on Social Thought at the University of Chicago, which he joined in 1962 and where he served as chairman for a time. But his participation in the life of the university has always been that of the artist and intellectual in search of answers rather than that of the academic dispensing scientific "knowledge." Indeed, Bellow would flaunt the separation of science, intellect, and art as artificial differentiations counterproductive to the purpose and well-being of society. In the fifties, well before this became an issue in the universities themselves, and well before he would address these dichotomies in his fictions as he later does in *Humboldt's Gift*, *The Dean's December*, and *More Die of Heartbreak*, Bellow publicly clarified his vigilant position in such essays as "The University as Villain" (1957) and "Deep Readers of the World, Beware!" (1959). In both, he cautions against intellectual posturing, culture-idolatry, and the downgrading of the imagination. It is an issue surfacing almost regularly throughout his career, culminating at the time he receives the Nobel Prize in the mid-seventies; here Bellow no longer considers the issue characteristic solely of American culture — it has become a world-wide phenomenon. In 1974, speaking at a conference in Italy, he accuses universities far and wide of breeding "educated philistinism" as "a new negative force."[4] And in his Nobel acceptance speech at Stockholm in 1976 he startles the festive audience with his thoughts regarding the universal fetishes of knowledge, attitude, and opinion and the deep-rooted antagonism among intellectuals to re-investigate their cherished "inventory of attitudes" about society, politics, the human mind, and art. Where attitudes replace thought, Bellow reminds us, the stabilizing center is lost. "What is at the center now? At the moment, neither art nor science, but mankind determining, in confusion and obscurity, whether it will endure or go under." And he demands: "At such a time it is essential to lighten ourselves, to dump encumbrances, including the encumbrances of education and all organized platitudes, to make judgments of our own, to perform acts of our own."[5]

Since then Bellow's bleak view and his contempt for "puffy-headed academics and intellectuals"[6] who have betrayed the arts has taken a slightly different turn. Today, Bellow asks more brazenly and directly how intellectual pursuits (the act of reading included) will affect our souls in a world that is attitude-ridden, fascinated by technological advancement, and bereft of spirituality. The human mind hovers in a void that has come to be the greater threat to humanity:

> To congratulate ourselves, however, on our educated enlightenment is simply an evasion of the real truth. We the "educated" cannot even begin to explain the technologies of which we make daily use. . . . Face to face with the technological miracles without which we could not live our lives, we are as backward as any savage, though education helps us to conceal this from ourselves and others.[7]

While such admonitions have been successful in keeping the American scholarly community mildly annoyed about Bellow's equable stance of "anti-modernism," what has apparently been more irritating are the answers he has proposed to counteract the decline of the human in the contemporary world. Such answers generally point to the forgotten or neglected spiritual realm of the human sphere and to art as its sole guardian. In the foreword to Allan Bloom's widely debated book about the decline of higher education in America, *The Closing of the American Mind* (1987), Bellow summarizes: "In the greatest confusion [of our age] there is still an open channel to the soul . . . and it is our business to keep it open, to have access to the deepest part of ourselves — to that part of us which is conscious of a higher consciousness, by means of which we make final judgments, and put everything together."[8] The irritation caused among contemporary readers by statements such as this stems from Bellow's persistent assertion of the existence of a spiritual world. It is a world as real as the physical, and all of

Bellow's protagonists struggle with its demands, which are the more pressing the more it is denied or rejected. That is Bellow's intent when, in the Nobel address, he speaks of the world's intoxicated consumerism, whose gravitational force pulls us into a collective apathy, a state where "the individual struggles with dehumanization for the possession of his soul."[9] A decade later, the argument is still the same, but the emphasis has become more focused, more openly defensive: "The soul has to find and hold its ground against hostile forces, sometimes embodied in ideas which frequently deny its very existence, and which indeed often seem to be trying to annul it altogether."[10]

The irritations Bellow seems to generate in America whenever he addresses matters of the soul are perhaps less a result of his alleged anti-intellectualism than of his allegation that artists as much as academics neglect their responsibility to instruct, enlighten, and heal. In effect Bellow says that the very beliefs of modernism run counter to the eminent spiritual needs of humanity. Since the publication of *The Dean's December* (1982), Bellow has dealt with the issues concerning the artist's social responsibility in ways more consistent, assertive, and perceptive than ever before, detailing a position that projects beyond polemics and marginalizations. Consequently, in what amounts to the writer's credo, Bellow today offers a more synchronized view of the artist as the voice of imagination and intellect:

> That poets — artists — should give new eyes to human beings, inducing them to view the world differently, converting them from fixed modes of experience, is ambition enough, if one must offer a purposive account of the artist's project. What makes that project singularly difficult is the disheartening expansion of trained ignorance and bad thought. For to put the matter at its baldest, we live in a thought-world, and the thinking has gone very bad indeed. Therefore the artist, whether or not he views himself as an intellectual, is involved in thought-struggles. Thinking alone will never cure what ails him, and any artist should be grateful for a naive grace which puts him beyond the need to reason elaborately. For me, the university has been the place of divestiture where I am able to find help in the laborious task of discarding bad thought.[11]

Throughout his career, Bellow has resorted to that "naive grace" as the condition which best defines — and protects — the artist's mind. It is a phrase inherited from Joseph Conrad, whose perception of the artistic process Bellow endorses. In fact, he builds his argument of the self as determined by spiritual forces largely on a Conradian notion when he observes that the artist appeals

> to that part of our being which is a gift, not an acquisition, to the capacity for delight and wonder . . . our sense of pity and pain, to the latent feeling of fellowship with all creation — and to the subtle but invincible conviction of solidarity that knits together the loneliness of innumerable hearts . . . which binds together all humanity — the dead to the living and the living to the unborn.[12]

This is the key to understanding Bellow and his protagonists — heroic in their "invincible conviction" of a common human bond, paranoid in their fear and pain of losing this connection, and comical or absurd in their pursuit of the "higher" worlds among the lower depths of urban America. It is also the key for many critical perceptions to unlock Bellow's technique of internal oppositions, of the intricate connections between the common and the extraordinary (*Mr. Sammler's Planet*), the quotidian and the eternal (*Herzog*), the material and the transcendent (*Humboldt's Gift*), memory and oblivion (*The Bellarosa Connection*). It is the unresolvable dialectic of the *marriage* of heaven and hell, that unmistakable Blakean world, to which Bellow always takes recourse. The images are multifarious, but the axiom is constant: Joseph's attempt at balancing incompatible worlds in *Dangling Man*; Augie's search for the "axial lines" in *The Adventures of Augie March*; Henderson's inner voice calling "I want! I want!" in the African jungle of *Henderson the Rain King*; Wilhelm's romantic impulse to be united with humanity in *Seize the Day* (an impulse Herzog will experience in his own version of the romantic self and Mr. Sammler in his version of the disillusioned modern):

> And in the dark tunnel, in the haste, heat, and darkness which disfigure and make freaks and fragments of nose and eyes and teeth, all of a sudden, unsought, a general love for all these imperfect and lurid-looking people burst out in Wilhelm's breast. He loved them. They were his brothers and his sisters. He was imperfect and disfigured himself, but what difference did that make if he was united with them by this blaze of love?[13]

And Bellow continues tapping the Conradian source of human frailty and compassion, albeit with stronger epistemological overtones, in *Humboldt's Gift* (Citrine's search for transcendence towards a higher self); *The Dean's December* (Corde's desire to resurrect truth from a world of "appearances"); and *More Die of Heartbreak* (Benn Crader's desire for purification of the soul and its consummation in Eros). While none of these passionate questers attain their objects of desire, their commitment to the contract they have established with their spiritual self remains intact; it is their perseverance against all odds — and consequently their dangling between states of self-aggrandizement and self-effacement — which renders Bellow's protagonists so absurdly heroic.

The parameters Bellow establishes with his major theme and his predominant mode of characterization have placed him squarely outside the major traditions and movements in the twentieth century. He writes against the grain of literary fashions and cultural dictum. As far as categorizations go, Bellow is unfashionably un-American — a novelist of ideas. His narrative patterns follow the models of Dostoevsky, Tolstoy, Conrad, and Thomas Mann. For him, plot stories are unreal. A reality created out of the imagination is more alive than factographic

accounts and perspectives "explaining" the world to itself. The epistemological weight of the issues he chooses to involve his characters in
seems to always point in the direction of European philosophical traditions. In fact, it can be poignantly argued that Bellow is the only
American writer of our century who has traversed the systems of
thought that have shaped our age, taking on in each of his novels a
particular school and its representatives, such as Romanticism and
existentialism in *Herzog*, the Enlightenment in *Mr. Sammler's Planet*,
or Transcendentalism (in both its American and European versions) in
Humboldt's Gift. In dealing so consistently with the values in the
Western hemisphere as formulated in these philosophies, Bellow has
often been accused of aloofness, a view he contests, noting that to be
literate in the twentieth century the individual must be thoroughly
exposed to modern ideologies, psychologies and philosophies. His own
exposure to these schools of thought, Bellow maintains, has been that
of the autodidact, and it is the nature of autodidacts to disregard intellectual boundaries and to open avenues of investigation where the
"learned" would tend to close them. Writers therefore should not be
expected to fashion their books to accepted thought and predominant
approaches to learning, but rather write for the "ideal" reader: "It may
well be that your true readers are not here as yet and that your books
will cause them to materialize."[14] As he does so often, Bellow takes
recourse to Conrad's defense of the artist's "separateness" from the
ordinary.

Positioning Bellow as a connecting point between American and
European traditions has been only one of the predominant critical
approaches to his work over the past five decades. Surveying the field,
the critical reader will find that the bases have been well covered, from
neocritical, psychological, and archetypal to structuralist, feminist, and
post-modern criticism. It is evident that the "Bellow industry" thrived
particularly in the 1970s, when canonical issues and the diversification
of critical theory found ample food in Bellow's oeuvre. Underlying this
multiplicity is a pattern which reveals that historically, Bellow criticism
has developed in three "generations."[15] The first of these, emerging in
the later 1960s, identifies in Bellow the writer who breaks with modernist orthodoxy, the tradition dominating American literary minds and
the critical profession since Eliot's "Wasteland"-projections and
Joyce's *Portrait of the Artist as a Young Man*. The first generation of
Bellow critics thus investigates the author's response to this tradition,
from *Dangling Man* to *Herzog*, using as a vantage point Bellow's own
assessment of cultural nihilism, the "unearned bitterness" projected by
the modernist position. Critiquing the post-war generation of writers,
Bellow finds it oddly ironic "that often the writer automatically scorns
contemporary life,"[16] and he clearly disavows this trend of obsessive
self-pitying and stylish negativism since it dodges the real issue at
hand, which for the artist is to portray individuals struggling with the

need to resolve by and for themselves the "bitterness" clutching at their hearts and minds.

At odds with this stylized pessimism, Bellow offers a mellowed optimism and a noticeable compassion with his characters' struggling determination, a stance which has earned him the label "affirmative humanist" from the critics. Several early monographs concentrate on this angle. The British literary historian Tony Tanner first sketches this position in *Saul Bellow* (1965), contrasting the author's approach to the American modernist tradition and detailing his European connections. In more systematic detail, Bellow's affirmativist stance is outlined in Keith Opdahl's *The Novels of Saul Bellow: An Introduction* (1967) and John J. Clayton's *Saul Bellow: In Defense of Man* (1968). Clayton clarifies three assumptions the moderns have made about our age which Bellow opposes: cultural nihilism, alienation, and the devaluation of the individual. Retracing Clayton's outline twenty years later, Brigitte Scheer-Schaezler summarizes Bellow's affirmativist humanism:

> Against cultural nihilism he posits that life is meaningful and that we can discover its meaning through art. Against alienation he holds the conviction of the brotherhood of human beings. Against the denigration of the individual he maintains that the individual is ennobled and dignified through pain and suffering, and that this is especially observable in our time.[17]

The second generation, largely of the 1970s and by now an international consortium of critics, broadens the critical spectrum to include investigations of individual issues arising from Bellow's humanist disposition, such as specific narrative devices and recurring thematic patterns. Sarah Blacher Cohen's *Saul Bellow's Enigmatic Laughter* (1974) explores humor as a rescuing device in the face of despair. Peter Bischoff, in *Saul Bellows Romane: Entfremdung und Suche* [*Saul Bellow's Novels: Alienation and Exploration*] (1975), examines the polarity of marginalization and the search for a center as a framework for each of Bellow's protagonists in their exploration of the self. Chirantan Kulshresta focuses on affirmation as a source of persistent anxiety in *Saul Bellow: the Problem of Affirmation* (1978). Yuzaburo Shibuya, in *Kaishin no Kiseki* [*Saul Bellow: The Conversion of the Sick Soul*] (1978), describes the patterns of the spiritual conversion from existential despair to transcending hope. Despite new objectives and an expanded thematic range, these perspectives do not principally challenge the first generation's assessment of Bellow as an anti-modernist and an affirmative humanist.

A reconsideration of such classifications comes with the new critical voices of the 1980s. Malcolm Bradbury, in *Saul Bellow* (1982), reassesses Bellow's relationship to the European and American intellectual traditions and the burdensome heritage of Romanticism in the modern age, and he repositions Bellow as creating, indeed as envisioning, his own historical self to be independent of any of these inherited traditions. Bradbury dispels the notion of the predominance of the transcendental in Bellow's works, as does Judie Newman in *Saul Bellow and History* (1984). Newman contests that Bellow's protagonists remain fully within a historical and experiential continuum, and that their inner tensions and anxieties reflect the outer tension created by the polarities of the temporal and the timeless. In *Les Romans de Saul Bellow: Tactiques Narratives et Strategies Oedipiennes* (1983), Claude Levy provides a structuralist interpretation of the narrative processes in Bellow's fiction, arguing for a clearer distinction between the narrational voice and the authorial voice. Liela Goldman, in *Saul Bellow's Moral Vision: A Critical Study of the Jewish Experience* (1983), reveals Bellow's debt to the Judaic tradition, arguing that this debt is more profound and functionally important in his novels than Bellow would concede. Daniel Fuchs sets a new standard in Bellow criticism with *Saul Bellow: Vision and Revision* (1984), which provides the first analysis of the writer's creative progress in a comparison of the different drafts of each work, thus displaying the process of artistic refinement of form, style, and idea. Jonathan Wilson, in a revisionist study titled *On Bellow's Planet: Readings from the Dark Side* (1985), addresses the dialectic nature of Bellow's "dangling" protagonists and the principle of indecision as characteristic of their/Bellow's contemporaneous attitudes, and thus provides a first energetic attempt to deconstruct the claims of the "affirmativists." Subsequently, Ellen Pifer has proposed a more moderate re-reading of Bellow in *Saul Bellow Against the Grain* (1990), although she does contend that Bellow's fictional stance is fundamentally radical in that he perpetually writes against the accepted notions of contemporary culture and, to the embarrassment of his trade, insists on the spiritual essence of the human being. Peter Hyland, in *Saul Bellow* (1992), espouses the idea that Bellow's eclecticism, his involvement in all the vagaries of twentieth-century traditions and intellectual ideas, is a positive signature of the writer's awareness of the polymorphous character of contemporary America. In a study based on Ken Wilber's theosophical model of transpersonal consciousness, Tetsuji Machida (*Saul Bellow's Transcendentalism*, 1993), disputes the notion that Bellow's transcendental stance replicates Emersonian transcendentalism.

With few exceptions, most of the summary readings of Bellow presuppose the existence of a common denominator by which to gauge his art. As singular perspectives, they represent individual approaches connecting Bellow's oeuvre as a unit to the (implied or expressed) unity of the critic's theoretical orbit. In contrast, this collection, in bringing together a multiplicity of voices over a historical distance of almost half a century, makes no attempt to present either Bellow's development or that of the critical responses as coherently connected. Instead, it presents Bellow criticism in all its divergence of thought and approach. The only parameters for selection applied here have been to connect, in each individual case, reviews with critical essays, and where feasible, to combine immediate responses (early reviews) with more distanced critical perspectives and revisions. Thus, Bellow's works and the responses they have received chronicle a major segment of the literary and intellectual life of post-war twentieth-century America. Bellow's oeuvre is particularly suited to such an exchange, since it presents, in all its facets, a rich reworking of the controlling concerns of our age, always perceived with the steady eye of the artist for whom his heritage has always been a condition rather than a tradition.

Notes

1. For more recent examples see "Mozart," *Bostonia* (Spring 1992): 31-35; "Intellectuals and Writers Since the Thirties" [Proceedings of "Intellectuals and Social Change in Central and Eastern Europe," Rutgers University, Newark, April 9-11, 1992], *Partisan Review* 4 (1992): 531-558; "There Is Simply Too Much to Think About," *Forbes* (14 Sep. 1992): 98-106.
2. Qtd. in Wayne C. Booth, *The Company We Keep: An Ethics of Fiction* (Berkeley: U of California P, 1988), 157.
3. Saul Bellow, *Humboldt's Gift* (New York: Viking, 1975), 32.
4. Saul Bellow, "A Matter of the Soul," *Opera News* (11 Jan 1974): 28.
5. Saul Bellow, "The Nobel Lecture," *American Scholar* 46 (1977): 324.
6. "Saul Bellow: An Autobiography in Ideas," Part 1: "A Half Life," *Bostonia* (Nov./Dec. 1990): 39.
7. "Mozart," 32.
8. "Foreword," *The Closing of the American Mind*, by Allan Bloom (New York: Simon & Schuster, 1987), 16-17.
9. "Nobel Lecture," 325.
10. "Foreword," 17.
11. Ibid., 17.
12. "Nobel Lecture," 316.
13. Saul Bellow, *Seize the Day* (Harmondsworth: Penguin, 1979), 84-85.
14. "Foreword," 15.
15. For a detailed account of the developments in Bellow criticism see Gloria Cronin and Liela H. Goldman's definitive "Bibliographical Essay" on Bellow in *Contemporary Authors Bibliographical Series,* vol. 1 ["American Authors"] (Detroit: Gale, 1986), 116-55; see also Ellen Pifer, "If the Shoe Fits: Bellow and Recent Critics," *Texas Studies in Literature and Language* 29.4 (1987): 442-57.
16. Saul Bellow, "Some Notes on Recent American Fiction," *Encounter* (Nov. 1963): 26-27.
17. Brigitte Scheer-Schaezler, "Saul Bellow and the Values of the Western World," *Saul Bellow Journal* 8.2 (1989): 3.

* * *

Dangling Man (1944)

Introducing an Important New Writer
Nathan L. Rothman

This is the journal of a man dangling between two worlds, or, perhaps more accurately, between two moments of existence in the one world we know, a split second of non-being extended immeasurably like a fissure growing beneath his feet. There might be many accidents in life to produce just such a hiatus: that time, for example, when a love affair that has crowded everything else out of the earth and sky is over and gone, and one gropes tenderly with hand and toe to learn to walk again; or a time when one is cast up out of the world, upon a reef somewhere, a magic mountain, as was Thomas Mann's Hans Castorp. In Saul Bellow's book it is a very common, contemporary accident that throws his man into the air to dangle. He is in that period between registration and induction, a matter of months filled with investigation (he is a Canadian and there is data to produce, papers, tests, records) and waiting. But this does not matter; it is a device for setting free the mind of Joseph (whose second name we do not ever learn) from the pattern of orderly living, and keeping it suspended out of pattern.

He is born again, free of the weight of accumulated attitudes, free of the people who reach to hold him (he is apart now, lonely and questioning), free of the emotions that have hitherto thought for him. He begins to see with the dispassionate eye of the painter — the mole in the armhollow, the vein beneath the surface of the skin, a stove's light in a room. He begins to think with the dispassionate mind of the anthropologist, beholding his wife, his father, his niece, his friends, the people in his boarding-house, as though he had just landed upon their continent, having foreknowledge of them with the freedom to examine coldly what he knows. And he examines his knowledge of himself, his world, the events in it, with a rare and miraculous

From *Saturday Review of Literature* (15 Apr. 1944): 27.

honesty. Now, as never before and probably never again, he can say exactly what he ought to feel, subtracting what he ought not. These pages, brief and pungent, are filled with inspired perception, from that true statement I have never seen anywhere else save in Joyce ("The child feels that his parents are pretenders; his real father is elsewhere and will someday come to claim him"), to such moments of self-searching as the credo on page 84, which begins: "I would rather die in the war than consume its benefits. . . . I would rather be a victim than a beneficiary. . . ."

Here, as elsewhere in literature when the mind is subject to the pressure of examination, it splits and turns upon itself in question. Joseph holds dialogue with his other self, whom he terms Tu As Raison Aussi, and even when he is talking to others it is not the ordinary words of outer discussion that he addresses to them, but the searching words that only he himself can answer. He understands their distrust almost as though he can see through them to the back; they are like cards he can turn over. The fact is he has been endowed with an extra dimension, and so long as he has it he has the gift of prophecy. It will drop from him, we feel, when he is at last inducted, when the spell breaks and he falls back into the heat of action. It is only at this point of suspension, where Bellow has caught him, that Joseph posses-ses this rare, cold clarity of vision. In this sense his is an interesting war document, his judgment upon the war world before he plunges beneath its surface. We shall read many afterthoughts when the war is over; this is a last forethought.

I have been trying to say also, in all this, that Saul Bellow is a writer of great original powers. Quite apart from the pressing interest of the material he has chosen for his book (a first novel, incidentally), he writes with obvious style and mastery, with a sharp cutting to the quick of language, with a brilliance of thought. This is a successful piece of work everywhere you examine it, and ought to be the herald of a fine literary career.

* * *

A Man in His Time
Delmore Schwartz

Here, for the first time I think, the experience of a new generation has been seized and recorded. It is one thing simply to have lost one's faith; it is quite another to begin with the sober and necessary lack of illusion afforded by Marxism, and then to land in what seems to be utter disillusion, only to be forced, stage by stage, to even greater

---

From *Partisan Review* 11.3 (1944): 348-50.

depths of disillusion. This is the experience of the generation that has come to maturity during the depression, the sanguine period of the New Deal, the days of the Popular Front and the days of Munich, and the slow, loud, ticking imminence of a new war. With the advent of war, every conceivable temptation not to be honest, not to look directly at experience, not to remember the essential vows of allegiance to the intelligence and to human possibility and dignity — every conceivable temptation and every plea of convenience, safety and casuistry has presented itself.

Joseph, the hero of *Dangling Man*, is remarkable because he has the strength (and it is his only strength) to keep his eyes open and his mind awake to the quality of his experience. He has been for a time a member of the Communist Party and he has been offered a business career by a successful older brother. He has rejected both. With the coming of the war, he undergoes the slow strangulation of being drafted but not inducted into the army because of various bureaucratic formalities. During this period in the inter-regnum between civilian and army life, he is gradually stripped of the few pretenses and protections left to him. A Communist refuses to speak to him; his brother attempts to lend him money; his niece taunts him as a beggar; his friends who have made their "meek adjustments" are repelled by his unwillingness to accept things as they are; he quarrels with his friends, his relatives, his wife who is supporting him and the people who live in the rooming house in which he spends his idle days. And finally, unable to endure the continuous emptiness and humiliation of his life, he sees to it that he is immediately taken into the army.

Is it necessary to emphasize the extent to which this experience is characteristic? Here are the typical objects of a generation's sensibility: the phonograph records, the studio couch, the reproductions of Van Gogh, the cafeteria; and the typical relationships: the small intellectual circle which gradually breaks up, the easy and meaningless love affair, the marriage which is neither important nor necessary, the party which ends in hysterical outbreaks or sickness of heart, the gulf separating this generation from the previous one and the family life from which it came.

What is not typical is Joseph's stubborn confrontation and evaluation of the character of his life. He insists on making explicit his dependency on his wife. He tells himself again and again that his days are wasted. He seizes the Communist party-member who tries to snub him, and insists that as a human being he has a right to be greeted. He tells himself and anyone who will listen that he does not like the kind of life his society has made possible. And he refuses to yield to the philistinism and the organized lack of imagination that consoles itself by saying: "It might be worse," "It is worse elsewhere," "It cannot be other than it is," "This is the lesser evil, hence it is good."

As a novel, the faults of *Dangling Man* come mainly from the fact that it is somewhat too linear in its movement and contained within too small an orbit. Thus, in seeking to keep Joseph's frame of mind constantly in the foreground. Bellow brushes over a number of dramatic possibilities, particularly those inherent in Joseph's marriage relation and his rejection of financial success. The narrative is perhaps too spare in its use of detail and background. And the use of the journal as a form blocks off the interesting shift of perspective that could be gained by presènting Joseph through the eyes of some person of the preceding generation. But, given Bellow's choice of a diary for conveying a larger social pattern, these limitations were perhaps hardly to be avoided, and this small book is an important effort to describe the situation of the younger generation.

*   *   *

Dangling Man: Saul Bellow's Lyrical Experiment
James Mellard

Dangling Man has never received the attention from critics that certain of Saul Bellow's other novels have drawn. Yet it has claimed careful attention, so the perplexing feature about the criticism is its failure to confront the serious formal experimentation in which Bellow engaged. Commentary usually begins with the remark that it is cast in the diary form: "*Dangling Man* was published in 1944 and consists of the diary entries of an unemployed man awaiting his call-up. These entries cover the four months prior to his decision to volunteer and they focus on the sequence of incidents, meditations, and moods which precede and precipitate that equivocal decision."[1] The commentary may continue with some appreciative remark about the appropriateness of that form: "Joseph's consciousness is the subject of the novel, and the journal form permits Bellow himself to maintain a certain distance from that consciousness at the same time that he makes the consciousness itself overwhelmingly immediate."[2] Or it may offer denigration, as in Tony Tanner's assessment that "Bellow's first novel is in some ways crude. One occasionally has the feeling that problems, preoccupations, and scraps of random reading are tumbled onto the pages rather unrelatedly. . . . And the diary form as here used carries with it the danger of solipsism,"[3] or as in Keith Opdahl's similar indictment: "Although it is short and intense, *Dangling Man* is as episodic as *The Adventures of Augie March*. Joseph ranges over the philosophic and the trivial, the past and the future, his guilt and his dreams, his walks and

From *Ball State University Forum* 15.2 (1974): 67-74.

his boarding house neighbors."[4] But in the end no analysis of this novel has gotten at its real mode. Understanding that mode allows us to resolve both the formal and the thematic problems Tanner, Harper, Opdahl, Joseph Baim, and others have pointed out.[5]

The way to approach *Dangling Man* is through the concept of "lyrical" fiction that has been carefully explained by Ralph Freedman working with some of those name novels Bellow may have used as models.[6] One of the problems associated with *Dangling Man* is its breakdown of point of view: one cannot always separate author and character, Bellow and Joseph, outer reality and inner perception, objective world and subjective image.[7] The opening paragraphs of *Dangling Man*[8] suggest the radical relationships among author, character, audience, and world in lyrical fiction. Though the tone of Joseph's opening suggests connections with *Augie March* and *Henderson the Rain King*, where we feel strongly that a first-person narrator is speaking to us, if we investigate the implications of what Joseph says and the form in which he says it we will see clearly enough the lyrical management of point of view. Joseph says, for example, that once people addressed themselves "and felt no shame at making a record of their inward transactions," implying of course that he shall address himself and record his inward transactions, whether or not it violates the code of the hard-boiled. He shall keep a journal and talk to himself, and he will not feel self-indulgent while doing it; given his condition, his "present state of demoralization," it has become necessary for him to keep that journal. Joseph's argument is precisely what lyrical fiction is all about, for he suggests how (and why) the lyrical point of view becomes author, audience, hero — all at once; he is talking to himself, becoming both subject and object, perceiver and perceived, an "individual communing with himself."[9]

Yet the form that Bellow creates through Joseph is objective. Bellow is not Joseph, nor are Joseph's experiences the sum of Joseph. "The experiencing self," as Freedman explains it, must be separated "from the world the experiences are about." Instead, actions, character, settings, and the like are absorbed in the lyrical pattern that seems to be the goal Joseph reaches in his diary. It is this distinction that suggests a major difference between *Dangling Man*, *Seize the Day*, and, perhaps, *Herzog*, on the one hand, and *The Victim*, *Augie March*, *Henderson*, and even *Mr. Sammler's Planet* on the other. Each of the latter novels finds its gestalt in "imitations of actions," which, as Freedman points out, are characteristic of the traditional novel. But in the former three novels structures are discovered, if they are perceived at all, in the interactions of patterns of imagery; where Augie sets out to discover his fate in Chicago, Mexico, and the Atlantic Ocean, Henderson sets out to discover his in Africa, and Leventhal and Sammler theirs on the streets of New York. Joseph can only discover his fate alone, writing to himself in his room, his "six-sided box." Of Bellow's introverted heroes, only Herzog discovers his fate through wide-ranging journeys, like Augie and Henderson, and yet there is a strong suggestion that Herzog's fate, like Joseph's, is discovered not in the journeying but in the patterned recollection of the images the journey provides.

Actions being limited to a claustrophobic space does not make the lyrical novel, but the spatial limits do make it clear that actions in time and space are not particularly important. The "contours" of the lyrical novel are drawn, not by the conventional temporal or spatial limits, but by the protagonist's point of view. The lyrical mode accounts for the problems of discontinuity both Tanner and Opdahl raised. What Freedman says of Rilke's *Malte Laurids Brigge* could as well apply to *Dangling Man*, "The individual encounters absorbed by the persona . . . only seem to be scattered at random. Actually they cohere as a texture, intermingling past and present, occult and real events, mythical and historical figures with persons in the hero's life. . . . Images . . . include not only objects and scenes but also characters, who exist as image-figures within the protagonist's lyrical point of view" (9). *Dangling Man*'s individual encounters are generally presented in dramatic scenes, but they are absorbed by Joseph's imagination and presented to us in his journal, that record of his efforts to map his "destiny" as he awaits, jobless, greetings from the Selective Service. Among the earliest dramatized encounters is the explosion of temper Joseph has at his old friend Jimmy Burns, a former Comrade who refuses to recognize him when they meet in a restaurant. Another is Joseph's similar explosion at his niece, Etta, on Christmas day at his brother Amos' home where Joseph and Iva, his wife, have eaten dinner. Later there is the recollection of Joseph's fight with his landlord, Mr. Gesell, over a lack of heat and electricity in the apartment, a blowup that Joseph recognizes now (5 Feb. 1943) as the first manifestation of his present ill temper, an early symptom of his spiritual poverty (97). All these encounters are capped by the ones occurring on 26 March, the foolish incident at the bank when Joseph, soiled and unkempt, is refused service by a clerk, a later argument with his wife, and, finally, a degrading encounter with his neighbor Vanaker, whom he maliciously accosts for his habit of leaving the bathroom door open at the end of the hall when he is relieving himself.

As randomly as these scenes appear to be presented, there is nevertheless a clear and climactic order in their presentation. This order is essentially the form that action takes in the plot itself, for these confrontations are what plot there is. Their ultimate significance is suggested in the word "incident" that Joseph uses to label the episode at the bank. All these episodes are only incidents to Joseph, who has come to the conclusion that neither chance nor incident nor coincidence may be allowed to govern his soul, spirit, mind, self — call it what one will. To label these encounters "incidents" is not to diminish their significance; to Joseph even the war that provides the background for all of them is only an incident, "a very important one; perhaps the most important that has ever occurred. But, still, an incident" (111). To label them so is only to suggest that they are not related to the essential Joseph. They do not create him as an individual, but as an individual he absorbs them. If all these incidents exist only in Joseph's experience of them, Joseph believes that he exists outside them, that his existence does not depend on them, that his essence exists in some ideal way beyond all the contingencies of the external world. He exists as much as an ideal as his diary's pattern.

If we can grasp the significance, perhaps really the insignificance of these "plotted" encounters, then we can probably also grasp the meaning of recurring images, of the encounters of Joseph's consciousness with characters, events, objects, scenes, ideas. What we learn from lyrical fiction is that we must read reflexively; our minds must range over a protagonist's experiences as associatively as his own might. Essentially, the rhythm of presentation in the lyric is association; as Northrop Frye suggests, the rhythm of association is "oracular, meditative, irregular, unpredictable, and essentially discontinuous."[10] In order to perceive the design of lyrical fiction such as *Dangling Man*, therefore, it is often imperative for us to be even more attuned to unexpected associative connections than the protagonist; his resolutions of tensions are likely to be emotional, but ours (if we are to be critics) will almost necessarily be intellectual. One can get an idea of how these associative processes work by looking at the connections among a few characters, both real and imagined — since one is no more important than the other in the lyrical mode. One could begin with Vanaker. He is only a fellow lodger with Joseph, but he has an expanding significance in Joseph's life that far outweighs this literal level. For Joseph, Vanaker has also a symbolic meaning and becomes associated with other figures, real and phantasmagorical. It is necessary, first, to recognize those figures associated with Vanaker in order to know what Vanaker himself means in Joseph's unconscious life.

Several of these associations appear in the journal on 26 January, a day on which Joseph is fever ridden and abed with a cold. The record of this day is almost a model of the disjunctive, associative, lyrical method. The journal passage begins with Joseph thinking how much it is a "day for a world without deformity or threat of damage." But his mood changes and shortly he writes that, on the one hand, there is "great pressure . . . brought to bear to make us undervalue ourselves. On the other hand, civilization teaches that each of us is an inestimable prize." He concludes, then, that there are "these two preparations: one for life and the other for death" (79). The preparation for death is that which teaches us to accept our insignificance, yet Joseph insists he must know what he himself is, whereupon he narrates a dream he has had recently, one more bare and ominous than "the old" Joseph's more prolix dreams. The central figure in this dream is a guide who is to lead Joseph on his "mission . . . to reclaim one for a particular family," who has been killed in a massacre, though Joseph claims not to be "personally acquainted with the deceased." He says, "I had merely been asked, as an outsider. . . . I did not even know the family well. At which my guide turned, smiling, and I guessed that he meant . . . 'It's well to put oneself in the clear in something like that.' This was his warning to me. He approved of my neutrality." Yet even in his dream, Joseph is disturbed about this guide, moving "brisk as a rat among his charges," the infantile corpses, and writes, "But it offended me to have an understanding with this man and to receive a smile of complicity from his pointed face." Joseph does not remember much more of the dream, though he does remember an atmosphere of terror that he associates with the descriptions he had heard his father give of "Gehenna and the damned" (80).

From this atmosphere of terror and only indirect threats of death, Joseph moves to another dream that threatens him directly. In this dream he is expected to "render harmless the grenade traps in one of the houses" of a North African town his army unit has entered. "I crawled through the window, dropped from the clay sill and saw a grenade wired to the door, ridged and ugly. But I did not know where to begin, which wire to touch first. My time was limited; I had other work before me. I began to tremble and perspire and, going to the far end of the room, I aimed my pistol long and carefully at the ridges and fired. When the din subsided, I realized that if I had hit the mark I could have killed myself. But I had scarcely a moment to feel relieved. Pincers in hand, I went forward to cut the first wire" (80-81). That these are death-dreams Joseph himself clearly indicates a bit farther on in his speculation about the modes of one's death: "How will it be? How? Falling a mile into the wrinkled sea? Or, as I have dreamed, cutting a wire?" (82).

But perhaps not surprisingly this archetypal dream symbolism also has sexual connotations, the processes of dream-work linking in a primary way concepts of death and sex, Thanatos and Eros. This dual symbolism comes not only from the ambivalence of the cutting of the wire, which may be the umbilical cord or the thread the Fate Atropos severs. It also comes in the scarcely veiled sexual imagery of the passage: the entry into the house, the phallic grenade, "ridged and ugly," and the phallic pistol. And it comes most insistently in the specific association that Joseph himself makes: "I recognize in the guide of the first dream an ancient figure, temporarily disguised only to make my dread greater when he revealed himself" (81). The "ancient figure" is a man who sexually attacks Joseph, presumably when Joseph is a child: "Suddenly I heard another set of footsteps added to mine, heavier and grittier, and my premonitions leaped into one fear even before I felt a touch on my back and turned. Then that swollen face that came rapidly toward mine until I felt its bristles and the cold pressure of its nose; the lips kissed me on the temple with a laugh and a groan. Blindly I ran, hearing again the gritting boots" (81). Occurring in a setting that is grimly emblematic, a cold, rutted, ash-drifted, muddy, back land lined with "snaggled boards" and denizened only by aroused dogs and a wandering goat, this event may well be the source of Joseph's greatest anxieties about both sex and death. Death we know he fears, but there is every indication, in his relation to both wife, Iva, and "lover," Kitty Daumler, that he also fears sex.[11]

It is clear enough that the "one fear" he suffers includes both, for this scene is followed immediately by a recollection of the "fallen man," the elderly man whom Joseph the week before has seen fall stricken in the street. It is both death and sex that the man's fall comes to mean to Joseph. In this recollection the policeman bending over the fallen man substitutes for the "ancient figure" of the molester, but he also represents "*the* murderer, the stranger who, one day, will drop the smile of courtesy or custom to show you the weapon in his hand, the means of your death" (81). Similarly, Joseph's over-determined images of the coming of Death combine with dual connotations of the primal sexual scene, as the italicized words in the following passage suggest clearly: "Who does not expect him with the opening of the door; and who, after childhood, thinks of flight or resistance or of *laying* any but ironic, yes, even *welcoming hands* on his shoulders when he comes? The moment is for him to choose. He may come at a *climax of satisfaction* or of evil; he may come as one comes to repair a radio or a faucet; mutely, or to pass the time of day, play a game of cards; or, with no preliminary, *colored with horrible anger*, reaching out a *muffling hand*; or, in a mask of calm, *hurry you to your last breath, drawn with a stuttering sigh out of his shadow*" (81-82). In fact, it becomes clear that Joseph's thoughts about everything from intellectual decay ("moral buggery") to physical death take the very image of the pervert's sexual attack.

Unquestionably, the guide, the attacker, and the fallen man are linked together in Joseph's imaginative experience. But how, one asks, does Vanaker fit into the associative pattern? Vanaker it is whose acts, character, and presence coalesce the formal pattern in which the associations operate. He draws together the varied associations and forces Joseph to act upon their meanings for his life. Vanaker is more a "queer, annoying creature" (12) than a man to Joseph, and the vague threatfulness of his "coughing and growling," which Joseph takes for "a sort of social activity," prompts Joseph's wife to call him a werewolf. He is of an indeterminate age, but apparently has a strong romantic interest in elderly ladies, being "engaged to marry a lady of sixty" (21) and having continually urged Mrs. Kiefer, before her eventually fatal illness, to go to the movies with him. "He is no gentleman," according to Marie the cleaning woman; he snoops about the house, and Joseph relates how "when he goes to the toilet he leaves the door ajar. He tramps down the hall, and a moment later you hear him splashing" (12). Perhaps his most ominous trait, however, is the energy that suggests a barely restrained aggression: "Hatless, he hurries in his black moleskin jacket up the street and between the snowy bushes. He slams the street door and kicks the snow from his boots on the first step. Then, coughing wildly, he runs up" (13). Dressed in his black coat (moleskin, no less) and hankering after dying old women, Vanaker is almost too easily associated with some dark, unfathomable power.

Vanaker is an interesting character, even if one cares for or sees nothing of his symbolic role. He does things, usually strange things: he takes Joseph's socks and Iva's perfume from their room, drinks heavily, coughing and grunting all the while, and throws his empties into the neighboring yards. On January first, Joseph says, he "observed the birth of the new year with large quantities of whiskey, with coughing, pelting the yard with bottles, with frequent, noisy trips to the lavatory, and ended his revels with a fire" (53). But most of all he comes to mean something to us and to Joseph. He represents the general malaise, the "derangement of days, the leveling of occasions" (54) that Joseph associates with his plight; he represents the "craters of the spirit" (26, 44, 102) toward which we are all drawn on a quest that Joseph comes to believe is the same for all men. "All the striving is for one end," he thinks. "I do not entirely understand the impulse. But it seems to me that its final end is the desire for pure freedom" (102). To Joseph freedom means choice, and the absence of choice means death (98); hence, the quest is essentially for life itself.

To the extent, then, that Vanaker is the objective correlative for Joseph's spiritual craters, the "anti-life" principle in himself, Vanaker is the death, both physical and spiritual, that Joseph must come to terms with before he can choose to go to war. Further, therefore, Joseph's confrontation with Vanaker at the toilet is the event in the plot that precipitates Joseph's decision and the resolution of the tensions created by all the old men who populate his imagination's landscape — the dream-guide, the fallen man, the policeman, the molester. Having fled from the confrontation, Joseph makes his final decision in a setting that almost exactly duplicates[12] the attack scene from his childhood:

> I walked over the *cinders* of a schoolyard and came into an *alley* approaching our windows. . . . I had halted near a *fence* against which a *tree* leaned, freshly *budding* and *seething under the rain*. . . . I turned and started back along the schoolyard *fence*. A steel ring on a rope whipped loudly against the *flagpole*. Then, for a moment, *a car caught me* in its lights. . . . *Something ran among the cans and papers*. A *rat*, I thought and, sickened, I went even more quickly, *skirting a pool* at the foot of the street where *a torn umbrella lay stogged in water and ashes*. (121; italics added.)

Much of the imagery here is similar to that of the attack scene —
cinders, alley, fence, ashes; Joseph's being "caught" in the lights of the
car as he had been by the attacker. But this scene also evokes the
dreams that haunt Joseph in the various sexual images — the wet, see-
thing tree, the flagpole, the umbrella in the pool of water, and especially the rat, which recalls the guide "brisk as a rat" scuttling among
the dead bodies of children. That the dual associations of the "ancient"
figures from dreams and reality are once more present suggests that
Joseph is overcoming a sexual trauma as well as a fear of death — a
theme that adequately accounts for the condensation of symbols from
both memory and dreams.

Yet, though all the images in the passage suggest the demonic
quality of this and other experiences for Joseph, perhaps the key image
is the one that ends the passage and is picked up in the paragraph following: "I took a deep breath of warm air." After his harrowing
descent into the reality of his dreams, the fantasm of reality, the deep
breath suggests that Joseph has finally come to terms with his own
"fate," his "destiny." The warm air he inhales signifies his ultimately
vigorous encompassing of all the contingencies of that fate — that is,
life itself. That, the willingness to accept the contingencies of life, is
the meaning of Joseph's ironic conclusion to his journal:

> I am no longer to be held accountable for myself; I am grateful for that. I
> am other hands, relieved of self-determination, freedom canceled. Hurray
> for regular hours! And for the supervision of the spirit! Long live
> regimentation! (126)

Joseph's ironic exclamations here are finally only self-protective
devices for concealing the truly problematic nature of the decision he
has made. Given the nature of Joseph's decision, it does not seem
appropriate to question, as Tanner, Opdahl, Baim, and others have, the
"success" or "failure" of Joseph to handle his freedom, his
responsibility, his spiritual craters. Joseph's decision is like that of any
tragic hero who commits himself to an irretrievable course of action. In
fact, this recognition, inherently tragic, though his journal is not
shaped as a formal tragedy, is precisely Joseph's: "I had apparently
come to a point where the perspectives of time appeared more contracted than they had a short while ago. I was beginning to grasp the
meaning of 'irretrievable'" (125). Arrived at through the essentially
therapeutic, lyrically expressive, form of the journal, Joseph's recognition is one that foreshadows those of most of Bellow's heroes in the
novels eventually to follow *Dangling Man*: Asa Leventhal, of *The Victim*, confronts life's natural contingencies through his alter ego, Allbee;
Tommy Wilhelm, of *Seize the Day*, and Artur Sammler, of *Mr.
Sammler's Planet*, both confront old mortality, weeping on the bodies
of dead men; and Herzog discovers the often grim facts of life in an
Orphean journey through a labyrinthine magistrates court; only Augie
March, still "circling" at the end, seems to escape the severe

psychological shocks Bellow's other heroes suffer, and yet even Augie hardly escapes an awareness of the contract with nature, fulfilled through death, that gives shape to man's life. *Dangling Man*, a lyrical record of a man's inward transactions, thus gives an objective form to a consciousness engagement with the varied craters of the spirit. In that objective, patterned, and finally aesthetic form, Joseph acts as his own therapist — as Dostoevski's underground man and Sartre's Roquentin (of *Nausea*) had done, and as Ellison's invisible man and Bellow's own Herzog were to do later. As Keith Opdahl[13] has shown, Joseph works his way through serious social problems; as Tony Tanner suggests, he works his way through traumatic psychological problems; and as Howard Harper and Joseph Baim argue, he works his way through an essentially religious and intellectual crisis in his felt tension between reason and faith, the rational and the irrational. But most of all, Joseph completes an aesthetic object that can absorb his conflicts and purge him of them.

Ultimately, it is not Joseph's decision to enlist that is final; it is his recognition that his formal pattern is completed. And as Herzog at last stops writing his letters, Joseph puts down his pen and closes his diary.

Notes

1. Tony Tanner, *Saul Bellow* (London: Oliver and Boyd, 1965), 18.
2. Howard M. Harper, *Desperate Faith: A Study of Bellow, Salinger, Mailer, Baldwin and Updike* (Chapel Hill, NC: U of North Carolina P, 1967), 15.
3. Tanner, 25.
4. Keith Opdahl, *The Novels of Saul Bellow: An Introduction* (University Park: U of Pennsylvania P, 1967), 30.
5. Baim's essay, "Escape from Intellection: Saul Bellow's *Dangling Man*," appeared in *University Review* 37 (Oct. 1970): 28-34.
6. See *The Lyrical Novel: Studies in Hermann Hesse, André Gide, and Virginia Woolf* (Princeton, NJ: Princeton UP, 1963). Freedman has also published a long essay on Bellow, "Saul Bellow: The Illusion of Environment," *Wisconsin Studies in Contemporary Literature* 1 (Winter 1960): 50-65, but he does not use the term *lyrical* to discuss the novels published up to that time.
7. Opdahl (37) considers some of the objections lodged against Bellow by early reviewers and critics of *Dangling Man*.
8. Saul Bellow, *Dangling Man* (New York: Signet, 1965), 7. Subsequent references in the text from this edition.
9. Northrop Frye, *Anatomy of Criticism* (Princeton, NJ: Princeton UP, 1957), 250.
10. Ibid., 271.
11. A molesting scene also appears in *Augie March* and *Herzog*, and apparently constitutes one form of what Norman Holland, in *The Dynamics of*

Literary Response (New York: Oxford UP, 1968), discusses as a "primal scene" in literature and dreams: "One finds several clusters of images in such fantasies: first darkness, a sense of vagueness and the unknown, mysterious noises in night and darkness; second, vague movements, shapes shifting and changing, nakedness, things appearing and disappearing; third, images of fighting and struggling, blood, and phallus as weapon" (46). There are other, perhaps less traumatic primal scenes imaged in *Dangling Man*: "in a curtainless room near the market, a man rearing over someone on a bed, and, on another occasion, a Negro with a blond woman on his lap" (57). An interesting parallel to these scenes is the one in *Mr. Sammler's Planet* in which the magnificent black pickpocket silently, contemptuously exposes himself to Artur Sammler, a scene that threatens the old man as much as the primal scenes threaten the imaginations of the children who become adults.

12. Opdahl (46) makes this same observation, though in a somewhat different context.

13. In note 6, Chapter 2, Opdahl identifies yet other critics who have judged differently Joseph's decision and suggests four ways in which the novel's conclusion might be interpreted: "Joseph's admission of failure, in which he is ironic about himself; his straight confession of failure, in which Bellow is ironic; his expression of gratitude, in which Bellow shows sympathy toward his weakness; and his claim to affirmation, in which he recognizes — with Bellow's blessing — that one cannot live without community."

*   *   *

From *Dangling Man* to "Colonies of the Spirit"
Bonnie Lyons

Saul Bellow's thirty-three years of publication, eight major novels, and one Nobel Prize all suggest that the time has come for an overview, a reconsideration. *Dangling Man*, Bellow's first novel, is an appropriate focus for such a discussion, for within its pages one finds the inherited intellectual and emotional starting point and the dialectical roots of all Bellow's later work.

Notes from Underground, the obvious forefather of *Dangling Man*, establishes the groundwork, or should I say *under*ground work, of one formulation of the modern condition. Predominant is the divided self ("opposite elements swarm in me") marked by a desire for greater consciousness (the underground man writes in order "to get to the bottom" of his condition) and a paradoxical fear of over-consciousness ("to be too conscious is an illness — a thorough-going illness"). The

From *Studies in American Jewish Literature* 4.2 (1978): 45-50.

same self-division is embodied in the disdain for decision and action ("an intelligent man cannot become anything seriously, and it is only a fool who becomes anything . . . a man must and morally ought to be preeminently a characterless creature") and a despairing inability to move ("the direct, legitimate fruit of consciousness is inertia"). The central focus and goal is existential freedom ("the whole work of man really seems to consist in nothing but proving to himself every minute that he is a man and not a piano key"); that is to say, that if there is no free will, man is "a stop in an organ." The means of discovering or achieving this goal is, paradoxically, mere talk, especially self-communion ("the direct and sole vocation of every intelligent man is babble").

Dangling Man recapitulates these themes, takes up the same pre-occupations, and in a sense is Bellow's debate with Dostoevsky (shades of Herzog's letters and Citrine's messages to Humboldt). But the nineteenth-century Russian theme is updated and Americanized; *Dangling Man* is very much a product and analysis of the American forties, a Bellovian rendition of the post-depression Chicago blues. The extent to which *Dangling Man* is a product of and comment upon the forties is apparent when the novel is viewed in conjunction with the contemporaneous "The Hand that Fed Me," a brilliant, self-conscious story about self-consciousness by Bellow's boyhood friend, Isaac Rosenfeld. Both *Dangling Man* and "The Hand that Fed Me" are stories of, in Rosenfeld's phrase, "bare, pared essential men." In both, the atmosphere is dense with memories of the thirties' depression and WPA, and with undercurrents of the present forties' ambience, the army and war background. In both we receive the outsider's position, the view from the cramped room in a boarding house. In both the quest for freedom, for moral engagement, resonates; psychic and moral breakthrough are glimpsed only dimly, while paranoia, isolation, and despair sit fatly in the foreground. Both pieces of fiction are clearly products of former radicals; both reflect the failure of political solutions and yet insist upon the reality of the political world, of economic and social relations and contingencies.

Less evident but even more important is the direction of Joseph's spiritual development. His celebrating words upon entering the army — "Hurray for regular hours! And for the supervision of the spirit! Long live regimentation!" — are no doubt ironic, but this is not simple defeat. What his spiritual journey suggests, and Joseph learns, is the paradoxical nature of both the quest for genuine self and the nature of human freedom. Holding himself aloof from all others and from the world in general, Joseph does not by any means discover his true self; rather he finds his sense of self disintegrating, his identity dissolving. And while not having a job superficially suggests pure freedom, in actuality Joseph discovers the paradox of unusable freedom: he is free from, not free for. Freedom is a kind of prison. True self and true freedom, he finds, are not found in extreme positions: they must be located, or invented, in at least partial engagement.

Dangling Man, then, is Bellow's dive into the underground, to the cellar floor of Dostoevskian alienation, and his encounter with and spring-back from this point of Absolute Zero, this bottom line of the spirit, his revelation of alienation as a destructive, useless path to solipsism and madness. Just as Bellow insists, through Joseph, upon the common man rather than the artist, the novel itself finally turns in favor of the common human condition. That is why Joseph's decision to give himself up to the army does not make him feel pained or humiliated, and instead fills him with "gratification and a desire to make my decision effective at once." To learn one's limitations — and the limitations of the human conditions — is no triumph, but it is *learning*.

Joseph's insistence that "the next move was the world's" accentuates his rejoining the world, his rejection of his inadequate notion of perfect freedom and unencumbered self, and it also stresses a "to-fro" attitude, a dialectic. That is to say, *only* the next move is the world's.

This dialectic suggests both the open-endedness characteristic of all of Bellow's fiction (nothing is final), and a key to the overt fictional pattern. Seen as a continuing debate with his various selves and a lively (if sometimes tendentious) dialogue with each unknown reader, the novels chronicle Bellow's various "answers" to the ultimate questions of self and society, the meaning of human existence, or, as Joseph says, "what we are and what we are for." The variety of selves and the depth and sympathy with which they are imagined are perhaps Bellow's greatest achievement: from the desperate underground man, to the self-conscious, anxious Victim, to the larky Augie, to the sad, touching schlemiel Tommy, to the turbulent, titanic Henderson, to the sweetly-sour intellectual Herzog, to the Olympian, disdainful Sammler, to the weary, comic, self-resurrecting Humboldt. While some of these characters experience aspects of Joseph's alienation (Herzog is alienated from the easy, cynical wasteland attitudes of his contemporaries, and Sammler completely rejects the libidinal freedom and "happiness now" of the sixties), in effect *Dangling Man* is Bellow's starting point away from the underground man, wherein he chronicles the given, establishes the literary, political, and personal donnée, makes the most radically negative claims, and starts the long debate. Since, as *Dangling Man* establishes, there are various "solutions" to the essential human questions, since no life is ended until it is over, the "to-fro" goes on. Bellow's novels offer us self after self, vision after vision, version after version, and in both their continuing spiritual quest and variety of questors, they fulfill what Isaac Rosenfeld called the function of the novel — which is "to bring us up to the level of our full human experience."

Despite its debt to *Notes from Underground* and its similarity to "The Hand that Fed Me," *Dangling Man* is not simply an updating of

Dostoevsky or an illumination of the forties' moral dilemma. It is the most explicitly negative of Bellow's novels, the clearest exposition of one pole of his work — his "No, in thunder." Despite Joseph's claim that "there's a lot of talk about alienation. It's a fool's plea," he (like his probable Kafkan namesake) is a thoroughly alienated man. The depth, degree, and variety of his alienation are staggering; his complaint endless; this December-to-April journal chronicles the winter of his discontent. Joseph is alienated from both his family and his friends. The two most memorable "scenes" are recreations of his social malaise: first, the party which reveals his friends' and his own just barely concealed nastiness and pettiness, the distance from Joseph's deeply desired, imagined "colonies of the spirit"; and second, the family dinner, in which his brother's complacent materialism, his sister-in-law's philistine snobbery, and his niece's teenage snottiness counter Joseph's self-righteousness and short temper. In essence, the minor characters are drawn to suggest social types; they represent unacceptable options to alienation. Joseph's brother is the smug middle-class man, mindful only of his own needs and those of his family, vainly priding himself on his ability to make money (a process seen as almost necessarily victimizing others), and on his ability to spend it — as if his large financial needs proved his value. Joseph's friend Abt represents the justification through personal achievement, through the insider's position: as an up-and-coming bureaucrat, he is proud of knowing what is going on. The most tempting option to Joseph's alienation is presented by another friend, the artist John Pearl, whose art permits him to feel cozily superior in his rejection of the world. For Pearl, "the only real world is the world of art and of thought"; for him "there is only one worthwhile sort of work, that of the imagination." Joseph's (and through him Bellow's) rejection of this position is the "throwing down of the gauntlet," Bellow's earliest rejection of the romantic tradition of the artist and especially of the implied transcendence and self-justification through art.

The very fact that Joseph himself is not an artist is central. Allowed no escape through artistic transcendence, Joseph is forced to seek a common solution, a way out of or beyond alienation that is generally applicable. As he puts it, his only talent is "for being a citizen, or what is today called, most apologetically, a good man." While he recognizes that in the strictest sense an artist's work is not personal, that through it he is connected with mankind, Joseph is also acutely aware that the artist is exceptional and thus unjustifiably superior. In his words, "Who does not recognize the advantage of the artist, these days?"

That Joseph is married is a striking and daring shift in the expected pattern, seemingly an anomaly: it is hard to imagine an underground man with a mate. Somehow marriage almost necessarily domesticates a burrow into a cozy nook. Both Dostoevsky's and

Rosenfeld's underground men are intensely solitary, obviously woman-less. By making Joseph married, Bellow clearly "extends the complaint": through the depiction of Joseph's marital relations and the cold, impersonal unconnubial rooming house atmosphere, he underscores and deepens Joseph's alienation and solitariness by making him lonely in marriage. Joseph's wife Iva "has a way about her that discourages talk," and we know how central talk is. She is also somewhat concerned about appearances, about getting on, and, perhaps most significant, she is impervious to Joseph's plans for her intellectual and moral uplift. Joyless sexuality pervades the novel. Even in his covert affair, Joseph maintains his sense of his own moral superiority and never really questions the meaning of his infidelity and lies. The depiction of the nice, boring, unmemorable wife who never really seems there and of the sexy, simple-minded girl friend suggests that Bellow does not see in sexuality a significant way out of the self, or the healing, connecting aspects of marriage. And the failure of the women in *Dangling Man* (or perhaps Bellow's failure to animate them fully) adumbrates the nags, bitches, and sex-pots of his later work.

In total, the early sections of *Dangling Man* establish an extreme polarity, a desperate choice between alienation and accommodation that is like choosing between death by drowning and death by hanging. On the one hand, there is the sour, solitary Joseph balanced on the edge of the "craters of the spirit"; on the other, those who prize convenience, comfort, accommodation, and their "terrible" ramified consequences.

Joseph's alienation is deeper than a feeling of separateness from other people. Besides being alienated from family, friends, and neighbors, he is alienated from the world's business, both the mindless, rote bustle of ordinary life and the war. A literary man, whose main connection with the outside world is books, he has depended upon reading to extend his horizons; but when he is no longer employed and has complete leisure to read, he finds himself unable to connect with any of his former beloved literary heroes. Perhaps the sharpest sign of his discontent is his identification with Barnadine of *Measure for Measure*, who is equally contemptuous of life and death.

Part of Joseph's problem is his rejection of contemporary conditions. At times he eulogizes the past when "something spoke in man's favor" and deplores the present for which the ugliness of the modern city (i.e., Chicago) is a fit symbol as well as product. But in general Joseph's alienation is not just a contemporary malaise (in no novel does Bellow permit a character to rest on simple renunciation of his time), and he moves toward something much more extreme — an alienation from reality and life in general. "Narcotic dullness" increases; at first he fails to distinguish holidays from other days, later each day blurs with the next, and finally time itself loses meaning, stretches, bends, collapses. As he comes to prefer fantasy to reality, sleep to awakening, Joseph dips perilously close to madness. Alienation, as Bellow presents it, is anything but slyly comfortable superiority. There is increasing desperation in Joseph's quest, and the obvious religious answer is denied him. Listening to music, which in the novel functions as a kind of voice of the soul, Joseph experiences extraordinary spiritual longing. Although the music "named only one source, the universal one, God," Joseph rejects religious consolation. He refuses to "catch any contrivance in panic." For him, to "sacrifice the mind that sought to be satisfied," to drown reason in religious faith, would be "a great crime." Likewise, while the novel's atmosphere may be vaguely Jewish, there is no suggestion of solidarity with the Jewish people, or hint of possible relevance of Jewish traditions.

Amid all the denying, negating, withdrawing, and dangling, several centers of positive value, of affirmation and hope, appear, however. All prefigure developments in later novels. The first is the nexus of childhood and poverty which in Joseph's remembrance is "the only place where I was ever allowed to encounter reality." His intense preoccupation and absorption with life at that period is the perfect contrast to his present estrangement. Also, despite the actual failure of his plan for a group united spiritually, for a colony of the spirit, Joseph's *desire* itself is neither denied nor belittled. As he says, "the plan could be despised, my need could not be." Finally, deeper than Joseph's alienation is his sense, however fleeting, of the basic goodness or value of each thing that exists. As he muses, "Good or not, it exists, it is ineffable, and for that reason, marvelous." This basic, if residual, life-affirmation is felt only minimally and intermittently in *Dangling Man*, but it explodes in the euphoric variety of the world created in *Augie March*, in Augie's rich appetite for life, and even in the novel's style of wonder, delight in simple enumeration, and Whitmanesque open-armed inclusiveness.

*　*　*

The Victim (1947)

Anti-Semitism Hits a Jew
Richard Match

Both the recent novels about anti-Semitism, *Focus* and *Gentleman's Agreement*, have featured what the Broadway fraternity call a "gimmick" — in each case a twist of identity whereby a Gentile character is exposed to the slings and arrows ordinarily reserved for Jews. *The Victim* is a novel of anti-Semitism as it hits the Jew, and Mr. Bellow is to get at the problem on a level less tangible than the "restricted" sign at a summer resort.

His book lacks the instant reader-identification both Arthur Miller and Laura Z. Hobson achieved, perhaps partly because its emphasis is universal rather than topical. What Mr. Bellow attempts is to compress into an arena the size of two human souls the agony of mind which has ravaged millions of Jews in our century. *The Victim* rates as a subtle and thoughtful contribution to the literature of twentieth-century anti-Semitism.

Asa Leventhal, editor of a minor Manhattan trade magazine, lived in a walk-up on Irving Place. He was a large, stolid-looking man, inclined to be rather short in speech, but his abruptness of manner actually masked a deep sense of personal vulnerability. In spite of his comfortable income, his six years with Burke-Beard publications, Leventhal could never erase from his mind the memory of the depression and the flophouse existence he had narrowly escaped. Nor could he forget that his mother had died in a mental hospital.

But on the whole life was fairly good for Leventhal — until Kirby Allbee's sudden appearance and monstrous accusation. Leventhal had known his accuser years before when he himself was a hungry job hunter and Allbee a prosperous journalist. Now their positions were reversed. Allbee was broke, unshaven, down and out. He smelled of

From *New York Herald Tribune Book Review* (23 Nov. 1947): 10.

cheap whisky and Bowery flophouses. And — impossible, senseless, maddening — he blamed Asa Leventhal, whom he had not seen in six years, for everything that had happened to him, from the loss of his job to the death of his wife. And he made his accusations sound plausible!

With a devious "logic" that would do credit to *Mein Kampf*, Allbee had built his case against Leventhal. There was the time, at a half-forgotten party, when he, Allbee, had made a slighting reference to the Jews. That was why Leventhal hated him. The rest was pure Jewish malice. Leventhal must have gone to Allbee's boss — there was an interview on record — undermined Allbee's position, cost him his job. As a result, Allbee's wife had left him and, while traveling South, been killed in an automobile accident. One thing had led to another, and clearly Asa Leventhal, the Jew, was to blame for everything.

Leventhal was outraged, then incredulous. Never very sure of himself, he began to crack, to half-believe in his own guilt. Mr. Bellow makes the steps in his disintegration suffocatingly real.

Asa Leventhal "felt that he had been singled out to be the object of some freakish, insane process, and . . . he was filled with dread." "Why me?" he asked himself. One wonders how many Jews have asked themselves the same question since 1933.

* * *

Among the Fallen
John Farrelly

One tends to have apprehensions about the second book of a talented writer. An incidental delight of *The Victim*, therefore, is that it solidly supports the position among contemporary American writers awarded Saul Bellow for *Dangling Man*.

The conditions and locale of the present novel are middle-class business life in New York. It is wonderfully witty (not in the texture of the writing — here the author has achieved a drabness without dullness, admirably suited to the colorlessness of the scene: cafeterias, rooming houses, subways, etc.), but witty in the delineation of its characters and in the manipulation of its themes.

In midsummer, lonely and depressed by family troubles, Asa Leventhal is a case of city nerves "that had made him acutely responsive, quick to feel." He senses insecurity, "feeling he was threatened by something while he slept. At this point, he is visited by Kirby Allbee, a former acquaintance obviously reduced to a derelict, who

From *New Republic* (8 Dec. 1947): 27-28.

returns to accuse Leventhal of ruining his life. The truth in the accusation is that Leventhal, indirectly and unintentionally, had been the occasion of Allbee's losing his job. To Leventhal, avid for security and moderately successful, Allbee is a convenient spectre of defeat, representing "that part of humanity of which he was frequently mindful . . . the part that did not get away with it — the lost, the outcast, the overcome, the effaced, the ruined." Allbee exploits these scruples, and making the "general wrong" of human inequality a particular one, points at Leventhal "and said '*You*'!"

In creating Allbee, the author let himself go and has produced the classic wreck. Having drowned his honor in a sea of whiskey, he rattles on about his New England ancestry. Blaming the Jews for destroying the traditions of that ancestry, he preys on Leventhal's virtues of order and justice to his own advantage. He is a philosopher who nourishes his mind on the half-truths of self-deception. He has perverted his cleverness and critical discernment to lies and bluff, carried on the hot wind of blustering rhetoric. He sobs about his dead wife into Leventhal's ear, and at a showdown escapes under cover of the whine, "I know I have a fallen nature."

His perfect counterpart is Leventhal, the Jew, honest and self-searching, who has equated his own personality and traditions with urban life and learned to make the current support him, while Allbee merely floats on the warm stream of liquor, expatiating: "The day of succeeding by your own efforts is past. Now it is all blind movement, vast movement, and the individual is shuttled back and forth."

The title, as it refers to Allbee, is ironic. He is the self-styled victim who preys on his persecutor, gradually usurping his life until he is settled in his bed. Actually, he is such a complete character that nobody could touch him. For Leventhal, on the other hand, unease is the condition of his being. He broods on some imaginary "blacklist" in the business world which proves the conspiracy he suspects. And the question always recurs: Was *he* a victim, as a Jew? If so, "then the turn he always feared had come and all good luck was canceled and all favors melted away."

Placed in relation to each other, the victim victimizing the victimizer, their opposite problems define their characters and contain their solution. This is the crux of the book, the wit of it and the wisdom of it. For Leventhal, a successful man, the problem is to rest upon the money-security he has achieved, and to believe in the possibility and efficacy of the good life he tries to lead. Allbee, the failure, must admit his collapse and believe in the reality of the evil he flaunts as a protective disguise.

*   *   *

Saul Bellow's *The Victim*
Malcolm Bradbury

In the period since the last war, American fiction has presented a number of exciting developments; and one of them has been an intensive, soul-searching kind of novel about a hero who, usually working from spare, existentialist premises, is attempting to realize his own character and duties and the significance of his humanity. Many of the writers who have written in this vein are Jewish, and the theme may be said to be related to a whole tradition of metaphysical Jewish speculation. Writers like Philip Roth, Bernard Malamud, Delmore Schwartz and Leslie Fiedler have made an intensive exploration of these properties; but the novelist who stands out both within this genre and in the whole activity of American literature since the war is Saul Bellow, one of whose novels I propose to analyse in some detail in order to indicate the kind of quality I think resides in his work.

Bellow, born in Canada in 1915, is the author of five novels — *Dangling Man* (1944), *The Victim* (1947), *The Adventures of Augie March* (1953), *Seize the Day* (1956) and *Henderson the Rain King* (1959) — and of a number of short stories. The novels are now all available in this country in various editions. They are predominantly city novels (with the exception of *Henderson,* which is a psychological myth) and frequently deal with Jewish communities within the city. Their heroes tend to be in some sense intellectuals or sensitives and responsive to, or representative of, modern intellectual dilemmas, uncertain of their nature and their responsibility, remote from their traditional faith, and concerned with their relationships to their fellow men and to their society. This last is conceived as, on the whole, an anonymous society, throwing the obligation for self-definition totally upon the individual; and the pattern of the novels is often that of the attempt to assert an individual act of will against the deterministic force of environment. I have chosen *The Victim,* Bellow's second novel, not because I think it his best but because it concentrates this central theme most clearly, just as *Dangling Man* concentrates the philosophical implications of it, and shows Bellow's clear debt to French novelists like Camus and Sartre, and to Dostoyevsky. *The Victim* is in spirit perhaps rather closer to Dreiser and the naturalists, but retains these philosophical and psychological emphases in an interesting mixture.

All Bellow's heroes in some way rise up against the constrictions of their environment and their society, and are concerned with moulding a morality, realising their humanity more intensely. Such is the subject of *The Victim,* a novel about a man's developing sense of

From *Critical Quarterly* 5.2 (1963): 119-28.

obligation to his fellows. The meaning of the novel is, in fact, greater than the experience of the hero; it is presented by the author as a third-person narrative, and it concerns a few days in the life of Asa Leventhal, a young Jewish professional man moving gradually from failure to success in his career, magazine publishing. Asa Leventhal has accidentally caused an acquaintance, a gentile named Allbee (the name has obvious significance) to lose his job, and through the larger part of the action he is pursued by the repulsive Allbee and forced to determine the degree of and the nature of his responsibility for him. This discovery forms the shape of the action. Though the novel lacks the width and largeness of *Augie March* or the exuberance and stylistic force of *Henderson,* it is a deep and penetrating tale, remarkable for rather than limited by its concentration. The soul-probings, the transcendentalism, that become the style and form of *Henderson* are here kept in check, bounded by the sense of a limiting society, and it is because of the intensity by which Leventhal's dilemma is seen as a social as well as a psychological problem that the book is important. It is indeed as much in the genre of Dreiser as of Dostoyevsky; its evocation of the immigrant, urban milieu with all the pressures in it that make life difficult and precarious, and man-to-man relations hostile and competitive, is essential to its meaning.

The book is set then in a densely realized society. The city is New York, the persons are largely low-grade professionals, the action takes place in offices, apartments, bars and cafes — places detached from much association, and permitting only tenuous relationships. The city, its heat ("On some nights New York is as hot as Bangkok,"[1] the novel begins), the crowds and the general abrasiveness of urban existence dominate the book; and in this context life is a rough, competitive struggle not only with other persons but with impersonal forces — with the subway doors that close upon one as one gets out of the train, as we find Leventhal doing as the novel opens. Leventhal is the lonely man in the crowded city, the man for whom the presence of so many other people is a permanent threat, as it must seem to anyone in the highly competitive petty bourgeois world to which he belongs. He has "got away with it" (20), found a niche, but it is an unsafe one and he is aware that he can easily fall again. This feeling of insecurity creates the mood of high tension in which the book is conducted. It is a world in which, as Allbee remarks, there are few opportunities for choices, and most of one's life is conducted accidentally:

> We don't choose much. We don't choose to be born, for example, and unless we commit suicide we don't choose the time to die, either. But having a few choices in between makes you seem less of an accident to yourself. It makes you feel your life is necessary. The world's a crowded place, damned if it isn't. It's an overcrowded place. There's room enough for the dead. Even they get buried in layers, I hear. There's room enough for them because they don't want anything. But the living. . . . Do you want anything? Is there anything you want? There are a hundred million

others who want that very same damn thing. I don't care whether it's a sandwich or a seat in the subway or what. I don't know exactly how you feel about it, but I'll say, speaking for myself it's hard to believe that my life is necessary. . . . Who wants all these people to be here, especially forever? Where're you going to put them all? Who has any use for them all? (193-94)

The world is then a jostling for places in which some go to the wall, and in which every man tries to ensure that it is not he. The city feels inhuman — Leventhal feels its presence like an animal — and the irritation of fighting and pushing makes every person intemperate, hostile. The awareness of the absence of any equitable mean of life (New York can be as hot as Bangkok; its inhabitants can be of all racial stocks) suggests too the overriding anarchy of this various city; no one moral scale fits all its cases, and no individual life is protected from the inroads that other persons choose to make upon it. Any personal order that a man makes out of the confusion is constantly challenged or threatened. In this sense the book is a "melting pot" novel, covering several different moral and emotional systems — Jewish, Anglo-Saxon, Italian-American. And the races are constantly set against each other; each has his own suspicion of persecution. Leventhal feels that there is a "black list" against Jews, Allbee that there is a Jewish set-up, the marriage of Asa's brother is disturbed by its mixed strains. Nobody knows his place, for there is no class system; no promises are made in advance. All feel isolated and detached and alienated. The contracts that take place between people are largely casual, often abrasive. Most of Leventhal's encounters are in fact with crowds — crowds on the ferry, on the subway, on the streets, in the parks and the cafeterias and the office-blocks — or with his own family, a broken unit, or with the disintegrating Jewish community. His brother has gone off, neglecting his family; his relationship with his wife is flawed by his memory of her previous lover; and during the substantial action of the novel she is away from home and Leventhal, alone in his apartment, is made at once aware of the thinness of the strands of love and of its importance in a world where so much works against it. The barriers between people — barriers of race and moral system, and even physical barriers (Leventhal's brother's family live on Staten Island, and he is forced to cross a ferry whenever he goes to see them) — are more evident than any ties; each man is thrown back upon himself alone.

Leventhal is very much a product of such an uncertain world. His character is a mixture of sensitivity and an aggressiveness that he feels is necessary in the city if someone is not to put something over on him. Security is of the utmost importance to him, since he is terrified of falling; and because he has been successful he is inclined to interpret the world as rewarding those who deserve it and pushing down those who do not. One of the things that he must learn in the book is that there is an element of chance and also of historical necessity in success and failure. By and large, however, Leventhal's insistence on responsibility is shown to us as just; his problem is simply to discern the true nature of his responsibility. Indeed, throughout the book, Bellow puts him into the position of having to distinguish between responsibilities of different kinds — to his work, and to his brother's family; to Allbee, and to his wife; to his general humanity, and to his Jewishness. And indeed, as I have indicated, the reason why the true and accurate discerning of responsibilities is of such importance is that it is precisely in this urban, competitive and morally confused situation that they are tenuous and *not* recognizable. Thus the important happening in the book is that in the course of its action Leventhal acquires a new understanding, an understanding about the nature of a general responsibility, and this involves a radical change in his view of what constitutes humanity, and of what way the social system works.

The confrontation with Allbee is the means by which this change in understanding is produced; and this confrontation is a great imaginative invention, the one event that makes the novel seem to us terrifyingly modern. Allbee is a face out of the crowd, come to claim from Leventhal a new attitude toward the world. He is a double — Allbee the ostensible victim, Leventhal the real one. He is the anarchistic principle that breaks up Leventhal's moral order, with its firm conviction of right and wrong, with its distant attitude toward others, with its touchiness about persecution. He is also the figure of that fall into the outcast state that Leventhal fears above all things. The chronological order of the book is so shaped as to give this confrontation all its possible force; although the plot chronologically begins when Leventhal goes for an interview with a prospective employer, Rudiger, and loses his temper with him, so helping to bring about the dismissal of Allbee, the book *actually* begins with the encounter with Allbee, now down and out, menacing, unrecognized by Leventhal. Leventhal himself is now in a state of reasonable good fortune; and he is completely unconscious of any duty or any link between himself and Allbee. Similarly, though the story is seen from Leventhal's point of view (we too experience his shock), yet at the same time the author provides us with sufficient detachment from him, so that we can notice his mixed character — he is a clerkly half-hero — and, at the beginning of the novel, his incomplete moral values.

The main plot is also widened and elaborated by a sub-plot which has to do with another kind of responsibility, this time for the death of his nephew, in a situation which is once again morally indeterminate; and Leventhal's experiences in this narrative are used to indicate to us what steps he has made in his contacts with Allbee. It is further widened by a speculative running discussion carried on among the Jewish community of the book, a discussion about the nature of humanity, which affects Leventhal considerably. In short, Bellow evolves elaborate means of commenting on, and giving breadth to, his fable, and it is no small kind of understanding that Leventhal must come to if he is

to do justice to the elaborate apparatus of the book. The whole inter-
lude with Allbee, in fact, provides Leventhal with a nightmare experience which is at once part of and a challenge to the workaday world in
which he lives. And it is worth remarking that the shape of the book is
a development towards a perception that Leventhal cannot permanently
use in his life, but only recall from time to time.

In one sense, what is required of Leventhal is an intellectual
change, the development of a better, more adequate account of the way
the world works. Thus Leventhal's philosophy at the beginning of the
book is highly moralistic and individualistic — he believes that people
are responsible for the quality of their own actions, and that they con-
trive their own fates. This philosophy to some extent debars sympathy
for others, since if they have done badly in life they only have themselves to blame; and to some extent, too, it cuts him off from his own
past of hardship. It is, curiously enough, the Anglo-Saxon, "aristo-
cratic" Allbee who taxes him with this, and confronts him with an
environmentalist philosophy (a kind of philosophy one more naturally
associates with the proletarian and the poor — but this, now, is what
Allbee is). Allbee challenges, repeatedly, Leventhal's Jewishness, and
does so on the grounds that it is a spirit closed to sympathy:

> You won't assume that it isn't entirely my fault. It's necessary for you to
> believe that I deserve what I get. It doesn't enter your mind, does it —
> that a man might not be able to help being hammered down? What do you
> say? Maybe he can't help himself? No, if a man is down, a man like me,
> it's his fault. If he suffers, he's being punished. There's no evil in life
> itself. And do you know what? It's a Jewish point of view. You'll find it
> all over the Bible. God doesn't make mistakes. He's the department of
> weights and measures. If you're okay, he's okay, too. That's what Job's
> friends come and say to him. But I'll tell you something. We do get it in
> the neck for nothing and suffer for nothing, and there's no denying that
> evil is as real as sunshine. (146)

In this way the moral and the social are closely intermingled, and
Leventhal is forced into suspecting that his moralizing does not adequately describe the competitive world in which he lives, a world in
which history has turned and the immigrant stock is on the upward lad-
der, while the Anglo-Saxon races are losing their traditional status.
Allbee puts the point when he refers to what has happened to his sense
of honor:

> You know, I'm from an old New England family. As far as honor's con-
> cerned, I'm not keeping up standards very well, I admit. Still, if I was
> born with my full share of it, in New York I'd have an even worse hand-
> icap. Oh, boy! — New York. Honor sure got started before New York
> did. You won't see it at night, hereabouts, in letters of fire up in the sky.
> You'll see other words. Such things just get swallowed up in these condi-
> tions — modern life. So I'm lucky I didn't inherit more of a sense of it.
> I'd be competing with Don Quixote. (141)

And he evinces a persecution complex that is just the reverse of Leventhal's — it is a Jewish "ring" that keeps him out of a job, a Jewish spirit that is on the rise to threaten the old stock, who are now just "remnants." In such a situation, as Allbee realizes, the old promises that are made in stable societies are no longer met; every man is uncertain about what place he may take up, and this leads to a general uncertainty of direction and standards:

> The world's changed hands. I'm like the Indian who sees a train running over the prairie where the buffalo used to roam. Well, now that the buffalo have disappeared, I want to get off the pony and be a conductor on that train. I'm not asking to be a stockholder in the company. I know that's impossible. Lots of things are impossible that didn't use to be. When I was younger I had my whole life laid out in my mind. I planned what it was going to be like on the assumption that I came out of the lords of the earth. I had all kinds of expectations. But God disposes. There's no use kidding. (232)

The message is simple and cogent, yet it is not the message of the book; and it is the measure of Bellow's complexity and of his characteristic interests that this idea contests in Leventhal's mind with another interpretation of the human condition expressed by Mr. Schlossberg, one of the Jewish community with whom Leventhal has casual dealings. He speaks for an extra-social standard that is neither environmental nor moralistic, a standard that is simply constituted as a lyrical hymn to human possibility. Schlossberg's opinions first appear simply as a judgment on stage-acting (the imagery of acting and the theatre is strong in the novel): "Good acting is what is exactly human. And if you say I am a tough critic, you mean I have a high opinion of what is human. This is my whole idea. More than human, can you have any use for life? Less than human, you don't either" (133). Most actors see people as packages; most businessmen believe simply in business. They have no idea of greatness and beauty. But, says Schlossberg: "I am as sure about greatness and beauty as you are about black and white. If a human life is a great thing to me, it *is* a great thing. Do you know better? I'm entitled as much as you. And why be measly? Do you have to be? Is somebody holding you by the neck? Have dignity, you understand me? Choose dignity. Nobody knows enough to turn it down" (134).

And the idea is returned to toward the end of the book, when Leventhal is moving toward his crisis, recognizing an essential human sympathy with Allbee, doubting the accuracy of his observations with respect to his brother's family. In a discussion about the way in which Americans seek to evade the thought of death, Schlossberg speaks of the fact that there is a limit to every man: "There's a limit to me. But I have to be myself in full. Which is somebody who dies, isn't it? That's what I was from the beginning. I'm not three people, four people. I was born once and I will die once. You want to be two people? More than human? Maybe it's because you don't know how to be one" (255).

What Leventhal has to find is the kind of responsibility he owes to Allbee, to himself and to mankind in general; and this involves his widening his moral system into an inclusive sense of humanity and a larger sense of human possibility — that possibility of which Schlossberg is the spokesman. It involves a paring down of social redundancy; and since truth never comes but in blows (as Henderson realizes) this requires a showdown:

> What he meant by this preoccupying "showdown" was a crisis which would bring an end of his resistance to something he had no right to resist. Illness, madness, and death were forcing him to confront his fault. He had used every means, and principally indifference and neglect, to avoid acknowledging it and he still did not know what it was. But that was owing to the way he had arranged not to know. He had done a great deal to make things easier for himself, toning down, softening, looking aside. But the more he tried to subdue whatever it was that he resisted, the more it raged, and the moment was coming when his strength to resist would be at an end. (157-158)

Leventhal, in short, comes to realize that every man contains within himself a principle toward order and a principle toward anarchy, and that for commitment to either principle one paid a price: "You couldn't find a place in your feelings for everything, or give at every touch like a swinging door, the same for everyone, with people going in and out as they pleased. On the other hand, if you shut yourself up, not wanting to be bothered, then you were like a bear in a winter hole, or like a mirror wrapped in a piece of flannel. And like such a mirror you were in less danger of being broken, but you didn't flash, either. But you had to flash" (98). Leventhal has thought this earlier in the novel, recognizing that people contain in themselves at once a something that is against sleep and dullness, and the caution that leads to sleep and dullness. And he repeats: "We were all the time taking care of ourselves, laying up, storing up, watching out on this side and on that side, and at the same time running, running desperately, running as if in an egg race with the egg in a spoon" (99).

When the showdown comes, it is an onrush of anarchy that destroys the "balance" that Leventhal has built up in himself. Allbee brings a woman into his flat; Leventhal breaks in on Allbee's "love" (much as earlier Allbee has broken in on Leventhal's); this disorderly act seems to bring about Leventhal's "release." In a dream the woman, who has been an anarchistic, unbearable principle, is related with his wife; then Allbee returns to the flat and tries to gas himself and incidentally Leventhal. It is an onrush of horror, the end of the nightmare, in which a kind of symbolic intermingling of identities takes place. It is also a death experience by which Leventhal is released, to be reborn into ordinary human life. He is invigorated; and when we see him in the last chapter, a coda, he has been "lucky," looks younger, and has done fairly well. But he now has firmly a sense of two orders of life. One is the workaday order, in which success is haphazard, and in which people nonetheless are expected to commit themselves entirely to their work; the other is an order which offers a different kind of duty and a different kind of promise — a promise of full humanity. One order refers to present social arrangements, which assign people to different roles and classes, to seats in various parts of the theatre in front of the varied display of life; the other, the order in which there are "more important things to be promised," refers to life fully lived, a hope which the book raises but cannot describe or include (in this sense it prepares for some of Bellow's later novels). Allbee, who reappears in this coda as seedily successful — "just a passenger" on the train he has spoken of before, living off an actress — has come to terms with society, the first order. But the novel closes with an unanswered question from Leventhal — "Wait a minute, what's your idea of who runs things?" he cries after Allbee (294) — which refers to the incompleteness of both their solutions.

One of the epigraphs to the novel is the *Thousand and One Nights* story about the merchant who eats a date in the desert and throws away the stone. An Ifrit appears and threatens to kill him, because the stone has struck and murdered the Ifrit's son. It is a tale about the ease with which we may violate the universe about us, and it will be remembered that Coleridge evoked it in connection with *The Ancient Mariner*. What Bellow chooses to heighten in his treatment is the accidental as well as the general nature of human responsibility to others and to the living fabric of the world. Like the Wedding Guest, Leventhal is picked out by someone who, as the novel puts it, emerges from the crowd and says *You!* The tale is told entirely from the point of view of the man thus accosted and changed. In the *Arabian Nights* tale the merchant redeems himself by his honorableness and his telling of stories; in *The Victim* Leventhal, who is both Mariner and Wedding Guest, makes a conscious and an unconscious repentance. More positive moral action is required of him than in the two previous fables. Nor is his redemption complete. Bellow's powerful awareness of the relevance and interrelatedness of *all* action, deliberate and accidental, is one of the great qualities that make his writing important (just as it is this that makes *The Ancient Mariner* so great a poem). In his novel there is a deep sense of the metaphysical, the supernatural, which elevates and stylizes the action. We are concerned in the book with the human condition as it relates specifically to competitive urban life in present-day New York, and Bellow certainly makes extensive use of the insights of the American naturalists. These writers, "veritists" concerned with the sordid and with the direct pressures of environment, are particularly relevant to the sense of uncertainty about rank and place that Bellow is concerned to convey; the intense economic competition in a labor market continuously expanded by immigration is a theme Bellow takes from their work, and one can see why he has confessed a debt to Dreiser. But, being realists, concerned with the representation of "actuality," they did not attempt to sustain any metaphysical insights, whereas Bellow most certainly does. This seems to me his essential strength. His concern is present, unobtrusively, from the start, and manifests itself in a subdued lyricism of style, and a slight heightening of effects. He avoids usually direct symbolic references, except in something like his naming of Allbee. But the way in which the jostling of people in crowds comes to dominate *The Victim* — reinforced by such touches as Leventhal's knocking his ring against the bedpost when visiting the sick child — and the crowds become crowds of the pleading damned, shows the sort of intensity he is trying to convey. The stylization is all in the direction of mythic and psychological intensification; the tale becomes a tale for all men. Thus his management of the confrontation of Leventhal and Allbee, his use of dream, his presentation of sickness of spirit, has that kind of preciseness and clarity only present in the writer with serious psychological concerns. For this kind of effect we must look for a comparison to the French existential writers and their Russian mentors.

In his article "Saul Bellow: Five Faces of a Hero," Ihab Hassan speaks of Bellow's aim as being "to convince us that reality or experience of life — call it what we will — is worth all the agonies of human existence without ever needing to be intelligible,"[2] and though there is indeed a search for intelligibility the predominant mode is indeed that of a kind of lyrical celebration of human existence, a pleasure at its mystery. Thus, despite his debt to the realists, he does extend far beyond realism, converting a limited deterministic philosophy into something very much larger, more "poetic." This lyrical intensity, this concern and celebration, forms the texture rather of his later novels; but in this one we are always conscious of its existence. To some extent Bellow is, like some of the realists, interested in the redeeming act of will, in the superman who can, without transcending his humanity, make his life meaningful; Leventhal falls short of this. But because of the dense texture both of the individual and the social, and the sufficient reality he allows to each, he can be found to deal with one of the most pressing of our present concerns, that of his relation to the social fabric which makes him and yet of which he feels himself to be insufficiently a part. He is, I think, among the most substantial of the younger novelists writing in English because of the intensity and the finesse with which he realizes this theme.

Notes

1. Saul Bellow, *The Victim* (New York: Vanguard, 1947), 3. Subsequent references in the text from this edition.
2. Ihab Hassan, "Saul Bellow: Five Faces of a Hero," *Critique: Studies in Modern Fiction* 3.3 (1960): 28-36. Hassan's article is extended in his *Radical Innocence: Studies in the Contemporary Novel* (Princeton, N.J.: Princeton UP, 1961).

*   *   *

The Holocaust in *The Victim*
S. Lillian Kremer

In the late 1960s two critical views of the treatment of the Holocaust in Jewish writing were prevalent. One position was that Holocaust treatment in American Jewish literature was inadequate, another that it was an ever present, though subdued, component of the fiction. In a 1966 essay dealing with Israeli Holocaust fiction, Robert Alter lamented: "With all the restless probing into the implications of the Holocaust that continues to go on in Jewish intellectual forums . . . it gives one pause to note how rarely American Jewish fiction has attempted to come to terms . . . with the European catastrophe."[1] In 1969, Lothar Kahn observed: "No Jewish writer . . . has written a book without the memory of Auschwitz propelling him to issue warnings, implied or specific against the "Holocaust."[2]

The Bellow canon illustrates these seemingly contradictory contentions, as it both subordinates and confronts the Holocaust. Although the Holocaust is generally absent from the dramatic center of Bellow's fiction, the works are rich in characters haunted by its specter. Moses Herzog repeatedly visits the Warsaw Ghetto, finding "the stones still smelling of wartime murders."[3] Humboldt Fleisher refuses an invitation to present a lecture series in Berlin because he is fearful that former Nazis will kidnap him. He reasons that a year in Germany would be a constant reminder of "the destruction of the death camps, the earth soaked in blood, and the fumes of cremation still in the air of Europe."[4] In addition to the substantive treatment rendered the subject in *The Victim* and *Mr. Sammler's Planet*, Bellow returned to the topic parenthetically in his non-fiction work, *To Jerusalem and Back*.

Saul Bellow was at the forefront of American readiness to cope with the European debacle. Most observers cite *Mr. Sammler's Planet* (1970) as his first Holocaust novel. Not so. Bellow's leadership in this area predates even Edward Wallant's admirable 1961 contribution, *The Pawnbroker*. Bellow's first contribution to Holocaust literature, *The Victim*, appeared in 1947, and to date has not been associated with the Holocaust in the critical press.

Discussion of *The Victim* has rightly centered on the dynamics of interaction between Jew and anti-Semite. Perhaps because Bellow was ahead of his time, perhaps because readers were not yet ready to face such horrors in literature, Holocaust matter in *The Victim* has passed unnoticed in the criticism. But the Holocaust symbolism of the novel is itself a matter of complexity and certainly of moment to critical evaluation. Bellow's method reflects historic pattern. Just as Nazi persecution

From *Saul Bellow Journal* 2.2 (1983): 15-23.

of European Jewry can be discerned as an evolutionary product of centuries of indigenous European anti-Semitism, so too can Bellow's Holocaust imagery be read as an organic outgrowth in a novel whose subject is the complex nature of anti-Semitism.

The Victim pits Asa Leventhal, a first generation American Jew, and Kirby Allbee, an anti-Semite, against each other. Leventhal believes himself a victim of social and economic manifestations of American anti-Semitism. Allbee's antagonism toward Jews stems from his feeling of being a member of an older order, traditionally bred to rule and influence American society but now being displaced by the descendants of non-English immigrants. Allbee's obsessive and irrational hatred is dramatized by frequent diatribes against American Jews for infiltrating and polluting American culture.

Bellow uses the conflict between Allbee and Leventhal to reveal the intricate and diverse nature of anti-Semitism. He invests Allbee with an amalgam of twentieth-century anti-Jewish arguments: economic displacement, cultural pollution, and racism, which had supplanted but had not eliminated the religious hysteria common to earlier centuries.

Illustrative of Bellow's allusive treatment of the Holocaust is his use of figurative language and imagery to relate Allbee's anti-Semitism to the heinous Nazi variety flourishing in the years preceding publication of *The Victim*. Allbee's language and imagery correspond to the Nazi propaganda of the 1930s. He believes that leaders of American society should be drawn from his class and reflect its values and he is, therefore, distressed by the growing Jewish influence in America. Allbee's insistence on the inordinate Jewish presence in American civilization is comparable to the absurd Nazi charge that Jews were gaining control of German life. "It's really as if the children of Caliban are running everything. . . . The old breeds are out."[5] With masterful economy of means, Bellow conveys not only the social and political implications of Allbee's remarks, but also uses Shakespearean allusion to evoke the peculiar rhetoric of Nazism. The Caliban reference implies the Third Reich's official classification of Jews as a subhuman species.

Not only does Allbee object to imposition of Jewish culture on American life, he also echoes the Nuremburg Laws of 1935 which forbade persons of more then twenty-five percent Jewish blood to play the music of Bach, Beethoven, Mozart, and other "Aryan" composers, when he insists that Jews not comment on or interpret American music and literature. This attitude is revealed at a party, when Albee admonishes a Jew for singing an American spiritual: "You shouldn't sing those old songs. You have to be bred to them . . . . sing a psalm, . . . any Jewish song. Something you've really got feeling for" (44). This exclusive attitude is reiterated during a later argument about Jewish encroachment on American culture. Albee despairs that a Jewish scholar has had the audacity to publish a book about the American Transcendentalists, Emerson and Thoreau. He is certain that "people of such background simply couldn't understand" (132).

Distressed by this blatant anti-Semitic insistence that the Jew, no matter how assimilated to the host culture, can never fully appreciate non-Judaic Western philosophy and poetics, Asa passionately associates cultural anti-Semitism with the ultimate violent variety, referring overtly to the Holocaust: "Millions of us have been killed" (133). This outburst provides internal evidence of Bellow's intention to link Allbee's remarks to Nazi propaganda. Although he uses only this direct correspondence with the Holocaust, Bellow's symbolic delineation of the atmosphere of the period, rendered in images commonly associated with Nazi persecution of European Jewry, is pervasive and yields an absorbing framework for *The Victim*'s thematic exploration of anti-Semitism.

Bellow consistently foreshadows or follows anti-Semitic verbal assaults on Asa with a single or fused reference to the archetypal images of the Holocaust: the yellow badge of shame, the resettlement trains, and asphyxiation by gas. Furthermore, the historic context of the Holocaust in European history is suggested by yellow, a symbol of degradation imposed on the Jewish people since the Middle Ages. Nazi insistence that the Jews wear a yellow identity badge was but a revival of a medieval ruling of the Catholic Church. Bellow supplements his use of yellow as traditional image of oppression with other symbols peculiar to the modern technological age. Asa's depression in crowded American trains induced by manifestations of anti-Semitism evoke the daily transports of European Jews crammed into cattle cars for resettlement in Nazi labor and death camps. Lethal gas, which the Germans perfected as a mass murder weapon, is an additional element in this imagery. Allbee's aborted assassination of his Jewish victim by gas from his apartment stove is a grotesque parody of Nazi use of gas showers and crematoria to effect the "Final Solution to the Jewish Question."

Consistently, yellow images surface when Asa is oppressed by the anti-Jewish remarks or behavior of his employer, Mr. Beard; his sister-in-law, Elena; and her mother. As Asa travels by train and ferry to Staten Island in muggy air, dampness, and gloomy yellow light to be with his terminally ill nephew, echoes of his employer's anti-Jewish comments reverberate in his ears. As he broods about Mr. Beard's statement that Jews take unfair advantage of others, he anticipates an unpleasant encounter with the child's grandmother, who he believes regards him with "spite and exultation as though he were the devil" (159). Asa is convinced that the old woman is full of hate because "a Jew, a man of wrong blood, of bad blood, had given her daughter two children" (61). Bellow objectifies Asa's anxiety during the ferry ride to Staten Island by means of color and burning imagery: "scorched, smoky gray and bare white . . . the light over them over the water was akin to the yellow revealed in the slit of the eye of a wild animal, say a lion, something inhuman that didn't care about anything human" (52).

In the early passage, Bellow begins the crucial juxtaposition of yellow with fire imagery, both operative on realistic and symbolic levels. The sun, sustainer of life, is thus transformed into an oppressive symbol as its glare beats down on the shoreline towers. Moreover, the oppressive yellow of the exterior environment is extended to the novel's interior setting. As Asa notes the surroundings of his nephew's sickroom "the yellowish, stiff web over the blackness of the window"(60), he imagines that the grandmother views the child's fatal illness as punishment for his mother's marriage to a Jew.

Asa grieves doubly for the loss of a child and for the loss of a Jew to the faith and people, as he suffers Elena's reproachful stare at her son's funeral. In the context of a Catholic funeral service which effectively obliterates any sign of the boy's Judaic identity, Asa considers the possibility that Elena has had the children baptized and the affront that would have been to their Jewish grandfather. Asa's mood is concretized in the imagist fusion of a yellow shine of a chauffer's uniform and the smoke of a priest's cigarette. During the return ferry ride to New York, Asa "caught a glimpse of the murky orange of the hull, like the apparition of a furnace on the water" (163). *Yellow* and *smoke* are transformed to the more intense *orange* and *furnace* corresponding to Asa's mounting and deepening sense of oppression.

Integration of realistic cityscape and metaphoric Holocaust landscape is sustained in train imagery. Bellow uses train imagery in conjunction with yellow and gas images to confirm Asa's anxiety about the Christianizing of his nephew. Following a condolence visit to his brother Max, Asa's pain is rendered symbolically as the "lead car with its beam shot toward them in a smolder of dust" (213) and the "concussion of the train" (213) is felt. Leaving his brother in the subway, Asa ascends to the open air and experiences difficulty breathing. Thus yellow light, train, and suffocation imagery, the archetypal images of the Holocaust, are encapsulated in a single scene of anguish stemming from Asa's feelings of anti-Semitic generated victimization.

In another train sequence, Bellow introduces dream, a device which is also frequently employed by European Holocaust writers who find in it a means to suggest the victims' disorientation and dislocation, their fear of chaos in a disordered universe, and their anxiety regarding personal survival.[6] Bellow skillfully combines train image and dream technique in order to evoke Asa's sense of desperation as the anti-Semite, Kirby Allbee, insinuates himself into his life:

> He had an unclear dream in which he held himself off like an unwilling spectator. . . . He was in a railroad station, carrying a heavy suitcase, forcing his way with it through a crowd . . . flags hanging by the hundreds. . . . He had missed his train, but the loudspeaker announced that a second section of it was leaving in three minutes. The gate was barely in sight; he could never reach it in time. There was a recoil of the crowd — the guards must have been pushing it back — and he found himself in a corridor. . . . It seemed to lead down to the tracks. . . . He began to run and suddenly came to a barrier. . . . Two men stopped him. "You can't go through," . . . "This isn't open to the public. Didn't you see the sign on the door? . . . You can't go back the way you came either," Leventhal turned and a push on the shoulder sent him into an alley. (150-151)

On a psychological level, the dream suggests the extreme anxiety created by Allbee's intrusion into Asa's life. On a symbolic level, it depicts Nazi transports of Jews to the death camps. Railroad station, flags, barriers, recoiling crowds pushed by guards, and sealed entrances are united to convey a Kafkaesque atmosphere. The dream crowd is herded by guards, much as European Jewry was herded to the death transports. By chance, Asa evades transport; by chance, American Jews escaped the fate of European Jewry.

Early in the novel, Allbee and Leventhal meet on a hellish summer night, "the redness in the sky, like the flame in a vast baker's oven" (28). In this manner, Bellow introduces the persecutor-victim relationship of anti-Semite and Jew and simultaneously foreshadows the novel's climax, the attempted suicide and murder in which Allbee uses Asa's oven to try to kill himself and the unsuspecting Jew. While Allbee is trying to play out the death scene, Asa suffers a tortured nightmare set in a surrealistic amusement park where he sees "round yellow and red cars whipping around and bumping together" (245). A dream composed of an environment which is visually disorienting and frenzied in atmosphere suggests Asa's anxiety which stems from his forced association with the anti-Semite. Asa is roused from his chaotic dream world to face a nightmarish reality: "Gas was pouring from the oven" (246). At the window, Asa observes that "long line of lamps hung down their yellow grains in the gray and blue of the street" (246). Thus the novel's climactic confrontation of anti-Semite and Jew merges dream and Holocaust imagery to delineate the Nazi dementia which Jewry had recently suffered and survived. Allbee's aborted attempt to gas himself and Leventhal is a powerful Bellovian parody of Germany's sinister "Final Solution to the Jewish Question," the gas chambers and ovens of Treblinka, Chelmno, and Auschwitz.

An ironic analogy exists in the correspondence of humanity's wartime disinterest in the slaughter of European Jews and the post-war failure of literary critics to note Bellow's symbolic evocation of those events. Aside from a desire to put the painful past out of mind, it is difficult to explain why the prodigious mass of Bellow criticism has failed to acknowledge the Holocaust imagery pattern in this early American fictional treatment of the century's most horrific crime.

The unprecedented vigor with which American novelists have explored the Holocaust in the late 1960s and through the 1970s must have assuaged Robert Alter's earlier dismay at the paucity of Holocaust treatment in our national literature. Publication from 1967-1969 of Richard Ellman's trilogy, *The 28th Day of Elul, Lilo's Diary*, and *The Reckoning*; Norma Rosen's *Touching Evil* and Ilona Karmel's *An Estate of Memory*; appearance at the dawn of the seventies of Bellow's *Mr. Sammler Planet* followed by Susan Schaeffer's *Anya* at mid-decade; and Styron's *Sophie's Choice*, Epstein's *King of the Jews*, and Roth's *The Ghost Writer* at the decade's end testify to this period as an era of substantial Holocaust exploration in American literature.

Cited repeatedly by many critics and readers as the foremost voice in contemporary American literature, it is Saul Bellow who paved the way in this hitherto unapproachable territory for American authors. It is Bellow, in the role of artist-seer, who has reminded us, after decades of the tendency of modern literature to be its own source, estranged from modern society,[7] that it is appropriate for the writer to accept the role of moral authority which society imputes to its men of letters.[8] Bellow's career is a testimonial to the vision of the writer as sage and guide. A distinguished moral voice of twentieth-century literature, Saul Bellow has confronted the central issues of our time, including the Holocaust, with intelligence and courage.

Notes

1. Robert Alter, "Confronting the Holocaust: Three Israeli Novels," *Commentary* 41 (1966): 67.
2. Lothar Kahn, "The American Jewish Novel Today," *Congress Bi-Weekly* 36 (1969): 3.
3. Saul Bellow, *Herzog* (Greenwich, Conn.: Fawcett, 1964), 37.
4. Saul Bellow, *Humboldt's Gift* (New York: Avon Books, 1976), 156.
5. Saul Bellow, *The Victim* (New York: New American Library, 1965), 133. Subsequent references in the text from this edition.
6. Lawrence L. Langer, *The Holocaust and the Literary Imagination* (New Haven: Yale UP, 1975).
7. Saul Bellow, "The Thinking Man's Wasteland," *Saturday Review of Literature* (3 Apr. 1965): 20.
8. Saul Bellow, "The Writer As Moralist," *Atlantic Monthly*, 211 (March 1963): 58-62.

* * *

The Adventures of Augie March (1953)

Portrait of an American, Chicago-Born
Arthur Mizener

This is a big book, not just physically but in purpose, by a writer of talent. Like most big books, it has failures, but its successes are very impressive. It has, to begin with, a great range of characters and events. Good as these are, however, they do not exist for their own sake. Mr. Bellow is acutely aware of the clutter of contingency in ordinary life, and Augie March has to deal with as much of it as the rest of us. This ordinariness, this almost overwhelming everydayness makes both convincing and impressive Augie's determination to understand his life, not just live it. He struggles to the end to keep his head above the welter of happenings, so that his adventures become almost a pilgrimage — through an endless Slough of Despond which Augie learns to understand without despair.

Most of what Mr. Bellow is up to is implicit in the first paragraph, where he has Augie March introduce himself. "I am an American, Chicago born — Chicago, that somber city — and go at things as I have taught myself, free-style, and will make the record in my own way: first to knock, first admitted; sometimes an innocent knock, sometimes a not so innocent."

So Augie makes the record of his life, commenting on himself and the world around him in this queer mixture of learning, homely figures and ironic diction, with an occasionally oddly moving touch like "Chicago, that somber city." It is the record of an impoverished, second-generation Jewish boy who seldom strikes out on a course of his own but always resists the courses set by others because he is determined "to have a fate good enough." He goes through childhood under the dominance of Grandma Lausch, "one of those Machiavellis of small street and neighborhood that my young years were full of,"

From *New York Herald Tribune Book Review* (20 Sep. 1953): 2.

through a young manhood of learning from a shrewd neighborhood operator and a queer North-Side family which tries to adopt him. After a period when he tries to follow the pattern of money and success because his brother Simon, whom he loves very much, has chosen it, he falls deeply in love with a rich girl named Thea, who carries him off to Mexico in order that they "man" an American Eagle and hunt the giant Iguana. This love affair — and the hunting scheme — ends in disaster, and the book concludes with Augie married to another girl and living in Paris, working for an Armenian named Mintouchian, who is an international operator.

But such a summary gives hardly an idea of the book's richness of detail or of its quality, which comes primarily from Mr. Bellow's special sense of the strangeness of people. At its best — when this special sense is probing for what drives recognizable people — it produces characters of great brilliance, like Einhorn, the neighborhood operator whom Augie compares to Caesar and Ulysses. This comparison has the initial charm of absurdity and the quite surprising merit, before Mr. Bellow is through, of being almost convincing. For the qualities are really there; only the circumstances differ. If a man's character is his fate, then Einhorn is a superior man. This is a genuine — and perhaps romantic — democratic vision; no wonder Mr. Bellow is fascinated by Machiavelli and Rousseau. But this way of seeing people has its dangers, too. Sometimes, as with Mintouchian, the characters seem merely grotesque.

This air of weirdness is increased by the novel's being written in the first person. The immediate advantages are great, for Augie's meditations are often exciting. The trouble is that he is a fully developed character with his own angle of vision and his own limitations and at the same time our only source of information about the way things really are, and we are constantly at a loss to know whether what we are told is only Augie's notion or really so. This difficulty even affects Mr. Bellow's prose. He piles up modifiers, splitting and spreading them until you can scarcely guess what goes with what; then he separates the clauses by periods as if they were sentences. Or he produces unlikely and confusing colloquialisms like "In the peculiar fate of people that makes them fat and rich, when this happens very swiftly there is the menace of the dreamy state that plunders their reality." Since nothing of this sort goes on in Bellow's earlier novels, it must be deliberate here; the novel would be better without it.

But despite these difficulties, this is an impressive book; it really makes you feel that there are underlying qualities in people which are often good and always touching. Or as Augie puts it:

> You take that poor Rousseau in the picture he leaves of himself, stubble-faced and milky, in a rope-wig, while he wept at his own opera performed at court for the monarch, how he was encouraged by the weeping of heart-touched ladies and fancied he'd like to gobble the tears from

their cheeks — this sheer horse's ass of a Jean-Jacques who couldn't get on with a single human being goes away to the woods of Montmorency in order to think of the *best* government or the *best* system of education. . . . That's what the more deep desire is under the apparent ones.

* * *

The Man With No Commitments
Robert Penn Warren

The Adventures of Augie March is the third of Saul Bellow's novels and by far the best one. It is in my opinion a rich, various, fascinating, and important book, and from now on any discussion of fiction in America in our time will have to take account of it. To praise this novel should not, however, be to speak in derogation of the two earlier ones, *The Dangling Man* [sic] and *The Victim*. Both of these novels clearly indicated Saul Bellow's talent, his sense of character, structure, and style. Though *The Dangling Man* did lack narrative drive, it was constantly interesting in other departments, in flashes of characterization, in social and psychological comment. In *The Victim*, however, Bellow developed a high degree of narrative power and suspense in dealing with materials that in less skillful hands would have invited an analytic and static treatment. These were not merely books of promise. They represented — especially *The Victim* — a solid achievement, a truly distinguished achievement, and should have been enough to win the author a public far larger than became his. They did win the attention of critics and of a hard core of discriminating readers, but they were not popular.

The Dangling Man and *The Victim* were finely wrought novels of what we may, for lack of a more accurate term, call the Flaubert-James tradition. Especially *The Victim* depended much on intensification of effect by tightness of structure, by limitations on time, by rigid economy in structure of scene, by placement and juxtaposition of scenes, by the unsaid and withheld, by a muting of action, by a scrupulous reserved style. The novel proved that the author had a masterful control of the method, not merely fictional good manners, the meticulous good breeding which we ordinarily damn by the praise "intelligent."

It would be interesting to know what led Saul Bellow to turn suddenly from a method in which he was expert and in which, certainly, he would have scored triumphs. It would be easy to say that it had been from the beginning a mistake for him to cultivate this method, to say that he was a victim of the critical self-consciousness of the novel in our time, to say that in his youthful innocence he had fallen among

From *New Republic* (2 Nov. 1953): 22-23.

the thieves of promise, the theorizers. Or it would be easy to say that the method of the earlier books did not accommodate his real self, his deepest inspiration and that as soon as he liberated himself from the restriction of the method he discovered his own best talent.

These things would be easy to say but hard to prove. It would be equally easy to say that the long self-discipline in the more obviously rigorous method had made it possible for Bellow now to score a triumph in the apparent formlessness of the autobiographical-picaresque novel, and to remember, as a parallel, that almost all the really good writers of free verse had cultivated an ear by practice in formal metrics. I should, as a matter of fact, be inclined to say that *The Adventures of Augie March* may be the profit on the investment of *The Dangling Man* and *The Victim*, and to add that in a novel of the present type we can't live merely in the hand-to-mouth way of incidental interests in scene and character, that if such a novel is to be fully effective the sense of improvisation must be a dramatic illusion, the last sophistication of the writer, and that the improvisation is really a pseudo-improvisation, and that the random scene or casual character that imitates the accidental quality of life must really have a relevance, and that the discovery, usually belated, of this relevance is the characteristic excitement of the genre. That is, in this genre the relevance is deeper and more obscure, and there is, in the finest examples of the genre, a greater tension between the random life force of the materials and the shaping intuition of the writer.

It is the final distinction, I think, of *The Adventures of Augie March* that we do feel this tension, and that it is a meaningful fact. It is meaningful because it dramatizes the very central notion of the novel. The hero Augie March is a very special kind of adventurer, a kind of latter-day example of the Emersonian ideal Yankee who could do a little of this and a little of that, a Chicago pragmatist happily experimenting in all departments of life, work, pleasure, thought, a hero who is the very antithesis of one of the most famous heroes of our time, the Hemingway hero, in that his only code is codelessness and his relish for experience is instinctive and not programmatic. This character is, of course, the character made for the random shocks and aimless corners of experience, but not merely irresponsible. If he wants freedom from commitment, he wants wisdom, and in the end utters a philosophy, the philosophy embodied by the French serving maid Jacqueline, big-legged and red-nosed and ugly, standing in a snowy field in Normandy, hugging still her irrepressibly romantic dream of going to Mexico.

But is this comic and heroic philosophy quite enough, even for Augie? Augie himself, I hazard, scarcely thinks so. He is still a seeker, a hoper, but a seeker and hoper aware of the comedy of seeking and hoping. He is, in fact, a comic inversion of the modern stoic, and the comedy lies in the tautology of his wisdom — our best hope is hope.

For there is a deep and undercutting irony in the wisdom and hope, and a sadness even in Augie's high-heartedness, as we leave him standing with Jacqueline in the winter field on the road toward Dunkerque and Ostend. But to return to the proposition with which this discussion opened: if Augie plunges into the aimless ruck of experience, in the end we see that Saul Bellow has led him through experience toward philosophy. That is, the aimless ruck had a shape, after all, and the shape is not that of Augie's life but of Saul Bellow's mind. Without that shape, and the shaping mind, we would have only the limited interest in the random incidents.

The interest in the individual incidents is, however, great. In *The Victim* the interest in any one episode was primarily an interest in the over-all pattern, but here most incidents, and incidental characters, appeal first because of their intrinsic qualities, and, as we have said, our awareness of their place in the over-all pattern dawns late on us. In incident after incident, there is brilliant narrative pacing, expert atmospheric effect, a fine sense of structure of the individual scene. In other words, the lessons learned in writing the earlier books are here applied in another context.

As for characterization, we find the same local fascination. The mother, the grandmother, the feeble-minded brother, the brother drunk on success, the whole Einhorn family, Thea, the Greek girl — they are fully realized, they compel our faithful attention and, in the end, our sympathy. As a creator of character, Saul Bellow is in the great tradition of the English and American novel, he has the fine old relish of character for character's sake, and the sort of tolerance which Santayana commented on in Dickens by saying that it was the naturalistic understanding that is the nearest thing to Christian charity.

It is, in a way, a tribute, though a back-handed one, to point out the faults of Saul Bellow's novel, for the faults merely make the virtues more impressive. The novel is uneven. Toward the last third the inspiration seems to flag now and then. Several episodes are not carried off with the characteristic elan, and do not, for me at least, take their place in the thematic pattern. For instance, the Trotsky episode or the whole Stella affair, especially in the earlier stages. And a few of the characters are stereotypes, for example, Stella again. In fact, it is hard to see how she got into the book at all except by auctorial fiat, and I am completely baffled to know what the author thought he was doing with her, a sort of vagrant from some literary province lying north-northeast of the *Cosmopolitan Magazine*. Furthermore, several critics have already said that the character of Augie himself is somewhat shadowy. This, I think, is true, and I think I know the reason: it is hard to give substance to a character who has no commitments, and by definition Augie is the man with no commitments. This fact is a consequence of Bellow's basic conception, but wouldn't the very conception have been stronger if Augie had been given the capacity for deeper commitments, for more joy and sorrow? He might, at least, have tried the adventurer's experiment in those things? That is, the character tends now to be static, and the lesson that Augie has learned in the end is not much different from the intuition with which he started out. He has merely learned to phrase it. There is one important reservation which, however, I should make in my criticism of Augie. His very style is a powerful device of characterization. It does give us a temper, a texture of mind, a perspective of feeling, and it is, by and large, carried off with a grand air. Which leads me to the last observation that the chief release Saul Bellow has found in this book may be the release of a style, for he has found, when he is at his best, humor and eloquence to add to his former virtues.

*   *   *

The New American Adam in *Augie March*
Steven M. Gerson

In the epilogue of *The American Adam*, R. W. B. Lewis contends that Saul Bellow's *The Adventures of Augie March* is written in the tradition of the earlier American Adamic myth. According to Lewis, Augie March, the protagonist in Bellow's novel, is similar to the nineteenth-century Adams evident in Cooper, Emerson, Thoreau, and Whitman because Augie is as youthful, innocent, optimistic, and adventurous as are the earlier Adams.[1]

Throughout much of Bellow's novel, Augie is similar to an early American Adam who seeks to make of America an earthly paradise and Lewis's mention of Augie as such an Adam is justified. However, as Augie matures and experiences heartbreak in love, the dissolution of family ties, the stock market crash, labor conflicts between the AFL and the CIO and World War II, he loses much of his youthful Adamic resilience and optimism. In fact, he becomes pessimistic, defeated, and broken, traits anathema to early American Adamism.

Nonetheless, inasmuch as Augie seeks paradise, he is still Adamic. But rather than envisioning paradise as the fulfillment of the American dream Augie envisions paradise as an escape from modern American dilemmas. Thus, in *The Adventures of Augie March*, Bellow deviates from Lewis's traditional concept of the American Adam applicable to the nineteenth century and creates a distinctly new and different character — a modern American Adam whose personality has been shaped by twentieth-century honors. An analysis of *The Adventures of Augie March* will reveal Augie's transformation from an early American Adam as defined by Lewis to a modern American Adam.

From *Modern Fiction Studies* 25.1 (1979): 117-128.

Lewis defines the early American Adam "as a figure of heroic innocence and vast potentialities, poised at the start of a new history." He also states that the image of the American Adam "had about it always an air of adventurousness, a sense of promise and possibility" (1). Lewis assumes that Augie fulfills these characteristics of the old American Adam inasmuch as Augie "takes on as much of the world as is available to him, without ever fully submitting to any of the world's determining categories." He "struggles tirelessly . . . to realize the full potentialities of the classic figure . . . [of] the simple genuine self against the whole world" (198).

The fact that Augie represents the Old American Adam is evinced clearly in the first sentence of the novel. Augie, the omniscient narrator, asserts, "I am an American, Chicago born — Chicago, that somber city — and go at things as I have taught myself, free-style, and will make the record in my own way."[2] Immediately Bellow develops a character who is adventurous, optimistic, self-reliant, and "poised at the start of a new history."

Moreover, in this first picture of Augie, he is similar to the Adamic figure in Whitman's poem, "As Adam early in the morning,"[3] who is the consummate example of the innocent and adventurous American excited at the prospects of beginning life. Augie recalls a sermon preached by a "Reverend Beecher telling his congregation, 'Ye are Gods, you are crystalline, your faces are radiant!'" (83). Though Augie is "not an optimist of that degree," he says, "I was and have always been ready to venture as far as possible" (83). As an idealistic youth, Augie is optimistic about his future and approaches all prospective experiences with an unflagging adventurousness.

The only qualification to his enthusiasm is that he questions how his desires can be fulfilled in Chicago, "that somber city." As an Adamic figure, Augie regrets the fact that Chicago, with its "deep city vexation" and "deep city aims," disallows the "nature-painted times, like the pastoral of Sicilian shepherd lovers" (92). He regrets that the city and the "crowd" yield "results with . . . difficulty," for what he desires is "happiness," "the misery-antidote" which he fails to discern in Chicago (92-93). Augie "longed very much" for excitement, and he sees himself as an innocent youth untouched by the "vice and short-comings" of the city or "the weariness of maturity" (92). Therefore, because Chicago fails to accommodate his idealistic desires, Augie yearns for the "early scenes of life . . . beginning with Eden" (92).

Despite the squalor of his surroundings and the vexations of the city, Augie maintains an optimistic view and is unbeaten by life. As he says, he "lacked the true sense of being a criminal, the sense that [he] was on the wrong side of the universal wide line with the worse or weaker part of humankind" (48). It simply "wasn't in [his] nature to fatigue [himself] with worry" (11).

Augie is able to avoid a sense of defeat primarily because he is consistently "too larky and boisterous" (11). Throughout the novel, he is usually able to overlook the faults in others, absorb his difficulties, and see his "crimes more tolerantly" (32). In fact, he is usually so affable and optimistic in the face of trouble that one character says to Augie, "A train could hit you and you'd think it was just swell and get up with smiles, like knee-deep in June" (297).

Possibly because Augie reveals this adventurousness, optimism, and cheerful immunity to traumas, characteristic traits of the early American Adam he is constantly challenged by "*Reality instructors*" who seek to deflate his affability. In *Herzog*, Bellow has his protagonist, Moses Herzog, confronted by cynical characters whom he calls "*Reality instructors*" because they seek "*to teach*" and "*to punish*" Moses with "*lessons of the Real.*"[4] Bellow further states that these instructors hope to teach Herzog to "suffer and hate" and attempt to drag him "down in the mire of post-Renaissance, post-humanistic, post-Cartesian dissolution, next door to the Void" (93). Though the term "*Reality instructors*" primarily is related to *Herzog*, it also applies to the cynics in *The Adventures of Augie March.*[5]

The first such instructor Augie encounters is Grandma Lausch, a boarder in the March home, who, though "not a relation at all," appropriates command of the house (3). Augie describes her as a Machiavelli (2) who enjoys making the Marches "take a long swig of her mixture of reality" (55). Primarily, her "mixture of reality" is "one more animadversion on the trustful, loving, and simple surrounded by the cunning-hearted and tough, a fighting nature of birds and worms, and a desperate mankind without feelings" (9). She preaches cynicism and ruthlessness as the only means of survival, while debunking Augie's type of optimism and innocence. Throughout Augie's youth, she commands his home by advocating her ideals: scheming, devising, intrigue (3).

When Augie is older and leaves the house to work, he escapes Grandma Lausch's cynical dogmatism, but encounters another Machiavellian instructor, William Einhorn. Augie states that if he had truly been Einhorn's disciple instead of an innocent optimist, he would have approached any important decision by asking himself, "What would Caesar suffer in this case? What would Machiavelli advise or Ulysses do? What would Einhorn think?" (65).

Initially, Einhorn is not a Machiavellian cynic advising deceit and cunning. Augie admits that "Einhorn had a teaching turn similar to Grandma Lausch's, both believing they could show what could be done with the world, where it gave or resisted, where you could be confident and run or where you could only feel your way and were forced to blunder" (79). But Einhorn's instructions, at first, enforce Augie's inherent optimism. Einhorn, a semi-corrupt entrepreneur who revels in the American system of free enterprise, compares the businessman to "the conqueror, the poet and philosopher" and assumes that business offers "a world of possibilities" (72-73). By working for Einhorn as an all-purpose secretary, Augie flourishes under the atmosphere of hope and accomplishment pervading Einhorn's home and offices. Einhorn preaches optimistically about "the machine age and the kind of advantage that had to be taken of it," and Augie gladly receives the lectures "from the learned *signor*" (78).

However, Einhorn's optimism is shattered by the stock market crash, in which he "was among the first to be wiped out" (117). After this debacle, Einhorn becomes like Grandma Lausch, a reality instructor overcome by cynicism and hoping to teach Augie of the "Void." Augie states that Einhorn now

> intended that, as there were no more effective prescriptions in old ways, as we were in dreamed-out or finished visions, that therefore, in the naked form of the human jelly, one should choose or seize with force; one should make strength from disadvantages and make progress by having enemies, being wrathful or terrible. (204)

Having lost his wealth and position due to the crash, Einhorn also loses his sense of hope in the "possibilities" of America and preaches a version of cunning and deceit even more sinister than Grandma Lausch's.

After Einhorn, Augie is forced to endure the cynical instructions of Mrs. Renling, an influential and wealthy woman, who seeks to adopt him and his brother Simon. Renling, whose vocation seems to be to "coach" and "instruct" (146), constantly pesters Augie with what he calls "damnation chats" (153). Like the previous reality instructors, she seeks to demean Augie's persistent "splendor of morning" attitude by calling "out her whole force of rights, apocalypse death riders, church-porch devils who grabbed naked sinners from behind to lug them down to punishment, her infanticides, plagues, and incests" (153). Augie, however, manages to ignore her pessimistic instructions and maintain his optimism, just as he manages to ignore his brother's reality instructions. Though Simon tells Augie to make himself "hard," Augie avoids Simon's cynical outlook, in which he "didn't fundamentally believe" (267).

Augie's final reality instructor is Mimi Villars. Like the other instructors, she berates Augie about how he "wasn't mad enough about abominations or aware enough of them, didn't know many graves were underneath [his] feet, was lacking in disgust, wasn't hard enough against horrors or wrathful about swindles" (233). She, too, tries to teach him her cynical viewpoint and tries to drag him down into the mire of nihilism. Augie, however, rejects her instructions. Though she asserts that "most people suffer," Augie can only tell her "about how pleasant [his] life has been" (284-85). He maintains an optimistic concept of life; he is unable to believe that "all was so poured in concrete and that there weren't occasions for happiness" (285).

Despite the instructions by Grandma Lausch, Einhorn, Mrs. Renling, Simon, and Mimi, all of whom attempt to destroy Augie's youthful and innocent views, Augie continues to illustrate traits of the early American Adam. He is adventurous, optimistic, and unbeaten by his experiences. He is self-reliant and chooses to approach life with his rosy attitude rather than be determined by the cynical instructions of his associates. Eventually Einhorn realizes that Augie is defiant and says: "But wait. All of a sudden I catch on to something about you. You've got opposition in you" (129). Augie agrees: "I did have opposition in me, and great desire to offer resistance and to say 'No!'" (129). He states, "No, I didn't want to be what [Einhorn] called determined" and "wouldn't become what other people wanted to make of me" (130). Primarily, Augie resists being beaten or tormented or made cynical; he chooses to maintain a youthful optimism even in the face of tribulation.

At one point in the novel, Augie clarifies his position further. He believes that there are two ways of approaching life. One can accept the "reality" of every day occurrences and thus submit to drudgery and the commonplace, or one can rise above normalcy and seek a more "triumphant" life. That Augie assumes life can be divided into only these two categories hints at his naiveté. That he chooses to ignore what he considers normalcy and yearns for adventure accentuates his role as the youthful optimist. He says,

> I had no eye, ear, or interest for anything else — that is, for usual, second-order, oatmeal, mere-phenomenal, snarled-shoelace-carfare-laundry-ticket plainness, unspecified dismalness, unknown captivities; the life of despair-harness, or the life of organization-habits which is meant to supplant accidents with calm abiding. Well, now, who can really expect the daily facts to go, toil or prisons to go, oatmeal and laundry tickets and all the rest, and insist that all moments be raised to the greatest importance, demand that everyone breathe the pointy, star-furnished air at its highest difficulty, abolish all brick, vaultlike rooms, all dreariness, and live like prophets or gods? Why, everybody knows this triumphant life can only be periodic. So there's a schism about it, some saying only this triumphant life is real and others that only the daily facts are. For me there was no debate, and I made speed into the former. (216)

What Augie does is describe a dichotomy between "reality" and fantasy; he ironically states that no one can really believe in the "periodic" triumphant life, but that one should surely accept "the daily facts" propounded by reality instructors such as Lausch, Einhorn, Renling, Simon, and Villars; then he asserts that he does choose triumph over reality, adventure over normalcy, and optimism over the "despair-harness."

An interesting scene in the novel which further reveals that Augie is like the early American Adam, living innocently before the fall, occurs when Augie first encounters Thea Fenchel, an Eve-like temptress. Augie has gone to a resort with Mrs. Renling where he sees and falls in love with Esther Fenchel, Thea's sister. Esther pays little attention to Augie, but Thea is attracted to him. One evening, Augie goes into an orchard to brood over Esther, and in the garden he hears

> someone light coming near, a woman stepping under the tree into the dusty rut worn beside the swing by the feet of kids. It was Esther's sister Thea, come to talk to me, the one Mrs. Renling warned me of. In her white dress and her shoes that came down pointed shapes of birds in the vague whiteness of the furrow by the swing, with lace on her arms and warm opening and closing differences of the shade of leaves back of her head, she stood and looked at me. (160)

In this Eden-like setting where Augie has gone to find solace from his defeated love for Esther, Thea intrudes and tries to seduce him. Beneath the "orchard leaves" she kneels beside him, seductively touches his feet and ankles with her thighs, and says she has fallen in love with him (161-162). Augie, the always innocent fantasist, is astonished that she would challenge his love for Esther by professing her own love for him. He stands up to leave and says to her, "Now, Miss Fenchel. . . . You're lovely, but what do you think we're doing? I can't help it. I love Esther" (162). Thea, however, is adamant and attempts to pursue him. Recognizing her intentions, Augie "had to escape from the swing and get away in the orchard" (163). He retreats further into the garden rather than confront Thea's seduction. In doing so, he exemplifies the type of innocence characteristic of the early American Adam.

His Adamic role is finally accented when, following the scene with Thea, Augie goes to a pier to wait for his brother Simon, who is planning a vacation near the resort at which Augie and Mrs. Renling have stayed. While he waits for his brother to disembark from a ship, he watches other vacationers and describes them as "tough or injured, . . . bearers of things as old as the most ancient of cities and older; desires and avoidances bred into bellies, shoulders, legs, as long ago as Eden and the Fall" (164). The implication is that these vacationers have suffered the ramifications of the fall from Eden and thus are "tough" and "injured." By juxtaposing these characters with Augie, who has just retreated into the garden to avoid consummation of "desires," Bellow underlines Augie's role as an innocent Adam.

However, despite Augie's attempts to remain innocent, optimistic, adventurous, and unbeaten; despite his attempts to remain like the early American Adams, he encounters a number of devastating occurrences which finally shatter his idealism. First, his friend Mimi Villars becomes pregnant, attempts to have an abortion, procures the services of an incompetent doctor, and almost dies from his butchering. Second, an acquaintance of Augie's sees him helping Mimi, assumes he is the father of the child, and runs to tell Lucy Magnus, Augie's fiancée, that Augie has been unfaithful. Though Augie is not the father but only has attempted to aid Mimi, Lucy and her parents break off the engagement. Next, Simon, who has chosen Lucy for Augie because she is wealthy, is offended that Augie has compromised himself and lost this chance at an economically promising marriage. In his anger, Simon more or less disinherits Augie and says he never wants to see him again. Though Augie is able to stand up under the pressures rather well, he suffers a final indignity which crushes his optimism. He is caught in a squabble between the AFL and the CIO, is beaten by agitators, and has to hide to avoid being killed.

After these traumas, Augie loses much of his innocence and states that he "was no child now, neither in age nor in protectedness, and [he] was thrown for fair on the free spinning of the world" (318). Though his reality instructors had been unsuccessful in shaking his optimism, the traumas he suffers succeed in forcing him to realize that life is brutal and that no one can remain as idealistic and youthfully innocent as he had been.

Augie recognizes that his initial innocence has been destroyed, and he finds that "in any true life you must go and be exposed outside the small circle that encompasses two or three heads in the same history of love. Try and stay, though, inside. See how long you can" (318). Once Augie concludes that he has lost Eden, he no longer is like the early American Adams; Bellow proceeds to depict Augie as a modern Adam who is defeated by life and who seeks to escape the world by envisioning a new Eden in which he can hide. Before, he had retreated into the garden to avoid Thea's seduction so that he could maintain his youthful innocence. Now, Augie has to seek a new Eden in which he can retrieve the innocence he has lost.

Ironically, Thea offers him his first vision of escape in Eden. Thea plans to go to Mexico to get a divorce, and she "assumed that [Augie would] go to Mexico with her" (350). Augie, having been wounded by reality, "never seriously thought of refusing" her primarily because he thinks Mexico will allow him to escape his traumas (350). He concludes this because Thea has suggested that in Mexico they will experience "something better than what people call reality" (353). To this suggestion, Augie thinks, "Very good and bravo! Let's have this better, nobler reality" (353). That Mexico will be paradisiacal for Augie is further indicated when we learn that Thea's house in Mexico is called "Casa Descuitada" — "Carefree House" (383). The implication is that Mexico will obliterate Augie's cares by allowing him a return to innocence in a new Eden.

However, as Patrick Morrow states, Bellow is a hopeful artist who has come to "believe that man's living within society is preferable to self-imposed alienation."[6] Bellow asserts that it is impossible to escape reality by envisioning paradise and that one must adapt to the world rather than attempt to flee it. To accentuate this assertion, Bellow surrounds Augie's trip to Mexico with portents and eventually depicts Mexico as a pseudo-paradise which is actually hellish. For instance, even before Augie departs for Mexico, he is made uneasy by his friends' warnings not to go. "Nobody, then, gave the happy *bon voyage* I'd have liked. Everybody warned me. . . . I argued back to myself that it was just the Rio Grande I had to cross, not the Acheron, but anyway it oppressed me from somewhere" (360-61). Immediately the tone is set. Though Augie hopes to find a paradise in Mexico, Bellow equates the trip to one into hell.

This portentous atmosphere is furthered when we learn that Thea, the temptress earlier in Augie's life, plans to travel to Mexico "with snake-catching equipment" (357). In fact, once Augie and Thea are in Mexico, Thea spends much of her time collecting snakes or visiting "snaky" areas (395). After a while, she has collected so many snakes and deposited them at her home that Augie says their porch became "a snake gallery" (402), and they "seemed in the age of snakes among the hot poisons of green and the livid gardenias" (395). In this sense, Thea compliments her earlier role as an Eve-like seductress who promises Augie, the Adamic character, pleasure, but who actually threatens his safety in Eden.

The final portent surrounding Augie's supposedly paradisiacal venture into Mexico is that Thea takes with her an eagle which she plans to train to hunt iguanas. Though the eagle is Thea's idea, the chore of handling it is relegated to Augie. Forced to spend a great deal of time with the eagle, which he names Caligula, Augie becomes almost possessed by it. Just as Thea is a snake-like temptress who corrupts Augie's paradise, Caligula, who glides "like a Satan," is a demonic invasion into Eden (377). The eagle becomes almost a demon reminder to Augie of his mortality. As he says, "In the most personal acts of your life you carry the presence and power of another; you extend his being in your thoughts, where he inhabits. Death, with monuments, makes great men remembered like that. So I had to bear Caligula's gaze" (374). Rather than finding Eden in Mexico, Augie resides with the satanic eagle whose gaze he must endure and whose deathly emanations enter and inhabit his thoughts.

These incidents which cloud Augie's quest for paradise prove to be portentous inasmuch as his stay in Mexico is disastrous. Not only does he suffer an accident in which his skull is cracked, but also Thea and he drift apart, fight, and end their relationship. Thea leaves him alone at her "Casa Descuitada," and for days he feels like one of "the damned" (445). Rather than retrieving his lost innocence, optimism, and adventurousness as he had hoped to do in the new Eden, he finds no solace. In fact, his having sought escape in paradise leaves him even more wounded than he was before he left for Mexico. Alone in Mexico, he says,

> suddenly my heart felt ugly, I was sick of myself. I thought that my aim of being simple was just a fraud, that I wasn't a bit goodhearted or affectionate, and I began to wish that Mexico from beyond the walls would come in and kill me and that I would be thrown in the bone dust and twisted, spiky crosses of the cemetery, for the insects and lizards. (447)

Perhaps one of the reasons Augie suffers so in Mexico is that his expectations are excessively romantic. He assumes that Mexico will be paradisiacal; when this assumption proves fallacious, he is destroyed. If he could learn to adapt to reality rather than seek escape, he possibly could avoid such pains. After Thea leaves him, he comes close to recognizing his penchant for fantasy and thus adapting to life. He states, "my invention and special thing was simplicity. I wanted simplicity and denied complexity" (449). At this point in the novel, he realizes that he has desired to hide from the complexity of life; he continues to say that "whoever would give [him] cover from this mighty free-running terror and wild cold of chaos [he] went to" (449).

With this realization, he decides to find Thea, ask for her forgiveness, and start a more realistic life with her. However, the more he thinks of her, the more he dreams of a perfect, paradisiacal life that the two could share. "Imagining how this would be, I melted, my chest got hot, soft, sore, and yearning. I saw it already happening. It's always been like that with me, that fantasy went ahead of me and prepared the way" (450). Rather than adapt to reality, Augie again chooses to fantasize about life with Thea.

Though Augie and Thea never get back together, his dreams of paradise continue. Later in the novel, he tells a friend of his that he hopes to buy "a piece of property and settle down on it" and start a school (508). Because his friend is leery of the idea, Augie attempts to remove his friend's fears. Augie states that his idea is not fantastic. "Oh, I don't expect to set up the Happy Isles. I don't consider myself any Prospero. I haven't got the build. I have no daughter. I never was a king, for instance. No, no, I'm not looking for any Pindar Hyperborean dwelling with the gods in ease, a tearless life, never aging" (508).

However, Augie kids himself by debunking his own idea. Despite his claims to the contrary, what he envisions is a paradise in which he will have a chance at beating "life at its greatest complication and *meshuggah* power" by starting "lower down, and simpler" (510). What he actually desires is a pastoral Eden. "What I had in my mind was this private green place like one of those Walden or Innisfree wattle jobs under the kind sun, surrounded by velvet woods and bright gardens and Elysium lawns sown with Lincoln Park grass seed" (575).

Because a number of characters in the novel see that Augie is a dreamer who will not adapt to reality, they try to correct him of his excessive idealism. Unlike the reality instructors who tried to force their cynicism on Augie, characters like Padilla and Clem Tambow simply try to teach Augie to be more realistic. Padilla tells Augie that he wants too much,

> and therefore if you miss out you blame yourself too hard. But this is all a dream. The big investigation today is into how *bad* a guy can be, not how good he can be. You don't keep up with the times. You're going against history. Or at least you should admit how bad things are, which you don't do either. (481)

Padilla recognizes that Augie is detached from reality and is unable to adapt to the world. He does not necessarily want to drag Augie down into the "mire" or the "Void" as did the reality instructors; he simply wants Augie to get in step with history and at least see the world clearly.

Clem Tambow tells Augie "practically the same thing" (481). He states that Augie's ambitions are too general and that Augie is "not concrete enough" (483). He says to Augie, "What I guess about you is that you have a nobility syndrome. You can't adjust to the reality situation" (484). Because of this, Tambow fears that Augie is "going to ruin [himself] ignoring the reality principle and trying to cheer up the dirty scene." He believes that Augie "should accept the data of experience" (485).

Considering Augie's experiences in Mexico, one can assume that it would be better for him to overcome his naive idealism and see the world clearly. However, Augie never is able to adapt to life. On the contrary, despite his traumatic experiences throughout the book, the novel ends with Augie "grinning again":

> That's the *animal ridens* in me, the laughing creature, forever rising up.
> . . . I am a sort of Columbus of those near-at-hand and believe you can come to them in this immediate *terra incognita* that spreads out in every gaze. I may well be a flop at this line of endeavor. Columbus too thought he was a flop, probably, when they sent him back in chains. Which didn't prove there was no America. (599)

Patrick Morrow says that Augie's comments at the end of the novel reveal that Augie has succeeded in adapting to the world, "accommodating through the comic, specifically by his good-natured grin" (402). Such a comment is difficult to accept inasmuch as Augie has grinned throughout the novel but has met with one dilemma after another. His grins seem to be not an accommodation but a naive and juvenile inability to perceive the facts of life and assess them maturely. Ihab Hassan supplies a more acceptable interpretation when he says that the novel offers "no proper ending." Whereas Morrow assumes that Augie's "good-natured grin" allows him to adapt successfully to the world, Hassan states that at the end of the novel, Augie is still one of the uninitiated. "Augie remains, like Huck, uncommitted, suspended, as it were, between native innocence and hard-earned knowledge, poised for the next adventure which, though it may not actually repeat a former escapade, guarantees no final knowledge or repose."[7]

The implication of Bellow's ending is that for Augie there is always some unknown land, some distant horizon that is fertile ground for his imagination and for his desire for escape in a paradise. At the end of the novel, Augie is searching for peace and happiness; though he might be "a flop" like Columbus and end up "in chains," as a modern American Adam he will not discount the possibility of a new Eden. He chooses to ignore reality and live in dreams; he fails to adapt to the world.

Notes

1. R. W. B. Lewis, *The American Adam: Innocence, Tragedy and Tradition in the Nineteenth Century* (Chicago, IL: U of Chicago P, 1955), 198. Subsequent references in the text from this edition.
2. Saul Bellow, *The Adventures of Augie March* (New York: Avon, 1977), 1. Subsequent references in the text from this edition.
3. Walt Whitman, "As Adam early in the morning," *Leaves of Grass and Selected Prose* (1921; rpt. New York: Modern Library, 1950), 92.
4. Saul Bellow, *Herzog* (New York: Viking, 1967), 125. Subsequent references in the text from this edition.
5. Tony Tanner, in *Saul Bellow* (New York: Barnes & Noble, 1965), 45-46, 94, and Brigitte Scheer-Schaezler, in *Saul Bellow* (New York: Ungar, 1972), 35ff. supply lengthy discussions of the extent to which the phrase "Reality Instructors" applies to numerous characters in *Augie March* who give the innocent protagonist their debased, cynical views of life.
6. Patrick Morrow, "Threat and Accomodation: The Novels of Saul Bellow," *Midwest Quarterly* 8 (Summer 1967): 389.
7. Ihab Hassan, *Radical Innocence: Studies in the Contemporary American Novel* (Princeton, NJ: Princeton UP, 1961), 311.

* * *

Looking Back at *Augie March*
Richard Pearce

Augie March was trying to save money for his college tuition. He was working at a luxury dog club — where his clients were entertained as well as steamed, massaged, manicured, clipped, and taught not only manners but tricks. And he found that he could make extra money by working for Manny Padilla, who was working his way through college by stealing books.

> Sooner than I had planned I quit the dog club, and it wasn't only confidence in my crook's competence that made me do it, but I was struck by the reading fever. I lay in my room and read, feeding on print and pages like a famished man. Sometimes I couldn't give a book up to a customer who had ordered it, and for a long time this was all I could care about. . . . Padilla was sore and fired up when he came to my room and saw stacks of books I should have gotten rid of long ago; it was dangerous to keep them. . . . "You can use my card and get it out of the library," he said. But somehow that wasn't the same. As eating your own meal, I suppose, is different from a handout, even if calorie for calorie it's the same value; maybe the body even uses it differently.[1]

From *New York Herald Tribune Book Review* (20 Sep. 1953): 2.

Three years ago, at a ceremony commemorating our new library addition, I was driven by some irrepressible adolescent impulse — and what I think was the spirit of Augie March — to read this passage. What a challenge: to get from stealing books to celebrating a library in five minutes. Now I would like to examine that impulse. For I have a hunch that Augie's urge to steal books — which derives from the spirit of play that animated Socrates, Erasmus, Rabelais, and a long line of rebellious humanists — is an expression of what captured the imaginations of so many American readers in the mid-fifties.

Right after World War II, many American writers and readers, identifying with the European experience, were profoundly influenced by the existentialism of Sartre and Camus. We were discovering or rediscovering Dostoevsky and Kafka. A religious revival, far different from the recent wave of fundamentalism, was generated out of "crisis theology" (Karl Barth and Paul Tillich emphasized original sin; Reinhold Niebuhr insisted on "moral man and immoral society"). Alienation was not just the result of social mismanagement or class exploitation; it was the human condition. We might aspire to be heroes but could never be more than victims of capricious powers that could be evoked only by the third-person, plural pronoun: "them." So words like *alienation* and *victimization* came into vogue — and the Jewish experience could become symbolic. Mark Shechner points out that *alienation* and *victimization* "became popular definitions of the Jewish sensibility, and the Jew became a stand-in for something known as 'the universal estrangement of man.'"[2] And he cites the Jewish fiction that contributed to this image: Isaac Rosenfeld's *Passage from Home* (1946), Lionel Trilling's *The Middle of the Journey* (1947), Delmore Schwartz' *The World is a Wedding* (1948), Paul Goodman's *The Breakup of Our Camp* (1949), Norman Mailer's *Barbary Shore* (1951), and Bernard Malamud's *The Natural* (1952). Bellow reinforced the image of the Jew as symbolic alien and victim in *Dangling Man* (1944) and *The Victim* (1947). None of these works achieved the recognition of Arthur Miller's *Death of a Salesman* (1949), though their effect was cumulatively significant. What brought Jewish fiction to the center of the cultural stage was *The Adventures of Augie March* (1953), and this was largely the result of a transformed Jewish hero. Though something of a schlemiel, no one had to say of Augie "attention must be paid!" Animated by self-confidence and "opposition," he commanded his own attention. And, since the novel was narrated in Augie's voice, attention was also paid to a new kind of fiction.

Even before it was published, Laura Z. Hobson was heralding Viking's "big fall novel" in the *Saturday Review of Literature*'s "Tradewinds" column. "Unless people like Robert Penn Warren, Lionel Trilling, Clifton Fadiman, and a host of others are all wrong, it's quite a book. . . . Mr. Fadiman, in his report for the Book-of-the-Month Club, calls the book 'a blockbuster of a novel, a howlingly American book,'

and predicts that 'it will set reviewers and public back on their haun-
ches.'"[3] And when *Augie March* appeared, the *Saturday Review*'s Harvey Curtis Webster said that reading this novel "in 1953 must be a
good deal like reading *Ulysses* in 1920."[4] Webster was fully aware of
the differences between Bellow and Joyce; he was comparing their
defiance of conventional technique and subject matter. Bellow's
innovations, we can see from today's perspective, may be far less striking than Joyce's. But we may appreciate Webster's point after even a
casual glance at many critics' objections to the novel's rambling structure, its inconclusive conclusion, the indeterminateness of its hero, the
inconsistencies of its narrative voice, to say nothing of its frank treatment of sex. Most important, though, this Jewish novel was hailed by
one influential critic as a "howlingly American book" and compared by
another to *Ulysses*, the modern work most noted for its universality.

Bellow began *Augie March* in the same spirit as *Dangling Man*
and *The Victim*. It was a "grim book," he recalls; in fact the writing
caused him "great revulsion." So he began conceiving something new:
"Augie March was my favorite fantasy. . . . Every time I was
depressed while writing the grim one, I'd treat myself to a fantasy
holiday."[5] Bellow's "fantasy holiday" is an American version of what
Mikhail Bakhtin calls "carnival" — a crude, sometimes farcical, open,
heterogeneous mode of expression, as opposed to the homogeneous,
closed, serious, "official" form. The American version is usually
restrained by vestiges of puritanism on the one hand and facile
optimism on the other. Neither Walt Whitman nor Huck Finn — with
whom Augie is frequently compared — could revel in the subversive,
indeed destructive, impulses loosened by the carnival spirit.

The Adventures of Augie March shocked and captivated readers of
the fifties because of what was considered crude humor and sexuality,
because of its heterogeneity, openness, and rebellious energy. But the
figure who approaches the comic subversiveness of carnival — and
who can only approach it, for important reasons I will explain later —
is not Augie but Grandma Lausch.

> She took her cigarette case out from under her shawl, she cut a Murad in
> half with her sewing scissors and picked up the holder. This was still at a
> time when women did not smoke. Save the intelligentsia — the term she
> applied to herself. With the holder in her dark little gums between which
> all her guile, malice, and command issued, she had her best inspirations
> of strategy. She was as wrinkled as an old paper bag, an autocrat, hard-
> shelled and jesuitical, a pouncy old hawk of a Bolshevik, her small rib-
> boned gray feet immobile on the shoekit and stool Simon had made in the
> manual training class, dingy old wool Winnie whose bad smell filled the
> flat on the cushion beside her. If wit and discontent don't necessarily go
> together, it wasn't from the old woman that I learned it. (5)

Grandma Lausch also taught Augie to lie. She coached him when,
as a nine-year-old, he took his mother to the free dispensary for eye
glasses. "The dispensary would want to know why the Charities didn't

pay for the glasses. So you must say nothing about the Charities, but that sometimes the money from my father came, and sometimes it didn't, and that Mama took boarders." Mama wasn't keen enough to lie with such delicacy. "That maybe one didn't need to be keen didn't occur to us; it was a contest" (2).

More than lying, Grandma Lausch inspired in Augie the love of contest. It was the love of contest that drove Augie to lie at the dispensary, to steal coal off the cars, clothes from the lines, rubber balls from the dime store, and pennies from the newsstands, to dump the Star Theatre handbills down the sewer, to join Gorman in robbing a leather goods store — and to steal books rather than use Manny Padilla's library card. Indeed, it is the love of contest that drives what R. W. B. Lewis calls the picaresque hero of the fifties through a world that is hostile and senseless.[6]

Einhorn characterizes Augie: "You've got *opposition* in you" (129). The opposition in Augie keeps him being defined by Einhorn, Mrs. Renling, Thea, Stella, Bateshaw, and Mintouchian. But Einhorn is only partly right. For along with opposition, Augie comes to discover, is "the *animal ridens* in me, the laughing creature, forever rising up" (599). The love of contest derives from both the spirit of opposition and the spirit of laughter or play. Remember, Grandma Lausch taught Augie that wit and discontent go together.

There is a precarious balance between the *no* of opposition and the *yes* of play. Grandma Lausch tips the balance toward opposition: her play is subversive. Augie's driving force, on the other hand, is affirmation. It enables him to find something positive in an enormous range of disagreeable characters, to see the world as open for new possibilities, to take up again after each failure — and to finally identify with Columbus, who also thought of himself as a flop, though that didn't prove there was no America (599).

Despite the opposition in him, Augie was not a rebel. His play was not subversive. He may have stolen coal off the cars and clothes off the clothes line and rubber balls from the dime store and pennies off the newsstand and cash from a leather goods store. He may even have stolen books rather than borrow a library card. But, unlike Grandma Lausch, he was never *that* engaged in the contest, and, therefore, was never a real threat to the established order. He read the books he stole, went to college, became a businessman, and remembered his family. He may have been naughty, but at heart he was always a good Jewish boy. So this was the new Jewish hero. This is why the Jewish experience could be universalized. This is why the novel sold so well in the mid-fifties.

America had lived through a depression without losing faith in the American dream and the open road. During World War II, we experienced the tenors of fascism and the devastation of bombings only through the news reports and the movies. According to a 1945 Gallup poll, only a third of the population was personally affected by the war; most "felt no great loss or deprivation." And when the war was over, *Look* magazine pictured the new American frontiers: the modern house, the automatic washer, express highways, the private plane, quick freezing.[7] By the year Augie appeared, one generation of women had been safely removed from the labor force to make way for returning veterans and another was raising large families in the suburbs. Thanks to the GI Bill, millions of young men were crowding into the universities or buying new homes. And the world was secure for "the organization man" in his gray flannel suit. If the first wave of postwar novels forced us to feel the *angst* of the modern condition, what a relief that, instead of another "grim book," we had Bellow's "fantasy holiday." And if this fantasy had the potential of carnival subversion, how nice that Augie's opposition was ameliorated by his affirmation.

Robert Alter may be right in calling our attention to affirmation, as opposed to *angst*, as the authentic Jewish response to a history of victimization.[8] But Bellow's affirmation derives from the tradition of Walt Whitman rather than the wandering Jew. And the cheeky, young Norman Podhoretz was indeed perceptive in detecting his "willed buoyancy."[9] Bellow's success was due to his Americanization of the Jewish hero. The urge to claim him as universal was an expression of our nascent imperialism, not to mention our need for new markets — which, at the end of the novel, Augie himself was helping to open up.

We should, of course, put "Americanize" and "universalize" in quotation marks, for Bellow's richly populated world contains no blacks, hispanics, or orientals, let alone native Americans. Indeed, it is important to recognize that Augie's ability to "go at things . . . free-style" (1) — in fact his very mobility — is only possible because he is a white male, who looks more like a Hollywood star than someone rooted in the Jewish ghetto of Chicago. Ralph Ellison's *Invisible Man*, published in the same year, depicts a black picaro who discovers that his mobility is only an illusion. His letter of recommendation to the powers of white society reads: "Keep this nigger boy running." He realizes his identity while hiding in a sewer. And his playfulness is truly subversive. Grandma Lausch — who taught Augie to lie — was trapped in the family apartment. Her subversive opposition precluded her from becoming anything more than a minor character in *The Adventures of Augie March*.

I don't mean to diminish our appreciation of Bellow's "howlingly American book," only to question the price of its success and define the nature of its impact. *The Adventures of Augie March* succeeded, first, by presenting a rebellious hero in a rebellious novel form — but the rebellion never threatened the established norms of writing, thinking, or acting. Augie could steal books from the library without losing the sympathy of the librarian or the respect of the professor. It also succeeded by seeming to Americanize and universalize the Jewish hero, but it actually perpetuated a role that was only available to white, acceptable-looking men.

In his autobiography *Making It*, Norman Podhoretz describes the letter Bellow sent to Robert Warshow, editor of *Commentary*, which published Podhoretz's review:

> "Your young Mr. P," he called me throughout, understandably not being able to bring himself to utter my despicable name; he said that I had charged his book with false spontaneity, but he himself, although only a graduate of the University of Chicago who had never enjoyed the advantages of so classy an education as I had had, knew this charge to be untrue. He had written the book and he knew. A writer knows these things and he knew. After repeating this point several more times, Bellow dismissed Warshow's avowal of admiration for the book, and ended the letter with an admonition from Cromwell: "I beseech you in the bowels of Christ, think it possible you may be mistaken."[10]

Despite Bellow's admonition, he too began making it in 1953.

Notes

1. Saul Bellow, *The Adventures of Augie March* (New York: Avon, 1977), 215-16.
2. Mark Shechner, "Jewish Writers." *Harvard Guide to Contemporary American Writing*, ed. Daniel Hoffman (Cambridge, Mass.: Harvard UP, 1979), 200.
3. Laura Z. Hobson, "Tradewinds," *Saturday Review of Literature* (22 Aug. 1953): 6.
4. Harvey Curtis Webster, "Quest Through the Modern World," *Saturday Review of Literature* (19 Sep. 1953): 13.
5. Bernard Kalb, "The Author," *Saturday Review of Literature* (19 Sep. 1953): 13.
6. R. W. B. Lewis, "Picaro and Pilgrim," *A Time of Harvest: American Literature, 1910-1960*, ed. Robert E. Spiller (New York: Hill and Wang, 1962), 144-153.
7. James Gilbert, *Another Chance: Postwar America, 1945-1968* (Philadelphia: Temple UP, 1981), ix, 8.
8. Robert Alter, "A Dissent from Modernism," *After the Tradition: Essays on Modern Jewish Writing* (New York: Dutton, 1969), 112-13.
9. Norman Podhoretz, "The Adventures of Saul Bellow," *Doings and Undoings: The Fifties and After in American Writing* (New York: Noonday, 1964), 218.
10. Norman Podhoretz, *Making It* (New York: Random House, 1967), 159.

* * *

Seize the Day (1956)

The Discovered Self
Herbert Gold

For the best of all reasons, *Seize the Day*, a collection comprising a novella, three short stories and a one-act play, is not an interim book between Saul Bellow's *The Adventures of Augie March* and his next novel. The reason is this: the long title story is a great one.

"Seize the Day" presents the essence of the life of Tommy Wilhelm, a yearning, youngish, middle-aged flop, crowded by New York, stunned by his dead marriage, manipulated by a crazy, fraudulent psychologist, under attack from his sly and malevolent old father, grasping wildly for significant relationship with himself and with others. He needs money, he needs love, he needs his own strength, and he seems at first to be sinking hopelessly in retreat from himself within the dense sea of Manhattan. Then abruptly the action turns around, and with the surge of magic which occasionally happens both in real life and in fiction, Tommy Wilhelm moves that redeeming vital inch from pity of self to perception of self. He weeps for a stranger's death.

The story presents an extension of Bellow's view of contemporary life, integrated here in a desperately focused action. We recognize his submissive, adaptable, strangely resilient hero; we find again the cagy, brilliant fraud who nuttily speaks the truth; the drama springs up within the blurring, blunting, bracing maelstrom of big-city life. Bellow is not much given to the besetting sin of American writers, a moral self-indulgence which we might call "Spokesmanship." Or when he falls, he falls with an indignant wit. Like Doctor Pep, Doctor Tamkin in this story is a stew of health and madness. As close to a spokesman as Bellow allows himself, Tamkin speaks from his own odd stance: "Now, Wilhelm, I'm trying to do you some good. I want to tell you, don't marry suffering. Some people do. They get married to it, and

From *Nation* (17 Nov. 1956): 435-36.

sleep and eat together, just as husband and wife. If they go with joy they think it's adultery . . . ." The truth of Tamkin's rant is demonstrated by real action (not symbolic action) in the life of Tommy Wilhelm.

The story, though an exhausting one and as close as "The Death of Ivan Ilyitch" to our primary experience, like Tolstoy's story escapes self-pity by the triumph of perception. A superficial reading might stimulate self-pity; the deeper sense of the story lies in something indicated by the energy of Bellow's prose in addition to the climactic incident itself — there is a redeeming power in self-knowledge, and a redeeming pleasure. Purged of hopelessness, Wilhelm can go on to some sort of self-determination in the world. A variety of stoicism seems to be emerging. A confrontation of the self can save us in a fragmented society — but this is an active, watchful stoicism which can do its part in putting the fragments back together.

"Seize the Day" enables us to take another look at Bellow's career. It represents an important integration of the dense unity of *The Victim* and the wide-ranging playfulness and pathos of *The Adventures of Augie March*. Bellow is working now with the born storyteller's directness. Incident does not distract from the underlying action; Tommy Wilhelm has the hallucinating fictional reality which Augie March sometimes sideslipped by irony. Irony is never used here to mask emotion; the humor bites without turning us away. The climactic scenes — with the father and at the end — are met climactically and feed each other. The value of Gertrude Stein's famous judgment, "Remarks are not literature," can be acknowledged in relation to the massive building, controlling and passion of this story. The rich play of incident and scene serves dramatic rather than symbolic purpose. The tale is of a magnificent piece.

The other work in the book is much lighter. "A Father-To-Be" shows a man in conflict about submitting to marriage; "Looking for Mr. Green" tells of a man ferociously working at a miserable job, for much more than the job's sake; "The Gonzaga Manuscripts" is a diversion and, despite its humorous moments, the only weak structure in the book. (Why isn't "The Sermon of Dr. Pep" included?) "The Wrecker" is a comic fantasy about marriage and the contrary passions toward security, toward freedom. The wife in it speaks a fine line about the needs of love and novelty: "Maybe the best way to preserve the marriage is to destroy the home."

"Seize the Day" gives contemporary literature a story which will be explained, expounded, and argued, but about which a final reckoning can be made only after it ripples out in the imagination of the generations of readers to come. I suspect that it is one of the central stories of our day.

*   *   *

Bellow Comes of Age
Robert Baker

It is a peculiarity of our age that the more significant statements about man are being made by people who speak in terms of the uptake of strontium-90 in human bone, or the release rate of serotonin in the brain. The throne once occupied by literature has seemingly been usurped (or abdicated — as you will) and so it is with some relief that we greet a new work by a novelist capable of saying something meaningful about life. With the novella from which this collection takes its title Saul Bellow demonstrates his attainment of full artistic maturity.

Briefly, "Seize the Day" depicts one crucial day in the life of a middle-aged New Yorker, Tommy Wilhelm (née Adler), whose own impulsiveness has brought him to the end of the trail, shorn of the conventional badges of identity. Jobless, separated from his wife, unable to marry his mistress, in conflict with his aged, successful father, Tommy is about to founder in the heavy seas of his financial and emotional obligations. The day in question is spent in frantic efforts to recoup his monetary losses by gambling his last seven hundred dollars in the commodities market under the guidance of a fascinating charlatan, Dr. Tamkin, with whom he has become embroiled. Interspersed with all this are Wilhelm's equally desperate attempts to review his past and discover some faint glimmer of meaning. Finally, at the funeral of a stranger he achieves a purgation, a sense of the value of merely being alive. But the action of "Seize the Day," so badly stated, conveys nothing of the work's concentrated power; it is all in the telling. Bellow has at last gained control of his never-questioned force: in earlier work he seemed unable to resist the temptation to digress, but here Bellow has piled scene upon scene, image upon image, building a marvelous focused crescendo that leaves the reader nearly as shattered as Wilhelm.

The three short stories and the one-act play that pad out the collection have all — like the title-piece — been previously published in periodicals. The principle (if such there be) behind their selection remains obscure, unless it is their common concern with the oppressive burden of the material world as symbolized by money: "Money surrounds you in life as the earth does in death," muses the protagonist of "A Father-to-Be." Undoubtedly competent, these stories do not match the brilliance of "Seize the Day," and so the less said about them the better.

"Seize the Day" logically culminates a line of development begun with *Dangling Man* (1944), and continued through *The Victim* (1947) and *The Adventures of Augie March*, Bellow's *Bildungsroman* that won

From *Chicago Review* 11.1 (1957): 107-10.

the 1954 National Book Award. Horace's *Carpe diem* furnishes the title for "Seize the Day"; for his work as a whole, Bellow could well adopt another Latin tag, the one found on the coins of his adopted country — *E pluribus unum*. For Bellow has tried to lasso the universe, to explore the splendid, profligate diversity of human experience, and to seek the ties that bind. His all-inclusiveness forces him to skip about from one level to another; the swift leaps from the sublime to the ridiculous and back have the flavor of the best Jewish humor — and are equally productive of brilliant insights into the human condition. Romantic at root, this impulse to embrace the world leads to, in his own phrase, "a mysterious adoration of what occurs." As Joseph says in *Dangling Man*, "In a sense everything is good because it exists. Or, good or not good, it exists, it is ineffable and, for that reason, marvelous." Bellow, recipient of a Guggenheim award, knockabout intellectual, and an intimate of the greatest living con man, Yellow Kid Weil, sees his role, as does Augie March, as that of "a Columbus of those near-at-hand." Since "judgment is second to wonder," in his work celebration of life takes precedence over criticism. (In "Day," all the major characters are partially right, partially justified. Bellow's compassion is the greater for being non-selective.) But what distinguishes this author from other "acceptors" is that with him acceptance is an outgrowth of full knowledge, not a substitute for it.

So much for *pluribus*. It is the vast tract Bellow must traverse in his search for the *unum*. Each man *is* an island, entire unto himself, and it is no good pretending otherwise. Bellow has few peers in delineating the particularity, the uniqueness of the topography of a single individual. But he also insists that individuals form archipelagos, and far beneath the surface all are rooted to the same ocean floor. Out of this awareness he draws two themes that pervade his work — the horrible price of insularity (far from rare in modern fiction) and, transcending this, the common humanity shared by all.

In his drive to illumine this latter motif Bellow has passed through four phases. Since each is organically related to the one preceding, they are not *that* sharply divided; they are, however, apparent enough to warrant noting. In *Dangling Man* the emphasis is ideational; what we get is mostly Joseph's thought and some of his speech. In *The Victim* ideas and action revolving around the theme of the difficulty of being human are neatly correlated, almost in a one to one ratio. In the sprawling *Augie* Bellow seems more confident of his abilities to convey attitudes through action rather than discourse, so that thought becomes the pungent seasoning and not the whole stew. Finally, in "Day" he descends deeply to a primal level of atmosphere and feeling that communicates in a way that defies analysis but that carries the moist, hot sting of truth.

The growth and ripening of Bellow's attitudes have been paralleled by the perfecting of his medium of expression. He has fused the varied and often conflicting elements of American English into a natural whole that is ours and yet remains peculiarly his own. Almost alone among today's writers he can select words and phrases, here from the gutter, there from the ivory tower, without the slightest hint of embarrassment of awkwardness.

For all his virtues (and they are considerable), Bellow is by no means flawless. If writing were dancing, the symbol of much postwar American fiction would be Fred Astaire: urbane, a bit wistful, it camouflages its lack of commitment behind a dazzling command of techniques. Bellow, on the other hand, is a Nijinsky, but one who takes an occasional pratfall. If at times he falls heavily, it is because he leaps higher, dares more, than those who are content to stay within the confines of competence.

The most apparent of Bellow's faults is his incapacity to deal convincingly with women. The female figures in his novels repeatedly fall into one of two categories; they are either nags or nymphomaniacs, and the Bellow hero is too often a passive figure, condemned to suffer verbal abuse on the one hand or a physical embarrassment of riches on the other. No Bellow novel has a heroine and in none of them does the protagonist's fate directly hinge upon his relationship with a woman. Joseph's wife Iva "has a way about her that discourages talk," and is alternately colorless and irritating. Joseph also has a mistress, Kitty, but it is noteworthy that she seduces him. The central action of *Victim* could not have occurred at all without the absence of Mary, wife of the protagonist, Asa Leventhal; and the little that we know about her relates almost entirely to the weird, abortive period of their engagement. In *Augie* many of the episodes that in other novels would be called "love scenes" are little more than rape fantasies with Augie as the assaulted. In the final chapters Augie is married to Stella, but matrimony seems to have transformed her from nympho to nag: "She sits and listens . . . and refuses me — for the time being, anyway — the most important things I ask of her." If and when Augie lights out for the territory, Stella will probably be left behind. In "Day," Tommy's wife Margaret, from whom he is separated, never gets closer than letters and telephone calls to refuse him a divorce and badger him for money. Nor is Tommy's mistress, Olive, ever clearly visualized.

The argument could be advanced that all this is intended, that Bellow uses these women as an analogue of the animal, natural side of life. Thus the abortive heterosexual relationships symbolize the twentieth-century American's failure to cope effectively with Nature. But if this be true, need it happen in all four of Bellow's novels? Surely, with the slow erasure of the distinction between the sexes that has been occurring in the past half-century, women are not incomprehensible and one could serve as *the*, or at least *a*, central figure in a Bellow novel.

Bellow's second failure — that his books don't end, they just stop — is perhaps more easily explained. With his avowal that "character is fate," sheer plot, the arrangement of events, has a diminished importance. Since life won't fit the neat forms of art, Bellow's flaw probably stems from his greater devotion to the former than the latter. It remains to be seen whether these faults can be transcended or whether they are logically outgrowths of the author's deepest beliefs. One rather suspects that his perceptions of women will remain the same, while predicting better resolutions for his future books. Bellow is certainly not insensitive to aesthetic issues, and the ending of "Seize the Day" is several cuts above those of the other three novels.

These strictures aside, it must be said that Saul Bellow is perhaps the major talent of the past decade. He has displayed magnificent fulfillment of his early promise and is now at an age — chronological and artistic — to produce his best work. Publication of his two works-in-progress will be awaited with uncommon eagerness, for he may very well be the fair-haired boy, *El Bello*, of current American letters.

* * *

Running Contrary Ways:
Saul Bellow's *Seize the Day*
Julius R. Raper

Saul Bellow's first novel, *Dangling Man*, opens with a spirited promise to eschew the hardboiled pose dominant in American life and literature, and to end the tradition of "closemouthed straight-forwardness" that runs, he implies, from Kipling through Hemingway to the literary offspring of Hemingway. For this tradition he wishes to substitute a confessional literature that feels no shame in being introspective and self-indulgent or in talking about feelings, emotions and the inner life. Among the other memorable passages of that flawed first novel are conversations Joseph carries on with the Spirit of Alternatives, an alter-personality that emerges to guide him beyond the position his reason guards to where he might discover his "inmost feelings." In one form or another, the Spirit of Alternatives appears in six out of the eight book-length works by Bellow. It makes its presence felt in the irrational attraction that pulls Leventhal toward Allbee the anti-semite of *The Victim*, destitute Tommy Wilhelm toward Tamkin the confidence man of *Seize the Day*, and introverted Artur Sammler toward the elegantly-dressed black pickpocket in *Mr. Sammler's Planet*; the Spirit of Alternatives also haunts Henderson as he exchanges roles with King Dahfu in *Henderson the Rain King*, and Bummidge the comedian in

From *Southern Humanities Review* 10.2 (1976): 157-68.

The Last Analysis when he madly wills to become Bummidge the Freudian intellectual. These variations in the Spirit of Alternatives and their hold upon the protagonists of Bellow's works reflect Bellow's belief that the conventional novel of the "unitary personality" offers little more than narcotic entertainment for an age that has grown used to discovering "dubious selves" within each of us. The old "personality" defended with "grace under pressure" by writers of the hardboiled school is viewed more and more as the "presentation self," the persona one improvises to play the limited roles required by society. The real self remains "unknown, . . . hidden, a sunken power in us," perhaps only "a quaintly organized chaos of instinct and spirit." The true identity, if there is one, "lies deep — very deep."[1] In Bellow's concern with the persona, the real self, and the Spirit of Alternatives, the influence of psychoanalysis, especially the Jungian school, appears central.

Of Bellow's six variations on the theme that a man's character develops by running contrary ways, none has as broad and immediate application to American society as the change in Tommy Wilhelm's personality in *Seize the Day*, a novel thought by many, despite its meager size, to be Bellow's finest achievement.

In *Seize the Day*, Bellow seems to have discovered a structure unusual, if not unique, in the impact achieved by what it leaves out. From the start, Bellow points every incident toward the final scene. The book opens with Tommy Wilhelm descending an elevator, very much afraid that he is in for a major crisis; the second paragraph ends with his awareness that "his routine was about to break up" and that "a huge trouble long presaged but till now formless" will have to be faced before evening.[2] From time to time thereafter, Tommy reminds us that this is to be his "day of reckoning," that he stands at the edge of a crisis. Often he experiences the confusion and anguish associated with the threshold of conversions, a possibility he seems to sense when at the end of the first chapter he prays, "Let me out of this clutch and into a different life. For I am all balled up. Have mercy" (26). Then, in the final scene, standing by the coffin of a total stranger and drowning in his own tears, he sinks "deeper than sorrow . . . toward the consummation of his heart's ultimate need" (118). This is a puzzling ending, for it leaves any reader habituated to the traditional dramatic rhythm of purpose-passion-perception, dangling. Where is the perception phase, the clarification? The novel gives a strong sense of preparation and struggle building up to the climax at the stranger's funeral, but just when one expects the falling action to unravel and explain, the book ends. What this truncation of the action accomplishes is the close identification of the reader with an initially unappealing character, Tommy Wilhelm, who remains a loser while all about him men are making fortunes in a rising market. At the end, the reader stands very much where Tommy stands: with a more or less profound emotional catharsis on his hands, wondering why this crying jag should be part of "the consummation of [Tommy's] heart's ultimate need." The answer to this question — had Bellow chosen to spell it out — would have constituted the perception phase of the novel. The solution, however, is implicit if we correctly answer a preliminary question: what is wrong with Tommy that he feels headed for a breakdown?

In his middle forties, Wilhelm finds himself out of work, separated (but not divorced) from his wife and two sons, and living again with his father — or, at least, in the same building, the Gloriana, a swanky retirement hotel on upper Broadway. Down to his last seven hundred dollars and with little prospect of a new position, he faces a future of endless payments of support money. Worse yet, his father, a wealthy and affable old gentleman named Dr. Adler, time and again refuses, on principle, to help his hopeless son out; the old man, who has settled down to long years of healthy old age surrounded by admiring contemporaries in the Gloriana, will tolerate none of Tommy's begging for money, advice and sympathy. All he offers is a contemptuous "I warned you!" Despite these rejections, Tommy says — and believes — when asked whether he loves his old man, "Of course, of course I love him. My father. My mother . . ." (92). Obviously he has never given the matter much thought; fathers are simply the other people that sons naturally love — along with mothers — even when the fathers will not step aside, or die. Love is essential to the son's role.

And Dr. Adler's son is the role Wilhelm has chosen to play in life, the role he has been unable to avoid, the role he has tumbled into even when he tried to escape it. His past record, marred with mistakes, is a story of his efforts to make himself worthy of being Dr. Adler's son without at the same time "outdoing" or even directly competing with his father (28). As he tells his father, "If anything, I tried too hard. I admit I made many mistakes. Like I thought I shouldn't do things you had done already. Study chemistry. You had done it already. It was in the family" (50). Avoiding thus the distasteful oedipal competition and yet trying indirectly to match his father's practical success, Tommy, in the early 1930s, turned his back on college after a few semesters, to begin a checkered career — as actor, hospital orderly, ditch-digger, public relations man, soldier, and toy salesman — that, a decade after the war, left him out of work altogether. No longer a young man, he feels he has failed to match the example of practical success his father set for him. This, more than oedipal guilt,[3] is the source of the anxiety that progressively incapacitates Tommy; he still lives in terms of his father's image of him.

But as three generations of Depression and post-Depression Americans have discovered, it is increasingly unrealistic and therefore unhealthy to attempt to model oneself after the nineteenth-century American ideal of success Dr. Adler embodies. Pampered, vain and self-centered, the bland old man[4] thinks of himself as totally self-reliant, a self-made man, the American Puritan-Protestant-Business ethic incarnate (50). Since Tommy does not fit his father's ideal, Adler rejects him as jittery, dirty, sentimental, weak, immoral, irresponsible — a "slob," the "wrong kind of Jew." Adler calls him the last even though the doctor in assimilating himself to the American formula has given up his own religion (86).

In following in his father's shadow, Tommy has had to make even greater sacrifices, for the practical, extroverted mask of success has forced him to neglect his true, introverted self. In the midst of a very important fit of self-castigation, he gains a glimpse of his other self: "From his mother he had gotten sensitive feelings, a soft heart, a brooding nature, a tendency to be confused under pressure" (25). It is this self which feels rather than judges, this "feminine" quality, that Tommy has been unable to accept — even though it is the dominant side of his personality — because he has not been able to cast off "his father's opinion of him." This he tried to do as an actor in California when he "cast off his father's name" and became Tommy Wilhelm rather than Wilhelm Adler. But the name change belonged to his earliest effort to match his father's success without directly imitating it and thus was, ironically, determined by his father's opinion of him. As a consequence, he never succeeded "in feeling like Tommy" and remained always in his soul Wilky. Wilky, he fears, is "his inescapable self," a doleful state of things for which he has developed an elaborate biological alibi; he thinks: "There's really very little that a man can change at will. . . . He can't overthrow the government or be differently born" (24-25). This explanation is clearly a rationalization, for it does not fit Tommy's case.

The real source of his anxiety is the double bind Dr. Adler has forced him into — a bind which keeps him alienated from either of his two selves. If he attempts to follow his father's example of practical self-reliance, he commits the crime of freedom against his father and remains tormented by his father's God-like voice internalized as conscience: "The changed name was a mistake, and he would admit it as freely as you liked. But this mistake couldn't be undone now, so why must his father continually remind him how he had sinned?" If, on the other hand, he feels as though he might really be Wilky, which has been his father's name for him for forty years, he sees himself through Adler's view of Wilky-like softness and introversion: "When he was drunk he reproached himself horribly as Wilky. 'You fool, you clunk, you Wilky!' he called himself" (25). It is not unhealthy to be a Wilky, but it is sick to judge one's own self so harshly. Thus separated from the vital center of his personality, his inner *daimon*, Tommy seems doomed to follow a path of progressively destructive self-judgment until at last *all* his creative possibilities are dead.

But this is not the psychic reality Bellow has described; for Bellow concurs with Jung that the personality runs contrary ways. Especially at middle-age, where Tommy now stands, does the personality,

like everything, "run into its opposite."[5] And today is the day of reckoning when Tommy must undergo what Jung calls *enantiodromia*, the
psychological process of "being torn asunder into pairs of opposites"
(*Essays* 83). Dr. Tamkin, in most things the opposite of Dr. Adler,
represents to Tommy the Spirit of Alternatives holding out to him an
alternative self. But to reach this new self the old must die.

Dr. Tamkin speaks for the unconscious attitude which Tommy as
an introvert and a loser cannot see in himself but projects upon external
objects. According to Jung, the unconscious contents of the psyche
stand in a compensatory relationship to those that are conscious.
Because an introvert fails to give external objects the importance they
possess, "a compensatory relation to the object develops in the unconscious, which makes itself felt in consciousness as an unconditional and
irrepressible tie to the object." Since the unconscious drives of an
introvert are thus extroverted, the object develops "an overwhelming
influence . . . because it seizes upon the individual unawares" (*Types*
477-78; *Essays* 186). Such powerlessness before external forces is typical for Wilhelm: "After much thought and hesitation and debate he
invariably took the course he had rejected innumerable times. Ten such
decisions made up the history of his life" (23). Because the introvert
attaches little conscious value to his external actions, his unconscious
needs often get him "swamped in inferior relationships, and his desire
to dominate [the external world with his mind or emotions] ends in a
pitiful craving to be loved" (*Types* 478). Thus Tommy, who has good
reasons to suspect Tamkin of being a sham and a confidence man, finds
himself nonetheless unable to resist his financial schemes: "He had
resolved not to invest money with Tamkin, and then had given him a
check" (23).

Bellow's image of Dr. Tamkin has been called "one of the most
singular condemnations in contemporary literature of what modern man
has become."[6] But even those who have judged him most severely or
have been puzzled by his role, have not missed the irony that the most
profound insights come from his mouth and that he is "wise, accurate
psychologically, and responsible for Wilhelm's final enlightenment."[7]
We would be wise not to judge Tamkin too harshly since we see him
only through a tissue of qualities Tommy has projected upon him. And
if Tamkin did not exist, Tommy would have had to invent him so that
there would be someone upon whom he might project the
unacknowledged contents of his own psyche.

The qualities projected by the introvert's unconscious "are primarily infantile and archaic" ones, the primitive contents that find
expression in the Jungian archetypes. Consequently, the objects which
receive such projections seem endowed with terrifying "magical
powers" (*Types* 479-80). The archetype Tommy projects on Tamkin is
the important figure of the magician, a dominant of the collective
unconscious embodying ego-inflating psychic energies capable of

producing what Jung calls the mana-personality (*Essays* 240-41). Tommy sees Tamkin variously as a "benevolent magician" (81), as "shrewd, and wizard-like, patronizing, secret, potent" (64), and as a "faker" (punning perhaps with fakir) who "knows what he's talking about" (98). As products of projected psychic energy which is morally neutral, spirit-figures are notorious for their moral ambivalence; Jung says of them: "We can never know what evil may not be necessary in order to produce good by enantiodromia, and what good may very possibly lead to evil."[8] Indeed, in dreams the spirit-figure may appear simultaneously as a "white magician" dressed in a long black robe and as a "black magician" clothed in a white robe, an archetypal equivalent of the paradox that Tamkin cons Tommy out of his last seven hundred dollars while guiding him toward the birth of his real self. Ethical neutrality enables the magician-figure to break through the sort of bind that incapacitates Tommy: "The archetype of spirit in the shape of a man," Jung writes, "always appears in a situation where insight, understanding, good advice, determination, planning, etc., are needed but cannot be mustered on one's own resources. The archetype compensates this state of spiritual deficiency by contents designed to fill the gap" (*Archetypes* 216).

Tommy's need for a new life, more than Tamkin's greed, lies at the bottom of the irresistible attraction this self-taught healer of humanity holds for Dr. Adler's son (95). For Adler's rational dogmatism Tamkin substitutes an appealingly intuitive view of things: a "keen nose for things in the bud pregnant with future promise," an "eye . . . constantly ranging for new possibilities," to use Jung's description of this type (*Types* 464). Tamkin's brand of extroversion stands as a bridge between Adler's absolutism and Tommy's introversion. Tamkin's long-range goal (aside from fleecing Tommy) seems to be to help him convert his self-image from slob to "King" (75-77). To reach this goal he must first alter Wilhelm's set of mind.

To prepare Tommy, he supplies him with readings, advice, informal lectures and mental exercises. A sympathetic surrogate father (although no more than ten years older than his victim/son), Tamkin, who understands the heart, teaches Tommy to value his emotions — rather than despise them — as a way to overcome loneliness, suffering and the death-wish (97-99). When, "under Dr. Tamkin's influence," Wilhelm begins "to remember the poems he used to read," they come back to him in pairs dealing with death (Shakespeare's "That time of year thou mayst in me behold") and rebirth ("Lycidas"), foreshadowing the pattern of his own development (12-13). In order to counter Wilhelm's obsessive anxieties about the past (his father and mother) and the future (the market and his sons), Tamkin proposes "here-and-now" mental exercises to immerse him totally in the present (61, 89-90). By focusing his attention upon increasingly small concrete details and thus driving anxiety from his consciousness, Tommy is supposed to achieve a state of pure being in which the "present, present, eternal present, like a big, huge, giant wave — colossal, bright and beautiful, full of life and death, climbing into the sky, standing in the seas," will break upon him (89).

Tamkin's immersion theory of self-discovery provides at base a method for releasing dammed-up emotions, as all the water imagery in the book implies.[9] In the language of Jung, Tamkin will use Tommy's secondary faculty for introverted sensation to develop his suppressed capacity for feeling ((*Types* 516). In this intermediate stage of sensation, with his mind fastened intensely upon an irresistible object, Tommy will, according to Jung, see the same thing as anyone else, but his mind will not stop "at the purely objective effect"; it will concern itself instead "with the subjective perception released by the objective stimulus." This subjective content will include mythological images, primal possibilities and dispositions of the collective unconscious — hints of an archaic reality within (*Types* 499, 503).

Bellow the trained anthropologist has turned up an incredible store of myth-laden particulars (mythemes) which Bellow the novelist employs to give the sense that Wilhelm might any moment turn a corner and break through into the mirror world of the collective unconscious. Aside from the sense that the entire novel has been set underwater[10] so that Hotel Gloriana resembles a submerged Mt. Olympus, Dr. Adler a submarine Zeus or Jehovah, and Tommy's day a descent into the waters of rebirth, there is a constant bombardment of mythemes which intensifies as Tamkin carries Tommy toward the climax of his enantiodromia. For Tommy, the commodity market is literally a great mechanical wheel of fortune that rises and falls with the seasons (78). The various father-figures (Adler, Rappaport, Tamkin) become gods who need only speak a word to provide the key that will liberate Tommy from his misery (87, 109). He begins to think of himself in terms of mythic animals: as bear (symbol of prime matter and instincts, 23), as bull (figure of fertility and chthonic power, 76), as hippopotamus (the river horse, to the Egyptians a figure for strength, vigor, fertility and water, 6), and, in his son's language, as "hummuspotamus" (a river of humus, source of organic life, 29). Street markets become cornucopias and a gilded cafeteria metamorphoses into a dreamscape: "Whole fishes were framed like pictures with carrots, and the salads were like terraced landscapes or like Mexican pyramids; slices of lemon and onion and radishes were like sun and moon and stars; . . . the cakes [were] swollen as if sleepers had baked them in their dreams" (91). A panicked trip to Tamkin's room followed by an elevator ride to the basement massage room takes on the proportions of an ascent to the zenith and a descent to the underworld (106-108).

As Tamkin's teachings about the need to kill the "pretender soul" in order to liberate one's "real soul" (terms *very* close to the Jungian "persona" or "ego" and "the Self"[11]) sink in, Wilhelm begins to catch glimpses of the collective nature of this "real soul"; "involuntary feelings" about the "larger body" of humanity break through to consciousness. A dark tunnel beneath Times Square becomes the collective unconscious externalized: "In the . . . tunnel, . . . all of a sudden, unsought, a general love for all these imperfect and lurid-looking people burst out in Wilhelm's breast. . . . They were his brothers and his sisters. He was imperfect and disfigured himself, but what difference did that make if he was united with them by this blaze of love?" (84-85). For Jung, it is the "sense of solidarity with the world" accompanying the assimilation of the collective elements of the unconscious which enables many sick individuals for the first time to love and be loved, and thus marks the turning point of their treatment (*Essays* 158).

Within this larger body, Tommy, who regrets that in a city like New York "the fathers [are] no fathers and the sons no sons" (84), discovers the role his "real soul" seems meant to play: a complex one combining important attributes of the archetypal son. Early in the novel he thinks of himself as the sacrificial son, a secular Isaac/Christ whose suffering gives life to others: "When I had it, I flowed money. They bled it away from me. I hemorrhaged money" (40, 76). By itself this role is totally unsatisfying; it belongs to his view of himself as loser and victim, an image he owes to his father. If the son must be sacrificed, he should, at least, be beloved and lamented. Under Tamkin's instruction he comes to the threshold of a second attribute of the son archetype, the previously unacknowledged oedipal hatred. With Wilhelm's mother dead, the rivalry between father and son has shifted to the other treasure that fathers, especially in a gerontocracy like the Gloriana, hoard from their sons — money. Midway through the novel in an argument with Adler, Wilhelm bursts out: "By God, you have to admit it. The money makes the difference." And continues: "Just keep your money. . . . Keep it and enjoy it yourself. That's the ticket!" (55). This rivalry produces another of Wilhelm's feelings that emerge involuntarily from the collective unconscious. He is discussing the possibility of his father's death with Tamkin. When Tamkin asks whether he loves his father, he answers, "Of course." Then Bellow adds: "As he said this there was a great pull at the very center of his soul. When a fish strikes the line you feel the live force in your hand. A mysterious being beneath the water, driven by hunger, has taken the hook and rushes away and fights, writhing" (92-93). The "fish" struggling under the waters of consciousness must be a negative or mixed answer to Tamkin's question, a shadowy awareness for the first time that his love for Adler is not innocent of hate and that his desire to see his father live is not free of the contrary wish. This is the great feeling Wilhelm must confront, and cannot, until Tamkin teaches him to seize the day.

But as guru, Tamkin can neither tell nor show Wilhelm what he needs to know — only lead him to the threshold and hope he will take the final step, make the necessary connections. And it is in panicked pursuit of Tamkin that Wilhelm, cut off from all other worldly connections, stumbles, at the end, into the huge funeral line which carries him toward the consummation of his heart's ultimate need (115). He is trying to get his money back; instead he undergoes the most unrestrained, powerful and intensely personal emotional experience of his life, one which stirs him to the vital center of his personality. At the same time as Tamkin's running away breaks Wilhelm's dependence upon him as a surrogate father, it leads the client/victim toward the most irresistible object his mind will ever fasten upon, and thus brings his immersion in the here-and-now to its highest possible intensity.

When Wilhelm's place in the funeral line reaches the coffin, there is a catch in his breath and he finds himself "so struck" that he cannot "go away" (116-17). As he stands by the dead man and his eyes begin to shine with tears, the most essential contents of his unconscious, images and associations released by this objective stimulus, flow forth. At first the dead stranger is gray-haired, proper but not old, calling to Wilhelm's mind his father and the oedipal wish to see him dead. Then the corpse becomes "a man — another human creature," an association that focuses the general sense of solidarity with mankind Wilhelm earlier felt in the dark tunnel beneath Times Square. Into this collective image the more particular one breaks again as Wilhelm addresses the stranger as "Father," and calls upon him (or is it his mistress Olive?) to protect him "against that devil who wants [his] life." Initially "that devil" seems to be his parasitic wife Margaret, but as he continues to speak to the corpse, the devil becomes his father: "If you want it [my life], then kill me. Take, take it, take it from me." This thought carries him to the furthest depth of the hatred that divides him from his father.[12] It also causes him to see himself (probably the Wilky-self his father created) as the dead man and carries him "past words, past reason, coherence" to "the source of all tears": the pure intimate self-pity that comes with the thought of one's own death. Somewhere well past reason, in the archaic content he has projected upon the dead stranger, Tommy has become the center of a wild cult of lamentation. As the chief mourner at a huge funeral for his father, himself, and all mankind, he sees "the flowers and lights fused ecstatically" in his wet eyes and hears "heavy sea-like music." Then, like Tammuz or Osiris, ancient son-gods and sacrificial quickeners of new life, he feels the sea of lamentation pour into him as he sinks "deeper than sorrow," where he must await rebirth.[13]

Identified thus with the archetypal contents of the collective unconscious, a "chaos of instinct and spirit," he becomes united with his real Self, the God or King hidden within him. How well he will, in the future, assimilate this "sunken power" and work out roles which acknowledge both his own psychic needs and the limits on self-expression created by society, depends upon the extent to which he understands a lesson Tamkin gave him earlier on the value of symbolic actions: in that episode Tommy is complaining about the way his wife Margaret lives only "in order to punish him." Tamkin interjects the story of his own wife: she was a "painful alcoholic" whom he loved deeply and "tried everything in [his] power to cure." But, he continues, he failed and she drowned, apparently a suicide. Wilhelm, whose distrust is especially intense at this moment, attacks Tamkin in his mind: "Liar! . . . He invented a woman and killed her off and then called himself a healer" (94-95). Wilhelm is probably right that this is one of Tamkin's lies — or fantasies. But being a liar does not keep Tamkin from being a healer. The ability to produce, recognize and "kill off" fantasies or symbols of man's deepest anxieties — his guilt about failure, his oedipal hatreds, need for security, wish to be loved, fear of his own death — furnishes the key to the method witch doctors, priests, psychoanalysts and sane individuals all employ. "The only person who escapes the grim law of enantiodromia is the man who knows how to separate himself from the unconscious, not by repressing it . . . , but by putting it clearly before him [often in symbolic form] as *that which he is not*" because its fears and needs are the burden of all mankind (*Essays* 83).

What lies immediately ahead for Tommy then is the sort of differentiation pursued in this essay, a process in which he may discover that the sources of the fantasies he experienced by the stranger's coffin lie in the collective mind of man and, through this realization, free himself of their destructive personal influence. It is well Bellow stopped with Tommy's fantasies, for lies that tell the deepest human truths are the most powerful tools a novelist can ever hope to control.

Notes

1. Saul Bellow, "Where Do We Go From Here: The Future of Fiction," *The Theory of the American Novel*, ed. George Perkins (New York: Holt, Rinehart and Winston, 1970), 443-45.
2. Saul Bellow, *Seize the Day* (New York: Viking, 1961), 4. Subsequent references in the text from this edition.
3. See Daniel Weiss, "Caliban on Prospero: A Psychoanalytic Study on the Novel *Seize the Day*, by Saul Bellow," *Saul Bellow and the Critics*, ed. Irving Malin (New York: New York UP, 1967), 123-25, 129. Weiss's position follows the classic Freudian line and argues that Tommy's suffering is the way his superego penalizes him with guilt for having willed his father's death. For a post-Freudian view of the oedipal wish closer to that of the present article, see Bruno Bettelheim, "The Problem of Generations," *The Challenge of Youth*, ed. Erik H. Erikson (Garden City: Anchor/Doubleday, 1965), 76-109.
4. Cf. C. G. Jung, *Psychological Types, or The Psychology of Individuation*, trans. H. Godwin Baynes (New York: Harcourt Brace, 1923), 435-36, 438-41. Subsequent references as *Types*. Adler fits the well-known

Jungian type of the extravert whom strangers consider a man of civic virtue but his own children know to be a cruel tyrant.

5. C. G. Jung, *Two Essays on Analytical Psychology*, trans. R. F. C. Hull (New York: Meridian, 1956), 82. Subsequent references as *Essays*.

6. Willam J. Handy, "Saul Bellow and the Naturalistic Hero," *Texas Studies in Literature and Language* 5 (Winter 1964): 542.

7. Weiss, 138.

8. C. G. Jung, *The Archetypes and the Collective Unconscious*, trans. R. F. C. Hull (New York: Pantheon, 1959), 215. Subsequent references as *Archetypes*.

9. Clinton W. Trowbridge argues this very convincingly in "Water Imagery in *Seize the Day*," *Critique* 9.3 (1967): 62-73.

10. Trowbridge, 62-73.

11. *Two Essays*, 250; M.-L. von Franz, "The Process of Individuation," *Man and His Symbols*, ed. Carl G. Jung (Garden City: Windfall/Doubleday, 1970), 161-62.

12. Cf. when Adler gives his son the impression that he resents the thought that his son will still be alive after Adler, "the better man of the two," is dead (*SD* 54).

13. In his descent into the archetypal unconscious, Tommy seems to approach most closely Tammuz or Dumuzi, the oldest known vegetation god in the Western tradition. As the power in the sap of the trees and plants, his death at the end of spring was lamented throughout ancient Mesopotamia by wailing women who regarded him variously as a dying son, brother, and husband. From Tammuz Bellow may have derived the names, Tommy, Tam-kin and Wilhelm's self-reproachful "dummy," as well as the water/descent imagery, the temporal setting (early summer), and the struggle between age and youth, death and rebirth. Cf. James G. Frazer, *The Golden Bough* (New York: Macmillan, 1951), 378-80, and Thorkild Jacobsen, "Toward the Image of Tammuz," *History of Religion* 1 (1961): 189-213.

*   *   *

Empathy and Self-Validation in Bellow's *Seize the Day*
J. Brooks Bouson

Wilhelm Adler, the protagonist of Saul Bellow's character study, *Seize the Day*, depends on others to support his threatened self. Indeed, he openly voices his sense of narcissistic entitlement and his desire for rescue. "I've never asked you for very much," Wilhelm says to his father in an anguished plea for sympathy. "One word from you, just a word, would go a long way."[1] "I expect *help*!" he insists (53). This

From *The Empathic Reader: A Study of the Narcissistic Character and the Drama of the Self* (Amherst: UMP, 1989): 64-81.

impassioned request for an empathic response from his father, which is central to the psychology of Wilhelm Adler, is also central to the critical responses Bellow's text has engendered.

In *Seize the Day* surface illuminates subsurface as Wilhelm's verbal pleas for sympathy shed light on the preverbal depths of his personality. Behind his desperate need for confirmation lie deep-rooted feelings of ambivalence, anger, and disconnection. As he undergoes a harrowing self-crisis, he perceives behind his "pretender soul" (71) — his socially adaptive, compliant counterfeit self — the deficiency at the core of his personality. A chronic mistake maker and a victim, Wilhelm has been variously described as a "*schlemiel*,"[2] a "moral masochist,"[3] and a symbol of "the failure of the American Dream."[4] And yet, despite his overt faults, most commentators have responded sympathetically to Bellow's character. Indeed, the word of confirmation Wilhelm fails to get from his father, as we shall see, has been spoken again and again by critic/readers. Legitimizing his struggles, they find a plenitude of meaning in his defective selfhood and read his suffering as a "mark of the chosen rather than of the rejected."[5] Reading *Seize the Day* in a new context — that provided by psychoanalyst Heinz Kohut in his pioneering studies in the narcissistic disorder — provides insight not only into the experiential core of Wilhelm's predicament but also into the critical responses Bellow's text has engendered.

Developing through the psychoanalytic process what he came to call the "psychology of the self," Kohut centers his attention on fundamental aspects of human behavior which other accounts of psychological man and woman ignore or minimize: the deep-rooted needs empathic responsiveness and for a sense of connection with others. "The self," in Kohut's words, "arises in a matrix of empathy" and "strives to live within a modicum of empathic responses in order to maintain itself. . . ."[6] Kohut's narcissistically defective individual — Tragic Man — suffers from a defect in the self because of traumatic empathic failures on the part of the parents during the early stages of self-development. As a consequence, such an individual lacks the inner resources of healthy narcissism: sustaining self-esteem and inner ideals. Instead, he is dominated by the regressive needs of the "archaic grandiose self" (which perceives itself as omnipotent, the center of attention, and in control of others) and/or the "archaic idealizing self" (which feels empty and powerless unless merged with an all-powerful other). Because the narcissistically defective adult cannot provide himself with sufficient self-approval or with a sense of strength through his own inner resources, he is forever compelled to satisfy these essential needs through external sources — by extracting praise from or exercising unquestioned dominance over others or by merging with idealized figures. Lacking a "stable cohesive self" — that is, a stable sense of himself as a unitary agent, an initiator of action and a continuum in time — he suffers from a fundamental weakness and deficiency in the center

of his personality. He may harbor feelings of greatness side by side
with low self-esteem. He may respond to the frustration of his exhib-
itionistic impulses with shame and to the failure of his grandiose ambitions with rage. Subject to what Kohut calls "disintegration anxiety" —
"dread of the loss" of the self[7] — he is, like Wilhelm Adler, compelled
endlessly to enact the same primitive, fixated behavior in his frustrated
search for wholeness.

In Tommy Wilhelm, as is typical of those with a self-disorder, we
find the uneasy coexistence of grandiose pretensions and an utter sense
of impotence and defeat. When Wilhelm searches his memory on his
"day of reckoning" (*SD* 96), he must sort out fact from fiction, truth
from grandiose myth, the "true" from the "pretender" self. His distorted grandiosity is conveyed in the novel's opening scene. Gazing at
his reflection in a glass cupboard full of cigar boxes, Wilhelm sees his
reflected image "among . . . the gold-embossed portraits of famous
men, Garcia, Edward the Seventh, Cyrus the Great. . . . Fair-haired
hippopotamus! — that was how he looked to himself" (6). Once
impressively handsome, Wilhelm, middle-aged, has gone to seed: "He
looked down over the front of his big, indecently big, spoiled body. He
was beginning to lose his shape, his gut was fat . . ." (29). Because
Wilhelm's self is not strong and resilient, he feels overburdened, that
he will be "crushed" if he stumbles, that his obligations will "destroy"
him (39-40), that he gets "taken" and is "stripped bare" (9-10), that
"the peculiar burden of his existence lay upon him like an accretion, a
load, a hump" (39). Narcissistically deficient, he looks to others to
shore up his sagging self and he looks to his father for support.

When Wilhelm, in his mid-forties and his life at an impasse,
comes to the ironically named Hotel Gloriana to be near his elderly
father, to be in the parental environment, he seeks some remedy for his
situation. In his reiterated attempts to elicit a word of sympathy from
his father, he acts out an anachronistic drama. "It's time I stopped feeling like a kid toward him, a small son" (11), Wilhelm thinks to himself
as he, clingingly dependent, demanding, and deeply angry, compulsively reenacts his childhood relationship with his father, endeavor-
ing to get from him, somehow or other, the empathic responsiveness he
feels entitled to. Emotionally, Wilhelm still is a child. In his crisis
situation, his needs for mirroring responses and support from an idealized selfobject — his father and Tamkin — have become acute. What
is at stake is his self-survival.

"I'm of two minds . . ." (29, 73), Wilhelm says in an unconscious
revelation of his split self. Similarly, the narrator appears to be of two
minds about Wilhelm. Mirroring Wilhelm's outer, sympathetic personality and his inner "gruff" voice that typically finds fault with others,
the narrator both comes to Wilhelm's support and devalues him. After
describing Wilhelm's "odd" habit of pinching out the coal of his
cigarette and dropping the butt in his pocket, for example, the narrator

makes mention of Wilhelm's ironic notion that he is capable of "outdoing his father" if he wants with his "perfect and even distinguished manners" (28). In contrast, when Dr. Adler's interior voice criticizes Wilhelm for being a "dirty devil," the narrator intrudes to defend Wilhelm: "He was not really so slovenly as his father found him to be. In some aspects he even had a certain delicacy" (42). And while the narrator consistently calls attention to Wilhelm's large, spoiled body, unkempt appearance, and untidy habits, he also describes some of the "slow, silent movements" of Wilhelm's face as "very attractive" (5). Occupying the shifting positions of the narrator, the reader both enters Wilhelm's consciousness and steps back, on occasion, and views him from a slight remove or through the critical eyes of his father.

Installed as an empathic listener and observer, the reader, as the narrative unfolds, becomes aware of Wilhelm's entrapment in his own stifling, interior hell. While the shifting narrative focus does serve to protect the reader from "the oppression of intense identification"[8] with Wilhelm, it does not, judging from the critical responses to this text, dilute reader sympathy for him. We are invited to feel a range of responses to Bellow's anti-hero. Like Dr. Adler, we may find things about Wilhelm disgusting, embarrassing, and annoying. But we are also urged to respond favorably to Bellow's character. "It is the neglected parts of Wilhelm," writes John Clayton, "that make us care about the man: the man who receives lines of poetry out of the blue . . . who thinks about the loneliness in New York, who has moments of peace. . . ."[9] And while we are forced to acknowledge Wilhelm's physical peculiarities, excessive self-pity, and childish irresponsibility, we are also urged to feel sorry for him and to become progressively concerned about his troubled life and hopeful of his rescue. Sarah Cohen's comments on the novel reflect the collective critical response this text has engendered. Bellow, she observes, "appreciates what Wilhelm is up against and therefore sympathetically pardons his buffoonish deviations and improprieties. . . . It is those who frown upon Wilhelm that meet with Bellow's censure."[10] Indeed, as we shall see, critics have repeatedly pardoned Wilhelm for his faults and denounced his accusers — Dr. Adler and Margaret — for their unempathic treatment of him. Reacting to Wilhelm's need for approval and rescue, most critic/readers have endorsed the conscious project of this text, which suggests Wilhelm's ultimate redemption and spiritual elevation through suffering. And what the text backgrounds, most readers have ignored and avoided. On the periphery of the text, another narrative is recoverable, one that inscribes Wilhelm's split-off anger. The weight of the unspoken, which haunts Wilhelm's interactions with others, haunts the reader of *Seize the Day*, vexing with unanswerable questions those critic/readers who have applied traditional expectations for narrative closure, character development, and resolution of conflict to Bellow's novel.

Providing a remarkable transcription of the strategies and defenses underlying the spoken and unspoken thoughts of Wilhelm and Dr. Adler, the conflict-ridden father-son confrontation that begins the novel gives the reader direct awareness of their colliding subjectivities and irresolvable differences. The narrator, acting the role of empathic listener, on occasion intrudes to explain what was really meant by their miscommunications. "On guard against insinuations" in whatever his father says, Wilhelm studies his father's remarks, looking for hidden insults and nuances. When his father says, "Here we are under the same roof again, after all these years," Wilhelm translates this into a rebuff: "Why are you here in a hotel with me and not at home . . . with your wife and two boys?" When Wilhelm, ostensibly trying to help his father remember how many years have elapsed, asks, "How many years has it been? . . . Wasn't it the year Mother died? What year was that?" (*SD* 27), he inwardly reacts with anger at what he perceives as his father's excessive self-involvement. His father has forgotten the date, was "set free" by his wife's death, and similarly wants to "get rid of" Wilhelm (29). When Wilhelm describes his mother's death as "the beginning of the end," Dr. Adler is "astonished" and "puzzled." But he defensively refuses to "give Wilhelm an opening to introduce his complaints," having "learned that it was better not to take up" his son's "strange challenges." Pleasant, affable in his response, Dr. Adler is a "master of social behavior." But inwardly he thinks, "What business has he to complain to *me* of his mother's death?" "Face to face," as the narrator describes it, each declares himself "silently after his own way" (28). Each is something of an actor, a pretender, the "great weight of the unspoken" lying between them (6).

In Wilhelm's interactions with his father, we find a typical narcissistic pattern: the thwarting of Wilhelm's demands for an empathic response stirs strong feelings of injury, resentment, and anger. On his "day of reckoning," Wilhelm strips away the protective myth of his happy childhood relationship with his father. "Maybe . . . I was sentimental in the past and exaggerated his kindliness — warm family life. It may never have been there" (26). "Filled with ancient grievances" (29), he recalls that his father "never was a pal" to him when he was young, i.e., was emotionally unavailable. "He was at the office or the hospital, or lecturing. He expected me to look out for myself and never gave me much thought" (14). While Wilhelm feels entitled to his father's sympathy and support — "I am his son. . . . He is my father. He is as much father as I am son . . ." — he also is aware that he doesn't "stand a chance of getting [the] sympathy" he craves (43). Nevertheless, he attempts to elicit an empathic response from his father. Wilhelm, trapped in his suppliant's role, is externally conciliatory. But inwardly he criticizes his father, finding him selfish, vain, insensitive. "He had always been a vain man," he thinks to himself. "To see how his father loved himself sometimes made Wilhelm madly indignant" (12). Predictably, Wilhelm's confession that he is "in a bad way" falls on deaf ears. "You might have told him that Seattle was near Puget Sound, or that the Giants and Dodgers were playing a night game, so little was he moved from his expression of healthy, handsome, good-humored old age" (11).

When Wilhelm tries "to unburden himself," he, instead, feels he must "undergo an inquisition to prove himself worthy of a sympathetic word" (52). Seeking sympathy, he ends up feeling rejected and enraged. He senses that he is "being put on notice" when his father comments that he keeps his "sympathy for the real ailments" such as that suffered by Mr. Perls who has a "bone condition which is gradually breaking him up" (42). Dr. Adler is unable to see what the reader recognizes all too clearly: that Wilhelm's fragile self is on the verge of breaking up. Rebuffed by his father, Wilhelm, at first, says nothing but instead compulsively eats, devouring not only his own breakfast but also the remains of his father's. Through this regressive behavior, Wilhelm acts out his desire to appropriate from his father the narcissistic sustenance he feels entitled to. When he, in his openly aggressive demands for sympathy, introduces his well-worn litany of complaints about his wife, Dr. Adler responds that it's Wilhelm's fault, that he doesn't understand his son's problems, and that Wilhelm shouldn't "carry on like an opera" (49).

Inwardly angry, Wilhelm towers and sways, "big and sloven, with his gray eyes red-shot and his honey-colored hair twisted in flaming shapes upward." Outwardly, he assumes the posture of the placater for he wants "an understanding with his father" and so he tries to "capitulate to him" (50). But to no avail. "You have no sympathy" (53), he tells his father. "When I suffer — you aren't even sorry. That's because you have no affection for me, and you don't want any part of me" (54). His urgent plea for sympathy and support — "I expect *help!*" (53) — is rejected. "I want nobody on my back. Get off!" (55), his father says to him.

In this father-son transaction we find important clues to Wilhelm's self-disorder. As we learn in this exchange, Wilhelm is acutely sensitive to what he perceives as his father's affective absence, his affable nonresponsiveness, his self-absorption, his chronic fault-finding, and his covert demand that his son live up to *his* standards of perfection. When Dr. Adler publicly boasts about him, Wilhelm feels that his father is making narcissistic use of him, bragging about Wilhelm's accomplishments for his own self-aggrandizement. "Why, that boasting old hypocrite," Wilhelm thinks to himself. "How we love looking fine in the eyes of the world . . ." (13). In an attempt to accommodate his father's wishes and driven by his archaic needs, Wilhelm tries to become a success. But his goals — his hypertrophied belief that he could become a Hollywood star, be appointed vice president of Rojax, and make a fortune in the commodities market — are unrealistic.

Again and again, Wilhelm's untamed grandiosity overwhelms his reality ego leading to a series of painful and predictable failures. And like the typical shame-prone narcissist, he protects himself through boasts and lies. He lies at "first boastfully and then out of charity to himself" about his Hollywood venture (15); he quits his job at Rojax out of hurt pride — "I told everybody I was going to be an officer of the corporation. . . . But then they welshed. . . . I bragged and made myself look big" (74); he defensively denies that "anything serious" has happened when he is wiped out in the commodities market, the "lie" helping him out (104).

But though such defenses can temporarily shield his attenuated self, they cannot counteract his underlying sense of defectiveness. "Ass! Idiot! . . . Slave! Lousy, wallowing hippopotamus!" (55), he mentally upbraids himself after his traumatic confrontation with his father. He has introjected his father's negative view of him. Years before when Wilhelm went to Hollywood, he, in a symbolic gesture, changed his name in the misguided belief that if he cast off his father's name for him — "Wilky" — he could also cast off his father's negative opinion of him. Ironically, the name he selected in his attempt to assert his identity — "Tommy" — suggests not autonomous selfhood but child-like dependency and arrested development. And "Wilky" has remained his "inescapable self." "You fool, you clunk, you Wilky!" he reproaches himself when drunk (25). In a similar vein, Wilhelm's inner, cynical "gruff" voice — an expression of his split-off anger and his fault-finding, parental introject — unempathically berates others. "Who is this damn frazzle-faced herring with his dyed hair and his fish teeth and this drippy mustache? . . . How can a human face get into this condition?" (31), Wilhelm asks himself when he meets Mr. Perls, an unacknowledged self-representation.

The fact that Wilhelm repeatedly attempts to provoke a reaction from his father through self-pity is also telling. For the self-pity response, explains psychoanalyst Samuel Wilson, expresses an "urgent attempt to counteract feelings of alienation and disintegration accompanying a severe narcissistic wound and to recover selfobject connectedness."[11] "The attack on the self," writes Wilson, "contains the hope that this will subserve the needs of the selfobject, as they are perceived, and therefore restore the tie. The appeal to the mercy of the selfobject subserves the needs for a comforting response." But the combination of "helplessness" and "hostility" underlying this response "provokes the already alienated selfobject into further withdrawal and anger" (183).

While Wilhelm provokes criticism and attack from his father, most commentators take his side in the father-son conflict, even though they may consider his self-pity excessive or confess themselves somewhat reluctant to give "sympathy to a man in his physical 'prime' who is asking support of an octogenarian."[12] Even a critic like Jonathan

Wilson, who sees many of Dr. Adler's criticisms of Wilhelm as "to some extent justified" and who faults Wilhelm for acting like "an overgrown child," feels that "it is Wilhelm's childishness that primarily recommends itself to us."[13] Given the critical responses to this text, there clearly is something in Wilhelm's urgent need for help that recommends itself to readers and prompts them to come to his support when his father turns away from him. In part because Dr. Adler is so callous in his response to his son's cry for help and also because the text associates him with the material values of a money-obsessed society, reader after reader has acted as Wilhelm's advocate and echoed his — and the text's — accusatory voice and split-off anger. While Wilhelm has been described as a "sensitive individual" who suffers financial failure in a milieu that determines a person's worth "exclusively in monetary terms,"[14] Dr. Adler, in contrast, has been harshly condemned for being "self-centered, uncompassionate,"[15] "irredeemably selfish,"[16] and for hoarding both his money and his "tight, withered, insulated self."[17] At one point Wilhelm thinks that "it was the punishment of hell itself not to understand or be understood"; in New York the "fathers were no fathers and the sons no sons" (*SD* 83-84). Drawn into Wilhelm's interior world, readers are urged, in effect, to enact the "good father" role by sympathetically responding to Wilhelm's need for understanding and rescue.

That Wilhelm's reality is narcissistically constituted is revealed in his involvement some twenty-five years before with Maurice Venice, the Hollywood scout, and in his current involvement with Dr. Tamkin. In Venice, Wilhelm unknowingly encounters a reflection of his own split grandiose/enervated self. When Venice talks about how the "downcast" need a "break-through, help, luck, or sympathy" (22), Wilhelm is moved. The "obscure failure of an aggressive and powerful clan" (20), Venice, like Wilhelm, is defensively concerned about the impression he is making on others and like Wilhelm he is a braggart and a liar. Physically grotesque, both powerful and weak, Venice is "huge and oxlike" but "so stout" that his arms seem immobilized, "caught from beneath in a grip of flesh and fat" (17). Prophetically, Venice typecasts Wilhelm as a loser. But he also appeals to Wilhelm's grandiose fantasies. "In one jump," Venice tells him, "the world knows who you are. You become a name like Roosevelt, Swanson. . . . You become a lover to the whole world. The world wants it, needs it. One fellow smiles, a billion people also smile. One fellow cries, the other billion sob with him" (22). Despite the negative results of his screen test and Venice's subsequent discouragement, Wilhelm, driven by his primitive belief in his "luck and inspiration" (15) and by his hankering after admiration, goes to Hollywood. Acting out a preestablished plot, he makes his "first great mistake" (17).

Similarly, when Wilhelm meets up with Tamkin, he is, again, "ripe for the mistake" (58). A "confuser of the imagination" (93), Tamkin is an important figure in Wilhelm's psychic life. In Tamkin, Wilhelm finds a potential need-fulfiller. "I've been concerned with you, and for some time I've been treating you," Tamkin tells Wilhelm (73). Making a hostile use of his empathy, Tamkin pretends he is concerned with Wilhelm so he can gull him. Snubbed by his father, Wilhelm transfers onto Tamkin his need for support from an idealizable selfobject. He sees Tamkin, who has "a hypnotic power in his eyes," as a "benevolent magician" (62, 81). While Dr. Adler says, "I want nobody on my back," Wilhelm imagines that Tamkin is supporting him, that he is riding on Tamkin's back, that he has "virtually left the ground" and is "in the air" (96). Narcissistically cathected, Tamkin is a father-surrogate figure. But he is also a complex self-representation.

Is Tamkin a "liar," Wilhelm asks himself, his question about Tamkin self-referential. "That was a delicate question. Even a liar might be trustworthy in some ways" (57). Like Wilhelm, Tamkin is a braggart who "believes he's making a terrific impression, and . . . practically invites you to take off your hat when he talks about himself . . ." (96). "I read the best of literature, science and philosophy," says the all-but-illiterate Tamkin (72). In Tamkin, Wilhelm finds an exaggeration of his own grandiose pretensions. Tamkin's "hints" about his life — he claims, among other things, to have been part of the underworld, to have been head of a mental clinic and a psychiatrist to an Egyptian royal family — grow "by repetition" into "sensational claims" (80). When Tamkin describes himself as a "healer" who belongs to humanity, Wilhelm's inner cynical voice calls him a "liar . . . a puffed-up little bogus and humbug with smelly feet" (95-96). An incarnation of Wilhelm's distorted grandiose/vulnerable self, Tamkin is a "rare, peculiar bird" with his "pointed shoulders, that bare head, his loose nails, almost claws, and those brown, soft, deadly, heavy eyes" (82). Potent and weak, he seems to achieve the "hypnotic effect" in his eyes through "exertion" (62), and when his "hypnotic spell" fails, his "big underlip" makes him appear "weak-minded" (96).

When Wilhelm gives Tamkin power of attorney over his remaining funds, he acts out a complex psychic script. To make or have money is to attempt to supply oneself with an external source of self-worth and power. Money also is a symbol of his father's power. When forced to accompany the self-involved and demanding Mr. Rappaport to the cigar store, Wilhelm displaces his angry feelings about his father onto Mr. Rappaport. "He's almost blind, and covered with spots, but this old man still makes money in the market," Wilhelm's angry inner voice complains. "Is loaded with dough, probably. And I bet he doesn't give his children any. Some of them must be in their fifties. This is what keeps middle-aged men as children. He's master over the dough" (101-02). At one and the same time Wilhelm believes that Tamkin will magically make a fortune and thus save him, but also expects to lose all his money. To be divested of his money is to make reparation for his covert angry impulses. But to be bankrupt is also to be rendered helpless, the hidden fantasy being that his father will relent and give him the money — i.e., the narcissistic support — he needs to sustain and strengthen his flagging self. As Wilhelm tells his father, "It isn't all a question of money — there are other things a father can give to a son. . . . One word from you, just a word, would go a long way" (109-10). Wilhelm is deeply angry with his father and afraid of his anger. But he also craves the healing response that only his father can give. Transferring his needs onto others, Wilhelm wants Mr. Rappaport to give him a winning tip on the market, "to speak the single word" that will "save him" (87). Similarly, he wants Tamkin to "give him some useful advice" and thus "transform his life" (72).

"How did you imagine it was going to be — big shot? Everything made smooth for you?" says Wilhelm's wife, Margaret (114). In his strained relationship with his wife, Wilhelm repeats the narcissistic drama he enacts with his father. Like Dr. Adler, Margaret is contemptuous, unempathic, fault-finding. Her emotional absence is reflected in her "hard" voice (112). Irritated with Wilhelm's hyperbolic talk, she tells him to "stop thinking like a youngster" and sardonically says that he deserves the "misery" he feels (112, 113). Also a self-representation, Margaret is an amalgam of Wilhelm's clinging dependency and disavowed anger. "A husband like me is a slave, with an iron collar," Wilhelm tells his father (49). "Whenever she can hit me, she hits, and she seems to live for that alone. And she demands more and more, and still more" (47). Her angry thoughts are lethal. "She just has fixed herself on me to kill me. She can do it at long distance. One of these days I'll be struck down by suffocation or apoplexy because of her" (48). "This is the way of the weak," Wilhelm says to himself in a self-referring description of his wife. "Quiet and fair. And then smash! They smash!" (112).

While the portrait of Margaret is extremely unsympathetic, Bellow's narrator explains and thus softens her hard words: "She had not, perhaps, intended to reply as harshly as she did, but she brooded a great deal and now she could not forbear to punish him and make him feel pains like those she had to undergo" (114). At one and the same time Bellow expresses his own dislike of the Margarets of this world and depicts himself as the empathic and mediating authorial presence behind the text. Critics, in their discussions of Margaret, follow the text's mandates and echo Bellow's anger as they, taking sides in the husband-wife conflict, come to Wilhelm's support and harshly judge Margaret. She has been depicted variously: as "parasitic,"[18] as a "resentful sadist,"[19] as a "murderer of the spirit,"[20] and as a "termagant wife" who endeavored to "rob" Wilhelm of his "identity during [the] marriage" and "is now determined to rob him of his waning funds."[21]

"I was the man beneath; Tamkin was on my back, and I thought I was on his," Wilhelm reflects when he, after his commodities loss, searches for Tamkin. "He made me carry him, too, besides Margaret. Like this they ride on me with hoofs and claws. Tear me to pieces, stamp on me and break my bones" (*SD* 105). His money gone, Wilhelm, desperate, seeks out his father. When, in this final father-son confrontation, his father disowns him, Wilhelm is struck by Dr. Adler's wide-open, "dark, twisted" mouth (110). A concentrated image, the angry mouth depicts not only the fault-finding father but also Wilhelm's split-off anger. Standing over his father in the massage room, Wilhelm also sees, in his father's "pale, slight" deteriorating body (108), a reflection of his own enervated, crumbling self. From the beginning of his "day of reckoning" Wilhelm has felt himself drowning in his quelled tears, this sinking sensation giving experiential immediacy to his crumbling self and the line from "Lycidas" which he recalls — "Sunk though he be beneath the wat'ry floor" (13) — giving further evidence of this feeling-state. Through his reiterated complaints that he feels congested and as if his head were about to burst, he communicates his feelings of strangulating anger and incipient fragmentation. "New York is like a gas. The colors are running. My head feels so tight, I don't know what I'm doing" (50). Sensing that he is about to confront "a huge trouble long presaged but till now formless" (4), he focuses on his verbalizable troubles to shield himself from what lies behind them: unbearable feelings of preverbal dread, rage, and despair.

"The past is no good to us" (66), says Tamkin, the self-styled "psychological poet" (69). "The future is full of anxiety. Only the present is real — the here-and-now. Seize the day" (66). All too often, Tamkin's advice to Wilhelm has been construed by critics as the novel's serious message. But is it? Wilhelm, in a moment of anguish, prays to be let out of his "thoughts," to be let out of the "clutch" he is in and "into a different life" (26). This prayer, significantly, follows his realization that he lacks "free choice," that "there's really very little that a man can change at will" in his life (25, 24). While Tamkin's seize-the-day advice reflects Wilhelm's *wish* to be different, Wilhelm cannot change merely because he wishes to do so. Just as years before Venice seemed to promise Wilhelm freedom from the "anxious and narrow life of the average" (23), now Tamkin seems to promise him freedom from his anxiety-ridden middle age. Claiming that he wrote his poem, "Mechanism vs Functionalism," with Wilhelm in mind, Tamkin describes the hero of the poem as "sick humanity," which, if "it would open its eyes . . . would be great" (77):

If thee thyself couldst only see
Thy greatness that is and yet to be, . . .
Witness. Thy power is not bare.
Thou art King. Thou art at thy best. (75)

After reading the poem, Wilhelm is "dazed, as though a charge of photographer's flash powder had gone up in his eyes." Consciously, he is enraged because he recognizes that Tamkin is illiterate. Unconsciously, he is angry because in the "mishmash, claptrap" (75) of Tamkin's poem he finds a parodic expression of his own grandiosity. Forced to "translate" Tamkin's words into "his own language," Wilhelm finds himself unable to "translate fast enough or find terms to fit what he heard" (68). "Why do people just naturally assume that you'll know what they're talking about?" he asks himself after reading Tamkin's poem (76).

Through his writing, Tamkin attempts to win the approval of, gain leverage over, and aggressively encroach upon Wilhelm. A subject of much critical discussion, the enigmatic Tamkin has been read as a coded representation of the literary artist. It is interesting that Gilead Morahg, one critic who pursues at length the Tamkin/artist parallels, transforms Tamkin into the novel's moral center and actively splits off his bad qualities. Describing Tamkin as a "morally motivated person who uses fiction in order to affect, and hopefully transform, the life of another," Morahg claims that Tamkin "is similar to the artist, the estimation of whose work is to be completely disassociated from any moral judgment concerning his personality and conduct."[22] While some critics claim that the "grotesque and eccentric Tamkin" gives voice to Bellow's "most-cherished ideas,"[23] others hold the opposite opinion, feeling that he "combines in caricature all the worst perversions of Modernist belief."[24] Latent in this critical split, one can speculate, is Bellow's own ambivalence toward his role as an artist. This text seems to suggest that the empathic artist who gives voice to healing ideas may also be a cold-blooded manipulator and an impostor.

In the novel's final, climactic scene when Wilhelm, searching for Tamkin, suddenly finds himself at the funeral of a stranger, he completes a drama whose script is largely unknown to him and one that actively fosters reader interpretation. "On the surface, the dead man with his formal shirt and his tie and silk lapels and his powdered skin looked so proper; only a little beneath so — black, Wilhelm thought, so fallen in the eyes" (117). In the psychic notation of the novel, the dead man represents the affectively absent father, the empty self that is subjacent to the social, pretender self, and Wilhelm's own self-demise. "What'll I do?" he asks himself. "I'm stripped and kicked out. . . . Oh, Father, what do I ask of you? . . . And Olive? . . . you must protect me against that devil who wants my life. If you want it, then kill me. Take, take it, take it from me" (117). Behind Wilhelm's verbalizable troubles lies a profound sense of vulnerability and despair. Soon "past words, past reason, coherence," he cries "with all his heart" (117-18). As the "flowers and lights" fuse "ecstatically" in his "blind, wet eyes" and the "heavy sea-like music" pours into him, Wilhelm, his self dissolving, hides himself "in the center of a crowd by the great and happy oblivion of tears." He sinks "deeper than sorrow, through torn sobs and cries toward the consummation of his heart's ultimate need" (118).

This final, ambiguous description has been read positively, as the inception of a healing process through mourning. But it also suggests both a loss of self-cohesion and a regressive retreat into the world of earliest childhood. Significantly, when Tamkin earlier enjoined Wilhelm to do "here-and-now" exercises, Wilhelm recalled how, years before when he was ill, his wife had nursed him and read to him the lines from Keats which haunt him on his day of reckoning: "Come then, Sorrow! / Sweetest Sorrow! / Like an own babe I nurse thee on my breast!" (89). These lines suggest not only Wilhelm's mourning for his lost self but also his regressive urge to return to the blissful world of earliest childhood, the "Mt. Serenity" described in Tamkin's poem: "At the foot of Mt. Serenity / Is thy cradle to eternity" (75). A narcissistic nirvana, Mt. Serenity is the introjected world of the good mother. In Wilhelm's mind this is the place inhabited by Ollve, his mistress, whom he associates with the peaceful, sunlit landscape of Roxbury (43). In the final scene, as Wilhelm's enfeebled self collapses, he returns to the formless oblivion and the oceanic oneness of this primal world. But this return offers him but a momentary respite. For Roxbury is but a stone's throw from the hell of New York where people howl like wolves from city windows and where it is impossible to communicate; Mt. Serenity is within reach of the "ruins of life . . . chaos and old night" (93). Wilhelm's introjected world of "the good things, the happy things, the easy tranquil things of life" (78) and his fantasy of merging into a mystical "larger body" where "sons and fathers are themselves" and "confusion is only . . . temporary" (84) are but fragile defenses against — and retreats away from — his more immediate feelings of anger, unrelatedness, and inner chaos.

"Let me out of my trouble. Let me out of my thoughts. . . . Let me out of this clutch and into a different life" (26), Wilhelm prays at one point, though he is fully aware that he lacks "free choice," that he cannot liberate himself from his "inescapable self" (25). While the tone of the closure is positive and suggests the possibility of Wilhelm's redemption through suffering, the weight of the novel conveys the opposite message. Critic Ihab Hassan questions whether the "particular mode" of Wilhelm's revelation "does not seem rather gratuitous, rather foreign to the concerns . . . most steadily expressed throughout the action."[25] The reader is enticed to believe, as does Bellow's hero, that Wilhelm can make a new beginning; can change midstream; can free himself from his introjects, his crippling dependencies, his defensive boasting and his masochistic self-depreciation; that he can be "let out of" his "troubles" and "thoughts" into a "different life." One critic who is seduced by the positive rhetoric of the closure writes: "Because he is able to transcend his personal grief, Wilhelm's tears are also tears of joy. In destroying the pretender soul, Wilhelm prepares the way for the coming of the true soul, who will not lead him to torture himself over an unworthy father, will not persuade him to go to Hollywood or marry unwisely or seek a quick fortune with a charlatan."[26] Wilhelm's "uncontrollable crying," writes another critic, provides a "release from the insoluble problems that tear at his heart" and marks the "beginning of his creative re-birth."[27] "Seize the day," free yourself from the past, Tamkin enjoins Wilhelm. How ironic such advice is in a novel whose protagonist is bound up in an ongoing process of consciously remembering and unconsciously reenacting his past.

What is the typical critic/reader's overall response to Wilhelm? Clinton Trowbridge's comments are illuminating. "Even when Wilhelm is being depicted least sympathetically, when he is most in the wrong, most the slob," he writes, "we are continually made aware that we are witnessing the strugglings of a drowning man and we want to see him rescued."[28] "I expect *help*!" Wilhelm says to his father, only to be rebuffed. But many critics have responded to Wilhelm's need for rescue by elevating and spiritualizing his struggle. While a few critics acknowledge and then excuse Wilhelm's anger, claiming that it results from his "sense of persecution,"[29] most keep intact their image of Wilhelm as a passive victim by totally ignoring it. They see Wilhelm as Keith Opdahl does, as a "good man" in a world "antithetical" to goodness.[30] While critics, as we have observed, echo Wilhelm's accusatory voice and the text's anger as they harshly condemn Margaret and Dr. Adler, they regard Wilhelm as an innocent buffoon who is "exposed to the world's sharkish materialism."[31] "Wilhelm's only weapon," writes Daniel Fuchs, "is love, and this is why he is in such a bad way among the money men. . . ."[32] Wilhelm's drowning is interpreted as a "baptism, a rebirth,"[33] his collapse as a "triumph."[34] Beneath the novel's "profound and moving sense of despair" Trowbridge finds "the birth of a soul."[35] Wilhelm is described as resisting modernist pessimism and as "holding fast to his transcendental dream."[36] "Wilhelm's sobs," as Fuchs comments, "have gained a following."[37] Indeed, they have. Wilhelm's suffering enhances his worth and gains the reader's attention and sympathy.

That the reader's impulse was shared by Bellow is suggested in Daniel Fuchs's analysis of Bellow's revisions of the novel. Particularly revealing is Fuchs's observation on how the "language of outrage" in the novel became "balanced somewhat by the development in the language and imagery of love and spiritual resurrection, most notably in the novella's conclusion."[38] The first version of the closure, unlike the final version, focused on Wilhelm's regressive collapse: "The lights and flowers fused in his blind wet eyes and the music shuddered at his ears. Wilhelm choked his sobs in his handkerchief, and bit his thumb but he failed to check his weeping."[39] Here attention is drawn, observes Fuchs, to the "neurotic, childish thumb in the mouth," an image totally eliminated from the final version with its suggestion of ecstasy and transcendence.[40] "Words such as *consummation* [and] *ecstatically*" and the "slow, deliberate, majestic rhythms" of the final paragraph, in the words of one critic, "compel the reader to participate in Wilhelm's moment of . . . transcendence."[41] Moreover, the measured speech of Keats, Milton, and Shakespeare which haunts Wilhelm serves to elevate his struggle. In effect, Bellow provides the healing word Wilhelm seeks through yet another type of father figure — the literary father. But the contrast between literary speech and Tamkin's garbled, illiterate romanticism works to subvert the author's intended literary reclamation of Wilhelm. We find a similar subversion in Bellow's description of Wilhelm's repudiation of his visionary "blaze of love" for all the "imperfect and lurid-looking people" he sees in the subway: "It was only another one of those subway things. Like having a hard-on at random" (*SD* 84-85). This has led at least one commentator to cross-question the positive tone of the closure and wonder if Wilhelm's "sour dismissal" of his subway experience isn't "predictive of a parallel dismissal" of his funeral home experience "once his tears have dried."[42]

While the closure can be viewed as a reparative gesture derived from Bellow's need to rescue the troubled self of his anti-hero, it also can be read as a reaction formation against his covert desire to "kill off" his hapless character. Tamkin, who, as we've observed, can be read as a clandestine representation of the author, is described as a storyteller who invents a woman, kills her off, and then calls himself a healer. Two contrasting but associated signifiers in the novel — the healing word and the angry mouth — can be read as coded references to the author who expresses his anger through his characters while enacting, in his narrator's guise, the role of mediator and empathic listener. "I can sympathize with Wilhelm," Bellow commented in an interview, "but I can't respect him. He is a sufferer by vocation. I'm a resister by vocation."[43] Fuchs asks, "Isn't Wilhelm the victim Bellow wants to delete from his own typology?"[44] While the closure of this text may represent a gesture toward resolution of conflict and aesthetic finality, its very abruptness and incompleteness undermine such an authorial intention. For just when the reader "expects the falling action to unravel and explain," comments J. R. Raper, "the book ends."[45] The closure is "unresolved," observes Richard Giannone, baffling reader expectations for "clarification and completion."[46] While the final potent image of Wilhelm in the funeral parlor provokes the reader's sympathy for his redundant suffering, it also, in effect, puts the reader in the place of the other mourners whose curiosity is provoked by his unexplained lament. The closure forces the reader to interpret and explain. It is also possible that the abrupt closure answers the secret wish of some readers — and the author — to abandon Wilhelm, to be let out of his troubles, and thus escape his stifling fictional presence.

Speaking informally on the novel, Bellow once described one of the novel's themes as the city dweller's attempt to fulfill his personal needs through strangers.[47] That Wilhelm craves empathic resonance is revealed in his open, compulsive sharing of his problems with others. "Other people keep their business to themselves. Not me," he realizes (*SD* 35). For him it is "the punishment of hell itself not to understand or be understood" (83-84). Despite this, Wilhelm finds it impossible to communicate, living as he does in a world in which "every other man" speaks a language "entirely his own" and where the fathers are "no fathers and the sons no sons" (83-84). When he, at the end, finally breaks down, it is at the funeral of a stranger and in a roomful of strangers who observe him from a psychic distance. Ironically, one of the bystanders comments that he must be "somebody real close to carry on so" (118). The tragedy is that Wilhelm, who wants to be "close," is so totally alone. "Howling like a wolf from the city window" (98), he knows the awfulness of living in an unempathic environment and in a world populated by reflections of his own distorted self. In a fantasy borne of deep necessity, he can imagine a world in which "sons and fathers are themselves" and "confusion is only . . . temporary" (84). But he also realizes that if he stops suffering, he will "have nothing" (98). For behind his verbalizable troubles is a formless oblivion, the wordless dread and inner emptiness of Tragic Man. His self defective, Wilhelm inhabits not the glorious here-and-now fantasied by Tamkin but the bleak here-and-now of his own crippled self.

Notes

1. Saul Bellow, *Seize the Day* (New York: Penguin Books, 1956), 109-10.
2. Sarah Cohen, *Saul Bellow's Enigmatic Laughter* (Urbana: U of Illinois P, 1974), 93-94.
3. Daniel Weiss, "Caliban on Prospero: A Psychoanalytic Study on the Novel *Seize the Day* by Saul Bellow," *Saul Bellow and the Critics*, ed. Irving Malin (New York: NYUP, 1967), 121.
4. Lee Richmond, "The Maladroit, the Medico, and the Magician: Saul Bellow's *Seize the Day*," *Twentieth Century Literature* 19 (1973): 15.
5. Cohen, 100.
6. Heinz Kohut, "Remarks About the Formation of the Self," *The Search for the Self: Selected Writings of Heinz Kohut 1950-1978*, ed. Paul H. Ornstein, vol. 2 (New York: International Universities Press, 1978), n. 5, 752.
7. Heinz Kohut, *The Restoration of the Self* (New York: International Universities Press, 1977), 104-05.
8. Keith Opdahl, *The Novels of Saul Bellow: An Introduction* (University Park: Pennsylvania State UP, 1967), 106.
9. John J. Clayton, "Saul Bellow's *Seize the Day*: A Study in Mid-Life Transition," *Saul Bellow Journal* 5.1 (1986): 41.
10. Cohen, 93.
11. Samuel Wilson, "The Self-Pity Response: A Reconsideration," *Progress*

in Self Psychology, ed. Arnold Goldberg, vol. 1 (New York: Guilford, 1985), 182.

12. Daniel Fuchs, *Saul Bellow: Vision and Revision* (Durham: Duke UP, 1984), 80.

13. Jonathan Wilson, *On Bellow's Planet: Readings from the Dark Side* (London and Toronto: Associated University Presses, 1985), 97, 100.

14. Joseph F. McCadden, *The Flight from Women in the Fiction of Saul Bellow* (Washington: University Press of America, 1980), 93.

15. Gilbert M. Porter, *Whence the Power? The Artistry and Humanity of Saul Bellow* (Columbia: U of Missouri P, 1974), 110.

16. J. Wilson, 103.

17. Eusebio Rodrigues, *Quest for the Human: An Exploration of Saul Bellow's Fiction* (Lewisburg: Bucknell UP, 1981), 85.

18. Julius R. Raper, "Running Contrary Ways: Saul Bellow's *Seize the Day*." *Southern Humanities Review* 10.2 (1976): 166.

19. Fuchs, 85.

20. McCadden, 106.

21. Cohen, 91.

22. Gilead Morahg, "The Art of Dr. Tamkin: Matter and Manner in *Seize the Day*," *Modern Fiction Studies* 25 (Spring 1979): 116.

23. J. Wilson, 98.

24. Gloria Cronin, "The Seduction of Tommy Wilhelm: A Post-Modernist Appraisal of *Seize the Day*," *Saul Bellow Journal* 3.1 (1983): 21.

25. Ihab Hassan, *Radical Innocence: Studies in the Contemporary American Novel* (Princeton: Princeton UP, 1961), 316.

26. Porter, 125.

27. McCadden, 91-92.

28. Clinton Trowbridge, "Water Imagery in *Seize the Day*," *Critique* 9.3 (Spring 1967): 65.

29. Porter, 114.

30. Opdahl, 112.

31. Cohen, 90.

32. Fuchs, 97.

33. Porter, 125.

34. Opdahl, 115.

35. Trowbridge, 62.

36. Cronin, 23.

37. Fuchs, 95.

38. Fuchs, 94.

39. Bellow, qtd. in Fuchs, 96.

40. Fuchs, 97.

41. Rodrigues, 105-06.

42. Carol Sicherman, "Bellow's *Seize the Day*: Reverberations and Hollow Sounds," *Studies in the Twentieth-Century* 15 (Spring 1975): 14.

43. Matthew Roudané, "An Interview with Saul Bellow," *Contemporary Literature* 25.3 (1984): 279. [see pp. 234-247 of this volume]

44. Fuchs, 79.

45. Raper, 158.

46. Richard Giannone, "Saul Bellow's Idea of Self: A Reading of *Seize the Day*." *Renascence* 27.4 (1975): 203.

47. Opdahl, 108.

* * *

Henderson the Rain King (1959)

The Search for Salvation
Granville Hicks

Saul Bellow's *Henderson the Rain King* is an adventure story with large and important implications. Like almost everything else Bellow has written, it is an account of a man's struggles to find and to transcend himself, but Henderson's quest takes him into strange and romantic places. It is as if Bellow were inventing for his hero physical perils commensurate with the inner hazards of his search. However one reads it, this is as exciting a novel as has appeared in a long time.

Bellow has created many bizarre characters, but Henderson is the most extravagant figure of them all. Fifty-five years old when he introduces himself to us, he is a giant of a man, six feet four inches tall and correspondingly heavy and strong. Rich and of good family, he has by his own account wasted his life. When he thinks of that life, he says, "a disorderly rush begins — my parents, my wives, my girls, my children, my farm, my animals, my habits, my money, my music lessons, my drunkenness, my prejudices, my brutality, my teeth, my face, my soul!" He is a man who is driven, but by what and towards what he does not know.

Henderson at this moment of his life has to go somewhere, and by chance he goes to Africa. Leaving his companions and striking off on his own with a faithful guide, he comes upon an isolated tribe, the Arnewi, gentle people, whom he likes. Eager to do them a great service, he brings disaster upon them, and, as so often before, is crushed with remorse.

He proceeds, this modern Gulliver, to visit the Wariri, a sterner tribe. But though his welcome is not cordial, he eventually finds himself on intimate terms with the king, Dahfu, who has studied medicine in missionary schools and who speaks English. This time Henderson's impulses lead him to expend his great strength in carrying a huge sta-

From *Saturday Review* (21 Feb. 1959): 20.

tue, and his success gives him an important role in rain-making ceremonies. And since rain does fall, he becomes the Sungo, the Rain
King.

All this is strange enough, but the strangest is yet to come. Dahfu
has a kind of private lion cult into which he tries to initiate the reluctant Henderson, the two meanwhile engaging in intense discussions of
the nature and destiny of man. Then comes the climax — a hair-raising
lion hunt conducted according to the risky precepts of Wariri ritual.
Dahfu is killed, probably as the result of a plot against him, and
Henderson has to flee to avoid becoming Dahfu's successor. He returns
to America with a lion cub and the conviction that he has found what
he was looking for.

No one has ever conveyed so well as Saul Bellow the anguish of a
man who is capable of honestly contemplating his nature but incapable
of changing it. This agony is to be found in his first book, *Dangling
Man*, and in his recent novelette, *Seize the Day*. The hero of the latter,
Tommy Wilhelm, might in some ways be regarded as a preliminary
study for Henderson, but there are great differences between them.
Tommy is a slob, and the best one can say for him is that he knows he
is and wishes he weren't, and this makes him pitiful. Henderson has
acted like a slob again and again, as he insists on reminding himself
and us, but one never doubts that he has good and even great qualities.
Often enough, as with the Arnewi, it is his good intentions that lead
him into disaster, and he is so genuine a seeker for salvation that his
predicament seems tragic rather than merely sad.

Because he has qualities of greatness, Henderson can have heroic
adventures as well as comic misadventures, and Bellow's uninhibited
inventiveness has given his virtues and vices full scope. I suspect that
resemblances between the Arnewi and the Wariri and existing African
tribes are purely coincidental, but whether this is true or not makes
little difference, for the main thing is that Henderson has a world in
which he can find himself. Bellow has also given him a style of his
own. Augie March expressed himself in colloquial language with rich
literary overtones. Henderson's style is more purely colloquial, and
what gives it its special quality is its headlong energy. The style is the
man, and Henderson is revealed to us not only by what he says but
also by the way in which he says it.

There was, I recall, a reviewer of *The Adventures of Augie March*
who spent much space in expounding the symbolism of that novel,
making everything stand for something else. (He then turned around
and scolded Bellow for the symbolism that he, the reviewer, had
dreamt up.) *Henderson* is likely to be misinterpreted in the same way,
although Bellow has been quite specific. The lions are lions, the pigs
are pigs, the bear a bear. That the lions have a special significance for
Dahfu, and that he hopes they can have a similar significance for
Henderson, he says flatly enough. In the same way Henderson knows
there was a reason why he raised pigs. But whatever meanings the

animals have, they have as animals, and they have these meanings to particular individuals. Lion does not equal this; pig does not equal that.

Although Bellow is dealing with deep mysteries, he does not indulge in mystification of any sort, but brings to his difficult theme as much clarity as possible. "Don't you believe in regeneration?" Henderson asks. He does, and so, with greater reason, does Dahfu. "Well, Henderson," Dahfu challenges, "what are the generations for, please explain to me? Only to repeat fear and desire without a change? This cannot be what the thing is for, over and over and over. Any good man will try to break the cycle." Earlier Dahfu has explained how the cycle can be broken: Imagination is a force of nature. Is this not enough to make a person full of ecstasy? Imagination, imagination, imagination! It converts to actual, it sustains, it alters, it redeems!"

Henderson differs from *Augie March* in many interesting ways. In the earlier novel Bellow uses a loose structure to illustrate, through a long series of essentially realistic episodes the vast possibilities of contemporary life. Beginning in poverty and illegitimacy, Augie ranges far, horizontally and vertically, to end in uncertainty. Henderson, on the other hand, born to every advantage, has lived fifty-five years of unquiet desperation. Of Augie's kind of patient pilgrimage he has never been capable. He is driven by the voice that cries, "I want, I want," and the story of his search is both romantic and dramatic. I cannot say that *Henderson the Rain King* is a better book than *Augie March*: the denseness of experience in the earlier novel is something almost unparalleled in contemporary literature. But it is a wonderful book for Bellow to have written after writing *Augie March*. It is a book that should be read again and again, and each reading, I believe, will yield further evidence of Bellow's wisdom and power.

*   *   *

Henderson's Bellow
Richard G. Stern

The first forty pages of *Henderson the Rain King* are packed with enough material for two or three novels, odd, intricate relationships between husbands and wives, fathers and children, landlords and tenants, all suspenseful, and all disposed of with a quick easy brilliance that is the first of this book's surprises. The next three hundred pages leap from this material into territory few novelists in the world are brave or energetic enough to enter. Or rather, to construct; for here lies the bravery: scanting a gift of which he has more than any writer alive, the gift of soaking in and then returning with shine the detail of

From *Kenyon Review* 21.4 (1959): 655-61.

the world, Bellow propels his book into the jungles of possibility to hack out a country that will both stage his hero's quest and partially slake his appetite, a country constructed for discovery.

> The way grew more and more stony and this made me suspicious. If we were approaching a town we ought by now to have found a path. Instead there were these jumbled white stones that looked as if they had been combed out by an ignorant hand from the elements that make least sense. There must be stupid portions of heaven, too, and these had rolled straight down from it. I am no geologist but the word calcareous seemed to fit them. They were composed of lime and my guess was that they must have originated in a body of water. Now they were ultra-dry but filled with little caves from which cooler air was exhaled — ideal places for a siesta in the heat of noon, provided no snakes came. But the sun was in decline, trumpeting downward. The cave mouths were open and there was this coarse and clumsy gnarled white stone.

This country is neither conscientiously symbolic nor artificial; seen through the eyes of the regal, knowledgeable, keening slob who narrates the book, its topography has personality, one which seems to both objectify and nourish the novel's bizarre notions.

Are there precedents for this sort of construction? In a way, there aren't. Utopians, satirists, dream visionaries have been contriving countries for millennia, but, to greater or lesser degree, their contrivances are unlikely. Either the landscape is unearthly and the brute creation articulate, or the hero arrives by time machine or dream. In Bellow's Africa, custom and belief are strange, but all — including a semi-domesticated lion — it seems, is real. The fantasy is kept in the realm of ideas where it can be legitimately accommodated as an early stage of knowledge.

There is a much more important difference in *Henderson*, and that is its hero. The Gullivers, Candides, and Connecticut Yankees may be scalpels, sensitometers, blank slates, mechanical pens, victims, physicians, P.A. systems, or even types, eccentric and amusing, but they are never characters whose fates mean more than their discoveries and situations. Eugene Henderson outlasts both what he learns and what happens to him, and constantly he pulls the book out of the perilous abstract. His American memories corkscrew through the African present tense with a backtracking ease which makes Ford and Conrad look elephantine; his grab-bag miseries and splendors — battered hulk, largess, sweet ambitions, ever aching conscience — weight the unfamiliar with familiar presence, and the book stays grounded in the real. *Henderson* is composed out of the expression of the narrator's want, its complicated genesis — he's had the world and found it wanting — and its satisfaction. It is partly the nature of the want and of the food which the novelist who instilled the want is obligated to supply for it that makes *Henderson* a different sort of reading experience for faithful Bellovians. An account of the difference might begin with a paragraph from *Augie March*:

In his office Simon wore his hat like a Member of Parliament, and while he phoned his alligator-skin shoes knocked things off the desk. He was in on a deal to buy some macaroni in Brazil and sell it in Helsinki. Then he was interested in some mining machinery from Sudbury, Ontario, that was wanted by an Indo-Chinese company. The nephew of a cabinet minister came in with a proposition about waterproof material. And after him some sharp character interested Simon in distressed yard-goods from Muncie, Indiana. He bought it. Then he sold it as lining to a manufacturer of leather jackets. All this while he carried on over the phone and cursed and bullied, but that was just style, not anger, for he laughed often.

There in a single paragraph out of Augie's thousand or so, the great know-how is at work, the skipping facts, the bunched variety more lively than life ever is, four or five different sorts of sentences, all held in and charged with Augie's tone. Places, things, people, pointed description, key movements — the alligator-skin shoes knocking things off the desk — and the characterizing summary, this is the way the novel goes, more brilliantly packed with the commodity and stuff of the world than anything in American literature. "It was like giving birth to Gargantua," Bellow said of it, and that comparison may indicate the reason it stopped, for, to the reader, it looks as if it might go on as long as the world supplied Augie with objects to handle and people to watch.

Henderson starts where Augie leaves off; where Augie was a knocker at doors, a Columbus of the "near-at-hand," Henderson is a Columbus of the absolute, fifty-five, not twenty, a man for whom doors have opened and whom the rooms have not satisfied. The problem for the writer here is that the absolute is barely furnished, and what furniture it has consists of those Biedermeier hulks of fiction, ideas.

When realist writers write novels in which ideas play important roles, the procedure is usually a form of concealment: the action is tied-into the idea either as illustration or contradiction of it. The big, organizing idea of a novel close to *Henderson*, Mann's *Felix Krull*, is something like the reality of fakery, and the book is cluttered with such detail as glorious looking champagne bottles containing miserable champagne, actors seen first under the lights and then backstage, crooks, magicians, illusionists of all sorts, a whole Mann spectrum drawn from department stores to interstellar space. The picaresque adventures are sunk into this detail which is assembled to illustrate, or rather, to compose the themes. On the other hand, in such a book as *The Magic Mountain*, the characters in action contradict the notions they expound and for which they sometimes seem to stand. (A humanitarian pacifist challenges a Jesuit convert to a duel, and the latter kills himself.) *Henderson* takes neither one of these classic routes; its actions are discrete from the notions which make up no small part of the book, those of Henderson himself, or of the two beautiful obesities, the women of Bittahness, or of the almost-MD, William James-reading totem king, Dahfu. The notions of *Henderson* glow like actions and the actions like ideas. This needs illustration.

Towards the end of the novel, King Dahfu is in the midst of a kind of Reichian analysis of Henderson's posture:

> You appear cast in one piece. The midriff dominates. Can you move the different portions? Minus yourself of some of your heavy reluctance of attitude. Why so sad and so earthen? Now you are a lion. Mentally, conceive of the environment. The sky, the sun, and creatures of the bush. You are related to all. The very gnats are your cousins. The sky is your thoughts. The leaves are your insurance, and you need no other. There is no interruption all night to the speech of the stars. Are you with me? I say, Mr. Henderson, have you consumed much amounts of alcohol in your life? The face suggests you have, the nose especially. It is nothing personal. Much can be changed. By no means all, but very much. You can have a new poise. It will resemble the voice of Caruso, which I have heard on records, never tired because the function is as natural as to the birds.

Then Dahfu tells him to get down on his hands and knees and bellow. "Be the beast!"

> And so I was the beast. I gave myself to it, and all my sorrow came out in the roaring. My lungs supplied the air but the note came from my soul. The roaring scalded my throat and hurt the corners of my mouth and presently I filled the den like a base organ pipe. This is where my heart had sent me, with its clamor. Oh, Nebuchadnezzar! How well I understood that prophecy of Daniel. For I had claws, and hair, and some teeth, and I was bursting with hot noise. . . .

Dahfu's speech is so wily a mixture of the lyric and admonitory, the descriptive and conceptual, that even if it were not couched in gorgeous Bellafrikanisch, it would seem to further the book's progress as more obviously dramatic action would. Indeed, as it is idea moving toward action, so the roaring of Henderson moves toward idea. "I was the beast. . . . [I roared]. . . . the note came from my soul. . . . This is where my heart had sent me. . . ." The scenic extravagance, a large man on hands and knees bellowing like a maniac, is implanted in an idea-context which not only makes it right but moving. Behind the action is the sort of momentum Swift supplied for the scene in which Gulliver kisses his Master's hoof, perhaps the most touching in eighteenth-century fiction.

As for the ideas themselves, they exist in terms of Henderson's need, and have as much relation to belief as Bellow's Africa to Tom Mboyo's. The major one — a version of the notion that we are in no small part the product of the images we absorb — can be found in such different places as the beginning of Plutarch's life of Timoleon, *Felix Krull*, and the somatic psychology of Wilhelm Reich. What counts in the novel is that Henderson's reaction to them is part of the revelation of his personality, and for Bellow, as for Malamud and some of the other fine novelists of the time, personality is back in the middle of the novel, not where their great predecessors — Proust, Joyce, and to somewhat lesser extent, Mann — put it, as part of a thematic scheme which apportions the size and intensity of every element. *Henderson* is a kind of bridge between *Augie, Seize the Day,* and these thematic novels; the difficulty is that the bridge must bear the weight of constant invention, which can draw hardly at all on the home detail in which the other novels luxuriate. An original like Bellow can't lean on the second-hand views of travellers and movies, and must be on the qui vive for the cliches which always threaten writing about the exotic. Consequently, much of Henderson's detail is landscape, physiognomy, and a few clothing props, and the investment there is great. Bellow readers, used to commodity markets, Mexican resorts, Evanston haberdasheries, and the Machiavellians and con men who in vintage Bellow load the pages, must go into another gear. They will be helped by the fact that *Henderson* is a stylistic masterpiece.

The Henderson prose had a kind of trial — and somewhat barren — run in a long story, "Leaving the Yellow House," which appeared a year or so ago in *Esquire.* The story's about a sort of female Henderson — but on her last legs — who drips out like hourglass sand in the Utah desert. The clean sentences of that story are now somehow galvanized by the popping energy of *Augie,* and the result is such paragraphs as this:

> Itelo protruded his lips to show that I was expected to kiss her on the belly. To dry my mouth first, I swallowed. The fall I had taken while wrestling had split my underlip. Then I kissed, giving a shiver at the heat I encountered. The knot of the lion's skin was pushed aside by my face, which sank inward. I was aware of the old lady's navel and her internal organs as they made sounds of submergence. I felt as though I were riding in a balloon above the Spice Islands, soaring in hot clouds while exotic odors rose from below. My own whiskers pierced me inward, in the lip. When I drew back from this significant experience (having made contact with a certain power — unmistakable! — which emanated from the woman's middle), Mtalba also reached for my head, wishing to do the same, as indicated by her gentle gestures, but I pretended I didn't understand and said to Itelo, "How come when everybody else it in mourning, your aunts are both so gay?"

There are, in my view, three very different sorts of literary experience, the writer's, the reader's, and the critic's, the last two being as distinct as the first from them. If we analogize the writer to an assassin, the reader may be thought of as the corpse, and the critic as the coroner-detective, The feelings of the assassin and his victim are notably different, but, at least for our purposes, they may be said to be powerful ones, and in the former's case organized by a sense of pupose as in the latter's by force — (scarcely conceived and rapidly terminated). The coroner-critic is the rationalist, the reconstructionist, and although he cannot alter the responses of the reader-victim, he can, in a sense, alter those of future readers in such fashion that their reactions

will be shaped in part by his notions. An early Monet critic could instruct viewers to stand back from the canvases. (Indeed, the feelings
of someone who knows he has been murdered — knows, because
"murder" is defined — are most likely different from the feelings he
would have if he thought he were dying a natural death.) I bring this
up because my reactions first as reader, and then as critic of *Henderson*, are distinct.[1] As reader, I respond more easily to the Bellow I am
used to, the parts of Henderson which deal with that hero's American
experience — his pig farm, bad teeth, Sevçik violin exercises, his
fights on Highway Seven, his high rides with the bear Smolak, his
wives and children. As critic, however, that part of me which reading
has not yet slain, I admire immensely the boldness and brilliance of the
whole, admire the "originality" and the style and the other tributaries
of great narrative, and I am hopeful that my feelings will in future
readings catch up with my admiration. This is the least credit one can
extend to greatness.

Notes

1. As a matter of fact, I feel in small part with the assassin, perhaps as acces-
    sory after the fact. I know Bellow, and have talked with him about this
    novel among other things. Indeed, I read an earlier version, and some of
    my initial reactions to it turned out to be similar to Bellow's as he went
    over the book, so that changes were made which make me feel — for no
    good reason — implicated. The point here is that I feel I know what
    effects were wanted at certain moments; I also feel "in" on such genetic
    factors as Bellow's interest in Reich. Such knowledge alters, and alters
    seriously, my responsiveness to the "magic" of the book and might well be
    taken into account by readers of the review.

*   *   *

Life Against Death in *Henderson the Rain King*
Donald W. Markos

> I found in myself, and still find, an instinct toward a higher, or,
> as it is named, spiritual life, as do most men, and another toward
> a primitive rank and savage one, and I reverence them both.
> Any nobleness begins at once to refine a man's features, any
> meanness or sensuality to imbrute them.
> Henry David Thoreau, "Higher Laws," *Walden*

In their introduction to *The Modern Tradition* (1965), Richard Ellmann
and Charles Feidelson assert "that the study of modern literature will
increasingly become a study of the modern in general," and that mod-

---

ernism, while not entirely dead, is far enough in the past to be seen "in historical depth."[1] Likewise, Irving Howe, editor of *Literary Modernism* (1967), notes that "signs of a denouement begin to appear" and fears that modernism faces the doleful prospect of popularization.[2] Indeed, one witnesses "existentialism" in such popular television series which feature the "outsider," the "rebel," the "fugitive," or the "authentic" individual who lives with the consciousness of death impending from some obscure but painless disease. Nor is the change from (or within?) modernism felt only by literary scholars. William Hamilton, co-author with Thomas Altizer of *The Death of God* (1966), senses a liberating, non-Barthian spirit of life in the sixties, witnessed in such disparate events as the civil rights movement, Herzog's decision to get well, and the Beatles' uninhibited horseplay in *A Hard Day's Night*.[3]

I do not intend to record here the signs of a new movement in literature, theology, or film, but will assume that the reader has been aware for some time now of similar rumblings of something beyond modernism and its hallmarks of despair, rebellion, alienation; its sometimes liberating, sometimes tragic, sense of changing or failing traditions; its bitter, often surreal, condemnation of civilization and, less frequently, the universe; and its celebration of the anti-hero as the authentic individual surviving as heel, rebel, rogue, underground man, artist, victim, and other marginal, anti-social, but not anti-human, categories.

Among significant post-war writers to feel the greatest dissatisfaction with the modernist movement in literature has been Saul Bellow. Though few writers understood the theme of alienation better than Bellow, Bellow from the first realized that alienation, marginal existence, indifference to nature, and fear of contamination from social involvement were too high a price to pay for whatever "authenticity" one was protecting. In all of his novels, Bellow has imagined, with increasing fullness, conditions and images that are alternatives to what he has called the "wasteland outlook." In *Henderson the Rain King* (1959), the alternative is most powerfully imagined, and we can see both the earlier modernist version of man's alienation and the tentative offering of a new attitude toward the world and man's conception of himself — a humanism grounded in a kind of intuitive naturalism. As in Bellow's best fiction and consistent with his stated views on the writer's moral allegiances, both views are developed with full strength — the often dogmatic modernist view of man trapped or adrift in a valueless universe and the other, more romantic, view of man integrated within an organic universe, sharing its principles of growth.

In the character of Henderson himself we find both the destructive symptoms of alienation as well as a potential vitality for regeneration. Bellow has made Henderson appear often larger than life, a mythical figure who embodies many of the fears and aspirations of a whole generation of Americans. Like America today, Henderson is big, restless, wealthy, confused, gamey, given to exaggerated utterance, afraid of death, and, most significantly, obsessed with the need for salvation. The reader will find resemblances in Henderson to many of our folk and literary heroes, not least of whom is Whitman whose descriptions of himself — "turbulent," "fleshy," "sensual," "eating," "drinking," "breeding," "hankering," "gross," "mystical," "nude" — quite literally fit Henderson. It is not inconceivable that many Americans, men of vitality now turning middle-aged, might dream of some journey on foot through heat and wilderness and hardship, living sparely off the land, stripping down, sweating off the fat and poisons of civilization, establishing contact with simple, primitive men — whether African warriors or Alaskan hunting guides. Something of this desire is behind Henderson's last resort drive for self-renewal. He is the American Adam turned middle-aged and on the verge of a breakdown, trying to recover some lost quality of himself — "All my decay has taken place upon a child."[4] Country-bred and rugged, facing "the biggest problem of all, which was to encounter death" (276), Henderson often seems to stand as a symbol for America itself — an America in need of change.

The first four chapters of the novel describe Henderson's turbulent life in the United States and try to explain the state of mind that drove him to Africa. Like Herzog, he has twice married but cannot get along with his second wife and has neglected his children. Henderson loses his temper with his tenants, tries to shoot their pet cat, threatens people, breaks bottles on a beach, quarrels with the state troopers, makes suicide threats, insults waiters, and suffers with comic exaggeration ("I am to suffering what Gary is to smoke" [258]). He is certain that the sound of his angry voice induced a fatal heart attack in an old woman — the incident directly prompting his trip to Africa. In short, Henderson is an apt embodiment of the instinct toward aggression which Freud put forth with such conviction in *Civilization and its Discontents*.

Yet the life instinct is strong in Henderson, too, though it has been grossly mis-directed. He has enough *grun-tu-molani* to realize that he must change his perspective, acquire new emotional habits. He has come to realize that if the world appears to be a pigsty to a man, that is because the man already has something of pig nature in him: "Reality is you" (123). Although his first name (Eugene) means well-born, Henderson feels he has "ruined the original piece of goods issued to me" (77). His soul is "like a pawn shop" — "filled with unredeemed pleasures, old clarinets, and cameras, and moth-eaten fur" (81). Henderson, then, is a man driven by violent, directionless energies, wasting effort, constantly in conflict with others and with himself, and yet yearning intensely for release. Recalling the time when he stood on his property thinking of how the carcasses buried on the land "have become humus and the grass is thriving" (29), Henderson, standing in the midst of grass and flowers, is not at all happy, because he has not yet undergone a needed transformation himself. And Henderson is profoundly excited by images of rebirth. He was greatly impressed by an article in a scientific magazine about a desert flower that blooms once in forty or fifty years and which bears seeds that will germinate only under natural conditions of rainfall and not by artificial soaking. The seeds have their own proper, organic means of growth and man must have his, too. The impulse toward renewal is at the heart of this novel; it is the source of motivation and symbolism as well as incidental imagery. We have moved from the modernism typified by Eliot's listlessly questing Fisher King to the energy and vitality of postmodernism where significant positive action is once again possible.

The impetus for change comes from within, organically, as Henderson hears a voice crying "*I want. I want.*" The voice does not express desire in the ordinary sense, but rather a need for "coming into" one's identity and a cessation from the neurotic, hyperactive flight from the inescapable human condition. Henderson's journey to Africa is an attempt to get back to that lost condition — the Africa of the imagination which, since Conrad and Hemingway, has stood as the place where man discovers the truth about himself and, by generic extension, about mankind itself. Henderson's search for "fundamentals" leads him to encounters with the Arnewi and Wariri. The meaning of the novel, in fact, emerges from a symbolic understanding of these tribes and their respective leaders. The simple contrast between love and hate (aggression) suggested by the tribes is complicated by the fact that their respective leaders transcend the limitations of their tribes and are personifications of completely integrated human beings.

The Arnewi, the first tribe Henderson encounters, are meek, docile, loving, and therefore "unlucky." They accept their fate (the drought, the frogs contaminating the drinking water) and suffer and are incapable of acting aggressively to better themselves. Hence they reveal the weakness of loving acceptance alone. Henderson, on the contrary, is quite full of eagerness and good intentions and wants to do something for the Arnewi; but because of his lack of self-knowledge, his impulsive actions are more destructive than beneficial. His bomb constructed from gunpowder and flashlight not only kills off the frogs but destroys the cistern, too. The incident is a parable of modern man's technical ingenuity backfiring on him.

The Wariri, in contrast to the Arnewi, are aggressive, hostile, cruel, and warlike, Like the civilization from which Henderson has fled, but much more overtly, they are in some way connected with death — as evidenced by the corpses hanging at the edge of the village, the dead man in Henderson's hut, the shrunken head of an assumed sorceress — and may represent a death instinct as well as an aggressive instinct. Their religious ceremonies include such barbaric acts as a wrestling match between a dwarf and an old woman, a contest in which two men whip each other, and a display of irreverence and brutality to the carved statues of their gods. These carved wooden statues of varying sizes represent gods who rule "the air, the mountains, fire, plants, cattle, luck, sickness, clouds, birth, death" (181). In short, they are the gods of life, and the harshness with which the natives treat them is a symptom of human resentment against life. Henderson, who has *grun-tu-molani* or love of life, is horrified by the spectacle: "To me it seemed like a pretty cheap way to behave, although I could see . . . plenty of grounds for resentment against the gods" (181). This resentment is the direct opposite of the Arnewi attitude of passive acceptance.

The Wariri attitude toward life is most fully revealed, however, in a later ceremony in which Henderson, now the Rain King, is caught up in a frenzied dance of screaming, chanting Amazons who strike the carved wooden statues with whips and soon are striking each other and Henderson as well. Some of them even force him to raise his hand and bring the whip down once or twice against his will. And in this way — through violent, aggressive force — the Wariri succeed in imposing their will upon life: the thunder claps and the rains come down. Dahfu, who disapproves of his tribe's behavior, explains to Henderson that the shrieking crowd represents the "earthly dominion," that man is a "creature of revenges" who receives blows from life and mechanistically passes them on to others — "it is a continuity matter" (213). But there are exceptions: "A brave man will try to make the evil stop with him. He shall keep the blow" (214). Henderson had tried not to render any blows, but found it very difficult to resist the chain of resentment.

If the Arnewi and Wariri represent dichotomous human instincts (or approaches to life), then we might reason that the complete human being would be one in whom these conflicting tendencies were somehow harmonized and made to work together rather than in conflict. According to N. O. Brown, it is a "Freudian theorem that the instinctual life of man starts from a primitive undifferentiated fusion of the two instincts."[5] And Dahfu, in fact, tells Henderson that the two tribes were once a single tribe "but separated over the luck question" (166). Each tribe still retains a vestige of their original union: the Arnewi prince, Itelo, insists upon a polite, formal wrestling match with Henderson, and one of the Wariri women, in an Arnewi-like gesture, puts the burning coals from Dahfu's pipe on her thigh as an expression of love and adoration for the king. But beyond these vestiges, the leaders of the two tribes, Queen Willatale and King Dahfu, represent — in different proportions — the full harmonization of human forces, and they therefore serve as examples of that equilibrium which Henderson needs to achieve.

One of the first things Henderson notices about the Queen of the Arnewi is that "good nature emanated from her" (71). Her greeting is full of benevolence. He feels the "radiant heat and monumental weight" of her breast; her heart beat is "as regular as the rotation of the earth" (72). Henderson feels as if he were "touching the secrets of life" (72). The Queen is huge, heavy, solid, and expresses "stability in every part of her body" (72). But a most significant detail in the Queen's appearance is the lion skin which she wears and which Henderson describes at length. It certainly must have some association with the lion which Dahfu keeps as a pet in the den beneath his palace. The fact that it is only the skin of a dead lion which the Queen wears suggests that animal nature plays a subordinate part in her psychological makeup. The Queen, a woman of Bittahness (suggesting the capacity to accept), is also considered to be bi-sexual and has both husbands and wives. She has transcended such limitations as sexual differences, which cause much torment for most of mankind, and is a complete being in herself. She is the very image of an impossible ideal — the fully integrated personality, without unsatisfied needs, in whom energies are not wasted or blocked or directed aggressively against oneself or others: " . . . there was no anxious care in her, and she was sustained. Why nothing bad happened! On the contrary, it all seemed good!" (79).

Henderson is likewise impressed with Dahfu's unmistakable reservoir of power and well-being: "He seemed all ease, and I all limitation" (160). While the Queen shows evidence of suffering transcended — old age, lost teeth, a defective eye — Dahfu seems to have gone unscathed by life. Henderson realizes that both Dahfu and Willatale are "Be-ers," though Willatale does not derive her power so exclusively from the lion, and she has reached an even more complete state of Being than Dahfu, for Dahfu must still capture a wld lion (believed to be his father) before he can firmly establish his kingship. While Dahfu admires the passive Arnewi virtues, his primary interest is with renewing mankind by restoring man's animal nature and hence his primitive connections with the universe. As Henderson explains it, "he's thinking of mankind as a whole, which is tired of itself and needs a shot in the arm from animal nature" (251).

Consistent with the transcendentalist faith in conscious self-transformation, Dahfu, a disciple of William James, declares that man can change himself by the power of his imagination, which in its present state of debilitation produces mostly grotesques — "the appetite, the agony, the fateful-hysterical, the fighting Lazaruses, the immune elephants" (269). As Emerson saw the human soul linked dynamically with a larger source of power and inspiration, the Oversoul, so Dahfu sees the human imagination as an agent of creative life force in nature; through the imagination, man has power to project himself beyond what he is, to shape himself into something better. If man would acquire a "noble self-conception," a "desirable model in the cortex" (268), then he would become what he thinks: "Think of what there could be . . . by different imaginations. What gay, brilliant types, what merriment types, what beauties and goodness, what sweet cheeks or noble demeanors" (269).

The ideal is best realized in the person of Dahfu himself, more than in his words. To Henderson, Dahfu is an enigma. His stylized African speech, his impressive stature, and his imperturbable dignity give his utterings an oracular significance. It is as if Dahfu's wisdom comes from some source which has been obscured in civilized man. Henderson is puzzled by Dahfu's combination of scientific interests and his apparent acceptance of some of the superstitions of tribe — a combination which suggests the unification of the ratio and instinctual which in Henderson are divided and opposed.

But the most impressive thing Bellow wants us to notice about Dahfu is the sense of well-being and relaxed vitality which radiate from his body. The power and inner harmony of Dahfu are suggested by his muscular well-proportioned physique and his graceful, athletic movements. Occasionally a low humming sound comes from Dahfu's lips and reminds Henderson "of the sound you sometimes hear from a power station when you pass one in New York on a summer night" (210). Like Queen Willatale, Dahfu is meant to symbolize the fully integrated human being. In Dahfu, man's animal nature, unrepressed and integrated with his conscious mind, is the source of his power. Because he is so close to nature, his energies are not wasted in neurotic conflict. He has achieved that state of Being which N. O. Brown in *Life Against Death* describes as "the condition of equilibrium or rest of life that is a full life, unrepressed, and therefore satisfied with itself and affirming itself rather than changing itself" (90). And part of Brown's cure for modern man, like Dahfu's cure for Henderson, is "the construction of a human consciousness strong enough to accept death" (108).

By helping Henderson to overcome his fear of death, Dahfu hopes to bring Henderson from the anxious state of Becoming to the serene state of Being. For Henderson embodies the paradox implicit in Brown's interpretation of Freud, that the man who represses death, who flees from knowledge of his mortality, actually brings death closer, becomes more anxiety-ridden, less alive, more dangerous to himself and others. Dahfu is right when he tells Henderson that "men of most powerful appetite have always been the ones to doubt reality the most" (232), that Henderson is an "avoider" and that the lion will cure him because "she is unavoidable" (260). Queen Willatale had made a similar diagnosis when she told Henderson that "the world is strange to a child" (84). Henderson acknowledged this truth and admitted that he had arranged to have himself "abducted" or estranged from life because of his dread of death. At the root of Henderson's self-avoidance and restless striving has been his fear of his animal nature, because to acknowledge this nature, this biological element, is to accept limitations on will and desire, to acknowledge one's capacity for death and savagery.

To restore Henderson to a full consciousness of his own nature, Dahfu proceeds to conduct the experiment deep in the lion's den under the palace. The experiment consists of exposing Henderson to the lion and also having him imitate the lion even to the point of getting down on his hands and knees and roaring. Thus the King tries to influence Henderson's mind through the body (Reichian somatic exercises) and the body through the mind (Emerson and William James). The experiment, however, is not a success — either because the theory behind the experiment is inadequate or else because Henderson is too far gone to be much influenced by a lion. Henderson had begun to feel a change for the better with the Arnewi, but not with Dahfu and the lion. "I feel that old self more than ever," he says, "like a Galápagos turtle. On my back" (275).

At this point the reader may wonder whether Dahfu's effort to recharge Henderson's animal nature, to give him lion qualities, is consistent with his desire to see "merriment types" and "sweet cheeks." This inconsistency occurs to Henderson, too, when he confronts the savage beast which Dahfu must capture: "And . . . the thought added itself that this was all mankind needed, to be conditioned into the image of a ferocious animal like the one below" (307). But in his enthusiasm for what he regards as a noble ideal, Dahfu fails to see that the return to animal consciousness may have undesirable consequences. The novel as a whole seems to criticize the primitive-transcendental ideal as well as celebrate it. Like Hawthorne in *The Marble Faun*, Bellow seems to have an ambivalent attitude toward the ideal of the natural man. While Donatello in his innocent state shared a union with "the inferior tribes of being, whose simplicity, mingled with his human intelligence might partly restore what man has lost of the divine,"[6] Hawthorne felt that man must, through sin, suffering, and sacrifice, complete some further human development beyond initial innocence. What some critics fail to see or emphasize is that Dahfu does not represent Bellow's unqualified view and that Bellow's rejection of primitivism as an ultimate ideal is consistent with his more cautious humanism.

Henderson gives several reasons for rejecting the lion image as appropriate for himself, but the main reason seems to be that he is too old and does not feel the kind of natural affinity for the lion which Dahfu feels. He also considers Dahfu's Lamarckian notion of transformation a "bourgeois idea of the autonomy of the individual mind" (288). Yet Henderson does accept from Dahfu the notion of conscious change in the direction of a chosen "noble self-conception": "I was willing to overcome my old self; yes, to do that a man had to adopt some new standard; he must even force himself into a part; maybe he must deceive himself a while, until it begins to take" (297-98). But the direction that Henderson wants conscious transformation to take is toward the human, not the animal: "Even supposing that an animal enjoys a natural blessing? We had our share of this creature-blessing until infancy ended. But now aren't we required to complete something else — project number two — the second blessing? I couldn't tell such things to the king, he was so stuck on lions" (288). Like Thoreau, Henderson comes to cherish his instinctual nature, but realizes that it is a stage that man must pass through. And he begins to see his participation in Dahfu's experiment as one more blunder in "a lifetime of action without thought," whereas he might better have spent his time "learning about grun-tu-molani instead, under Willatale" (288). He regards the lion experiment as a mistake except in so far as it cemented his friendship with the king.

And yet the lion does have an influence on Henderson — not the pet lion which the king keeps in his den but the much larger and fiercer male lion which the king must capture. The change in Henderson is effected as he waits with the king for the lion to approach. The snarl of this lion batters "at the very doors of consciousness" and Henderson sees within the wrinkled, contracted face of the lion "the darkness of murder. . . . The snarling of this animal was indeed the voice of death" (306-307). The roaring of the lion pierces through whatever illusions Henderson might have held about reality: "Unreality, unreality! That has been my scheme for a troubled but eternal life. But now I was blasted away from this practice by the throat of the lion" (307). Waiting with Dahfu, Henderson is forced into a full realization of the reality of death and savagery which belong to the natural world of which man is a part.

But while the result of this incident is an awakening for Henderson, it means death for Dahfu who is a victim both of the savagery of the men who sabotaged the lion-catching rig and of the savagery of the lion. The symbolic significance of Dahfu's death may be that it is dangerous for man to regress too far back into nature. With his pet lion, Atti, Dahfu had been able to maintain an equilibrium between the forces of his nature, influencing the lion as much as being influenced. But with the completely untamed and much larger beast, Dahfu received, so to speak, an overdose of animal nature. If there is any symbolic connection between the lion skin which Willatale wears, the pet lion of the king, the lion which kills him, and the lion cub which Henderson brings back to civilization, it must have something to do with the proportion of animal nature which man can safely assimilate. Henderson does not completely reject Dahfu's primitivism, for he names the cub Dahfu. Such an explanation as this may seem overdone, but then much of the symbolism in *Henderson* (e.g. the carved wooden statues, the game with the skulls, the contrasting tribes, the lion in the den) seems to be quite consciously and elaborately worked out.

Dahfu had been the image of the perfect natural man, man in a state close to nature, free from all frustration, including sexual frustration. Henderson sees that such a state of natural perfection and satisfaction is not enough for him — he wants a more human condition ("project number two — the second blessing") but without completely disowning the natural as he had hitherto done. Henderson cannot take

Dahfu's place in the natural world because he has needs which are more specifically human: "And it isn't only that I'm scared of all those wives, but there'll be nobody to talk to any more. I've gotten to that age where I need human voices and intelligence, that's all that's left. Kindness and love" (316). With this affirmation Henderson appears to be close to the resolution of a middle-aged identity crisis. His rejection of primitivism looks forward to Herzog's similar repudiation of sexualism as a cure-all, along with other twentieth-century -isms which isolate the self.

While Dahfu has brought Henderson to a consciousness of death, Henderson senses that only love and brotherhood can keep such consciousness from becoming morbid. Dahfu's return-to-nature philosophy was not adequate for coping with death and aggression. His dying words reveal that he had not been strong enough to break the chain of blows, for when Henderson wants to know why the king put him in such a hazardous position as Rain King, Dahfu's answer is, "It was done to me" (312).

After the king's death, Henderson, no longer quite so rash, devises an effective plan of escape and returns with his guide and the lion cub to civilization. He is now committed to realizing his "service ideal." The change he had sought has come about ("the sleep is burst, and I've come to myself"), and he wonders "why this has to be fought by everybody for there's nothing that's struggled against so hard as coming-to. We grow these sores instead" (328). Henderson professes his change of heart a bit too stridently at times, yet Bellow manages to make his awakening convincing. He is over-excited and buoyant, yet happy and at peace, too. The sight of the Atlantic Ocean thrills him because it is a symbolic reflection of the newly-discovered depths in himself. His mind is filled with valuable recollections, among which is the memory of the age-worn, battered, tragic-looking bear named Smolak. In despair and fear Henderson and the bear rode the roller coaster, clinging to each other for safety "I enbeared by him and he probably humanized by me" (339). Therefore Henderson reasons, "I didn't come to the pigs as a tabula rasa. It only stands to reason. Something deep already was inscribed on me" (339). The language of this passage, not all of which is quoted here, is very suggestive; and I do not know whether Bellow simply means that a unity is possible between man and the world, that man absorbs influences from the external world, or whether the meaning is more inclusive, the bear perhaps being a symbol of suffering nature — an idea familiar to Melville — and further evidence of that shared unity between man and nature. But the bear is also, like Willatale, a Be-er with a capacity for accepting all of life: "He had seen too much of life, and somewhere in his huge head he had worked it out that for creatures there is nothing that ever runs unmingled" (339). Henderson, too, has learned to accept the intermingled existence of love and aggression, of death as a part of life.

At the very end, Henderson expresses his new awareness and sense of being by leaping exuberantly over the arctic snows while the plane refuels in New Foundland. His confidence and optimism, however, are qualified by the cold snowy blankness surrounding him and the airplane, just as Augie March's final affirmation was symbolically qualified by the threatening wintry sea on one side of him and the war ruins on the other, The arctic snow may symbolize innocence, but there is something ominous about it, too. Henderson's new-found identification with man and nature is asserted in the face of a potentially meaningless universe. The balanced acceptance of life symbolized by Willatale and the bear is not, we suspect, something that Henderson can acquiesce in. Most human beings cannot sit out their lives in Buddha-like serenity. Henderson realizes this, and he intends to live for others, to fulfill the "service ideal" which has been a constant, though often eccentric, characteristic of his family and of American history, too. The ambiguous symbolism of the arctic snow, the comic impulsiveness of Henderson's leaping around the plane, the impracticability of his becoming a doctor at the age of fifty-six, the fact his good intentions are still just intentions — all of these things qualify the final note of affirmation, but that note still remains strong.

It should be evident from this analysis that the attitudes and value assumptions which inform *Henderson the Rain King* are often contrary to those of literary modernism, that there is something in the tone that distinguishes this novel from such paradigmatic modernist works as *Notes from Underground*, *The Wasteland*, *Waiting for Godot*, *The Sun Also Rises*, *Miss Lonelyhearts* — the world-rejecting literature of impotence. Against the dualistic view of the universe which make death unacceptable and nature hostile and alien, the novel has posed the possibility (tentative vision) of a universe in which "God does not shoot dice with our souls" (175), an organic universe in which man can feel more at home, more related to sun and earth, to childhood, animals, death, and his own body. Against the modernist hostility toward civilization — its restrictions, artificialities, and worn out forms — the novel poses the possibility of an integration or accommodation which is not destructive to one's sense of authentic being.

The point of the novel is that one must return from Africa. Henderson's quest stops short of the hidden mysteries (and self-destruction) granted to Conrad's Kurtz. Once Henderson learns about himself what he needs to know, the logic of the novel requires that he return to civilization. This novel does not celebrate the anti-hero: it does not uphold Henderson's vices and weaknesses, his moral deformities as evidence of a true individuality. Rather than endorsing alienation as a desirable life-style, Bellow emphasizes Henderson's basic decency, his desire to be a good man, to take some constructive action, to live for something more than himself. In placing his focus on the individual spiritual awakening to sources of hidden "grace" or inspiration, Bellow stands in a tradition that unites Jonathan Edwards, Ralph Waldo Emerson, Walt Whitman, William James, Wallace Stevens, and William Carlos Williams.

Yet, while emphasizing the need to cultivate one's best self and to find a positive relationship with society, the novel by no means condones conformity to the status quo. *Henderson* shares with much postwar literature the increasing sense that civilization is a madhouse, steadily accelerating, in Mailer's terms, toward cancer. Although the critique of society is not so detailed in *Henderson* as it is in Bellow's other novels, there should be no doubt in the reader's mind that the civilization to which Henderson is returning is, in many of its manifestations, mad — feeding upon its own collective death instinct.

How does the book manage to convey this impression? Partly through certain minor characterizations, partly through the allegorical Wariri, partly through Henderson's remarks about the destructive bent of mankind, and partly through the sometimes maddened Henderson himself who is a product of his times and who knows that one cannot entirely expect to escape the malaise of a sick civilization: ". . . in an age of madness," he says, "to expect to be untouched by madness is a form of madness" (25).

Henderson, then, is both a victim and a representative of the spiritual madness of his society, yet he is also the one who wants to live. In him, Eros is finally stronger than Thanatos. The novel suggests that the source of malaise in society is the effect of instinctual renunciation (something more comprehensive than sexual repression) which N. O. Brown describes in *Life Against Death* as man's loss of the biological and emotional actuality of his being, his flight from nature, his sublimations in the form of technology, wars, business carried to dehumanizing extremes. The cure would require a deepening of personality through some awareness of the instinctual sources of one's being before one could effect a worthwhile integration with one's society. *Henderson*, then, like the older modernist literature, maintains a vision of the absurdities and life-denying tendencies that are part of modern civilization, but departs from modernist literature in suggesting that alienation is, or should be, only a transitional condition for the more sensitive alive protagonist.

Notes

1. Richard Ellmann and Charles Feidelson Jr., *The Modern Tradition* (New York: Oxford UP, 1965), v-vi.
2. Irving Howe, *Literary Modernism* (New York: Fawcett, 1967), 40.
3. "The New Optimism — from Prufrock to Ringo," in Thomas J. J. Altizer and William Hamilton, *Radical Theology and the Death of God* (New York: Bobbs-Merrill, 1966), 157-169.
4. Saul Bellow, *Henderson the Rain King* (New York: Viking, 1959). Subsequent references in the text from this edition.

5. N. O. Brown, *Life Against Death* (New York: Vintage, 1959), 52. For the relevance of Brown's book toward understanding Bellow's work, I am indebted to Keith Opdahl, *The Novels of Saul Bellow* (University Park: Pennsylvania State UP, 1967).
6. *The Complete Novels and Selected Tales of Nathaniel Hawthorne* (New York: Modern Library, 1937), 630.

*   *   *

Saul Bellow's Henderson as America
Eusebio L. Rodrigues

By 1959 Bellow had put in all the labor that a major writer needs to, according to T. S. Eliot, before triumphantly entering and altering a tradition. *The Adventures of Augie March* (1953) had been too deliberate a territorial invasion: the title nods a greeting at Mark Twain; the opening sentence — "I am an American, Chicago born" — is an aggressive echo of the opening sentence of *Moby Dick*; Augie flaunts a Whitman-like pose — "being democratic in temperament, available to everybody and assuming about others what I assumed about myself";[1] and the reference to Columbus in the last paragraph of the novel loudly insists that Augie is the discoverer of a new America. *Henderson the Rain King* (1959) is an orbic (the word is Whitman's) romance that has close affinities with *A Connecticut Yankee* and with the many Jamesian fables about the complex fate of being an American. Bellow proceeds to extend the tradition by creating a daring parable about America and the American Dream.

Set beside Henderson, Gatsby loses a whole dimension as mythic figure. For Henderson is America itself, gigantic, gargantuan, monumental. Bellow endows him with huge, physical dimensions: Henderson is six feet four inches tall, weighs two hundred and thirty pounds (he weighed fourteen pounds at birth), his neck size is a formidable twenty-two. His face is enormous, almost as big as the entire body of a child, half the length of another person's body. New York, suggests Henderson, is stamped upon his face: "My face is like some sort of terminal; it's like Grand Central, I mean — the big horse nose and the wide mouth that opens into the nostrils, and eyes like tunnels."[2]

Henderson is continentally large; more significantly, he contains multitudes. He is acutely conscious of the swirl of ancestral forces inside him that drives him to bursts of furious action: "Now, I come from a stock that has been damned and derided for more than a hundred years, and when I sat smashing bottles beside the eternal sea it wasn't only my great ancestors, the ambassadors and statesmen, that

From *Centennial Review* 20.2 (1976): 189-95.

people were recalling, but the loony ones as well" (86). Powerfully aware of the martial blood that flows through him, proud of the service ideal that exists in his family, sadly recognizing the crazy elements in his makeup, Henderson seems to have leaped straight out of the melting pot of American history. The founder of the family was a Dutch sausage-maker who became "the most unscrupulous capitalist in America" (82); Henderson's great-grandfather was Secretary of State, and his father was a famous scholar, a friend of William James and Henry Adams. Through Henderson flow the currents of American history, including the very beginning of it all. "My ancestors," he confesses, "stole land from the Indians" (21). Henderson, the millionaire, is truly a strange heir to a great estate.

Like America, Henderson is an amalgam of contradictory forces. Violent, impetuous, a buffoon at times, restless — "From earliest times I have struggled without rest" (68) — he is also an idealist, childlike in many ways, a romantic who clamors for instant salvation. He cannot be contained in any rubric, according to King Dahfu. Henderson is partly, as L. Moffitt Cecil points out, the American Imago of the 1950s.[3] He can be seen as the embodiment of mid-twentieth-century America, bursting with vital energy, victorious in war, triumphant in technology, at the very peak of its prosperity. And yet, out of the depths of this America comes a cry of desperate yearning, I want, I want, I want.

It is at the moment when the voice that tortures Henderson is introduced into the narrative that the correlation between Henderson and America becomes unmistakably clear. The voice that springs from his harried American soul is the secret promise of hope and rejuvenation that was made when the old world came to the new. But modern America with its technological routine, its nine to five business day, its dreams of material success, has forgotten its original dream and has lost sight of the fresh, green breast of the new world that beckoned the Dutch sailors. The voice within torments Henderson and drives him to despair: "By three o'clock I was in despair. Only toward sunset the voice would let up. And sometimes I thought maybe this was my occupation because it would knock off at five o'clock of itself. America is so big, and everybody is working, making, digging, bulldozing, trucking, loading, and so on, and I guess the sufferers suffer at the same rate" (25). What Henderson, like America, wants is to stop the suffering and achieve this true destiny. Like Whitman, he wants to complete true being. He equates his own plight with that of America during his first meeting with King Dahfu: "Enough! Time to have Become. Time to Be! Burst the spirit's sleep. Wake up, America! Stump the experts" (160).

Henderson wants the dormant national consciousness to arouse itself and awaken to its true greatness of soul. He does not know how to arrive at this greatness, but he is convinced that the experts are wrong. The "experts" are those advocates of doom, wastelands who predict the downfall of the West and the collapse of industrial America. Bellow does not accept such a vision of apocalyptic despair based on a facile rejection of technology. His faith in contemporary civilization and his belief that mankind will ultimately make it come through forcefully in *Herzog* (1964). Bellow deliberately makes Henderson a New Yorker, modern urban man conditioned and affected by the new technology. Henderson loves New York, he has traveled on its subways, he knows the hock shops and army-navy stores on Third Avenue. His experiences in Africa are frequently measured by New York standards. The noises of the Wariri rain-festival are like "Coney Island or Atlantic City or Times Square on New Year's Eve" (169). When he manufactures a bomb to rid the Arnewi of the frogs, he bases his design on the diagrams of the bomb-scare man in New York.[4]

As a representative of modern technological America wanting desperately to burst the spirit's sleep, Henderson ventures into primitive Africa. In Arnewiland, which has a plague of frogs, he makes "one of those mutual-aid deals" (87): he will help the Arnewi with his technology in exchange for the wisdom of life they have. However, the bomb he concocts destroys the cistern, and the Arnewi have to go on a long trek in search of water. The incident signifies that unless technological power is put to proper use in the right spirit (Henderson's heart was filled with violence against the frogs), the result will be disaster and suffering. Henderson and America have to learn how to control this tremendous power, a lesson they learn in Waririland.

Henderson is fascinated by the magnificent, rhythmic power displayed by the Wariri King Dahfu in all his gestures and actions. The voice of the king reminds him "of the sound you sometimes hear from a power station when you pass one in New York on a summer night; the doors are open; all the brass and steel is going, lustrous under one little light, and some old character in dungarees and carpet slippers is smoking a pipe with all the greatness of the electricity behind him" (210). The king, who is in perfect control both of himself and of his people (he too smokes a pipe and wears slippers), is closely parallel to the old man who is in charge of the power station that lights up a city and has luster of its own. Henderson learns the lesson that technological power and the power of the human spirit, incarnate in King Dahfu, are essentially the same. He can now understand and respond to the great achievement of a dedicated American engineer like Slocum, who has such power and who built the great dams in the Punjab Valley. In the letter to Lily, Henderson celebrates the marriage of the human imagination with man's technical capability. The airplane flight to Africa testifies to mankind's capacity to realize its own marvelous dreams: "We are the first generation to see the clouds from both sides. What a privilege! First people dreamed upward. Now they dream both upward and downward. This is bound to change something, somewhere" (280).

King Dahfu, with the aid of Atti and her animal power, awakens Henderson to a new awareness of human possibilities, to the reality and need of love and human brotherhood, to the fact that human nobility can be realized even in our terrible technological day. The spirit's sleep has burst and Henderson now has a vision of what America can be. He knows that America can transform and renew itself now as it had done in the past:

> Americans are supposed to be dumb but they are willing to go into this. It isn't just me. You have to think about white Protestantism and the Constitution and the Civil War and capitalism and winning the West. All the major tasks and the big conquests were done before my time. That left the biggest problem of all, which was to encounter death. (276)

What Henderson celebrates so emphatically here is the shaping spirit in the American past that propelled its peoples to magnificent achievement. In today's age of madness America faces the greatest challenge in its history — death, the death of the human spirit damaged by a technology it cannot control, valuing junk (like Mrs. Lenox, who dies after listening to Henderson's terrible rage), swollen with empty success and purposeless power. Henderson himself has come to realize that the tremendous power compressed within his own being has to be controlled and unselfishly directed towards the welfare of others. He is sure that America can, Whitman-like, go forth again and achieve true greatness:

> Millions of Americans have gone forth since the war to redeem the present and discover the future. I can swear to you, Romilayu, there are guys exactly like me in India and in China and South America and all over the place. Just before I left home I saw an interview in the paper with a piano teacher from Muncie who became a Buddhist monk in Burma. You see, that's what I mean. I am a high-spirited kind of guy. And it's the destiny of my generation of Americans to go out in the world and try to find the wisdom of life. (276-77)

Armed with such healing, prophetic knowledge, Henderson has to return to America so that both their destinies may be fulfilled. In Africa, the primitive abyss, the fundamentals of life were revealed to him, the radiant realities of love, suffering, death and brotherhood. With marvelous fictional tact, Bellow dramatizes not Henderson's arrival in America, but his journey thereward. It is a journey attended by auspicious omens and by intimations of a new America, a journey that ends with a highly significant rite of celebration.

Henderson travels towards his childhood dream that had been inspired by a medical missionary, Sir Wilfred Grenfell of Labrador; at fifty-six he will enroll in medical school as Leo E. Henderson, the first name signifying the nobility he has recovered, the initial (for Eugene) revealing that he is truly well-born. After graduation, he will take up missionary work, perhaps in India. The lion cub, an enigmatic form of his dead friend, King Dahfu, travels with him in a wicker basket. On the plane Henderson meets a stewardess from the Midwest who reinforces his faith in his people and in their ability to resurrect and renew themselves: "She was from Rockford, Illinois. Every twenty years or so the earth renews itself in young maidens. You know what I mean? Her cheeks had the perfect form that belongs to the young, her hair was kinky gold. Her teeth were white and posted on every approach. She was all sweet corn and milk" (333-334). Here is a marriage of soil and soul. The stewardess is the corn maiden, an emblem of fertility, the incarnation of the innate power of the American spirit to revitalize itself. Henderson feels a religious propulsion to pronounce a psalm-like blessing on her: "Blessings on her hips. Blessings on her thighs. Blessings on her soft little fingers which were somewhat covered by the cuffs of her uniform. Blessings on that rough gold. A wonderful little thing; her attitude was that of a pal or playmate, as is common with Midwestern young women" (334).

Henderson is also sustained by an idea out of Emerson, that "corporeal things are an image of the spiritual and visible objects are renderings of invisible ones" (338). Everything he sees and experiences on his journey toward America is a spiritual sign. He identifies himself with Ishmael, Melville's Ishmael surely, one who has unflinchingly faced the evil in the world and is saved at the end to tell his tale. And the stewardess introduces Henderson to the American-Persian orphan on the plane, one who "was still trailing his cloud of glory" (339). Henderson looks into the child's eyes and sees intimations of immortality there, his own past and man's future in them: "Two smoothly gray eyes moved at me, greatly expanded into the whites — new to life altogether. They had that new luster. With it they had ancient power, too. You could never convince me that *this was for the first time*" (339). The luster and the power call to mind the radiant energy of King Dahfu and suggest that here is a "power station" in miniature. The eyes proclaim a victory over death and the continual renewal of the human spirit.

Henderson's plane lands at Newfoundland, the name as in Donne's poem powerfully suggesting an America to be. Henderson now feels impelled to rejoice and to express his joy in his own fashion. Carrying the child in his arms and the lion cub too, he begins a ritual dance, leaping and bounding like a very lion around the motionless plane. It is a dance of triumph, a reenactment, but now with hope and a sense of glory, of the dance with King Dahfu and Atti in the African jungle. It is the dance of human life, past, present and future circling together in absolute harmony. And it is a dance to celebrate a new and vital America.

Bellow discards as irrelevant earlier myths and metaphors that interpret America in terms of the American Adam, the lost Eden or the wasteland. In the nineteenth century, Thoreau and Hawthorne had seized on the locomotive, that power of blackness, as a graphic image of the technological demon that was beginning to ravage their virgin land. Leo Marx has described how the sensibilities of their twentieth-century successors, Frost, Faulkner, Hemingway and West, were thrown into turmoil as they faced the metaphysical horror of "the machine's sudden entrance into the garden."[5] The tensions thus generated did not allow these writers to design "satisfactory resolutions for their pastoral fables."[6] Bellow's resolution is both optimistic and Emersonian. In an 1843 journal entry Emerson had noted rather simply: "Machinery and Transcendentalism agree well."[7] *Henderson the Rain King* offers us what Leo Marx requires of the contemporary American artist, that he create new symbols of human possibility. One such symbol is the stewardess on the plane, a virgin who works in perfect accord with the dynamo, Henry Adams' other kingdom of force.

The last paragraph of *Henderson the Rain King* is an epiphany of awakening and hope:

> Laps and laps I galloped around the shining and riveted body of the plane, behind the fuel trucks. Dark faces were looking from within. The great, beautiful propellers were still, all four of them. I guess I felt it was my turn now to move, and so went running — leaping, leaping, pounding, and tingling over the pure white lining of the gray Arctic silence. (340-341)

Here is a vision of a technological America that can be transfigured by the noble ideals of love, service and brotherhood when they are set in motion. The twin sources of America's strength are vividly presented. Her twentieth-century technological power is symbolized by the lustrous plane with the great, though now still, propellers that brought Henderson to Newfoundland. And the unquenchable and radiant power of the human spirit is now incarnate in Henderson, and will lead both him and America to true glory.

Notes

1. Saul Bellow, *The Adventures of Augie March* (Greenwich, Conn.: Fawcett Crest, 1965), 155.
2. Saul Bellow, *Henderson the Rain King* (New York: Compass Books, Viking, 1965), 51. Subsequent references in the text from this edition.
3. L. Moffit Cecil, "Bellow's Henderson as American Imago of the 1950's," *Research Studies* 40.4 (1972): 296-300.
4. In 1956-57 a real bomb-scare man who planted pipe-bombs everywhere threw the city into a state of panic. Diagrams of his bombs were published in the New York papers.
5. Leo Marx, *The Machine in the Garden: Technology and the Pastoral Idea in America* (New York: Oxford UP, 1967), 365.
6. Ibid., 364.
7. Qtd. by Marx, 232.

* * *

Herzog (1964)

Bellow the Brain King
Philip Rahv

With this new work, *Herzog*, his sixth novel, Saul Bellow emerges not only as the most intelligent novelist of his generation but also as the most consistently interesting in point of growth and development. To my mind, too, he is the finest stylist at present writing fiction in America.

For some time now the critical consensus has been, expressed not so much formally in writing as in the talk of literary circles, that *Seize the Day*, published some nine years ago, was his best single performance. However, I think *Herzog* is superior to it, even if not so tightly organized and in fact a bit loose on the structural side. For one thing, it is a much longer and fuller narrative than *Seize the Day*, which is hardly more than a novella. For another, it is richer in content, in the effective disposition of tone and language, as well as in intellectual resonance and insight of a high order in the makeup of modern life — insight into what is really new and perhaps all too hazardous about its strange, almost inconceivable mixture of greater freedom and maddening constriction.

Above all, this novel positively radiates intelligence — not mere brightness or shrewdness or that kind of sensitiveness which all too often passes for mind among us. This intelligence is a real endowment, coherent, securely founded, and of a genuine intellectual quality which, marvelously escaping the perils of abstractions, is neither recondite nor esoteric. It is directed toward imaginative ends by virtue of a true and sharp sense of the pain that rends the human world, of its ills both curable and incurable, and equally by a bracing, unfailing sense of humor and irony serving to counteract such chronic vulnerabilities of intelligence as oversolemnity of mind on the one hand and perversity of sensibility on the other.

From *New York Herald Tribune Book Week* (20 Sep. 1964): 1, 14, 16.

It is important to stress this element of intellectual mastery in Bellow, for in the milieu of our creative writers intellect has by no means played a conspicuous part. Hence the immaturity of even the best, like Hemingway for instance, and the aborted careers of not a few other gifted writers, aborted among other things by the repetition compulsion that results not so much from neurotic disturbance, though that may be present too, as from thematic poverty and narrowness of the mental horizon. To be sure, intellect is not art; in some ways it might even be said to be corrosive in its effect on artistic production. But without intellect it becomes impossible for the artist, the verbal artist particularly, to transform into consciousness what is offered by experience and the manifold and at times infinitely varied and subtle emotions it gives rise to. After all, thinking too is an experience. Without thought the writer may be able to relate the particulars of experience well enough, though usually at inordinate length, but he is at a loss when it comes to extracting values from experience that will make it meaningful to the reader (and perhaps to himself also).

Herzog is far and away the most personal novel Bellow has written, and the most immediate in self-reference. But the personal element in this case in no way strikes us as an intrusion, as it makes for a clear gain in impact and reality-mindedness. By comparison, *The Adventures of Augie March* seems like a wonderfully inventive exercise in mere narrative fantastication, projecting an affirmative message that falls short of conviction. *Herzog*, moreover, despite its deeply personal provenance, betrays none of that orgastic self-glorification that you may find in our hipster writers who make do with the self (the ravenous, raging self of erotic fantasy and adolescent daydreams of power) when talent and moral intelligence fail them. As a maker of prose fiction, Bellow is far too scrupulous and his personality too complicated to engage in such capers. He has put a great deal of himself into his protagonist Herzog, but always with a twist of irony and a minimum of self-display.

Herzog is a Chicago professor, author of a work entitled *Romanticism and Christianity* (a good stroke, that, for the novel is in its own way a kind of exploration of latter-day versions of romanticism), who is suffering a near breakdown when his second wife, Mady, leaves him. She appropriates house and child to take up with his best friend, Gersbach, a purveyor of the latest cultural goodies, like Buber's "I and Thou" relationship, the more portentous varieties of existentialism, and Yiddishisms of phrase and stance. At the very start of the story we are told that some people thought Herzog was cracked, and he himself is uncertain whether this is so. The truth is, however, that he "had fallen under a spell and was writing letters to everyone under the sun," feeling an irresistible need "to explain, to have it out, to justify, to put in perspective, to clarify, to make amends." The letters teem with ideas, thus converting Herzog's personal crisis into the more impersonal crisis of modern thinking. Herzog moves from place to place carrying a valise full of papers, which he takes with him from New York to Martha's Vineyard and back again almost at once. Two days later he flies to Chicago, keyed up to the highest pitch, to have it out with his wife and her lover (at this stage the latent violence almost erupts), and then back again to a village in western Massachusetts where, hidden in the country, he again "writes endlessly, fantastically, to the newspapers, to people in public life, to friends and relatives, and at last to the dead, his own obscure dead and finally the famous dead." The story ends in this village, where Herzog evades his brother's efforts to get him to a psychiatrist even as he makes ready for a visit from his New York mistress, a superbly rendered figure of "sex and swagger."

There is nothing in any novel I have read quite like these letters Herzog writes. In no sense formal in tone, they represent at once a fictional device and a prodigiously productive aggression of the mind. The writer is richly ironic, at his own expense too, and intolerant of the typical platitudes of modern thought, letting go in a strange intermixture of "clairvoyance and spleen, *esprit de l'escalier*, noble inspiration, poetry and nonsense, ideas, hyperaesthesia." To the philosopher Heidegger he addresses himself, "I should like to know what you mean by the expression, 'The Fall into the Quotidian.' When did this fall occur? Where were we standing when it happened?" Another letter, to Nietzsche, opens with the sentence, "Dear Herr Nietzsche — my dear sir, may I ask a question from the floor?," followed by an outburst against the German thinker's celebration of the Dionysian spirit's pride in allowing itself the luxury of pain and evil. In still another letter, to a fellow scholar named Shapiro, he writes that "we must not forget how quickly the visions of genius become the canned goods of the intellectuals. The canned sauerkraut of Spengler's Prussian socialism, the commonplaces of the wasteland outlook, the cheap mental stimulants of Alienation, the cant and rant of the pipsqueaks about Inauthenticity and Forlornness. I can't accept this foolish dreariness. We are talking about the whole life of mankind. The subject is too great, too deep, for such weakness, cowardice. . . . A merely aesthetic critique of modern history! After the wars and mass killings! You are too intelligent for this. You inherited rich blood. Your father peddled apples."

Herzog, with his talent for polemics, bears down with particular force on those German existentialists who tell you that guilt and dread are good for you; their story is that "God is no more but Death is." Human life, writes Herzog, "is far subtler than any of its models. Do we need *theories* of pain and anguish?" Now such ideas will scarcely please our academic popularizers of existentialism who imagine that with delusions of concreteness borrowed from Germany and France, they are actually escaping the basic and very comfortable abstraction of their professorial stance. Herzog protests vehemently against the seeming profundities of the modern cult of pain and suffering. Himself in a state of extreme anguish, he needs no theories to rub it in.

Among the characters of the novel other than Herzog (of whom there is a richly varied cast, some beautifully drawn), Ramona, his mistress, is an outstanding creation. Mady, the treacherous wife, does not really come through except as an object of hostility, though a weirdly interesting one, whereas Ramona is the best portrait I have encountered in contemporary fiction of the modern woman *par excellence* who has made good on the sexual revolution. That kind of woman is the chief beneficiary of the revolution, made mostly by men. How is it possible, muses Herzog, to run out "on fragrant, sexual, high-minded Ramona? Never in a million years. She has passed through the hell of profligacy and attained the seriousness of pleasure." She believes in no sin but "the sin against the body, for her the true and only temple of the spirit." If you are under stress and Ramona likes you, then the only thing to do, the perfect restorative indeed, is to fly to her at once; she will "feed you, give you wine, remove your shoes, flatter you, put down your hackles, pinch your lips with her teeth. Then uncover the bed, turn down the lights, disclose the essentials."

In his state of feeling betrayed, Herzog voices a certain animus against women, and this animus is not without heuristic value. He notes: "Will I never understand what women want? What do they want? They eat green salad and drink human blood." This short last sentence, with its startling juxtaposition of the tame and the fierce, is good vivid writing and by no means purely rhetorical. For nowadays women do expect all the privileges of the sex-inhibited past plus all the freedoms of the swinging present. In other words, the modern female is hugely avid and expects nearly everything, and from her husband most of all. She expects him to provide nightly erotic "gratification, safety, money, furs, jewelry, cleaning women, drapes, dresses, hats, night clubs, automobiles, theater!"

As the story progresses it becomes clear that poor Ramona will receive none of those valuable things from Herzog, who is much too ironically observant of her modern ways to fall in love with her, even though, far from young, she is touching enough as a woman who more than once has taken matters into her own hands. It is scarcely easy to live on an ideological diet of permanent sex, and Ramona is "fairly fanatical about that." On the theme of the erotic, Herzog has his mordant say: "The erotic must be admitted to its rightful place, at last, in an emancipated society," but why put such a great value on the sexual act as "actually socially constructive and useful, an act of citizenship" no less? Salvation through sex is among the more fatuous illusions of our age. In this novel there are sexual scenes galore, but none of them clinical, none of them fired with the vulgar *ne plus ultra* fervor of our contemporary sexologists in fiction.

Bellow's style in this narrative, as in most of his fiction, provides a very meaningful pleasure in its masterful combination of the demotic and literary languages. At once astringent and poetic, it neither muffles nor distends his themes. Among the elements back of it is, no doubt, a deep sense of humor derived from his Jewish background and thoroughly assimilated to his sensibility. This style is sensibility in action.

* * *

Hurtsog, Hairtsog, Heart's Hog?
George P. Elliott

Herzog; what a title. On the realistic surface, the word is a name you can find in telephone books, free of English meaning or association. But there are cracks in the realistic façade. The name is German but is it also Jewish? And how is it pronounced, Hurtsog, Hurzog, Hairtsog? In the pidgin of the (American) unconscious, it puts "heart" and "hog" together in all sorts of silly ways, with "sog" in the offing. These, then, are juxtaposed to the literal German meaning "duke." Duke Heart's Hog. . . . No more silliness: Professor Moses Herzog, scholar. *Moses* Herzog! This middle-aged nut, this writer of unsent letters, this naive cuckold — a law-giver! Don't laugh. He suffered a lot. His second wife betrayed him with his best friend, he tried with all his mind to make sense of the crazy world, God knows he had his weaknesses, he was a little crazy himself there for a while. That's true, he suffered, he really did, even though he is a bit snobbish about his suffering like a good many Jews. . . . Herzog, a complicated man worth knowing.

Ceaseless mental play of words — the life of this book is in the high-wire play of mind. Without this verbal play, Herzog would not be worth knowing: neither the book nor the man. When knowing the central character is the point of a book — biography, confession, novel — then the radical question is: "Why is this person worth knowing?" Usually he has some extraordinary qualities of his own (Dr. Johnson) or is part of a good tale (Cortez). It takes real nerve to build a whole book on an uneventful day in the life a Leopold Bloom. Still, there are ways to write stories which can ruin the most interesting subject. Set a definitive biographer to work piling up facts, and even Gandhi's life would disappear shapeless under the cairn.

Herzog, like most characters, is neither a Gandhi, so interesting that it would take a perverted anti-writer to make him dull, nor a Bloom, so uninteresting that only a perverted super-writer would think

---

From *Nation* (19 Oct. 1964): 252-54.

of telling his non-story. The book has no plot, but at least Herzog is in an intense situation, full of hate for the treacherous wife and friend; at least he does something, nowhere near enough to keep you reading for the story's sake, but something. He is a rather typical character in modern American fiction, alienated, baffled; but he has an intellect almost exactly as extraordinary as Saul Bellow's, one which raises him to a realm altogether brighter than the smog in which Chicago characters usually deem to live, Sister Carrie, Studs Lonigan, Bigger Thomas, Frankie Machine. But intellectual vigor is not in itself enough to make a character worth knowing. As a subject, Herzog is down toward the Bloom end of the scale: meager of story, somewhat colorless of person, his life is sustained in the reader's mind by his creator's prose. The play of Bellow's prose causes in the reader's mind a play analogous to the play of Herzog's mind. Of no live character, real or fictional, is it truer to say: "The style is the man."

Take those letters he is forever writing, seldom finishing, never sending:

Dear Mama, as to why I haven't visited your grave in so long . . .

Dear Wanda, Dear Zinka, Dear Libbie, Dear Ramona, Dear Sono, I need help in the worst way. I am afraid of falling apart. Dear Edvig, the fact is that madness also has been denied me. I don't know why I should write to you at all. Dear Mr. President, Internal Revenue regulations will turn us into a nation of bookkeepers. The life of every citizen is becoming a business. This, it seems to me, is one of the worst interpretations of the meaning of human life history has ever seen. Man's life is not a business.

Quirky, leaping, sometimes silly, sometimes piercing — such is Herzog's mind, such the prose of the letters and of the entire novel. It is far from the self-effacing prose of most fiction, of realistic novels. It is much closer to the style of the "anatomy," Rabelais, Robert Burton. Among novelists, it has a good deal in common, functionally, "with the prose of *Tristram Shandy* and *Ulysses.* That is, it is erudite, allusive, and full of tricks, and in itself it is the main source of the reader's pleasure. Because of the prose, Herzog is the first intellectual in American fiction whose mind is fully a part of him, who is all there in the reader's imagination. This is not the least of the reasons why the first round of literary-intellectual reviewers liked the book so much. To be sure, a style sets its own limits. How *Herzog* works on a willing reader who is nonliterary, nonintellectual and non-American, I cannot guess. Meanwhile let us revel in the book who can. Besides, as soon as Herzog gets to Chicago, everything picks up and the style expands to include all who will.

Of course Herzog isn't identical with the style. The book is not a confession, an arrangement of words projecting a self directly and immediately. The man personally is not as funny as the style. He is humorous, he sometimes does ludicrous things, he laughs at himself. But we readers laugh a lot more than he does. Our laughter may often be painful, since we do not cease to sympathize with him in his silliness and misfortune. Still, we do laugh.

Try telling someone what *Herzog* is about, all the time insisting that it's funny. Loneliness, betrayal, disillusionment, near murder, humiliation, half-madness, sorrow, severance, confusion, waste — comic, all comic! A strange combination. Why does Bellow insist on making the novel comic? In this book, the style is the man *plus* his author's looking at him. For example, Herzog goes to Chicago to visit his widowed stepmother, a strong, shrewd old woman. He gets her out of the room so that, on the pretext of taking some Czarist rubles from his dead father's desk he may finch his father's loaded pistol. (Neither he nor we are fully conscious of why he wants the pistol; it turns out he takes it with him when he goes to spy on his former wife and her lover, though he does not shoot.) Immediately after he pockets the gun, he goes to the old woman, Taube, and Bellow represents his thoughts as follows:

> *He knew it was not proper that he should think her expression sheeplike. This figurative habit of his mind crippled his judgment, and was likely to ruin him some day. Perhaps the day was near; perhaps this night his soul would be required of him. The gun weighed on his chest. But the protuberant lips, great eyes, and pleated mouth were sheeplike, and they warned him he was taking too many chances with destruction. Taube, a veteran survivor, to be heeded, had fought the grave to a standstill, balking death itself by her slowness.*

There is nothing comic about either the situation or his reflections. It is their juxtaposition which is comic, and this juxtaposing Bellow has caused so that he and we alike may keep our distance from Herzog.

Without the double distance of comedy, near and far simultaneously, all would have descended into a glop of free association and self-justification; no Herzog, no *Herzog*. As it is, the character and his self-justifyings remain *over there*; we see him, we laugh at him even as we feel for him, we can understand him. Usually. Nearly always, but not quite always. In one important respect, Bellow fails. Herzog's non-comic, anti-comic loathing of his false friend, Gersbach, almost totally obliterates that character for the reader. The faithless wife, Madeleine, we can see somewhat better, though nowhere near so well as his present stress. But wife and friend we get only glimpses of, usually distorted, and we need to know them well if we are to size up Herzog fully. Here, and here only, Bellow allows Herzog's fantasy to supplant the reality almost entirely, rather than to play counterpoint to it. A serious flaw, fatal if the book had been realistically serious.

That is, according to realistic psychology, we know that Herzog, even in his middle age, was false-naive. Looking at a photograph of himself taken at the time he got his M. A., he thinks:

> *His younger face expressed the demands of ingenuous conceit. A man in years he then was, but in years only, and in his father's eyes stubbornly*

un-European, that is, innocent by deliberate choice. Moses refused to know evil. But he could not refuse to experience it. And therefore others were appointed to do it to him, and then to be accused (by him) of wickedness.

This is the naiveté which made it possible for him to be so thoroughly duped, and his natural rage at his betrayers is magnified by rage at himself. As he knows: he puts himself into the position to shoot them, and then does not. He knows and Bellow knows, but we readers must know too. We must know more about Gersbach than externals, than that he was a poet-announcer with a wooden leg; we must know him in our hearts. *We* weren't victimized by him. After all, Herzog, an arrogant, intellectual, experienced man, had no business being so innocent at his age; he is guilty of innocence. The evil of Gersbach and Madeleine we cannot take on Herzog's word; Bellow must prove it, if we are to credit it fully enough to hate them on our own, and he does not. He seals us inside Herzog's mind too much, as he does not with the other secondary characters.

But, happily, the book is only partly about the rape of Herzog's naiveté. There is more to him than that, much more. According to another, older, moral psychology, Herzog is a man of sloth. He has his quota of the other sins, lust, pride, anger, but sloth dominates him. Not merely indolence, but busy-work too, furiously doing a thousand other things instead of what he ought to be doing. His soul wallows, and all the time his mind is thinking wildly, surrounding it with swarms of thoughts, attacking it, darting every which way, always coming back to it, prodding it till it shifts and grunts, jabbing at it. Sometimes the heaviness gets into the book. Late one afternoon his mistress phones and invites him over to dinner. He says he will be right there. It takes him thirty or forty minutes to get to the door of his apartment, during which time he does nothing but have twenty pages of thoughts. There is a lot of energy in these thoughts, but the inertia beneath them makes the passage drag.

Realistic or moral, whatever the psychology, there is the flaw in Herzog's character which we are grateful for and which the novel could not do without. He can't stop thinking: he is out of control of his thoughts a good deal of the time, he spills over, he darts all over the place. A lot of the thoughts he has are worth having, their energy is abundant, and they reek with vitality, even the silly ones. And the way Saul Bellow has put them together is a delight, a treat. On the next to last page occur the last words of Herzog's last imaginary letter: "'But what do you want, Herzog?' 'But that's just it — not a solitary thing. I am pretty well satisfied to be, to be just as it is willed, and for as long as I may remain in occupancy.'" When you read this, you believe it. This is not just an easy upbeat ending. Herzog has earned the right to say this.

Still.

"For as long as I may remain in occupancy." Here he is, an English professor whose scholarly writing is good enough to put him in *Who's Who*, and he writes a sentence like that! The language of it may be more or less in character, but Bellow uses the locution to hold Herzog *over there* to the very end, so you won't take his sentiments too much to heart. You believe him, but you also believe Bellow's prose: Herzog has got through, all right, but only just and there's plenty of trouble ahead. How long has Herzog, to our knowledge, ever been satisfied with anything, much less existence? "I am pretty well satisfied to be, to be just as it is willed." Come off it, Moses, we know you, Duke, you won't rest for long, you're about to get married again, your heart is gluttonous as a hog.

* * *

Moses-Bloom-Herzog: Bellow's Everyman
David D. Galloway

At first glance, Saul Bellow's *Herzog* would appear to be a return to an earlier narrative mode, recalling Joseph's digressive journal and his long dialogues with self, or even the tormented but essentially static trials by conscience to which Asa Leventhal is subjected. *Herzog* owes much to those early exercises in what Bellow himself has called "victim literature," but it owes an equal debt to the picaresque structures and assertive conclusions of *The Adventures of Augie March* and *Henderson the Rain King*. Moses Herzog is both victim and victimizer, whose own worst enemy is his "narcissistic, masochistic, anarchistic personality,"[1] but he is also the comic hero — bumptious, often self-contradictory, occasionally roguish. Like Augie March, he is "a sentimental s.o.b." (293) in an unsentimental and selfish world; like Henderson, a dedicated opponent of the wasteland mystique and a comic champion of extreme emotional versatility. Augie's picaresque wanderings through Montreal, Chicago, Mexico, Rome, and Paris are presented in a realistic manner which owes much to the American naturalists who have influenced Bellow; Henderson's voyage is the stuff of romance — more fantastic and more highly charged with symbolic nuances. Like Conrad's Marlowe or Hemingway's African hunters, Henderson moves into an Africa of the heart which exists without relationships to time and space. Herzog is a wanderer in the mind as well as the heart — the picaro flat on his back; his actual travels to Europe, the abortive trips to Martha's Vineyard and Chicago, the retreat to the ruined house in the Berkshires — these are sharply detailed episodes, but the real pilgrimage is more internalized even than that of Hender-

From *Southern Review* 2.1 (1966): 61-76.

son, for whom Africa is a subsuming metaphor. In *Herzog* there is no metaphorical representation of the quest; there is only the quest itself.

Thus Bellow unites the two traditions in which he has formerly worked — one devoted to the characterization of the meditative, highly ratiocinative, but essentially impotent victim, and the other to the depiction of the comic, instinctual rebel. Though the fusion is not entirely successful, the effort itself makes *Herzog* Bellow's most ambitious novel to date. He himself has described the process as

> a break from Victim literature. . . . As one of the chieftains of that school I have the right to say this. Victim literature purports to show the impotence of the ordinary man. In writing *Herzog*, I felt I was completing a certain development, coming to the end of a literary sensibility. This sensibility implies a certain attitude towards civilization — anomaly, estrangement, the outsider, the collapse of humanism. What I'm against is a novel of purely literary derivation — accepting the canon of Joyce and Kafka. With Dostoevsky, at least, his eyes are turned freshly to the human scene. This view of life as literature is the modern disease — a French infection. Inevitably, it puts all hope into the performance, into virtuosity.[2]

Herzog becomes the extreme extension of all Bellow's earlier themes and devices — beginning with the victim, morose, almost paranoid, consumed by self-pity, tottering on the brink of nihilism and alienation, but clinging (like Augie and Henderson) to a transcendent view of man's fate, though all life seems to negate that vision; and finally mastering the courage to live in terms of the resulting tension. If there is fault in the execution, it is that Herzog's determination to fasten himself to the real in life-giving combat is heavily dependent on that very "virtuosity" which Bellow ironically cites as a false source of hope.

Augie's quest is preeminently emotional, despite his philosophical reverence for "axial lines," and it is often supported chiefly by the rhetoric which Bellow admits he did not have under consistent control in that book. With Henderson the quest begins with a sense of emotional vacancy, gradually and dynamically — especially in the dialogues with Dahfu — assuming an enriched spiritual significance. What Herzog calls "my vague pilgrimage" (17) is charted not only in emotional and spiritual terms — but in intellectual terms as well. Though the final form of his resolution seeks its references in the heart, Herzog must also do battle with the windmills of philosophy, law, psychology, biology, and political theory.

Bellow is the only contemporary novelist who can speak repeatedly of sincerity (indeed, he rarely speaks about anything else) without sounding maudlin, clichéd, or merely irrelevant. The subject is given flesh in Moses Elkanah Herzog, the man of "*Herz* (n., neut.) heart; breast, bosom; feeling, sympathy; mind, spirit; courage; center; vital part; marrow; pith; core, kernel. . . ." He is "*Herzog* (n., masc.), duke" — as James Dean Young has suggested,[3] the man of "noble heart," who has given his adult life to a study of "the importance of the 'law of the heart' in Western traditions, the origins of moral sentimentalism and related matters" (*H* 119). But he studies these laws *in vacuo*, detached from the objective external world, a profound dilettante at last undermined and "awakened" by the unfaithfulness of his wife and his best friend. Thus, Herzog's "stage sets" collapse; when they do so he samples various alternatives of conduct — indiscriminate "potato love," the nihilism of Reality Instructors, the final and unredeemable retreat into self, only to find each one lacking. Herzog must learn to live with reality without sacrificing heart, without crippling the "vital part," without denying "spirit; courage; center." Only contact and engagement can keep the law of the heart alive; only brotherhood can legitimatize feeling. In a world dominated by "actors" who depress and exploit and distort this law, such an intention is as absurd as loving Seymour Glass's Fat Lady; it is also as essential.[4]

Herzog's compulsive letter writing offers a brilliantly versatile conceit for the absurd predicament: these letters are the calling cards by which he attempts to revisit the world from which he had once abdicated, and they also chronicle the absurd conflict of his intention (heart) with the hostile reality which he encounters. Nonetheless, so long as Herzog maintains the conflict only on paper, until he is willing to engage it fully and consciously in life, he is only an absurd man — not an absurd hero. Only when he has learned to live in terms of the conflict does he earn the name Moses, archetype of prophets, or Elkhanah, the one whom "god possesses." The names are, of course, richly allusive. Tony Tanner displays acrobatic zeal in suggesting a possible relationship between the hero of Bellow's novel and Maurice Herzog, who led a famous mountain-climbing expedition into the French Himalayas; Maurice is a possible derivation of the Biblical name Moses. Discussing his dangerous expedition, Maurice Herzog argued that

> in overstepping our limitations, in touching the extreme boundaries of man's world, we have come to know something of its splendor. In my worst moments of anguish I seemed to discover the deep significance of existence of which till then I had been unaware. . . . The marks of my ordeal are apparent on my body. I was saved and I had won my freedom. This freedom, which I shall never lose, has given me the assurance and serenity of a man who has fulfilled himself. It has given me the rare joy of loving that which I used to despise. In this narrative . . . we bear witness.[5]

So broad and sensitive is Bellow's literary experience that his knowledge of Maurice Herzog's narrative is not unlikely, and indeed, the passage which Mr. Tanner cites might almost have been drawn from the concluding pages of *Herzog*. But even if Bellow is acquainted with this source, its discovery would have been little more than coincidence, for Herzog's final peace, in which he too can accept that which he used to despise, and in which he wins his freedom despite the marks of ordeal etched in his face, is the logical conclusion of the quest on which all the author's earlier heroes have embarked.

Indeed, if there is a specific literary source for Bellow's intense hero, it is to be found in Joyce's *Ulysses*, though here, too, any possible literary derivation must be thought of in terms of syntactic convenience — at best, a reinforcement of Bellow's own nominal shorthand — rather than as a direct source of imitation or even of inspiration. The sole reference to the Jewish merchant Moses Herzog occurs near the beginning of the Cyclops episode in *Ulysses*. The unnamed, garrulous narrator encounters Joe Hynes "dodging along Stony Batter," and the following is part of the dialogue between them before they decide to visit Barney Kiernan's:

> — What are you doing round these parts? says Joe.
>
> — Devil a much, says I. There is a bloody big foxy thief beyond by the garrison church at the corner of Chicken Lane — old Troy was just giving me a wrinkle about him — lifted any God's quantity of tea and sugar to pay three bob and said he had a farm in the country Down off a hop of my thumb by the name of Moses Herzog over there near Heytesburg street.
>
> — Circumcised! says Joe.
>
> — Ay, says I. A bit off the top.[6]

There shortly follows a statement of Michael Geraghty's legal transaction with Herzog, who is clearly fated never to collect that debt, due to be repaid in weekly installments of three shillings; similarly, Joe Hynes is unlikely to repay the three shillings borrowed from Leopold Bloom.

The opening section of the Cyclops episode contains various parodies of public rhetoric, of which Herzog's legal agreement (quoted in full) is the first example — and singularly appropriate to a public house favored by the legal profession. In examining the possible significance which this passage in *Ulysses* may have had for Saul Bellow, however, it is necessary to note the degree to which Bloom himself is not only a complex, but also a composite character; he is every older man (ultimately everyman) in search and in need of mature resolution; he is many-sided and, as Homer said of Odysseus, "polytropic." Thus, in Bloom Joyce fuses a complex set of literary and historical personalities in addition to Ulysses: "Jesus, Elijah, Moses, Dante, Shakespeare, Hamlet, and Don Giovanni" are among the antecedents noted by William York Tindall. Similarly, many of the occasional figures who appear or are referred to in *Ulysses* also represent aspects of Bloom's polytropic experience. Thus, in light of Bellow's novel, Tindall's analysis of the parallel figures incorporated in Bloom takes on enriched significance: "That Jesus gets along with Ulysses is not so surprising as it seems; for allegorical fathers of the Church had found Ulysses a moral prototype of Jesus, who is, of course, a kind of Everyman. Moses is another exile seeking home and leading others there. Jesus and Moses are analogues for Bloom, and since Stephen is a potential Bloom, for Stephen too."[7] The text of *Ulysses* contains many references to Moses, usually in association with Bloom himself, though occasionally with Stephen. Thus, Bloom's thematic relationship to Moses Herzog is strongly reinforced: both are aliens, Jewish exiles in Irish Dublin, and both are owed "debts" by society which it is unlikely they will ever collect.

In speculating about the Moses—Leopold Bloom—Moses Herzog parallel, one finds in Joyce's Cyclops episode numerous arguments and devices which would seem to foreshadow the method and the themes of Bellow's novel. One must, to be sure, keep in mind Bellow's own prejudice against the novel of literary derivation and his warning to "symbol hunters," even if the latter is essentially a contemporary translation of Mark Twain's famous notice to critical poachers in *Huckleberry Finn*. The critic would perhaps be well advised to think of Moses E. Herzog as a collateral descendant (via the force of Bellow's imagination) of Joyce's Herzog-Bloom. Certainly Bellow is familiar with *Ulysses*, whereas his knowledge of Maurice Herzog's story — however tantalizing to the critic — is highly speculative, and would, in any event, have proved far less germinal than the Cyclops episode in Joyce's novel. While an understanding of *Herzog* is in no way dependent upon literary sources and hence not what Bellow would condemn as "the novel of literary derivation," the reader can, without violating Bellow's belief in the independent integrity of the work of art, look to *Ulysses* for the themes and motifs which would have reinforced his own examination of the limitations, the strengths, and the significance of the contemporary hero. In terms of the Cyclops episode, the major reinforcement would seem to rest in three closely related areas: Bloom (the composite hero) as an outcast whom society greets with stony incomprehension, dramatized by the characters who surround him at Barney Kiernan's bar; Bloom's external lassitude, contrasted with his vitally active attempts to understand the world about him — woman, the Citizen, friendship; and Bloom's statements about love, which Bellow's Herzog occasionally seems to be echoing. To his cynical fellow drinkers (Reality Instructors, all), Bloom responds:

> — But it's no use . . . Force, hatred, history, all that. That's not life for men and women, insult and hatred. And everybody knows that it's the very opposite of that that is really life.
> — What? says Alf.
> — Love, says Bloom. I mean the opposite of hatred. (333)

We know that Bloom maintains this belief despite his own failed marriage, and even though his literal-minded companions make him an object of grotesque ridicule. In addition to such thematic parallels to Joyce, there are stylistic correspondences in Bellow's skillful juxtaposition of legal terminology, philosophical jargon, and historical formulations with a vigorous, often bawdy conversational tone, as well as in his kaleidoscopic narrative manner.

   The immediate and present action of Bellow's novel describes the
period of extreme crisis when Moses E. Herzog fears that he is not
only unable but unworthy to live according to "the law of the heart"
which he has expounded; though his withdrawn condition can be psychologically described as depressive and occasionally paranoid, he himself best identifies it as "*Heartsore*" (17). This intellectualized Leopold
Bloom sums up his despair when, after temporarily losing radio contact
while on maneuvers with the Army, he manages to croak asthmatically
(and so that the entire force hears him), "We're Lost!" (160). Dressing
to visit Ramona, Herzog summarizes for himself the factors which col-
laborate to give him this profound feeling of alienation:

> Well, for instance, what it means to be a man. In a city. In a century. In
> transition. In a mass. Transformed by science. Under organized power.
> Subject to tremendous controls. In a condition caused by mechanization.
> After the late failure of radical hopes. In a society that was no community
> and devalued the person. Owing to the multiplied power of numbers
> which made the self negligible. Which spent military billions against for-
> eign enemies but would not pay for order at home. Which permitted
> savagery and barbarism in its own great cities. . . . On top of that, an
> injured heart and raw gasoline poured on the nerves. (201)

The description is a microcosm of the absurd world in which many
modern heroes are compelled to function, but to the harshness and
impersonality of external reality is added "an injured heart," injured
not only by those who have betrayed him, but injured by its very
owner, for "he, Herzog, had committed a sin of some kind against his
own heart, while in pursuit of a grand synthesis" (207). That heart is
finally healed by Ramona's love and by the self-analysis which Herzog
undergoes while writing his interminable, unmailed letters.

   Herzog's violation consisted in believing that life is a "subject"
which could be looked at with intellectual detachment (hence his apparent indifference to his mother's death) and counted on to yield itself to
logical principles, to be encompassed in "systems." This fault is not
simply the result of misguided and overstimulated intellect; it also
grows from Herzog's fear of "the depths of feeling he would eventually
have to face, when he could no longer call on his eccentricities for
relief" (10). Like most of Bellow's heroes, Herzog must learn to face
both inner and external reality; he must rejoin the world. The result of
his failure to do so is spiritual, emotional, and intellectual sickness. In
the critical interim, he becomes masochistic and depressive; he experiences "the sickness *unto* death" (105); he is "no better than any other
kind of addict — sick with abstractions" (123); and in this condition,
when an airline stewardess offers him a drink, he feels "incapable of
looking into the girl's pretty, healthful face" (241).

   Herzog chronicles this agonized man's attempt to rejoin the world
without sacrificing the principles of heart for which his integrity demands defense. This entails not only a new understanding of the world

which surrounds him, but a purification and revaluation of self. Herzog's most immediate parallel in this regard is Bellow's Bummidge, the hero of *Last Analysis*, whose comical autotherapy is similarly motivated though executed with a greater flair for the burlesque. As Bummidge's harassed agent describes this self-analysis, "He recaptures the emotions. He fits them into a general framework. He thinks, and thinks, and talks and talks, and the girl takes it all down, and types it in triplicate, in leather binders." Herzog's syndrome is not unlike Bummidge's "Humanitis": "It isn't that I don't like people. I need 'em, I even love 'em. So why can't I bear 'em?" And Bummidge's lament is precisely that of Herzog: "Oh, how can I pull the plug and let the dirty water out of my soul. Value, value, give me value. Oh, for some substance."[8]

With a variety of intentions — most of them selfish — Herzog's friends suggest therapy for his condition, offering two major alternatives to his intellectual retreat. Sandor Himmelstein is a part-time exponent of Potato Love, that "amorphous, swelling, hungry, indiscriminate, cowardly potato love" (91) which shields man from reality by enveloping him in emotional fantasies. Far more insidious are the Reality Instructors, whom Sandor himself joins with brutal intensity when the irrational potato love fails him. The teacher of reality denies heart entirely, emphasizing that "we're all whores in this world, and don't you forget it" (85). Simkin is another of the Reality Instructors who love "to pity and poke fun at the same time" (30), and all of them point the way to a pessimism, even a nihilism, which Herzog cannot in honesty accept, however much such a principle might simplify his own dilemma. He must come to terms with reality, but first he is compelled to understand it, and for Herzog (as for Bellow's other heroes) reality cannot be encompassed by "*the commonplaces of the Wasteland outlook, the cheap mental stimulants of Alienation, the cant and rant of pipsqueaks about Inauthenticity and Forlornness. I can't accept this foolish dreariness. We are talking about the whole life of mankind. The subject is too great, too deep for such weakness, cowardice*" (75). Similarly, he writes testily to Heidegger, "*I should like to know what you mean by the expression 'the fall of into the quotidian.' When did this fall occur? Where were we standing when it happened?*" (49). He is repulsed that "the very Himmelsteins who had never even read a book of metaphysics, were touting the Void as if it were so much salable real estate" (93); that despair is almost a voting requirement; that an entire generation imagines "that nothing faithful, vulnerable, fragile can be durable or have any true power" (290); and that "*comfortable people playing at crisis, alienation, apocalypse and desperation*" (316) dominate the fashionable magazines.

Herzog searches not for rest or escape or illusion, but for that state in which he can exercise the intention of his heart in full knowledge and presence of reality — however antagonistic the latter may seem. He can deny neither term — unlike the Potato Lovers who deny reality, and the Reality Instructors who deny heart. Herzog himself has been an intellectual Potato Lover, and the results of this sort of abstracted humanism include an unhealthy absorption with the past, to which the scholar looks "with an intense need for contemporary relevance" (5), writing many of his letters to the dead because "he lived with them as much as with the living — perhaps more" (181). Herzog's intellectualized emotionalism, without anchor in reality, is shown at its most perverted extreme in Lucas Asphalter, who humanizes his animals to a grotesque degree: "Now Herzog had to consider some strange facts about Asphalter. It's possible I influenced him, my emotionalism transmitted itself to him. . . . I suspect Luke may be in a bad way" (45-46).

Through his meetings with Asphalter, the sordid courtroom trials which he observes, the bizarre automobile accident, the healing love of Ramona, and his questioning, argumentative letters, Herzog finally achieves an objective view of his absurd predicament: "He too could smile at Herzog and despise him. But there still remained the fact. I *am* Herzog. I have to be that man. There is no one else to do it. After smiling he must return to his own self and see the thing through" (67). Herzog learns to "be," and his progress is recorded in the letters with which he phrases a lover's quarrel with an essentially unloving world; he is schooled in the absurd tension between intention and reality and is at last content to exist in terms of the tension: "*But what do you want Herzog?*" he asks himself at the conclusion of the book. "*But that's just it — not a solitary thing. I am pretty well satisfied to be, to be just as it is willed, and for so long as I may remain in occupancy*" (340). Thus, he is prepared to renew what he calls "universal connections," the equivalent of Augie's "axial lines," but defined now in more specific humanistic terms. First, he conceives of his struggle as being significant in terms of "the human condition" (107) as a whole: "The progress of civilization — indeed, the survival of civilization — depend on the successes of Moses E. Herzog" (125). This is not simply narcissism or a distinctive lunacy; it is an index of Herzog's struggle for a stance which will allow him existence in terms of mankind — not merely in terms of intellect, of the exacerbated self, or of a hostile, external reality. Without this broader significance, Herzog loses all sense of time and space: he glances at his watch without being able to fix the time in his mind; he tries to orient himself in space, but from his apartment window he can see: "Nothing in particular. Only a sense of water bounding the overbuilt island" (159). And all he can fix firmly in his mind is his own face in the mirror.

The central paradox of Herzog's experience is that only through self can man renew universal connections, but too much involvement in self may cancel out the universal: "If ever Herzog knew the loathsomeness of a *particular* existence, knew that the *whole* was required to redeem every separate spirit, it was then, in his terrible passion, which he tried, impossibly, to share, telling his story" (156-57). Thus, he becomes increasingly aware of the grotesquerie of his own peccadilloes, and becomes the subject not only of the author's comic sense, but of his own as well. As comic detachment grows, Herzog becomes aware that the letters themselves, though crucial in helping him to resist the Potato Lovers and the Reality Instructors, are a means to an end which can be fully experienced only when he no longer needs to write them. As he explains to Asphalter with grim humor: "I must be trying to keep tight the tensions without which human beings can no longer be called human. If they don't suffer, they've gotten away from me. And I've filled the world with letters to prevent their escape. I want them in human form, and so I conjure up a whole environment and catch them in the middle. I put my whole heart into these constructions" (272). Herzog sees the average intellectual as a "Separatist" — hence he himself has hoarded food in the Ludeyville house in a scheme for solitary self-sufficiency, which seems ludicrous to him once he has become a "specialist in . . . in spiritual self-awareness" (307), for that very awareness teaches him that no definition of the self is complete unless it embraces other people — even such actors as Gersbach and Madeleine.

Madeleine is essential in forcing the crisis through which Herzog comes to terms with reality, and Ramona is the crucial counterbalance which saves him from insanity and gives him strength to keep his absurd intention alive. He confesses to Simkin that he is not a realist (convinced now of the necessity of confronting reality but uncertain how to interpret it), and his ultimate vision embraces all the ambiguities of the world about him, resisting both romanticism and nihilism:

> The air from the west was drier than the east air. Herzog's sharp senses detected the difference. In these days of near-delirium and wide-ranging disordered thought, deeper currents of feeling had heightened his perceptions or made him instill something of his own into his surroundings. As though he painted them with moisture and color taken from his own mouth, his blood, liver, bowels, genitals. In this mingled way, therefore, he was aware of Chicago, familiar ground to him for more than thirty years. And out of these elements, by this peculiar art of his own organs, he created his version of it. Where the thick walls and buckled slabs of pavement in the Negro slums exhaled their bad smells. Farther West, the industries; the sluggish South Branch dense with sewage and glittering with a crust of golden slime; the Stockyards, deserted; the dullness of bungalows and scrawny parks; and vast shopping centers; and the cemeteries after these — Waldheim, with its graves for Herzogs past and present; the Forest Preserves for riding parties; Croatian picnics, lovers' lanes, horrible murders; airports; quarries; and last of all, cornfields. And with this, infinite forms of activity — Reality. (278)

Madeleine had hampered such an inclusive vision by driving him, through her own ambition, further onto the shoals of intellectualism, and by giving him additional evidence to support the nihilists' conclusions that man is by nature whorish. As a bitch goddess who coolly applies lipstick after a meal by looking at herself in a knife blade, Madeleine has a polite and morally rigid ancestress in James's Madame de Mauves, a frivolous one in Fitzgerald's Daisy Fay Buchanan, and a serious competitor in West's Faye Greener, with her "long sword-like legs." Herzog's spirit is too active, too resilient, to be completely dominated by this woman (though she does give him cause to question his own potency); she appropriately chooses a one-legged lover named Valentine: a paper imitation of the real man of heart, an *ersatz* Herzog, though physically more powerful, as his name implies.

Ramona, on the other hand, offers regeneration through love: "She, Ramona, wanted to add riches to his life and give him what he pursued in the wrong places. This she could do only by the art of love, she said — the art of love which was one of the sublime achievements of the spirit. . . . What he had to learn from her — while there was still time; while he was still virile, his powers substantially intact — was how to renew the spirit through the flesh (a precious vessel in which the spirit rested)" (184-85). And Ramona can succeed because she knows not only how to produce sensual gratification (as cook, florist, lover), but because she too has been tested and tempered: "she knew the bitterness of death and nullity, too" (185). In the conclusion of the novel, Herzog offers Ramona not one of the letters he has written for months, but a bouquet of wildflowers. Ramona, the friendship of Asphalter, his two children, the rich memories of Napoleon Street all reinforce the man of heart as he passes through this crisis of consciousness. They reaffirm his belief that man only *seems* lost, only remains alienated when he blindly accepts the fashionable stance of alienation as a condition of existence. Despite the new barbarisms of a machine age, well known to Herzog as a moral historian, he can reaffirm that "*civilization and even morality are implicit in technological transformation*" (164); that "*there are moral realities*" (178) as well as physically unstable, destructive ones; and even as he scents the odor of decay rising through a waste pipe, he notes "unexpected intrusion of beauty" (218).

Herzog's Jewishness, a question to which many reviewers of the novel peremptorily turned their backs, seems a vital factor insofar as it gives Herzog a sense of the significance of family ("He could be a patriarch, as every Herzog was meant to be. The family man, father, transmitter of life, intermediary between past and future, instrument of mysterious creation. . . " [202]); a richness and complexity of experience, heavy with love as well as deprivation, which causes him to rebel against the simplistic clichés of popular nihilism ("much heavy love in Herzog; grief did not pass quickly with him" [119]); and an almost dauntless compassion ("a great schooling in grief. I still know these cries of the soul" [148]). It is true that he possesses these traits in greater degree than the other members of his family; that he himself feels that modern experience has made much of the traditional Jewish heritage inapplicable; and that other backgrounds might have resulted in a constitution similarly resistant to nihilism, dedicated to children and the principle of family. Nonetheless, the relevant fact remains that such values as Herzog embodies are not, at least in this degree, the common stock of modern industrialized America. Herzog *is* a Jew, and many of his values grow directly from his Jewish immigrant background rather than from his adult experiences as a liberal intellectual. Though he was brought up in an eccentric and only erratically "religious" family, he himself repeatedly refers to his Jewishness. The critic who urges that this "Jewishness" is unimportant to the novel is correct to the same degree that Leopold Bloom's Jewishness is unimportant; he is right if he intends to suggest that the character is a symbolic alien whose struggle has significance for all of us. But he is clearly wrong if he means to suggest that a Jewish background is irrelevant in terms of the particular character's dramatic development. Similar arguments apply to all of Bellow's Jewish heroes.

In Moses E. Herzog, Saul Bellow presents the most rich and diverse of his band of questing men who dissipate their powers and energies in fruitless, often comic quests for salvation which are resolved only through the character's realization that man's triumph comes when he has learned to sustain the vital equilibrium between reality and intention. One need only recall Joseph's remarks in *Dangling Man* to observe the consistency of Bellow's heroes while, at the same time, appreciating the mature development which these concepts are given in the person of Herzog: "We are all drawn toward the same craters of the spirit — to know what we are and what we are for, to know our purpose, to seek grace. And, if the quest is the same, the differences in our personal histories, which hitherto meant so much to us, become of minor importance."[9] In every case the Bellow hero is aggravated into self-awareness and into revaluation of the world around him as preparation for engaging the vital tensions in the most fruitful manner. The hero shouts, "Hurray for regular hours!"[10] He develops conscience, orients himself to the axial lines of life, learns to confront death, returns to society, renews "universal connections." Bellow's knights progress in orderly file from one novel to the next — increasing in complexity of treatment, if not, consistently, in depth. If Bellow has, in effect, only written one book from six different points of view, the book has constantly improved, although it would seem to have reached its most extreme extension in *Herzog*. Further elaboration on the theme might well force the novelist to yield to the rhetorician — a danger already apparent in the concluding pages of both *Henderson the Rain King* and *Herzog*. Perhaps Bellow may have had such dangers in mind when he noted, "In writing *Herzog* I felt I was completing a certain development, coming to the end of a literary sensibility."[11] It is, perhaps, the end of monologue as well, for the technique comes to a crisis in *Herzog*. Here the struggle to externalize, to escape the trap of self and renew universal connections, depends on Herzog's seeing his own dilemma in an objective light: that he cannot do so consistently is indicated by the shifting narrative voice, which moves erratically between first and third persons until at last, after Herzog has made his resolution that "*I am pretty well satisfied to be, to be just as it is willed, and for as long as I remain in occupancy*" (340), the third-person voice takes over entirely; with the exception of the opening sentence, the first section of the novel, which similarly describes Herzog at the end of his ordeal, is also in the third person. It is almost as though the objective narrative voice were a further indication of Herzog's restoration to life, a proof that he is now "confident, cheerful, clairvoyant, and strong" (1), just as significant as his "weirdly tranquil" face and the "radiant line . . . from mid-forehead over his straight nose and full, silent lips" (2). The alternating voices of the remainder of the book constitute monologue despite the constantly shifting person; there is dialectic but not dialogue. If *Herzog* seems Joycean in its circular structure (though it is a formal, not a thematic circularity), in narrative manner it also owes a debt to *Tristram Shandy*, that "history book . . . of what passes in a man's mind."

Perhaps Herzog's victory is only temporary, but we leave him in the conclusion of the novel a far wiser man than any of Bellow's earlier heroes, one who has now affirmed and legitimatized the absurd struggle on all levels of experience — emotional, spiritual, and intellectual. Perhaps now Bellow has prepared himself for the novel of dialogue, which can begin with the engagement toward which his diverse knights have struggled — in short, perhaps he can move beyond affirmation of the absurd experience to examine the consequences of those "tensions" which he has detailed with such skill and integrity.

Notes

1.   Saul Bellow, *Herzog* (New York: Viking, 1964), 4. Subsequent references in the text from this edition.
2.   Qtd. in David Boroff, "Saul Bellow," *Saturday Review* 47 (19 Sep. 1964): 38-39.
3.   James Dean Young, "Bellow's View of the Heart," *Critique* 7.3 (1965): 11-12.
4.   The concept of the absurd referred to in this article is of a different nature from that commonly used in conjunction with the contemporary theatre. The principle on which my thesis rests is derived from Camus' discussion, in *The Myth of Sisyphus*, of the absurd man as one who displays "a disproportion between his intention and the reality he will encounter." The absurd *hero* learns to accept the terms of this disproportion, and his

ultimate victory comes when he learns to live in accordance with the tension and without denying either term of its composition: intention or reality. For a more detailed examination of this principle, see my article "The Absurd Man as Picaro: The Novels of Saul Bellow," *Texas Studies in Literature and Language* 6.2 (1964): 226-54.

5. Tony Tanner, "Saul Bellow: The Flight from Monologue," *Encounter* 24 (Feb. 1965): 65-66.

6. James Joyce, *Ulysses* (New York: Vintage, 1961), 292. Subsequent references in the text from this edition.

7. William York Tindall, *A Reader's Guide to James Joyce* (London: Thames and Hudson, 1959), 130.

8. These passages are excerpts from an early draft of *The Last Analysis* entitled "Scenes from Humanitis — A Farce," which appeared in the *Partisan Review* 29.3 (1962): 327-49.

9. Saul Bellow, *Dangling Man* (New York: Vanguard, 1944), 154.

10. Ibid., 191.

11. Boroff, 39.

* * *

"Weirdly Tranquil" Vision: The Point of View of Moses Herzog

M. Gilbert Porter

The consensus among Bellovian scholars and critics is that, all things considered, *Herzog* remains Bellow's best novel. Here artistic vision finds its appropriate concretions; meaning is achieved through form. Point of view is complicated and directly reflective of the emotional and intellectual condition of the protagonist. The end of the novel grows organically out of the exposition and resolves the initial conflict without making larger claims than the condition of the central intelligence can support. The theme is significant and presented with intensity. Views opposite to those of Herzog are given more than ample play in the characterizations of a large cast of antagonists and in the fundamental ambivalence in Herzog himself. The conflict in Herzog between his intellect and his sensibilities provides the integrating principle in the novel, setting up the complex point of view, inviting the "lessons" of the reality instructors, intensifying Herzog's anguish, and leading him, finally, to his transcendental affirmation, in which he frees himself from the compulsion of intellectual systematizing and relaxes in the freedom of an emotional/intuitional synthesis. "*The intellectual has been a Separatist,*" says Herzog as he approaches clarity. "*And what kind of synthesis is a Separatist likely to come up with?*"[1]

From *Saul Bellow Journal* 8.1 (1989): 3-11.

What passes for plot in the novel is a narrative strategy that moves Herzog from a state of agitation to a state of rest, from a frantic search for direction to a discovery of that direction. The events that attend Herzog's transformation, though, are presented mainly through Herzog's own perceptions as the central intelligence in a sophisticated and often convoluted narration. Thus, point of view is central to the assessment of Bellow's achievement in *Herzog*, yet most critics have settled for summary statements rather than detailed examinations of narrative technique. Earl Rovit, for example, observes that Bellow "reshuffles time sequences expertly, shifts Herzog's point of view from first- to third-person, employs the device of the fragmentary "mental" letters as a masterly bridge between solipsism and communication, and casts an ambience of irony over his entire construction."[2] According to Peter Bischoff,

> the novel is located essentially in the consciousness of the protagonist. The "psychodrama" of Herzog is played out in a technically refined labyrinth of descriptive and scenic flashbacks, and of letters which are conceived in the mind, sometimes recorded, but never sent. Through the artifice of the changing perspective, Bellow grants to the solipsistic self-analysis of his protagonist a psychical dynamism which combines the descriptive and scenic narrative elements in a mixture of various time levels. The narrative point of view alternates between character, persona, and omniscient author; thus the point of view of the protagonist varies constantly between "I," "you," and "he." Such a change within the character-perspective is made possible by the fact that Herzog is always conscious of his own consciousness. In observing himself not only as subject but also as object Herzog becomes a stranger to himself.[3]

In a similar vein, Eusebio L. Rodrigues writes that "the narrative angle jumps around shifting wildly from one mode to another without warning and often within the same paragraph, creating an illusion of constant rapid nervous motion and a continuity of tempo that offsets the tortoise pace of the action and the cramping time schedule."[4] And Malcolm Bradbury comments that "this is a book set primarily *within* consciousness, and there is a parallel formlessness or oblique design in the novel's structure — until, finally, both Herzog and the book transfigure the plurality of words and explanations into significant silence."[5]

These remarks are all thoughtful and perceptive but remain, as far as point of view is concerned, within the realm of general observation. What follows here is an attempt to explore in some detail, but without becoming tedious, the actual functioning of narrative technique in the novel as it contributes to the development of Herzog's character.

The opening section of the novel presents Herzog as seriously distracted. The adulterous Gersbach and Madeleine are saying he is insane, and others have agreed with them. Herzog reports the rumor accurately without being disturbed or intimidated by it, behaving oddly but feeling "cheerful, clairvoyant, and strong" (1). In a Wordsworthian exercise, Herzog is recalling emotion in tranquility — and he

approaches total recall — in the interest of justifying, putting into perspective, and clarifying the events that have led him to distraction.[6]
Although the opening section precedes the ending section by only a few
days of the week of the narrative time covered by the novel, the bulk
of the book between beginning and end focuses on the domestic strife
of the past year and includes memories and reflections extending as far
back as Herzog's childhood. Most of the events of the novel, then, are
images recreated and relived — in pain, trembling, and humor — by a
suffering mind, but the recollection leads ultimately to peace, though
the journey is circuitous indeed.

The end of the introductory section shows Herzog viewing himself
in the windowpane of the old house in Ludeyville that is as imposing
and disordered as Herzog himself: "He was taking a turn around the
empty house and saw the shadow of his face in a gray, webby window.
He looked weirdly tranquil. A radiant line went from mid-forehead
over his straight nose and full, silent lips" (2). The reflection of the
self — "weirdly tranquil" — in the murky pane and the line bisecting
the head are emblematic of both a divided consciousness and a narrative technique. Herzog is at once involved in and detached from his
experience — pained, amused, bewildered, evaluative. The shifts in
narrative from past to present, from private to public, from abstract to
concrete, and from third to first person are reflective of Herzog's
ambivalence. His intellectual fervor and emotional pain heighten his
perceptions, making his observations in all areas vivid, intense, and —
at least in terms of his own character — reliable.

Like Mr. Sammler in *Mr. Sammler's Planet*, Herzog looks both
inward and outward. He is in his experience as participant; he is
detached from it as spectator, witness, and judge. The shifting point of
view keeps the reader aware of a protagonist who is consciously experiencing his experience. "Awareness was his work; extended consciousness was his line, his business. Vigilance" (278). That Herzog is
a self examining himself is fundamentally revealed by a series of
reflections in glass, water, and various mirrors, beginning with the
image of the divided self in the murky windowpane. When Herzog
recalls the scene in which Madeleine announced her intention to obtain
a divorce, he looks back from his New York apartment on himself in
Chicago putting up storm windows on the house Madeleine had
ordered him out of:

> . . . lying with no more style than a chimpanzee, his eyes with greater
> than normal radiance watched his own work in the garden with detach-
> ment, as if he were looking through the front end of a telescope at a tiny
> clear image. *That suffering joker.* (11)

The present self sees the past self here through the perspective
provided by elapsed time, but the subject and object are still one; the
suffering joker in the garden is now the suffering joker on the couch.
Shopping for clothes on Ramona's suggestion, Herzog examines him-

self in the store's "triple, lighted mirror": "His body seemed unaffected by his troubles, survived all blasts. It was his face that was devastated, especially about the eyes, so that it made him pale to see himself" (20). This is one of many such assessments of his condition. He is frightened by his condition, but he refuses to be intimidated by it or to take himself and his suffering too seriously: "Alone, he put his tongue out at himself and then withdrew from the triple mirror" (21). Looking back further still, Herzog remembers a moment in a subway after a visit with Marco in Philadelphia:

> The mirror of the gum machine revealed to Herzog how pale he was, unhealthy — wisps from his coat and wool scarf, his hat and brows, twisting and flaming outward in the overfull light and exposing the sphere of his face, the face of a man who was keeping up a front. Herzog smiled at this earlier avatar of his life, at Herzog the victim, Herzog the would-be lover, Herzog the man on whom the world depended for certain intellectual work, to change history, to influence the development of civilization. Several boxes of stale paper under his bed in Philadelphia were going to produce this very significant result. (104-05)

The pattern is constant. Recalling pain in the past produces a smile in the present, mitigating the pain but certainly not negating it. Although his anguish often ambushes him in the form of involuntary tears, Herzog tells Himmelstein, "I'm going to shake this off, I'm not going to be a victim. I hate the victim bit" (82). Herzog's recurrent smile despite his tears signifies both resilience and resistance, acknowledging the pain but promising to transcend it.

The desire for transcendence sometimes assumes the form of imaginative reflection. Waiting for the ferry at Woods Hole, Herzog looks into the water "at the net of bright reflections on the bottom. . . . There was no stain in the water, where schools of minnows swam. Herzog sighed and said to himself, 'Praise God — praise God'"(91). Like the Ancient Mariner blessing the water snakes, Herzog is moved to prayer by the clarity and beauty of the water. He yearns to see his essential being at one here with the brilliance of nature. "If his soul could cast a reflection so brilliant, and so intensely sweet, he might beg God to make such use of him. But that would be too simple. . . . The actual sphere is not clear like this, but turbulent, angry" (91). Despite Herzog's yearning, the albatross of his mortality does not drop from his burdened neck, and he must continue his quest for clarity in the realm of the actual. In the mirror in Ramona's apartment he sees reflected the same struggling self, and in the police station Herzog reads in Madeleine's eyes the vote for his death, his total non-existence, a reflected wish that frees him from any residual hold Madeleine could have over him. These reflections of the self are symbolic of Herzog's anguished spirit, his heightened consciousness, his compulsion to revisit his pain, to tell all in order to overcome chaos and prevent nervous collapse. The reader — a transfixed Wedding Guest — is thus compelled to attention and to sympathy, and the narrative framework is neatly established for the credible juxtaposition of memories, letters, dramatic scenes, philosophical discourses, *obiter dicta*, social commentary, and assorted musings in a convolution of Herzog's present and past.

Herzog's struggle toward clarity and balance as revealed in various physical reflections is established further through Bellow's use of the shifting point of view in the modified technique of a central intelligence who requires the reader to share his pain, his humor, his humanity, and his process of discovery and transformation. The pattern usually starts with traditional third-person objective point of view (Herzog in the narrative present), shifts to first person (Herzog recalling an antecedent event, reliving it in scenario), shifts to first-person editorial (Herzog analyzing the event in retrospect), and then shifts back to third-person (Herzog from authorial perspective resuming the pace of narrative present). The letters typically provide the stimulus for the interruption of third-person narrative to follow Herzog, in dialogue and dramatic episode, through one of his excursions into his past. One example will suffice to illustrate the technique:

En route on the train to visit Libby Sissler, Herzog, in a New Haven car, is described in the third person from the point of view of an objective author: "He sat in a cramped position, pressing the valise to his chest, his traveling-desk, and writing rapidly in the spiral notebook. *Dear Zelda* . . . "(34). Addressing Zelda in the second-person vocative places Herzog in the first-person role, in which he returns in memory to hockey games with Herman and conversations with Zelda both before and after the divorce — these memories presented dramatically and through narrative summary, but here the third person is Herzog describing himself, and the first person is Herzog in action: "He tried to get a grip on himself. Half buttoned, red-eyed, unshaved, he looked disgraceful. Indecent. He was telling Zelda his side of the case: 'I know she's turned you against me — poisoned your mind, Zelda'" (37). As Herzog dramatically renders the scene from the past with himself as both first and third person, he recreates what he said as well as what he thought, and this scenario is interrupted in its turn by the continuation, in italics, of the letter to Zelda in the narrative present:

"Well, I know you aren't like the other wives out here. . . ."

Your kitchen is different, your Italian lamps, your carpets, your French provincial furniture, your Westinghouse, your mink, your country club, your cerebral palsy canisters are all different.

I am sure you were sincere. Not insincere. True insincerity is hard to find. (38)

With sarcasm, with equivocal attempts at fairness, with bemusement and discomfort, the "he" of the present relives the "I" of the past: "(Recalling, in the still standing train, the thwarted and angry eagerness of these attempted explanations, he had to laugh. Nothing but a wan smile passed over his face). . . . He saw himself in the train window, hearing his own words clearly. I think you're on the level" (40). With this reflection of the self viewing the self, Herzog ends his letter in the narrative present — and this episode into the antecedent past — with an editorial comment in first person evaluating himself and Zelda: "*But I'm no criminal, don't have it in me; frightful to myself instead. Anyway, Zelda, I see you had tremendous pleasure, double excitement, lying from an overflowing heart*" (41). The self-effacing author now resumes control in the narrative present and advances the movement of Herzog in the third person: "All at once the train left the platform and entered the tunnel. Temporarily in darkness, Herzog held his pen" (41). Bellow then records his central intelligence making a Freudian-inspired notation suggested by the memories of Madeleine and Zelda as they have conditioned his present state of mind: "Herzog wrote, *Will never understand what women want. What do they want? They eat green salad and drink human blood*" (41-42).

The whole novel, of course, is a reflection, beginning and ending with Herzog practicing the self-examination that Socrates and Thoreau advocated to make life worth living. The section immediately preceding provides a paradigm of the technique that makes the novel work as an extended reflection in which Herzog prepares himself through hyper-awareness for a better future. In a typical passage, Herzog describes his own rhetorical stance:

> We must be what we are. That is necessity. And what are we? Well, here he was trying to hold on to Ramona as he ran from her. And thinking that he was binding her, he bound himself, and the culmination of this clever goofiness might be to entrap himself. Self development, self-realization, happiness — these were the titles under which these lunacies occurred. Ah, poor fellow! — and Herzog momentarily joined the objective world in looking down on himself. He too could smile at Herzog and despise him. But there still remained the fact. I am Herzog. I have to *be* that man. There is no one else to do it. After smiling, he must return to his own Self and see the thing through. (66-67)

Bellow's use of strategic shifts in person and time — the special employment of an intricate central-intelligence point of view — embodies particularly well the condition of the protagonist, torn as he is between the realm of thought and the realm of feeling, between the evidence for despair in the world and the desire for affirmation in himself, between the active man and the reflective consciousness.[7] The intimacy of the first person enlists our sympathy; the objectivity of the third person, whether Herzog's voice or Bellow's, lends credibility to the perceptions. The vacillations in Herzog find engaging and natural expression in the vacillating point of view in a masterful narrative technique that enables Bellow as an artist to display his shiniest wares.

Notes

1. Saul Bellow, *Herzog* (New York: Viking, 1964), 322. Subsequent references in the text from this edition.
2. Earl Rovit, *Saul Bellow* (Minneapolis: U of Minnesota P, 1967), 24.
3. Peter Bischoff, *Saul Bellows Romane: Entfremdung und Suche* (Bonn: Bouvier, 1975), 96. ["Der Roman ist zum wesentlichen Teil im Bewußtsein der Hauptfigur abgesiedelt. In einer technisch sehr ausgefeilten Verschachtelung von beschreibenden und szenischen Rückblenden sowie im Geiste konzipierten, mitunter aufgezeichneten, jedoch nie abgesandten Briefen spielt sich das 'Psychodrama' Herzogs ab. Durch den Kunstgriff der wechselnden Perspektivierung verleiht Bellow der solipsistischen Selbstanalyse seines Protagonisten eine psychische Dynamik, die die beschreibenden und szenischen Erzählelemente in einer Mischung verschiedener Zeitebenen verbindet. Die Erzählperspektive wechselt zwischen figürlicher, figürlich-auktorialer, und auktorialer Erzählweise, wobei die figürliche Perspektive des Protagonisten ständig zwischen 'I,' 'you,' and 'he' variiert. Ein solcher Wechsel innerhalb der Figurenperspektive wird dadurch ermöglicht, daß sich Herzog seines Bewußtseins stets bewußt ist. Indem Herzog sich nicht nur als Subjekt, sondern auch als Objekt betrachtet, entfremdet er sich von sich selbst." Translation mine.]
4. Eusebio L. Rodrigues, *Quest for the Human: An Exploration of Saul Bellow's Fiction* (Lewisburg: Bucknell UP, 1981), 162.
5. Malcolm Bradbury, *The Modern American Novel* (London: Oxford UP, 1983), 138.
6. For a discussion of elements of English romanticism in *Herzog* and elsewhere in Bellow's work, see Allan Chavkin, "Bellow and English Romanticism," *Studies in the Literary Imagination* 17.2 (1984): 7-18.
7. Time is kept strategically vague in the novel, but as Herzog gathers his forces in the Berkshires toward the end of the narrative, he muses, "But was it only a week — five days? Unbelievable!" (326). The narrative goes on, then, with Herzog's report of his desultory activities ("For the next two days — or were there three? — Herzog did nothing but send such messages, and write down songs, psalms, and utterances" [327]) before he shaves to meet his brother Will, makes a date with Ramona, and ends the novel with "no messages for anyone" (341).

* * *

Plays (1954, 1965)

Saul Bellow on the Drag Strip
Robert Brustein

There is an awful lot of noise issuing from the stage of the Belasco these days, but the loudest explosion of all can be heard only with the inner ear: it comes from the head-on collision of a gifted writer, Saul Bellow, with the crassness and incompetence of the whole commercial theater system. Since this has been an accident with no survivors, and since the vehicle being driven was smashed beyond repair, it will probably never be known that *The Last Analysis* was, potentially, a remarkable play, or that its protagonist, Philip Bummidge, was among the most flamboyant comic characters ever written for the American stage. Any interested in rooting around amidst this wreckage, however, will find the major cause of the accident to be the complex and ambitious nature of the work itself. There is only one actor in our theater capable of realizing the intricacies of its central character, and that is Zero Mostel — but he has elected to entertain the Hadassah ladies in *Fiddler on the Roof*. Sam Levene, who inherited the role by default, apparently doesn't understand one word of it, and to hide his bafflement, he plays this one too as if it were written for the Hadassah ladies, to the crash of splintering intentions. As for directors, William Ball is the only one I can think of whose touch would have been dual to the play's delicate balance, but Joseph Anthony handles himself in the driver's seat with all the grace of a teen-age drag racer at the wheel of his father's Rolls Royce. The result is vehicular homicide, for which the major victim, the author, alone has been arraigned. But never before, in my experience, have a play and its production been so at odds.

I have some quarrels with the work, though nothing that a competent director could not have ironed out with the playwright. It suffers, like much of Mr. Bellow's writing, from a lack of focus; its struc-

From *The New Republic* (24 Oct. 1964): 25-26.

ture is sprawling; its form is not always integrated with its theme; and its theme is somewhat impacted in the author's ambivalence toward his subject. But it contains, at the same time, some of the most magnificent rhetoric to be heard on the American stage since Clifford Odets, and it is rippling with energy and intelligence. Mr. Bellow is not — as the condescending tone of the dailies seemed to imply — merely another novelist writing dialogue. He has natural dramatic gifts. And in *The Last Analysis*, he is working out a fascinating theater experiment, trying to combine depth insights with popular American forms.

The form of the play is cartoon farce of that broad knockdown variety common to the thirties — and Bellow's stage is alive with vaudeville jokes and uninhibited action. Despite all the slammed doors, embarrassed confrontations, hidden eavesdroppers, and Jiggs-and-Maggie battles, however, the farce is rather dark, for, inside it, Mr. Bellow is fashioning a melancholy play-within-a-play, somewhat on the order of Pirandello's *Six Characters*. The pivot of the action is Bummidge, an aging, neurotic Jewish comedian, afflicted with the dread plague of "Humanitis," a kind of metaphysical *Angst* over the plight of human existence. This has so infected his career that he is now seeking, through a process of rigorous self-analysis, to undertake "an expedition to recover the lost Self," fishing around in his past for the secret of his life. Being an entertainer, he is preparing to act out his memories over closed-circuit television (piped directly to a convention of psychoanalysts at the Waldorf). And using his family, friends, and parasites as histrionic pack carriers, he begins a safari into the jungle of time, reliving his memories and subjecting them to his own hilariously mordant Freudian commentation.

Moving always back in history, he reenacts his burlesque and vaudeville days; his marriage to a pregnant girl friend; his early hostility toward his father; his childhood difficulties with his mother ("You didn't want the breast, and your Mamma said, 'All right, I'll give it to the conductor'"); his early toilet training. At last, with the rest of the cast playing Greek chorus to Bummy's Oedipus, he reenacts his own conception ("Ma, no, no, no! Too late, my number's up"); his development in the womb ("It's great in here. I like it"); and finally the trauma of birth itself ("I hear screams. I'd holler too if I could breathe"). At the climax, resurrected like Lazarus, he rises from a tomb to the playing of "America the Beautiful" and the unfurling of an American flag.

The upshot of all this fine madness is that Bummidge is showered with television offers — but turns them down in order to form a Platonic Academy of Comedy for failing comics like himself; and though his parasites desert him, he is reunited with his family. The ending is shallow and sentimental, inspired more by the conventions of farce than by the pressure of the author's insights, and it demonstrates how the various elements of the play have been improperly fused. For example, Bummy is apparently meant to be a representative of the artist in our time — his need to understand himself, to transcend his sense of futility, to achieve freedom, and to lead an austere life in the midst of American plenty — but we are never told precisely what is typical about a television comic, or why his experience should invite such generalizations. Mr. Bellow states that his theme is "the link between the individual and the universal," but although he tantalizes us with suggestions, he never really shows us how this link is forged.

Still, if Bellow has failed to formulate his play sufficiently, he has certainly created a wild, anarchic theater piece that would have yielded ample rewards if only his collaborators had not made attentiveness impossible. The cast — with three exceptions (Tresa Hughes as Bummy's wife, Ann Wedgeworth as his mistress, Will Lee as his tailor) — is dismal; and poor Sam Levene, who is almost never off stage, has been abysmally miscast. At a loss with the part, he has fallen back on the only character he has confidence in, the Jewish garment manufacturer, mugging, grimacing, and ogling until he has flattened the values of the play. As for the direction, Joseph Anthony's major contribution is a resounding tumult — typical of which is the recurrent gurgle of a flushing toilet — but he has made no effort whatsoever to grasp the work, or to clarify its line of development.

Then there are the theater reviewers who, exposing that awful gap that exists between the theatrical and the literary worlds, dismissed Mr. Bellow as if he were simply another hack writer of the Broadway school. From the tone of some of their reviews, this response was partly motivated by a desire for revenge against those who have kept them in an abject state of inferiority; but its effect, I fear, is to have frustrated a potentially fine dramatist from ever writing plays again. The next time these men begin asking "Where are the playwrights?" let them look at the corpses they have buried under their own reviews.

* * *

The "Mental Comedies" of Saul Bellow
Keith M. Opdahl

Saul Bellow has always been interested in the theater. He wrote a survey of Broadway for the *Partisan Review* in 1954, and published his first one-act play, *The Wrecker*, that same year. His novels are filled with references to the theater, from the actor Alf Steidler in *Dangling Man* to the pervasive allusions to acting in Herzog.[1] Citrine in *Humboldt's Gift* is a playwright, Allbee in *The Victim* takes up with a movie actress, and Tommy Wilhelm in *Seize the Day* quits college to

From *From Hester Street to Hollywood: The Jewish-American Stage and Screen*, ed. Sarah Blacher Cohen (Bloomington: Indiana UP, 1983), 183-196.

become an actor. Bellow often uses theater imagery to suggest something false, pretentious, inauthentic, as he does in the play *The Last Analysis* or in the climactic scene of *Herzog*; but at other times he uses it to suggest something real and moving, perhaps the spectacle of our human life or the mystery of our social place (our "seat"), as at the end of *The Victim*.

Thus when Lillian Hellman suggested, in the late 1950s, that Bellow write a play, he didn't need to have his arm twisted. "In a short time, my play was ready," Bellow wrote in *The New York Times*. "Miss Hellman found it amusing and estimated it would run about eight hours without Wagnerian orchestration."[2] He let the manuscript sit for a few years, read it to a group known as the "Theatre of Living Ideas," and then in 1965 saw the play produced on Broadway, with Sam Levene in the major role. Bellow has said privately that he suspected in this period that *Herzog* might flop and that *The Last Analysis* (with Zero Mostel in the lead) might succeed. Instead the novel was a best-seller and the play folded in three weeks. Walter Kerr gave it a bad review, but it was praised by several reviewers who felt the production failed the play. John Simon summed up this last viewpoint when he charged that "there is still no excuse for reviewers and audiences not to have come to the rescue of *The Last Analysis*. It was, in the last analysis, far more provocative than anything else around."[3]

Bellow wasn't done with Broadway, however. After publishing a refurbished version of *The Last Analysis* in 1965, he wrote two one-act farces, *A Wen* and *Orange Soufflé*, which he gathered together with an unpublished one-act farce, *Out From Under*, to form the entertainment *Under the Weather*, so named because all three protagonists are not quite themselves. It was produced in 1966 and was praised in Spoleto and London, but it failed on Broadway, where Walter Kerr felt both the play and the production were frivolous.

By the end of 1966, then, Bellow had written a total of five plays, four of them one-act farces, and had seen two Broadway productions fail. And that (as of 1982) is the extent of his career in the theater, although his work is still produced on occasion in such places as Philadelphia or the Saul Bellow Conference in Brussels in 1978. None of the five plays is considered a masterpiece, although critics cite Bellow as the best of those contemporary novelists attempting drama, and at least two of the plays, *A Wen* and *The Last Analysis*, are delightful. We might even say that Bellow has done very well, given the essentially untheatrical cast of his imagination. His fiction consists largely of observation and meditation, and the driving force of his story is less often a suspenseful action than a description — a scene, an image, an emotion, precisely that texture which a play leaves up to the director and actors. And yet Bellow's gifts *do* lend themselves to the theater, too, as Bellow achieves not only some of the most dramatic characters around, but the kind of large, complete image or situation that will play — the human situation that can penetrate the footlights and yet retain its subtlety.

Bellow's problems, such as they are, seem due rather to what the theater means to him. In his review of *Under the Weather*, Walter Kerr objected to Bellow's writing "with what seemed more a giggle than an accepted obligation, [for] he gave the impression of toying with the stage, of idly building sandcastles that were bound to be swept away."[4] Kerr defines this "giggle" in terms of a lack of narrative drive, which is fair enough, but his impression is also that of a writer at play, which is precisely how Bellow regards the stage. "I wrote a play . . . because I thought it would be easier than a novel," Bellow confessed to an interviewer. "You have to worry less about moods and details, and one is freer to come to the point."[5] To Bellow the theater means freedom, which is reflected, too, in his choice of the farce, which he saw as liberation. The farce would permit him to mix the high and the low, as he puts it, or a sexy obsession with a metaphysical speculation, all in a play that, like the Yiddish theater, is swept along by its energy and emotion rather than any careful structure, mixing the earthy and the sublime, the passionate and the sentimental, the insightful and the grand. Bellow also remembered the joy of vaudeville (in which Jews were prominent) and thought that a string of sketches, if acted broadly and energetically, could be a lot of fun.

In this desire for liberation one hears, of course, echoes of *Augie March*. One could do worse than define Bellow's history as a writer in terms of his struggle to free himself, for his desire to be free cuts across not only his work and his attitude toward the theater, but also his attitude toward his Jewishness. How many novels begin with the energetic rush of an uncertain or forced liberation? One thinks not only of *Augie March*, but *Henderson* (freed from WASP conventions, which is very much to the point) and *Herzog*, who doesn't care if people think he's mad, and then *Dangling Man*, which shows its own strain. All of these novels announce a rejection of shackles. And what are the shackles? They are the formal restrictions of a WASP art and a WASP society. Bellow is very much like Walt Whitman in paralleling aesthetic forms with political ones — and in seeking liberation in both areas. "A writer should be able to express himself easily, naturally, copiously," Bellow has said,

> in a form which frees his mind, his energies. Why should he hobble himself with formalities? With a borrowed sensibility? With the desire to be "correct"? . . . should add that for a young man in my position there were social inhibitions, too. I had a good reason to fear that I would be put down as a foreigner, an interloper. It was made clear to me when I studied literature in the university that as a Jew and the son of Russian Jews I would probably never have the right *feeling* for Anglo-Saxon traditions, for English words.[6]

Bellow's use of his Jewish heritage in his writing is, of course, complex. Even as he's struggled with religious prejudice — and his interviews reveal how painful it has been — Bellow has resisted the label of "Jewish novelist," describing himself instead as a Jew who writes fiction, a description that does justice to both his citizenship in the larger European-American culture and his experience as a Jew, which ranges from that of a child of Russian-Jewish immigrants who has experienced the pain and pleasure of assimilation into America to that of the immigrant himself, coming to Chicago at the age of nine. One is struck in fact by how unselfconscious Bellow's characters are of their Jewishness. With the obvious exception of Asa Leventhal in *The Victim*, the protagonists are so absorbed by personal and metaphysical issues that they pay only occasional mind to their cultural and religious identity. And in the plays it is notable that Bellow deals most directly with Jewish experience when the characters are identified as Jews — in the *Orange Soufflé*, which dramatizes the relations of an East Chicago Pole and a millionaire WASP, and in *The Wrecker* in which only an allusion to Samson among the Philistines implies a Jewish identity, as the middle-aged husband seems to express the frustration of immigrants cramped in small apartments and of Jews forced to swallow resentment in an alien culture. In the other two plays, Bummidge in *The Last Analysis* is a Jew who suffers from "humanitis," which is actually a personal malady, and Ithimar in *A Wen* is alienated not from a society (though that plays a part) but from a birthmark.

Bellow uses Jewish characters, then, but not necessarily as Jews. They are characters who happen to be Jews, and whose Jewish experience is important but not dominant in the story. Believing that "it is impossible for men to be rejected in great literature,"[7] which by definition recognizes our common humanity, Bellow fulfills David Daiches' observation that "the American Jewish writer has been liberated to use his Jewishness in a great variety of ways, to use it not aggressively or apologetically, but imaginatively as a writer probing the human condition. . . ."[8]

And yet we can't really understand Bellow's plays without recognizing the profound and often unconscious effect on him of his Jewish background. One of the most interesting definitions of the Jewish writer is that of Alfred Kazin, who refers to the intermingling in the *shtetl* of the spiritual and material worlds: "The so-called Jewish novel (there really is one, though only a few Jews have written it, and those who write it are not always Jews) takes place in a world that is unreal, never *our* world." Kazin thus fuses alienation and transcendence: Bellow's fiction, he wrote in 1971, "tells, as the best Jewish stories always do, of the unreality of this world as opposed to God's."[9] If many critics have rather curiously overlooked this quality of Bellow's work, it nonetheless suggests Bellow's deep kinship with the culture that provided the West with its concept of God. From Joseph in Bellow's first novel, whose story climaxes in a personal sense of the "strangeness" of existence, to Charles Citrine's rather desperate search for a form for his transcendental intuitions, Bellow has written about the sense of the transcendent in the midst of a materialistic and distractingly gaudy society.

As one reads Irving Howe's *World of Our Fathers*, moreover, one is struck by how many of Bellow's attitudes belong to the Jewish immigrant experience. The protagonist's deep suspicion of the street outside his window, for example, epitomized by Asa Leventhal's feeling that "he really did not know what went on about him, what strange things, savage things,"[10] might be related to the Jewish suspicion of a strange culture, in which, as Howe says, "the street enclosed dangers and lusts, shapeless enemies threatening all their plans for the young."[11] Bellow's fiction is filled not only with the famous Jewish literary types, the *schlemiel* and the *schlimazel*, but also with the lesser known.[12] When Earl Rovit decribes the character "generally known in the old Catskill Borscht Belt as the *meshuggah* — the wild, irresponsible, disconnected buffoon who oscillates between frenetic edges of obscenity and tearful sentimentality," he could be describing Bummidge.[13]

And then Bellow's prose is deeply influenced by Yiddish, ranging from the very specific qualities of repetition, question, inversion, allusion, and inflection — giving to a populace starved by the dry Hemingway manner a strongly human voice — to the more general and profound strategies of "verbal retrieval," in which the beset and overpowered Jew wins a victory by virtue of wit or language.[14] Bellow himself in the introduction to *Great Jewish Short Stories* describes language as a refuge for the oppressed as they right wrongs and express pain. And some critics have claimed that the mixture of the realistic and fantastic, so often characteristic of Bellow's style, even in subtle ways, is characteristically Jewish. Indeed, Bellow theorizes that storytelling itself is especially important to the Jew.

Thus Bellow reflects a typically Jewish love of language when he says that a writer would feel the American stage has "no language" and "lacks rhetoric or gesture" and that he wanted "to bring rhetoric back to the theater."[15] For the most striking influence of Jewish culture on a writer such as Bellow must be the emotional openness of his style, the ease and directness with which he negotiates the distance not just between the object and the feeling, but between the objective and subjective worlds, the external and the internal. To some extent the key here is energy, for the enthusiasm in a typically Jewish-American style picks up all, sweeping objective and subjective together in a rich mixture of motive and setting, present and history, quotidian and mythic, action and feeling. The grandiloquence of Yiddish explains quite a bit of this, of course, as does the emotional openness which, "ranging from a rich abundance to a wanton excess," in Irving Howe's words, "permeated the whole of Jewish immigrant life."[16]

I am not talking about sentimentality, of course, nor excessive emotion, but rather inwardness, the interior experience which involves will and desire and sensation and thought — all of which we mean by "our feelings." To note that a Jewish story tends to revolve around the feeling of the character is to say that it gives the human being his due, recognizing the importance of human reactions. How many Jewish-American writers give the interior of their subject, writing with the ease of a writer at home with feeling? To a non-Jew this is the most striking similarity among the Jewish-American writers, accounting for their warmth and perhaps even for their great appeal to the general American public. Just as Jewish prose sweeps up allusions to the creation and to the daily wash, so it moves from action to feeling, assuming remarkably in our Cartesian world that both the object and the human attitude are crucial, and equal.

Thus Bellow can worry that "the Jewish imagination has sometimes been found guilty of overhumanizing everything, of making too much of a case for us, for mankind, and of investing externals with too many meanings."[17] And thus, too, Bellow has defined his identity as a writer, a Jewish writer, in terms of human emotion. Joseph begins *Dangling Man* by attacking the emotional reticence associated with Hemingway. "Do you have feelings? There are correct and incorrect ways of indicating them. Do you have an inner life? It is nobody's business but your own. Do you have emotions? Strangle them."[18] Joseph will give in his book his "inward transactions," which is exactly what Bellow ten years later calls for in "The Pleasures and Pains of Theater-Going." Reviewing the year's plays, Bellow charged that audiences attend the theater "to test their powers of resistance to emotion. . . to find whether they can eat without tasting, view without suffering, make love without feeling and exist between winning and losing." What Bellow would prefer is an audience seeking to "be diverted, delighted, awed, and in search of opportunities to laugh and to cry."[19]

What can we make of this recurrent theme? Bellow began to write in an era when reticence, among other stiff-upper-lip WASP attitudes, was prized and practiced by the likes of Hemingway, Eliot, and John Crowe Ransom. A tight, careful form tended to parallel a tight, careful — and exclusive — social order, so that Bellow's plea for energy and sensation in the face of correctness was a demand for an open society. It also involved a new model for the American, for Hemingway and Eliot spawned an ideal of the unemotional and the understated, perhaps as a reaction to the "wasteland" they portrayed. To the WASP who'd had things pretty much his way for a while, the response to chaos was a buttoned lip. A thing doesn't exist if you don't acknowledge it, and at any rate, the situation was dire. But the Jews over the centuries had learned to live with chaos, and so could offer a more open kind of model, a type well-worn, harassed, and suffering, but large and dignified and persevering, finding his ideal in the human being itself. Such a character is Schlossberg in *The Victim*, a drama critic in the

Yiddish press who calls for emotion, for liveliness, for a sense of the magnificence of the character — sexual and otherwise. "She had mouth, she had flesh on her, she carried herself," he says of an ideal actress. "When she whispered tears came in your eyes, and when she said a word your legs melted."[20] She was simply a handsome, open human being.

Such was the dialectic in which Bellow engaged in the late forties. David Daiches has suggested a shift in American literature at this time and in these terms from what I will call an aesthetic of distance, involving precisely the emotional reticence of Hemingway, Eliot, and the New Critics (based on irony, control, and paradox) to an aesthetic of empathy or passion that stressed emotion, story, and a renewed interest in the human experience.[21] If such a shift occurred — and the plethora of writers who are now at home with feeling (John Updike, for instance) suggests that it did, evolving into a new, enriched realism — it was led and nurtured by such Jewish writers as Bernard Malamud and Saul Bellow.

But whatever its effect on literary history, the expression of feeling is absolutely central to Bellow's drama. The four plays[22] we have in print are almost uncannily alike in the themes they share — different though they are in character and setting — and in their celebration of emotion against the background of a middle class unable to deal with it. Bellow's plays tell us a great deal about his novels, in fact, as though the long, tricky passage across the footlights (or into dialogue) filtered out the subtlety and diversion that complicate his novels. The protagonists in the plays are cruder than those of the novels, and more naked in their needs and emotions, which is, of course, both the challenge of drama for a novelist and the liberation, as Bellow is free to indulge his love of the broad, farcical stroke.

The most striking fact about these four plays is that the protagonist is in every case an enthusiast. He has a vision, a dream that excites him, much to the discomfort of the more literal-minded, less emotional types about him. What is more, the protagonist gives up worldly concerns, money, position, power, for this dream — a sacrifice based upon a biting criticism of the American middle class. Bellow clearly feels the enthusiast is funny, often because he deals with ideas that are beyond him, but Bellow sympathizes with him too, and even champions him, giving the victory in both plays and novels to the imaginatively liberated.

We can see this theme in Bellow's first play, *The Wrecker*, in which the dream is that of tearing down an apartment which has been condemned by the city and from which the protagonist, "The Husband," refuses to move until the end of his lease. "The Husband" wants to vent with his axe the reservoir of resentment he's built up in fifteen years of married, middle-class life. "I'm getting rid of a lot of past life, dangerous to the soul," he says. "The past, you understand, is very dangerous if you don't deal with it" (203).

The Wrecker is a decent play in spite of the fact that Bellow is not quite sure where to take his idea. The concept is at once striking and familiar, revealing human emotions in a form that is dramatic and visible. One of its most attractive qualities is the good humor of the characters, as "The Husband" does not turn against "The Wife" in his disappointment — he's too active here, too much the happy maniac for any nastiness — and the wife for her part handles the implied insult of his frustration with patience. The play finds its true story, in fact, in the wife's struggle with what the wrecking implies about her marriage, even though the husband clearly means something general ("I learned my own limitations"), so that when she joins the husband, confessing that she, too, has stored up some resentments in the bedroom, we are delighted — and he's not sure this wrecking is a good idea.

Bellow has fun with this small, unconventional visionary; we laugh at the husband's obsession even as we nod in agreement with its content, the need to vent the accumulated emotions of an ordinary life. Bellow plays the man-woman relationship off the rigidity of an idealist. And he does the same thing in the next one-act play he published, *A Wen*. The protagonist, a scientist, does not so much attempt to destroy the resentments of his life as to leap beyond them, back to the moment of childhood ecstasy when the girl next door favored him with a glimpse of the birthmark on her inner thigh. At the time of the play, the scientist (Ithimar, or Iggy) has found nothing to compare with the beauty and delight of that feminine favor. Though powerful and famous, he tells Marcella (when he finds her in a flea-bitten Miami hotel) that his life is empty. To fill it, he desperately wants another look.

Bellow suggests a certain inevitable process of aging in this, perhaps reminiscent of Wordsworth's concern over the loss of childhood radiance. Bellow also means to criticize our middle-class American life, for Marcella's chiropodist husband is, she says, "typically American. . . . He acts cheerful but feels gloomy. . . . And you have to call him Doc, or he blows up. It's an ordinary life" (73). Ithimar is so familiar with such emptiness that when Marcella insists, he willingly risks his position and power for her favor.

A Wen is good theater for several reasons. Since Iggy wants only a look, Bellow enjoys the comedy of female modesty. A middle-aged Hadassah matron, Marcella worries that Ithimar is not interested in her as a *person*. Isn't it just the birthmark he's after? We laugh at Iggy's obsession even as we like him — he refuses to lie down and die. And in calling his obsession grotesque, Iggy is really too apologetic, for his desire catches not only the immense and innocent pleasure of intimacy as a gift, together with the sense in which things were larger and purer in our youth, but something real about the importance and impersonality of sex.

We can see in fact how much Bellow had grown in the ten years since *The Wrecker*, for Bellow offers not only a complete, sustaining situation and psychology, he has the playful pleasure of explaining the meaning of the wen. Its meaning is immeasurable to Iggy, of course, and so the small apricot-colored mark expands in its symbolic significance: it suggests the female favor, and then the central importance of small beauties and then, as Iggy makes like Henry Adams, the correlation of human emotion and physical power. The small mark becomes the occasion of a religious ecstasy that is at once great fun and convincing. Ithimar recalls to Marcella (as a hurricane develops outside) his first glimpse, "the secret moment of intimacy which silenced the whole world. When you disclosed that personal object, you and I were sealed in stillness. Then my soul took form, a distinct form. I experienced all the richness and glory for the first time consciously. I recognized beauty" (74). He later tells her that the wen contains the "secret of life" and is "the same diameter as the sun." When he thought of it, he says he felt "explosions within me like whole novae, scattering my matter through sidereal space. . ." (74).

If the hurricane striking just as Iggy gets his wish seems pat, it is not because Bellow has not prepared us for it; the power of the storm comically parallels the power of his emotion — and of the social taboos they are breaking. At bottom, *A Wen* is about the power of the imagination, but it's playful, mixing in a way we can call Jewish the earthy and the grand, the sad and the comic, the psychologically real and the farcically fantastic. Bellow gets some of his best comic effects in this potpourri, for in all of these plays he mixes — with comic inappropriateness — the sexual with something as solemn as urban renewal or Henry Adams. In *Orange Soufflé*, as light as its title promises, Bellow combines sex and sociology in a rather disturbing way. The visionary here is Hilda, a Polish whore who entertains Pennington, the WASP millionaire, once a month. After ten years, she'd like a little recognition ("If I were one of your employees I'd have plenty of seniority by now" [130]), but even more, she foresees a deadly existence when her sister moves in. Like Iggy and "The Husband," she is desperate to escape her middle-class life, and Pennington, so feeble he can't even don his own trousers, is her answer. She, too, has a vision: wouldn't it be grand if he set her up in Palm Beach as his hostess? She's learned to be a gourmet cook and has actually been out of the trade for years. The play begins as a light, sexy farce but becomes more serious as the desperate Hilda begs. Pennington does not want anything as complicated as a human being around, and so, in the one play with a downbeat ending, Hilda's soufflé fails to rise.

Thus the plays have the same kind of unity as Bellow's novels, returning within their different stories to similar themes. All three plays are about sex, about the emptiness of middle-class life, and about the imaginative individual attempting to persuade his more literal-minded and cautious associates to adopt an exciting and original idea. The three visionaries seek to break out of their seclusion, even though they are surrounded by a middle class that is narrow and even antithetical to the imagination. And as all three seek a new life — involving always the persuasion of another — they attempt to deal in their separate ways with the past, to break it up like "The Husband" or to recover it like Iggy or to build upon it, like Hilda — who would erase it, too.

This emphasis upon confronting the past is at the center of Bellow's work, for Bellow not only champions the emotional and the imaginative, he discovers the deepest function of his art in catharsis, which is one of the keys to the nostalgia that informs his work.[23] Almost all of the novels explore the past in some way, and by the time of *Humboldt's Gift*, reminiscence has become the central activity. Herzog portrays a man in the past remembering a man in the past remembering his childhood. Joseph reviews his many memories, past and present. Allbee is the living embodiment (he says) of a past wrong, while Tommy Wilhelm remembers vividly moments of his life-destroying error. More important, in each of the works the protagonist comes in contact with violence of death, whether in a dream, as in *Dangling Man*, or in a suicide or murder attempt, as in *The Victim* and the Basteshaw chapter in *Augie March*, or in a corpse, as in *Seize the Day* and *Henderson the Rain King*. Herzog almost commits murder, almost kills himself in an accident, and is almost incarcerated in a penitentiary. Mr. Sammler witnesses the corpse of Elya as well as the near murder of the black pickpocket, and *Humboldt's Gift* involves direct messages from a dead man about whom the protagonist broods.

What can we make of these patterns? It is clear that the play or novel works for the reader (and no doubt the author) in much the same way as the protagonist's memories work for him, offering an opportunity to vicariously rehearse an event (often violent or fatal) and thus discharge the emotion connected with it. Bellow's art drives to discover the hidden emotions of protagonist and reader. Its point is less theme than experience, a fact we have been slow to recognize: our modern realists like Bellow and Updike offer their readers (and audience) a vicarious experience that is *necessary* to them, purging as it does the accumulated emotions of daily life.

But in *The Last Analysis* Bellow uses this mechanism openly and for the purposes of comedy. He makes fun of his own art, presenting a comedian who has slipped because of his seriousness and who now, in his New York warehouse studio, seeks to combine laughter and homestyle psychoanalysis. Bummidge seeks a cure for "humanitis," and his technique he says is to act out "the main events of my life, dragging repressed material into the open by sheer force of drama" (74). In the first act he struggles to get enough money to go on closed-circuit TV before a gathering of psychoanalysts, and talks about performance with his associates and relatives — his agent Winkleman, his mistress Pamela, his sexy but platonic secretary Imogen, his sister, his wife, his son — many of whom resent the money he is squandering. He rehearses his method, remembering a few minor traumas such as getting caught fondling his sister's step-ins. In the second and last act, Bummidge gives his lecture-demonstration, taking himself through the birth trauma, conflict with his father, sexual adolescence, marriage and then death, the experience of the last triggering an ecstatic state in which he disposes of all those who had obstructed him and determines to proceed with an institute to advance his new therapy.

One of Bummy's chief motives is his rebellion against our shallow culture, for he sees that as an entertainer he had distracted people from the truth that lies beneath the surface confusion of our lives. He will now drive deep, as Bellow has always done, engaging in what is no less than a metaphysical quest. Bummy tells us that he is "on an expedition to recover the forgotten truth. . . . It's fantastic, intricate, complicated, hidden. How can you live without knowing? Madge, look deep! Infinite and deep!" (18). The "truth" is psychological too, for Bummy, like all the protagonists, fears something is wrong with him. Having pandered to his audiences, he now seeks an independent, dignified manhood — this, too, to be discovered by means of the Bummidge method. Bellow finds his climax in Bummy's reliving of his own birth, a play within a play, which Bummy entitles "The Birth of Philip Bomovitch" and plays lying on a sofa behind which, heads sticking through holes in a black cloth, his associates declaim. As the chorus talks, he is born, undergoes an unplanned attack of humanitis ("Farce follows horror into darkness. Deeper, deeper" [96]) and then undergoes his own death, too, from which to the "Hallelujah Chorus" he is reborn.

The result is a witty and imaginative play that ought to work quite well as theater, especially since the published play is a reworking of the version that flopped. Bellow reduced the number of characters, he tells us, and emphasized the "*mental* comedy" of Bummidge, making for greater consistency. For the truth is that Bellow did not find in farce the freedom he had sought. Although some have worried about the ending, it is clear that Bellow did too: the revised play makes good formal sense. Why does Bummy now cure himself, on camera as it were, having used this technique for years? The answer is that the actual performance was necessary to heighten the emotion, creating the pressure that drives the repressed material into the open. Bummy does not discover any insights into himself, moreover, because the point is less insight than catharsis — or say that the imagined experience of his own death offers insights that cannot be articulated. Psychoanalysis slides into religion, self-analysis becoming epiphany, but then psychoanalysis has always had a kind of religiosity, and Bellow prepares us for Bummy's revelation by Bummy's comic assumption, at the end of Act I, of Christ's position on the cross.

Bummy does die, comically, and his ghostly, abstracted demeanor at the end of the play combines serenity, rebirth, and high humor. Theater professionals tell me *The Last Analysis* not only plays well, but that Bellow knows a great deal about the theater.[24] The first act reminds us of *Volpone*, for example, as a series of rapacious characters visit the protagonist. Bellow also gets high marks for daring — the concept of a character dredging up repressed material is inventive, offering risks the playwright accepted. Bellow has typically conceived of a grand idea within which he can present a more or less chaotic potpourri of characters, events, and comic bits. As character after character comes on stage, the influence of vaudeville is clear: each encounter could be viewed almost as a sketch.

We like Bummy then, and we enjoy Bellow's wit, as he develops a series of punchy, aphoristic lines, parodying academic research and professional meetings, self-help and deep theories, existentialists and back-room messiahs. And yet the play is flawed, or offers dangers to the unwary director. For what Bummy has repressed and must now purge — what he recalls throughout the bulk of the play — is family friction, bad feeling, resentment. His obstacle in the present, the real antagonist in the play, is once again family and friends. If the main business of the play is Bummy's obsession with an idea, as Bellow has said, its basic conflict is between Bummidge and the people around him. What does he do when he is reborn, strength discovered? He tells them off, one by one — wife, mistress, agent, son — and then orders them hauled away.

Beat it, the whole gang of you. . . .
A device appears above. Bella, Pamela, Winkleman, Mott, Madge, Fiddleman and Max stare up.
Winkleman: A net! Duck! Look out!
All are caught in the net. Bertam runs up like the ratcatcher he is to see what he has trapped. (116-17)

The farce often sweeps away the hangers-on in a catharsis of hostility and justice, but in this play the high spirits are marred by a certain misanthropy, as though the farcical form permitted Bellow's own personal feelings to come to the fore. And indeed, Bellow defines "humanitis" in precisely such terms. In a version of the play published in *Partisan Review* in 1962, Bellow had Bummidge say that "Humanitis means that you begin to come on with another person, but all of a sudden you can't bear him anymore. Take the sonofabitch away!"[25] He softens this in the final version, but "humanitis" remains other people. The reborn Bummidge, having relived some very unpleasant experiences, confesses a revulsion: "Please — please don't crowd. Oh, don't touch! It makes me cold in the bowels. I feel you breathing on me. See how my skin is wincing" (109).

Such lines give the lie to a more or less accepted view of Bellow as the champion of community. Certainly the protagonist desires community, but he desires the opposite too, for the people around him are distracting. He can triumph only by escaping them — and by surmounting an unclean world too, rendered here not in the description of the novel, but in dialogue, characters, attitudes. Bummidge has stopped making people laugh, he says, because "I can't stand the sound they make. And I feel hit by the blast of sickness from their lungs" (8). Bummy's colleague is a ratcatcher who offers chopped liver prepared with his own hands. Bummidge exhorts his colleagues, "Onwards to the Tilby. We have to clean up the floors and purge the smell of blood" (118).

Bummy's rejection of his associates makes *The Last Analysis* a notably non-Jewish play. Bummy is himself a Jewish character, as we have seen, but he ends up alone, like the American cowboy with a sidekick or two. So, too, do the protagonists in the novels, so that we must confess that the Bellow hero defines his final victory in terms of solitude. Or is the truth about us to be found in such solitude, since we fantasize about it so much? Bellow seems to tell us that we are not nearly as gregarious as we think we are, and after such novels as *Portnoy's Complaint* and *Good As Gold*, not to mention Bellow's own stories, "The Old System" and "The Silver Dish," we might want to argue that discomfort with a close family is indeed Jewish. Perhaps it is now the tension between the self and the relatives that captures the imagination of Jewish writers.

Or is such ambivalence very Jewish indeed? We might well argue that "humanitis" is a personal or emotional equivalent to the very real Jewish ambivalence about assimilation. To join the larger community is to end a painful alienation, obviously, but it is also to risk losing one's identity. No wonder characters such as Augie March first join and then resist the smothering community of their fellows. And then, perhaps deeper than the problem of assimilation, is a Jew's knowledge of the world's treachery: in a very personal way, Bellow's protagonists live out the conflicts of a people who have been persecuted.

Is there any doubt that many of the other themes and situations in this play are Jewish? The emphasis on purity certainly is, though not many cultural historians comment on it. God's demand that the Jews be holy and righteous requires — as orthodox law suggests — a life of physical purity, including diet. Like the other protagonists, moreover, Bummidge is a visionary, and is surrounded by unbelieving companions, living a personal form of Jewish alienation. Bummy's concern with the past is obviously Jewish, for, as Irving Howe puts it, "nothing is more deeply ingrained in the Jewish experience than the idea of the past," and the problem of dealing with it in some way "forms the major burden of their art."[26] Psychoanalysis has been called the "Jewish science," since it was invented and widely practiced by Jews, and we have already commented on the Jewish emphasis on ideas, on talking, on language. Alfred Kazin describes Bummy with precision when he cites "the age-old Jewish belief that salvation is in thinking well — to go to the root of things, to become a kind of scientist of morals, to seek the ultimate forces that rule us."[27]

And the Yiddish theater? Certainly it stressed energy and spectacle and emotion over form or coherence, but I think it influenced Bellow in an even stronger, though more subtle, way. For in the Yiddish theater actors sought to be larger than life, as Schlossberg tells us in *The Victim*, to act in the open and sweeping Russian manner, indulging their emotions and projecting their nobility. Part of Bummy's need for a new self derives from his sense of having fallen away from a richer, deeper humanity, of being somehow smaller than his ancestors. Though the delightful Bummidge seems large enough, the fact remains that he is driven by an image of humanity that owes something to the large, full, exuberant character of the Yiddish theater. But even more important than that, in terms of Bellow's Jewishness, is the play's striking internality. In *Great Jewish Short Stories* Bellow cites the old man who, in his despair at lightening a burden, summons death. But when the Angel of Death appears he changes his mind: "I can't get these sticks upon my back and wonder if you'd mind giving me a hand."[28] We find the old man funny and lovable in his will to live, his wit (as he retrieves the situation verbally) and his sass. But most importantly, we find him vivid because of the flash of the internal; as we stand outside of him, watching the old man talk to the Angel of Death, we get a glimpse of his inner self, a change of feeling that makes him at just that moment blossom into life.

Such it seems to me is the Jewish genius. And certainly it is Bellow's, at least in these plays, since they, too, are based on feeling, gaining their power from the pleasure of a middle-class verisimilitude: we are delighted by our surprised recognition of the emotions portrayed. What is important perhaps is the fact that Bellow finds an external way of expressing those feelings — the point of his use of farce. For Bellow can give us in farce the character turned inside out, a character revealing his inner life in an imaginary external world. The plays thus bring forth to public view emotions that would otherwise remain unarticulated. They make us recognize our community, really, since we share those feelings, or many of them, and thus are in on the secret. And they make us laugh, providing comedies that are the world writ funny — comedies that permit Bellow to say what he really thinks (as Bummy's method makes a kind of sense) and to express what he must.

Notes

1. For an interesting discussion of this point, see James M. Mellard, "Consciousness Fills the Void: Herzog, History, and The Hero in the Modern World," *Modern Fiction Studies* 25 (Spring 1979): 81-85.
2. Saul Bellow, "My Man Bummidge," *New York Times*, 27 September 1964, Section 2, p. 1. In the late 1950s Bellow also collaborated with Mary Otis on an adaptation of "Seize the Day" for the stage. This manuscript, which is in The University of Chicago collection, received only a reading (with Mike Nichols playing Tommy Wilhelm). See Richard Gil-

man, *Commonweal* (29 March 1963): 21. Another Bellow novel, *The Victim*, was adapted to the stage by Leonard Lesley in 1952. See Wolcott Gibbs, *The New Yorker* (10 May 1952): 54.

3. John Simon, "Theater Chronicle," review of *The Last Analysis*, *Hudson Review* 17 (1964-65): 557.

4. Walter Kerr, "Three Writers New to the Theatre," *New York Times* 25 December 1966, sec. 2, 3.

5. Gerald Nachman, "A Talk with Saul Bellow," *New York Post Magazine* (4 October 1964): 6.

6. Saul Bellow, *Writers at Work*, Third Series, ed. George Plimpton (New York: Viking Compass, 1967), 183.

7. Saul Bellow, "The Jewish Writer and The English Literary Tradition," *Commentary* 8 (1949): 366.

8. David Daiches, "Breakthrough?" in *Contemporary American Jewish Literature: Critical Essays*, ed. Irving Malin (Bloomington: Indiana UP, 1973), 37-38.

9. Alfred Kazin, *Bright Book of Life* (Boston: Little, Brown, 1973), 132-33.

10. Saul Bellow, *The Victim* (New York: Viking Compass, 1956), 94.

11. Irving Howe, *World of Our Fathers* (New York: Harcourt Brace Jovanovich, 1976), 261.

12. Sanford Pinsker, *The Schlemiel as Metaphor* (Carbondale: Southern Illinois UP, 1971).

13. Earl Rovit, "Jewish Humor and American Life," in *Herzog*, ed. Irving Howe (New York: Viking, 1976), 515.

14. Sarah Blacher Cohen, *Saul Bellow's Enigmatic Laughter* (Urbana: U of Illinois P, 1970), 20.

15. Bellow, "Bummidge," 5; and Robert Gutwillig, "Talk with Saul Bellow," *New York Times Book Review* (20 September 1964): 40.

16. Howe, 222.

17. Saul Bellow, "Introduction," *Great Jewish Short Stories* (New York: Dell, 1963), 10.

18. Saul Bellow, *Dangling Man* (New York: Meridian, 1960), 9.

19. Saul Bellow, "Pleasures and Pains of Playgoing," *Partisan Review* 21 (1954): 312, 313.

20. *The Victim*, 126.

21. Daiches, 33.

22. Pages in parentheses are to the following editions: *The Wrecker*, in *Seize the Day* (New York: Viking, 1956), 193-211; *A Wen*, *Esquire* (January 1965): 72-74, 111; *Orange Soufflé*, *Esquire* (October 1965): 130-31, 134, 136; *The Last Analysis* (New York: Viking, 1965).

23. For an extended discussion of this, see Keith Opdahl, "'Stillness in the Midst of Chaos': Plot in the Novels of Saul Bellow," *Modern Fiction Studies* 25 (Spring 1979): 15-28.

24. I am indebted here to Fred Nelson, director, playwright, and teacher.

25. Saul Bellow, "Humanitis," *Partisan Review* 29 (1962): 345.

26. Irving Howe, "Introduction," *Jewish-American Stories* (New York: National American Library, 1977), 4.

27. Kazin, *Bright Book*, 134.

28. *Great Jewish Stories*, 11.

*   *   *

Mr. Sammler's Planet (1970)

Mr. Sammler's Planet
Irving Howe

From book to book, ornament and variations apart, Saul Bellow has really had one commanding subject: the derangements of the soul in the clutter of our cities, the poverty of a life deprived of order and measure. His work has in part continued the line of sensibility established by T.S. Eliot in *The Waste Land*, for in Chicago and New York one can ask as urgently as in London, "What branches grow out of this stony rubbish?" But Bellow has also diverged, in the more original portions of his work, from the Eliot line of sensibility, for he has come to feel that the once-liberating perceptions embodied in Eliot's great poem have, through the erosion of popularity, become clichés. Bellow now writes from a conviction that even today men can establish a self-ordering discipline which rests on a tentative-sardonic faith in the value of a life without faith. As he remarks in his latest and extremely brilliant novel *Mr. Sammler's Planet*:

> . . . people exaggerated the tragic accents of their condition. They stressed too hard the disintegrated assurances; what formerly was believed, trusted, was now bitterly circled in black irony. The rejected bourgeois black of stability thus translated. That too was improper, incorrect. People justifying idleness, silliness, shallowness, distemper, lust — turning former respectability inside out.

There is always a danger in the work of an urban novelist like Bellow that his books will turn into still another tiresome afterword to the literary talk about Angst and Alienation; but what has saved Bellow from that common fate has been his fierce insistence that, no matter how heavy the cloud of despair hanging over this (or any other) time, we can still find some pleasure in sociability and our bodies, or, at least, still experience that root sense of obligation which the mere fact of being human imposes on us.

From *Harper's* 240 (Feb. 1970): 106, 108, 112, 114.

It is from such sentiments that Bellow moves into his latest book. More and more, in recent years, he has found himself cast as an adversary — not always openly, sometimes too cagily — of the dominant styles of our culture. Growing older, entering those hard years when one realizes that the middle of the journey is past, Bellow has not only become a master of his own special idiom, that verbal impasto which mixes demotic richness with mandarin eloquence, racy-tough street Jewishness with high-flown intellectual displays; he has also found his place, no longer a dangling man, as person and writer, and set forth on a stubborn, uncertain quest for the cup of wisdom: that cup, if it exists at all, in which the veteran artist hopes to squeeze some essence of contemplation out of the wastes of experience.

For putting it so bluntly Bellow isn't likely to thank me, and indeed his characteristic strategy, at least until this new book, has been to protect his flanks through smoke screens of elaborate comic rhetoric. He has maintained two narrative voices signifying two world-outlooks, the first sententious and the second sardonic, yet with the declamations of the sententious voice never quite undone, and sometimes even slyly reinforced, by the thrusts of the sardonic voice has kept the reader on his toes, precisely where he belongs.

Mr. Sammler's Planet is set in a milieu that has become Bellow's own, a created province of the imagination quite as much as Wessex is Hardy's and Yoknapatawpha Faulkner's. The Upper West Side is a grimy place, at once unfit for human habitation and the scene of what must, I suppose, be called an advanced civilization. It is ugly, filthy, dangerous; it reeks with dog shit; its streets are crammed with the flotsam of society: winos, junkies, pushers, whores, grifters; yet here too are stately refugees, stuffy reformers, literary intellectuals, eager Puerto Ricans, and most of all, elderly Jews haunted by memories of sweatshops and concentration camps and no longer able to take life as incessant struggle. In this menagerie of integration, anomie, and good feeling, people still manage to live.

Bellow first immortalized this neighborhood in *Seize the Day*, but the Upper West Side in that great novella was mainly a bright-colored backdrop to a personal drama. In *Mr. Sammler's Planet*, however, the Upper West Side is more than setting, it becomes a tangible sign of the nature of our time. In the Upper West Side, as Bellow sees it, the continuities of ordinary living, by no means always a triumph but never to be sneered at, manage somehow to coexist with the raspy notional foolishness our culture casts off like smoke. The Upper West Side becomes transformed in Bellow's fiction into a principle of sorts, a mixture of health and sickness exemplifying our condition, and not merely through his great gift for evoking every street, every figure, every shade of light and dark, but still more through the saturation of his characters with the spirit of the place. On a smaller scale, Bellow does for the Upper West Side what Lawrence has done for the Midlands and

Hardy for Dorset: a linkage of setting and figure so close that the two come to seem inseparable parts in a tradition of shared experience.

Mr. Sammler is a Polish Jew in his seventies. In his early years he had worked as a correspondent in London, which accounts for his old-fashioned liberal courtliness and values; later he escaped miraculously from a death convoy in the Nazi camps. Sated with experiences beyond absorption and reflections forever conjectural, Artur Sammler looks out upon America in the sixties: its violence, its coarseness, its jabbery mindlessness, its sexual cult. He is not surprised, having lived in Europe after the first world war; he is alarmed, knowing that history can repeat itself. Yet Sammler is not a polemicist, he is too canny for easy visions of apocalypse. Preparing for death, he knows the world is no longer his. He looks, wonders, muses.

Sammlen means "to collect" in Yiddish, and Sammler, like all those compulsive talkers, half-clown and half-philosopher, in Bellow's novels, is a collector of experience, sometimes a tentative sorter of conclusions. First of all his *Sammlung* consists of relatives, mostly female, the lot of whom are presented by Bellow with wonderful vivacity and good-humored tartness. Shula, Sammler's daughter, was saved by a Polish convent during the holocaust and now is "almost always at Easter" a "week-long Catholic." Mercilessly devoted to the higher things in life, this amiable loon believes her father is writing an inspired memoir of H. G. Wells. The complications of the plot, if there is a plot, devolve partly around Shula stealing an Indian scholar's manuscript because she thinks it will help her daddy. Any day on Broadway, our garbaged Mortality Row, you can see Shula between 72nd and 86th Streets:

> She turned up in a miniskirt of billiard-table green, revealing legs sensual in outline, but without inner sensuality; at the waist a broad leather belt; over shoulders, bust, a coarse strong Guatemalan embroidered shirt; on her head a wig such as a female impersonator might put on at a convention of salesmen.

Next, Sammler's niece Margotte, also mad for culture but in a more *gemütlich* Weimar way: a dumpy lady prepared to discuss Hannah Arendt's theory of evil (or anyone else's theory about anything) all day long, while looking helplessly for a piece of salami with which to make a sandwich. And last, Angela, "one of those handsome, passionate, rich girls . . . always an important social and human category," who is driving herself crazy through sheer sexual concentration. The derangements of the first two women are of earlier decades, Angela's of this very moment.

This cast, with several supporting players, is more than a bit mad yet not at all insufferable. Human all too human, it is presented by Bellow with an affectionate sardonic detail, and the incidents that pile up with seeming casualness bring them into quick changes of relationship, all calculated to set off Sammler's dilemmas and reflections. He detects a black pickpocket, superbly elegant and powerful, working the Riverside bus; the pickpocket, aware that he has been seen but not frightened, follows Sammler into an apartment lobby; and there, as evidence of his superiority of being — quite as if he'd been reading certain reviews — he exposes to Sammler his formidable penis. It is an act of symbolism Sammler is prepared to understand, if not quite appreciate.

In another episode, again shot through with the fevers of our moment, Sammler accepts an invitation to lecture at Columbia about England during the thirties:

"Old Man! you quoted Orwell before."

"Yes?"

"You quoted him to say that British radicals were all protected by the Royal Navy? . . ."

"Yes, I believe he did say that."

"That's a lot of shit."

Sammler could not speak.

"Orwell was a fink. He was a sick counter-revolutionary. It's good he died when he did. And what you are saying is shit." Turning to the audience, extending violent arms and raising his palms like a Greek dancer, he said, "Why do you listen to this effete old shit? What has he got to tell you? His balls are dry. He's dead. He can't come."

Lively-odd figures, brilliantly managed incidents — but what does it all come to? That, until the very last paragraph, is the question one keeps asking about *Mr. Sammler's Planet*.

Perhaps there's an answer of sorts in the lectures and speeches, more in the style of *Herzog* than *Seize the Day*, that Bellow scatters through his pages? For whole sections the book moves into a genre somewhat like those conversations Thomas Love Peacock wrote in the nineteenth century, in which voices of varying refinement representing disembodied but fixed opinions are set up in an interplay of friction. There are readers who have always felt these portions of Bellow's novels to be digressive or pretentious, in any case lessening the immediate emotional impact of his work. I think such criticisms mainly — not always — ill-conceived, first because Bellow is a man of high intelligence so that his generalized commentary is intrinsically absorbing, and second because he has the rare gift of transforming dialectic into drama, casuistry into comedy, so that one is steadily aware of the close relationship between his discursive passages and the central narrative. [. . .]

Yet we are still dealing with fragments, episodes, set pieces: our most gifted novelist turning somersaults and negotiating leaps like Villella on a spree. Is that all? Are we not bound to expect some ultimate unity of action and theme, no matter how slyly achieved?

It is there, but so risky in execution that many readers, I suspect, will deny its presence. Throughout the book Sammler keeps returning to the hospital room of a friend, Dr. Arnold Elya Gruner, a rich and crafty man, sometime Mafia abortionist, soured father of Angela the handsome nymph, and yet, as we come to see, a decent man in quite commonplace ways. Elya had rescued Sammler and Shula after the war, had given them money with which to live: a not very costly, and if you wish, a *bourgeois* gesture. Sammler knows his faults, but knows too that in this ordinary man there are strengths and resources of a kind we must have if we are not to perish on this earth.

An old man implicated, despite his wish for detachment, in the lunacies of his daughter, the gabble of his niece, the suicidal thrust of Angela, the brutalities of the Columbia heckler, the threat of the pickpocket, and a host of other menacing fantasies and realities that rise out of the very pavements of the Upper West Side, Sammler all the while keeps yielding himself to the most fundamental themes of gravity: a man is dying, a man who has been good to me. He has shown himself responsible to me, I must be responsible to him. Gradually all the foolishness of Sammler's days, all the absurdity and ugliness of his encounters, all the brittleness and bravura of his thought, give way. There remains only the imperative of the human obligation. Standing over the dead body of his quite unremarkable friend, Sammler speaks the final words of the book:

> He was aware that he must meet, and he did meet — through all the confusion and degraded clowning of this life through which we are speeding — he did meet the terms of his contract. The terms which, in his inmost heart, each knows. As I know mine. As all know. For that is the truth of it — that we all know, God, that we know, that we know, we know, we know.

These lines, like all of Bellow's endings, constitute an overwhelming stroke. Carrying its truth as a precious cargo I yet find myself wondering whether Eliot, a writer of different persuasion, might not ask, "Yes, in our inmost hearts we know, or at least remember, but how do we know? Is it not through the memory of traditions lapsed and beliefs denied?" What Bellow might say in reply I would not presume to guess, but the strength of the position from which he would speak seems very clear to me. Of all the American Jewish writers of the last few decades, Bellow is not merely the most gifted by far, but the most serious — and the most Jewish in his seriousness. In him alone, or almost alone, the tradition of immigrant Jewishness, minus the *Schmaltz* and *Schmutz* the decades have stuccoed onto it, survives with a stern dignity. Sammler speaking at the end is something like a resurrected voice: experience fades, explanations deceive, the iron law of life is the obligation we owe one another. The *Sammlung* is complete.

*   *   *

Though He Slay Me . . .
Alfred Kazin

The great thing that some Jewish writers have — sometimes the only thing they have — is coming up against the cumulative, unendingly extreme, anomalous, "absurd" experience of being Jews. What has happened to "Jews," not just certain Jews, is so terrible and "unbelievable" that again and again with Jewish writers the thing to notice is this often innocent contact with the inexpressible that for many Jews is their only recognition of the supernatural. There is that touch of something "unnatural," not to be understood in and through history alone, positively magical and awesome in its concentrated maleficence. This can be — is — often too much for ordinary intelligence. It is often too much for those many young Jews today who prefer not to absorb the fact that between 1942 and 1945 a million Jewish children were done to death for reasons unclear also to many of their murderers.

Of all contemporary "Jewish" novelists, Saul Bellow seems to me the most responsive, the most penetrating, the most unyielding in his ability to express the extraordinariness of the Jewish "situation." The great thing to me about his work is the ability to express the texture, the vibration, the extremity of experiences that do not make Jews nobler or more intelligent than other people, but that have certainly been different. Jewish experience has been too much for many Jews who have been too conventional in intelligence, too conformist, even too terrified to rise to the apocalyptic demands of the subject in this first great era of "Jewish" imaginative writing. Bellow has in every way made intelligence, independence, and terror the texture of his work.

Unlike the more purely imaginative but now gently cynical Isaac Bashevis Singer writing about a country of the dead, Bellow evidently sees the whole Jewish "experience" as immediately present in the streets of New York or Chicago. Although he is now in his middle fifties and has "succeeded" in every way that a "leading American novelist" can, each of his fictions is a recurrent *agonia*, describes the same desperate struggle for life — by which he means a more refined consciousness. It is the most concentrated example I know of in contemporary fiction of the age-old Jewish belief that the only possible salvation lies in thinking well, which is thinking one's way to the root of all creation, thinking one's way to the ultimate reason of things.

Thinking is for Bellow the most accessible form of virtue. Probably he is the only contemporary American novelist who just now equates virtue *wholly* with thinking well rather than with any particular form of action. It may be that the romantic emphasis on "action," now so popular with intellectuals who are usually as passive as they have

---

From *New York Review of Books* (3 Dec. 1970): 3-4.

always been, sits especially badly with a middle-aged intellectual Jew who has good reason to have a horror of what the Nazis used to call "an action." But Bellow is in any case not a very dramatic novelist, and melodramatic things tend to occur in his novels as a way of interrupting the hero's reflections. He is utterly unusual among contemporary novelists both in his fierce insistence on right thinking, wisdom, *philosophia* — and in the evident way his personae attain their interest for *him* by their ability to express the right opinion.

The protagonists of Bellow's novels are generally the voices of his own intellectual evolution, from Joseph the dangling man in 1944 to old Artur Sammler in 1970. If an anthology is ever put together from his novels, it will take the form of a breviary, an intellectual testament, from protagonists whose most felicitous brilliancies were expressed not to other characters but in diaries, letters to public men and dead philosophers that were never mailed, arias to the reader like Augie March's, thoughts that like Artur Sammler's are neural dreams wholly in the privacy of one's consciousness and that *cannot* be expressed to the other characters — they are too severe, too disapproving.

Mr. Sammler's Planet is a brilliantly austere set of opinions, more than usually impressive because of the decisive intellectual elegance that by now Bellow has turned into a language of his own. But Sammler's opinions are set in a context so uncharitable, morally arrogant toward every other character in the book but one, and therefore lacking in dramatic satisfaction, that the book becomes a *cri de coeur* that does not disguise the punitive moral outrage behind it. Bellow has always had a remarkable ability to find narrative forms for the urgency of his own undisguised thinking, but I suspect that his more lasting fictions will be those whose heroes are not *exactly* as intelligent as he is — *The Victim* and *Seize the Day*.

In these books the weight of the world's irrationality and injustice falls heavily upon human beings who earn our sympathy by their inability to understand all that is happening to them and why it is happening to *them*. Asa Leventhal at the end of *The Victim*, having been persecuted, terrified, exploited by a Gentile who accuses the Jew of having persecuted *him*, ends up civilly saying to Albee, "Wait a minute, what's your idea of who runs things?" Tommy Wilhelm, who in one day realizes that he has lost his wife, mistress, father, money, God, can sense something of the unknown depths of his suffering only by identifying with a dead stranger into whose funeral he has stumbled by accident. These perplexities and incomprehensions are truly evocative of what remains in fact the "existentialist situation" — the tragedy of Jews and non-Jews who in the course of human events are never up to their own suffering, cannot fully take it in, and have learned only that their suffering has its reasons of which reason knows nothing.

Artur Sammler, on the other hand, is so openly Bellow's mind now, in its most minute qualifications, that I am torn between my ad-

miration for the man's exemplary intellectual style and my amazement
that Bellow's hero should lack opacity in every side of life except his
relations with other human beings. Of course Sammler is an old man, a
widower, with only one eye left to him by the Nazis, whose wife was
shot to death in the same Polish pit from which he managed to escape
past so many dead bodies (the fable that haunts certain Jewish writers).
Sammler is too old, too experienced, too intelligent, too cultivated and
well-bred (and too much at the mercy of relatives on the Upper West
Side of New York for whom he is the only Wisdom Figure) to be
"with it" in the numerous pseudo-events now so dear to the young. He
also spent years in England, a correspondent for Polish papers, learning to furl his umbrella and to keep his opinions to himself.

But none of these things really accounts for the fact that Artur
Sammler dislikes everyone he sees on the ugly alarm-laden streets of
the West Side and disapproves of everyone he knows except a vague
kinsman, a doctor who got him to America and supports him. He dislikes all the women especially. The evident fact is that Mr. Sammler is
The Jew who, especially after Hitler, has taken the measure of this
world, of the treacheries and lusts that are its greatest pleasure, and has
decided, exactly as the less official but more profound sages among the
Jews have always decided, that this world can be a very bad place
indeed, that the human heart *is* the world, and that the only thing for us
is the soul in its intelligence of the Creator, the soul in its exclusive
and excluding disposition to "know" what is real and what is not.

The unsatisfactory thing about Mr. Sammler is that he is always
right while most other people are usually wrong — sinfully so. More
than most Jewish intellectuals, Artur Sammler is right and has to be
right all the time. The Jewish passion for ideological moralism, for
ratiocination as the only passion that doesn't wear out (and doesn't
interfere with other passions), that passion has never really been done
in fiction — there is no precedent for its peculiar self-assertiveness, so
different from luxuriating in one's own ego in the style of Stephen
Dedalus. In Bellow's novel, profoundly moralistic and world-weary,
the hero's total identity with his own thought, his total rejection of
other people because of *their* thought, thus poses a lack of incident, an
invitation to symbolic politics, like the now celebrated scene in which a
Negro pickpocket follows old, delicate Mr. Sammler to his apartment
house and exposes his gigantic penis, or the corollary scene in which
Mr. Sammler's mad Israeli son-in-law beats the same Negro almost to
death near Lincoln Center.

Bellow is even cleverer in finding a *style* for Sammler's silent
thinking than he was in finding the form of unsent letters for Herzog's
equally continuous meditations. The style is one of the lightest,
featheriest, mental penciling, an intellectual shorthand, in brusque city
images, that answers to the traditional contractedness of Jewish
thought. The great historian of Jewish mysticism, Gershom Scholem,

points out that the favorite form for Jewish sages has always been the shortest. (Bellow's fiction is best when it is shortest; his recent stories are particularly striking.) His intellectual at-homeness with Sammler's thoughts is so assured that over and over again one has the Blakean experience of reading thoughts expressed as sensations.

But what are certainly not Blakean are the austere, dismissive jeremiads, the open contempt for the women in the book as crazy fantasists, improvident, gross, careless sexpots, "birds of prey." There is a brilliantly immediate, unsparing knowledge of other human beings' limitations and appearances which in its moral haughtiness becomes as audible to the reader as sniffing, and is indeed that. There is so strong a sense of physical disgust with all one's distended, mad-eyed, pushing neighbors on the West Side that there seems nothing in the book to love but certain past opinions, Meister Eckhardt, and Sammler's wife's "nephew" Dr. Gruner, who earns our sympathy by his disgust with this greedy errant children as much as by his love of Mr. Sammler himself.

American fiction today is so topical in its interests, so plain and non-experimental in style, so consumed by what novelists, too, have come to think of as the "public interest," that *Mr. Sammler's Planet* is distinguished from other novels only by the formidable intelligence of its author and the profoundly intellectual wit that has formed Bellow's style. In a fiction that seems more and more disposed to express only our public troubles, to discourage the invention of any great new myths, *Mr. Sammler's Planet* seems a normal political novel of our day, didactic to a fault. With his stern sense of justice, Bellow wants to right the balance after so much evil. God lives.

* * *

Bellow on Modernism
Charles T. Samuels

Mr. Sammler's Planet is middling Bellow: better than *Henderson*, *Herzog* and *Dangling Man*, though it shares with those books defects in dramatic or conceptual plausibility; not so good as *Augie March*, *The Victim*, and *Seize the Day*, whose palpable urban setting and memorable grotesques it also shares. But even middling Bellow approaches the zenith of contemporary fiction. Who else gives us so much vitality and such deep thought, such pleasure in an imagined world and so much concern for the one we inhabit?

This last quality makes Bellow more than a novelist, places him in the company of our major writers, all of them men who would tell us how to live. In his Hopwood lecture on "The Future of Fiction," he

From *New Republic* (7 Feb. 1970): 27-30.

proclaimed that "the imagination is looking for new ways to express virtue"; and expressing virtue negatively, by exposing the ways in which men evade it, has always been his primary goal. Therefore, Bellow's characters are usually egomaniacal enemies of human community whom the author, sometimes through a lone hero, relentlessly criticizes.

Because the action in Bellow typically proves the presence of vice while the rhetoric argues for virtue, none of his books (except *Seize the Day*) is fully coherent or convincing. Comic caricatures and scintillating ideas abound to a degree that makes Bellow the only contemporary novelist who entertains and informs in equal measure; and it therefore seems ungrateful to point out that the two halves of his appeal do not cooperate. I don't enjoy having to make the point again about *Mr. Sammler's Planet* — an intelligent, beautifully written book — but its imperfect connection between action and idea invites criticism.

Bellow's hero and *raisonneur* is a refugee intellectual with one good eye, survivor both of early twentieth-century optimism (via H. G. Wells) and of the Nazi holocaust that exposed its pretensions. Resettled in America during the sixties, Mr. Sammler is distressed to learn that madness and solipsism continue to thrive, that modern life has brought not the progress envisioned by Wells but a new cult of unbridled egotism, validated by modernist thought. Sammler is a traditionalist, a believer in institutions and constraints, and their apparently universal breakdown makes him doubt if the world he knows — his planet — has much future.

As the story begins, he accidentally sees a black pickpocket working an uptown bus. To his surprise, he finds himself fascinated. Later, he discovers crime in his own family. Shula, his middle-aged batty daughter steals an Indian scholar's manuscript about moon-colonization because she thinks it essential to her father's research. Compounding this disillusionment, Sammler is begged by Wallace Gruner, son of a dying relative who had been Sammler's benefactor, to discover the whereabouts of money he believes the old man to have illicitly earned and then hidden. In short, a wise survivor of mankind's worst brutality is confronted by vice and selfishness close to home, thereby confirming his doubts about the whole species, and inspiring a flood of rumination on which the novel moves.

The ruminations are splendid, but they are insufficiently warranted by the behavior of Sammler's relatives who mostly parody vice. Shula does cause a great deal of trouble, but nothing that can be taken seriously. Moreover, her motives are sweetly filial (though Bellow unconvincingly solicits our sense of outrage by darkly intimating she stole the manuscript to meet its author). The paragraph in which Bellow links Shula with a more obviously demonic pickpocket suggests inflation of a peccadillo:

. . . even Shula, though a scavenger or magpie, had never actually stolen before. Then suddenly she too was like the Negro pickpocket. From the black side, strong currents were sweeping over everyone. Child, black, redskin the unspoiled Seminole against the horrible Whiteman. Millions of civilized people wanted oceanic, boundless, primitive, neck-free nobility, experienced a strange release of galloping impulses and acquired the peculiar aim of sexual niggerhood for everyone.

Nor is sufficient cause given for this thumping denunciation by Wallace Gruner, whose zealous search for his father's cash causes him to burst the water pipe he suspects of being a hiding place, thereby farcically flooding the old man's house.

The book contains several other representatives of modern vice but, like Shula and Wallace, they are too comic, or their actions are too trivial to serve as adequate stimuli for Sammler's powerful responses. More acceptable as a representative of chaos and dark night is the pickpocket, for after learning that Sammler has been watching him, he corners the old man in an apartment house lobby and by forcing Sammler to see his blackman's powerful penis, symbolically warns him of a potency that cannot easily be fought. Although this action is obtrusively meaningful, it does have a certain sinister effect that typifies the first part of the book, for which it provides a conclusion. But Bellow obscures the function of his one powerful embodiment of evil by showing that Sammler, the moralist, is obscurely attracted. This might be understood as the ironic appeal of wickedness even to the good, but the hero explicitly denies such an explanation. However, in a blatantly contrived scene near the end of the novel, Sammler saves the criminal's life when he is set upon by Sammler's friends. If the thief does stand for the imperious ego — which the novel consistently identifies with sex and crime — why isn't he condemned by Sammler, who overreacts against Shula and Wallace? And if the ego is admirable in special circumstances, why doesn't Bellow spell them out instead of falling back on that hoariest of primitivisms: the prepotent savage beyond morals? In a novel whose manner was less judgmental, whose symbolic dramatization of discursive ideas was less obviously intended, such intellectual obscurity would not be damaging. Here it is.

Bellow's representation of vice through trivial or ambiguous figures is matched by an equally unconvincing representation of good. Throughout the book, one character is judged by Sammler to exemplify virtue: Dr. Gruner, Wallace's father. To be sure, the man has characteristics admirable to Bellow: traditionalism and charity. But these are represented by occasional trips to Israel and his financial support of the Sammlers, phenomena no weightier than Shula's theft and Wallace's bad plumbing. Furthermore, like the pickpocket, Gruner is a crook. He made extra money performing illegal abortions, possibly for Mafia cronies. Again, Bellow may be admired for representing the moral complexity of all persons, since no one is purely good or purely evil.

But morally complex characters belong in novels where they are amply revealed objects of inherent interest — whereas Bellow's are symbolic grotesques rhetorically labelled — or in books whose theme is the mysterious human soul, whereas *Mr. Sammler's Planet* is fundamentally an argument against modernism and for tradition. It is therefore disconcerting to find that Bellow's embodiments of opposing values give these neither clear nor impressive form.

The clearest, most impressive things in the book are Sammler's monologues, performed with or without audience. Significantly, these are frequently surrounded by apologies (before beginning a long lecture, Sammler announces, "Excuse me, I am . . . heavy-hearted and talkative"), apologies that suggest Bellow's consciousness that Sammler is a thinly fabricated mask for his creator and that *Mr. Sammler's Planet* lives less powerfully as a novel than as an angry meditation on modern libertarianism, with interludes of action to sugarcoat the pill.

In fact, the pill required no sugar-coating sweeter than the delicious language in which Sammler delivers his opinions. Since there is as little difference between Sammler's language and that of his author as there is between their ideas, we can read the book as Bellow's personal testament, in which case it becomes intellectually fascinating. On madness: "Madness makes interest. Madness is the attempted liberty of people who feel themselves overwhelmed by giant forces of organized control. Seeking the magic of extremes. Madness is a base form of the religious life." — On the wildness of selfhood: "The idea of the uniqueness of the soul. An excellent idea. A true idea, But in these forms? In these poor forms? Dear God! With hair, with clothes, with drugs and cosmetics, with genitalia, with round trips through evil, monstrosity, and orgy, with even God approached through obscenities? How terrified the soul must be in this vehemence, how little that is really dear to it it can see in these Sadic exercises." — On neo-Freudianism: ". . . what was it to be arrested in the stage of toilet training! What was it to be entrapped by a psychiatric standard (Sammler blamed the Germans and their psychoanalysis for this)! Who had raised the diaper flag? Who had made shit a sacrament? What literary and psychological movement was that?" — And, in a less sublime mood, on hippies: "These poor kids may have resolved to stink together in defiance of a corrupt tradition built on neurosis and falsehood . . . in their revulsion from authority they would respect no persons. Not even their own persons."

But the very dazzlement of Bellow's criticism, of which these are mere examples, makes lame his answer to the contemporary passion for overturned barricades and stormed outposts of experience. His negations are validated not by his plot and characters but by what we know of the real world; his affirmation is validated by nothing, is scarcely even asserted but rather exhaled as a kind of pious hope. "You certainly take a traditional line," Angela Gruner tells the hero in the last pages of the novel as it appeared in *The Atlantic Monthly* (November & December, 1969). To this, Sammler replies, "But there are two traditions here. Yours is even older, I think. One has to do with the setting of limits, and the other doesn't recognize limits. Without limits you have monstrosity, always. Within limits? Well, within limits monsters also appear. But not inevitably."

Perhaps recognizing the weakness of this retort, Bellow eliminated it from the novel's current version. Now, Angela rebukes Sammler with his ignorance of the stresses of modern life, and the hero walks off feeling futile. But Bellow doesn't permit this sense of futility to last. At Gruner's deathbed, Sammler delivers the same speech as in the magazine, reasserting the claims of traditional restraints and duties.

In either version, Bellow shows himself incapable of presenting a convincing argument for his conservative position. Since its negative side is not proven by the plot or characters, this failure to be persuasively positive confirms the book as a sermon designed for the already converted. Such readers will find *Mr. Sammler's Planet* delightful. Others, I suspect, will find it provocative, entertaining, and ultimately frustrating.

* * *

Mr. Sammler's Planet:
Wells, Hitler, and the World State
Judie Newman

Mr. Sammler's Planet, Bellow's seventh novel, met with a mixed critical reaction. In general, critics assailed the novel for its failure to integrate ideas with imaginative action. In *Modern Fiction Studies* David Galloway claimed that the novel displayed "the bankruptcy of Bellow's novelistic imagination," arguing that the imaginative structure of the novel failed to provide sufficient support for the intellectual structure. Jennifer M. Bailey described the events of the novel as heavy pieces of symbolic machinery, and Mas'ud Zavarzadeh lamented its "aesthetic and ideational thinness."[1] These criticisms can however be challenged by a close study of the relation between the ideas of the novel and the action in which they are inscribed, a study which depends upon an understanding of Bellow's attitude to history in the novel.

In *Mr. Sammler's Planet* Bellow's primary interest lies, as the title suggests, in global history. Two historical events govern the action of the novel: the Holocaust, in the past, of which Mr. Sammler is a survivor, and the Apollo moonshot which occupies the immediate future of the novel. Each involves a "planetary" metaphor. The identification

From *Dutch Quarterly Review of Anglo-American Letters* 13.1 (1983): 55-71.

of the world of the concentration camps with "another planet" is a common procedure in the literature of that experience. In a recent article Edward Alexander argues that the "planet" of Bellow's title is precisely that other world of the Holocaust.[2] The second planet of the title is however the moon, identified with the future. The novel is set shortly before the Apollo moonshot, from which Dr. Lal hopes to gain publicity for his book, "The Future of the Moon." Like the world of the camps the moon is another planet, a world beyond man's comprehension. In a general sense these two opposing planets, past and future, offer the opposition which dominates the novel, that between history-as-nightmare and history-as-progress. Where the Holocaust provides a locus for the discussion of evil in history, a discussion centered on Hannah Arendt's classic study of the war criminal, the moonflight introduces a view of history as progress, as a Utopian and visionary project, initiating a discussion which is centered on H. G. Well's ideas on space colonization and technological advance.

Mr. Sammler's planet is, however, also the earth of the present, described as the novel opens as "an earth of ideas."[3] In the action of the first chapter of the novel — Sammler's conversation with Margotte about Eichmann, his lecture on H. G. Wells, and his encounter with the pickpocket — Bellow develops the opposition between optimistic and pessimistic visions of global history. Sammler is invited to lecture at Columbia on the British scene in the thirties. As a younger man Sammler was a friend of Wells, and was invited by him to participate in the "Open Conspiracy," Wells' Utopian plan for a World State. Wells' Utopia was to involve the subjection of industry, capital, transport, and population to world-wide collective control, and the abolition of national sovereignty and thus of war. When Sammler outlines the plan, however, he is shouted down by a heckler who yells: "You quoted Orwell before. . . . You quoted him to say that British radicals were all protected by the Royal Navy" (36).

This comment indicates that Sammler's account of the Open Conspiracy incorporates Orwell's pessimistic attack on Wells. In "Wells, Hitler and the World State," an essay which provides an illuminating subtitle to *Mr. Sammler's Planet*, Orwell expresses his revulsion from Wells, whom he identifies with the belief in progress. Orwell points out that, while sensible men may agree with Wells' views, sensible men nowhere hold power. Men's motives are not as reasonable or as progressive as Wells maintains. For Orwell there are immediate problems to be solved in the present, that of Hitler in particular, and these problems are being met from quite unreasonable motives. Atavistic patriotism, he claims, has kept England on its feet during the war, a type of motivation which Wells' Cosmopolis would outlaw. Orwell particularly assails the intellectual inability to recognize evil: "The energy that actually shapes the world springs from emotions — racial pride, leader worship, religious belief, love of war — which liberal intellectuals mechanically write off as anachronisms."[4] He goes on to argue that those who perceive Hitler as Antichrist are closer to the truth than intellectuals who persist in seeing him as a figure from a comic opera. This latter view is, in his explanation, a product of the sheltered conditions of English intellectual life, where "the Left Book Club was at bottom a product of Scotland Yard, just as the Peace Pledge Union is the product of the Navy" (162).

How far Sammler shares Orwell's sentiments becomes very evident when he and Margotte discuss Arendt's *Eichmann in Jerusalem*. Margotte expounds the book as a work which discounts evil: "The idea being that here is no great spirit of evil. . . . A mass society does not produce great criminals" (15). Sammler disagrees totally, and the terms of his disagreement suggest a debt to Orwell: "Intellectuals do not understand. They get their notions about matters like this from literature. They expect a wicked hero like Richard III" (17). In Sammler's view, Arendt is "making use of a tragic history to promote the foolish ideas of Weimar intellectuals" (17). Sammler is quite clearly Bellow's mouthpiece at this point. In 1975 Bellow restated Sammler's view as his own, dismissing Arendt and arguing that man has an innate sense of evil.[5] Where Wells discounts evil out of progressive futurism, Arendt, in Bellow's view, discounts it from an overactive concentration on historical explanation, seeing man as totally conditioned by his historical circumstances. In 1964 Bellow was asked to comment on an article by Harold Rosenberg which considered Arendt's book, by then a *cause célèbre* in America. In his comment, Bellow agreed with Rosenberg in attacking popular philosophies of doom, anomie and alienation as "simple-minded historicism" and expressed the hope that "the imagination will free itself from the clichés of culture history."[6]

When Mr. Sammler wakes in America, his first impulse is to lament the dominance of historical explanations. Eying his books he surmises that

> they were the wrong books, the wrong papers. . . . Being right was largely a matter of explanations. Intellectual man had become an explaining creature. Fathers to children, wives to husbands, lecturers to listeners, experts to laymen, colleagues to colleagues, doctors to patients, man to his own soul explained. The roots of this, the causes of the other, the source of events, the history, the structure, the reasons why. (5)

Just as Sammler is now less than certain of Wells' Utopian views, so he discounts the writers of culture history, on the grounds that looking only backwards to historical conditions is as morally paralyzing as the longsight gaze into the future. In America Sammler "had been reading historians of civilization" (32) — he names Ortega, Valéry, and Burckhardt among others. As we shall see Bellow does draw upon these historians in *Mr. Sammler's Planet*, but as a part of a critical evaluation of historicism. The opposition between the governing planets of optimism and pessimism is contained within this larger question. Bellow rejects historicism, in the sense in which Karl Popper understands the term, as the appeal to history as a determined order.[7] Yet he accepts the phenomenon of historicism as the sudden hypersensitivity of modern man to the sense of history.

Mr. Sammler is particularly influenced by Ortega. When he visits Israel he is struck by its confusion of cultures, as demonstrated in the person of a Bessarabian-Syrian-Spanish-speaking Israeli from the Argentine. He comments:

> The many impressions and experiences of life seemed no longer to occur each in its proper space, in sequence, each with its recognizable religious or aesthetic importance, but human beings suffered the humiliations of inconsequence, of confused styles, of a long life containing several separate lives. In fact the whole experience of mankind was now covering each separate life in its flood. Making all the ages of history simultaneous.(23)

Sammler's stress on the mass and multiplicity of life, and the rise of the historic floodwaters to cover man, takes its metaphors from Ortega. In *The Revolt of the Masses*, Ortega argued that historicism is intimately connected with the rise of the mass-man. "Now the average man represents the field over which the history of each period acts; he is to history what sea level is to geography . . . the level of history has suddenly risen."[8] We recall that Sammler, overwhelmed by pullulating historical explanations, opened the novel by describing the mind as "a Dutch drudgery . . . pumping and pumping to keep a few acres of dry ground. The invading sea being a metaphor for the multiplication of facts and sensations" (5). Ortega also sees modern life as planetary: "Life has become, in actual fact, worldwide in character; I mean that the content of existence for the average man of today includes the whole planet; that each individual habitually lives the life of the whole world" (41). Unlike Wells, however, Ortega views this new Cosmopolis with unalloyed disgust. The widespread dissemination of culture, of information and technology, produces in his view only a new barbarian: the mass-man. For Ortega there are two fundamental traits of the mass-man: "the free expansion of his vital desires and therefore of his personality, and his radical ingratitude towards all that had made possible the ease of his existence. These traits together make up the well-known psychology of the spoilt child" (63). Bellow introduces these spoilt children of the West in Sammler's pervasive hostile comments on the youth culture of America, and in particular, in the characters of Angela and Wallace, spoiled children of Elya Gruner. Ortega argues that the spoilt child is unable to distinguish the works of history from nature. When Wallace floods the Gruner house he makes this point himself, intrigued to discover that he cannot shut off the water because he has no idea of its source: "It's supposed to be a sign of the Mass Man that he doesn't know the difference between Nature and human arrangements. He thinks the cheap commodities — water, electricity, subways, hot-dogs — are like air and sunshine, and leaves on the trees

. . . Ortega y Gasset thinks so" (*MSP* 196). The point of Ortega's argument is that civilization demands continual vigilance; it is neither infinite advance nor regress:

> If you want to make use of the advantages of civilization, but are not prepared to concern yourself with the upholding of civilization you are done. In a trice you find yourself left without civilization. Just a slip, and when you look around everything has vanished into air. The primitive forest appears in its native state. (Ortega 64)

Ortega founds his morality on the assertion that human nobility involves, not the passive enjoyment of rights, but the active attempt to meet one's obligations to civilization. Mr. Sammler's own life illustrates the point. As a young aristocrat in Poland, Sammler enjoyed, as of right, his cultural privileges, flattered by the gift to him on his sixteenth birthday of Schopenhauer's *The World As Will and Idea*, delighting in its cosmic pessimism. In London Sammler is equally flattered by his involvement in Wells' Utopian schemes. While Sammler plays with ideas of cosmic pessimism and Utopian Cosmopolis, however, the Second World War is looming. In Poland he suddenly discovers that civilization has disappeared, and finds himself, a murderous savage, in the Zamosht forest.

It is only in the action of the novel, however, that Sammler learns the full lesson of his past: the dangers of intellectual distance, and the obligations of the present. In the first chapter Sammler watches the pickpocket at work but does not intervene. Intellectually he condemns the thief, and yet Mr. Sammler seeks out opportunities to watch the man in action. He connects the experience with a detail of his reading:

> The moment in *Crime and Punishment* at which Raskolnikov brought down the axe on the bare head of the old woman, her thin grey-streaked, grease-smeared hair, the rat's-tail braid fastened by a broken horn comb on her neck. That is to say that horror, crime, murder, did vivify all the phenomena, the most ordinary details of experience. In evil, as in art, there was illumination. (11)

After being heckled at Columbia, Sammler admits to a similar "intensification of vision" (37). After the lecture, Sammler converts the experience into matter for intellectual diversion, pondering the heckler's comment from a safe distance. Bellow comments: "Individuals like Sammler were only one stage forward, awakened not to purpose, but to aesthetic consumption of the environment" (38). When Sammler is seen by the pickpocket he adopts a similar strategy: "Confronted by the elegant brute . . . he adopted an English tone. A dry, a neat, a prim face declared that one had not crossed anyone's boundary; one was satisfied with one's own business" (7). "Mr. Minutely-Observant Artur Sammler" (12) enjoys registering the details of the world around him, converting them into matter for intellectual and aesthetic diversion, but he does not feel called upon to act. In exposing himself to Sammler, the Negro mimics Sammler's own position: he does not cross Samm-

ler's boundaries or assault him, he does not speak, he merely gives
Sammler something to look at. Ironically catering to Sammler's desire
to observe, he displays his penis: "Sammler was required to gaze at
this organ. No compulsion would have been necessary. He would, in
any case, have looked" (42). When the thief leaves, Sammler is for
once singularly unilluminated by this experience, unable to convert it
into "safe" intellectual material. He feels only "a temporary blankness
of spirit. Like the television screen in the lobby, white and grey, buzz-
ing without image" (43). For once Sammler gains nothing from an
experience, finding that rather than vivifying the phenomena, it erases
them altogether.

Sammler is, however, fatally attracted to distancing strategies,
ways of escaping from the present. In the novel the image of the moon
serves as a focus for each of his three principal strategies: imaginative
vision, an ironic perspective, and mystic transcendence. Here Sammler
is attracted to the latter. Collapsing onto his bed he finds Lal's book
under the pillow:

> "How long," went the first sentence, "will this earth remain the only
> home of Man?"
>
> How long? Oh, Lord, you bet! Wasn't it the time — the very hour to go?
> For every purpose under heaven. A time to gather stones together, a time
> to cast away stones. Considering the earth itself not as a stone cast but as
> something to cast oneself from — to be divested of. To blow this great
> blue, white, green planet, or to be blown from it. (43)

Sammler's description of the earth as stone borrows its terms from
Ecclesiastes 3, suggesting that the earth is a place of stony confinement, burying the individual soul in earthly matter, as opposed to the
changeless eternal moon, where: "Stone crumbles but without the usual
erosion" (44). History reappears as nightmare, the horror of man's
confinement within space and time. The central experience of Sammler's life, his burial, choking on stones and earth in a mass grave, has
reinforced Sammler's vision of the finite world as confinement, its concerns merely irrelevant in the light of mystic vision. Sammler now
embarks on a lengthy reflection upon Kierkegaard. Kierkegaard distinguishes in *Fear and Trembling* between the moral realm and the realm
of faith, using as his example Abraham's readiness to murder Isaac at
God's command, an act which is immoral by human standards. Feffer
describes the heckler as a product of the divorce between the ethical
and the religious realms, a man who thinks himself "a pure Christian
angel because you commit murder" (88). Sammler is now not so sure
that the two realms can be so easily divorced. In the passage which he
paraphrases from *Fear and Trembling*[9] Sammler connects the question
of finite and infinite with that of travel to other worlds:

> This brought to mind Kierkegaard's comical account of people travelling
> around the world to see rivers and mountains, new stars, birds of rare
> plumage, queerly deformed fishes, ridiculous breeds of men — tourists

abandoning themselves to the bestial stupor which gazes at existence and thinks it has seen something. This could not interest Kierkegaard. He was looking for the Knight of Faith, the real prodigy. That real prodigy, having set its relations with the infinite, was entirely at home in the finite. (51-52)

Sammler sees in Kierkegaard's theology a possible solution to the problems of space and time. By accepting that his life is finite, a mere preamble to infinity, the Knight of Faith accepts that life is his duty, a contract to be honored. Yet there is a difficulty for Sammler in accepting Kierkegaard's ideas:

Mr. Sammler was worried. He was concerned about the test of crime which the Knight of Faith had to meet. Should the Knight of Faith have the strength to break humanly appointed laws in obedience to God? Oh yes, of course! But maybe Sammler knew things about murder which might make the choices just a little more difficult. (52)

What Sammler knows of murder includes of course his own murder of the German straggler. Before Sammler murders the German, he has come to the conclusion that the world is only a spatial-temporal prison, and when the man pleads for his life, he sees "the soil already sprinkled on his face. He saw the grave on his skin. The grime of the lip, the large creases of skin descending from his nose already lined with dirt — that man to Sammler was already underground" (112). Sammler's vision of the earth on this man's face, of the finitude of the individual confined in the earth, actually assists him in the act of murder. Acting with one eye on eternity appears as radically immoral. Sammler is also an exponent of Meister Eckhardt, a German mystic. The choice of this particular figure underlines the ambiguity. Eckhardt was adopted by the Nazi party as giving religious sanction to its racist views. While this is based on a vulgarization of Eckhardt's writing,[10] it is a reminder to the reader that mysticism may also foster amoral and violent energies. The transcendental, while not entirely discarded, is subjected to moral criticism here.

The action of the novel develops the point. At the bedside of Elya Gruner, Sammler meets his son, Wallace. Wallace's adventures clearly illustrate the description by Kierkegaard of those who are ill at ease in the finite. When Sammler lends Wallace Burckhardt's *Force and Freedom*,[11] a work which attacks on moral grounds the belief in historical determinism, Wallace ignores the moral message to rush off to Turkey, Morocco, and Albania to observe peoples at different stages of historical development. Farcical and spectacular events dog Wallace's trajectory as he rushes from project to project, and from world to world. Wryly Sammler sees in Wallace an alternative sense of the lunar metaphor: "Wallace was genuinely loony. For him it required a powerful effort to become interested in common events . . . so often he seemed to be in outer space. Dans la lune" (76). Elya Gruner, however, presents an image of the man who is entirely at home in the finite, accom-

plishing his daily tasks to the best of his ability and meeting his obligations in the present. Sammler dismisses Elya's faults as "dust and peb-
bles, as rubble on a mosaic which might be swept away. Underneath, a
fine, noble expression" (70). Contemplating Elya's face Sammler sees
the "dirt" of ordinary human existence as unimportant, arguing that a
few "may comprehend that it is the strength to do one's duty daily and
promptly that makes saints and heroes" (76). As Knight of Faith,
however, Elya has met the test of crime all too well. Wallace reveals
Elya's Mafia involvement to Sammler. Suddenly Sammler sees Elya as
akin to the pickpocket who is in fact described as a surgeon at three
separate points (6, 10, 39), reinforcing his kinship with Elya.

No longer certain of the value of mystic transcendence, Sammler,
returns to the imagination, approving of Lal's description of it: "The
imagination is innately a biological power seeking to overcome impossible conditions" (87). Feffer, however, who now accosts Sammler,
offers less than comforting evidence of the ability of the human
imagination to create new forms. In the past, as he explains, Feffer had
been delighted by his psychiatrists' ability to give new names to his
problems. Labeled as "manic," "reactive-depressive" or "Oedipal,"
Feffer had felt like a new man. As he explains: "When you set up a
new enterprise, you redescribe the phenomena and create a feeling that
we're getting somewhere" (90). New names, however, don't alter old
problems. Wallace and Feffer are planning a new business enterprise,
flying over suburban gardens to identify and label their shrubs, an
enterprise which ends in old-fashioned disaster when Wallace crashes
his plane into a house. This lunatic flight of Wallace's imagination
casts an ironic light on Sammler's new optimism in relation to the
moonshot as evidence of the triumph of the creative imagination.

Feffer also reveals that Shula, Sammler's daughter, has stolen
Lal's manuscript. Shula has committed this crime out of a belief in the
imagination; she sees her father as a "Prospero" (93) able to conjure up
wonderful cultural visions, and hopes that Lal's book will remind
Sammler of his own projected book on Wells. Apologizing to Dr. Lal,
Sammler describes Shula as a believer in the scientific future who is
also anachronistic: "Psychologically archaic — all the fossils in her
mental strata fully alive (the moon too is a kind of fossil) — she
dreams about the future" (104). In Shula's action Sammler sees evidence that the human imagination cannot be counted upon to transform
itself and the world. The way in which he makes this point significantly develops his assessment of Utopian writers: "New Worlds?
Fresh beginnings? Not such a simple matter. . . . What did Captain
Nemo do in *20,000 Leagues Under the Sea*? He sat in the submarine,
the Nautilus, and on the ocean floor he played Bach and Handel on the
organ. Good stuff, but old" (110). The remark is remembered from
Paul Valéry's essay on politics and history, in which Valéry considers
the imagination as irremediably backward-looking:

What would an inventor of imaginary worlds, such as a Wells or a Verne, do today? Please observe that though they invented imaginary worlds, neither of them tried anything in the realm of the mind. For instance they never attempted to picture the arts of the future. The famous Captain Nemo, whom everybody knows, played the organ in his Nautilus at the bottom of the sea, and on it he played Bach and Handel.[12]

As Valéry sums it up, man is entering the future backwards. The danger of history is that it acts upon the present with violence. According to Valéry: "Our feelings and ambitions are stirred by memories of what we have read, memories of memories, to a far greater extent than they result from our perceptions and the data of the present moment. The real nature of history is to play a part in history itself" (12-13).

Anachronistic Shula, lost in her memories of H. G. Wells and of Sammler's long abandoned memoir, steals Lal's book, a vision of the future. Sammler has already experienced the anachronism of history. Saved by Polish partisans he had fought alongside them. Yet as peace drew near the Poles returned to older loyalties, to anti-Semitism, and massacred the Jewish fighters. Saved once again by another Pole, Sammler corresponds with him for a time until a tinge of anti-Semitism creeps into Cieslakiewicz's letters. Sadly Sammler considers the persistence of outdated historical ideas — the Russian desire for a Mediterranean port in an era of air power, the stupid sultanism of Louis Quatorze reproduced in General de Gaulle, the Arabs in Israel once more killing Jews. The fact that the ideas are anachronistic makes little difference: "No more than the disappearance of Jews from Poland made a difference to the anti-Semitism of the Poles. This was the meaning of historical stupidity" (115). When Sammler confronts Shula she argues that she stole from concern for the future, appealing to the creative imagination, maintaining that "for the creative there are no crimes" (159). Sammler, however, reiterates his beliefs that human beings know what is right and wrong, and that these categories are not redefinable. Crime is crime, whether committed under the influence of a nightmare past, out of desire for the future, or as a means of bringing to birth the "new" thing, creatively redefined. Gently, by a demythologizing of Wells, Sammler communicates to his errant daughter that the world cannot be made afresh by the efforts of the imagination, that he is no Prospero, and that "there is nothing left remarkable Beneath the visiting moon" (157).

Shula's theft, however, leads Sammler to the last of his distancing strategies — that of cosmic irony. The alternation between the planets of moon and earth now appears as an image of the meaningless recurrence of history, its errors cyclically repeated. The plot of the novel suggests the farcical nature of this repetition. Shula actually steals Lal's book twice, once from Lal and again from Sammler's room. When Sammler discovers the second theft, he connects Shula in his mind with the pickpocket. In the plot Shula's theft, and Sammler's pursuit of her, form a comic parody of his involvement with the black thief. The low, farcical tone of the chase, culminating in the discovery of Shula, naked in the Gruner tub, discredits the view that crime has overtones of glory. Murder and intense sexuality may be seen as vivifying the phenomena. Low pilfering by the grotesquely bewigged Shula can have no such overtones. Confronted with Shula's second theft Sammler gains a horrified awareness that "humankind kept on doing the same stunts over and over" (140). Whirled off by the lunatic Shula into the circus of her fancy dress activities, Sammler sees life as a cyclic dance in which "anyone can clutch anyone, and whirl him off. The low can force the high to dance. The wise have to reel about with leaping fools" (141). Images of cyclic action, of circles and circuses, multiply in the text.[13] In the structure each major idea is encircled, ironically, by parodic reenactment. Wells celebrates technology and space travel. Lunar Wallace, looking for money to insure his future as a flyer, prepares a technological blueprint before searching the plumbing of the Gruner house, thereby causing a flood. In his desire to "crash out of the future my father has prepared for me" (197), Wallace crashes his plane into a house. Apocalyptic visions of flood and fire yield to domestic engulfment. Oriental mysticism is horribly parodied by Shula in a sari. Sammler's own life is repetitive. He "dies" in Poland in a mass grave, emerging to a second life in which he merely repeats the errors of the former, assuming once again the position of distant intellectual. This distance, tragically irrelevant in the thirties, becomes merely comical in America. The novel conveys a sense of future-in-past and past-in-future, as technological progress is accompanied by anachronistic urges, as Wells, prophet of the future, becomes the mainspring of anachronistic action in the present.

And yet, there is a sense in which repetition is not without value. In the Gruner house Sammler begins his lengthy monologue by inveighing against those historical writers who have, he feels, in their analysis of the past, violently conditioned the present: "history follows their words. Think of the wars and the revolutions we have been scribbled into" (170). Supposed progress is ambivalent, as Sammler sees the manner in which revolutions cycle back, ending in more violence and terror than that which they sought to remedy. Yet Sammler does speak, engaging in an activity which he acknowledges as cyclic: "Once you begin talking, once the mind takes to this way of turning, it keeps turning and it dips through all events" (172). "Like a Ferris wheel" (173), comments Lal. Sammler's monologue describes the sea of ideas around man, the anachronistic savagery of the mass-man, the dangers of the transcendental view, the horrors of individualism without obligations. These ideas have already been expressed, even repetitively, in the novel. Yet Sammler makes no apology for this repetition. He argues that "it is sometimes necessary to repeat what we all know. All mapmakers should place the Mississippi in the same location, and avoid originality. It may be boring, but one has to know where he is. We cannot have the Mississippi flowing towards the Rockies for a change" (183).

The point of Sammler's monologue, circling back to his previous arguments, restating and repeating, is precisely that while these ideas may appear to be boringly known, there is a need for continual restatement, lest they go into eclipse; much as in the life of the individual there is a need for constant vigilance, for repeated moral activity. Continual restatement is necessary to keep such truths as have been attested before men's eyes. The cyclic dance of human activity, advancing only to retreat, may appear as a circle of "black irony" (9) but it may also express the essential truths of human existence. Significantly, Elya, the moral touchstone of the novel, now appears, in Sammler's mind, in cyclic motion: "Elya reappeared, strangely and continually, as if his face were orbiting — as if he were a satellite" (179).

The monologue is interrupted by the flood which flows over a mosaic floor. Elya's face has previously been compared to a noble mosaic (70) and when the mosaic floods there is the clear implication that this is the moment of Elya's aneurysm, a flooding of the brain in blood. While events in the Gruner household attest the necessity of human repetition, they also stress the importance of immediate, practical action within time. Sammler has to abandon large ideas in order to bale out the attic; the need for practical action in the present to maintain the structure of the house takes precedence over abstract thought. In the final chapter of the novel Sammler is forced out into the present. The action emphasizes the pressure of time. While Sammler has now realized that he cannot attempt to live outside the world, in philosophical detachment, he has realized this too late to allow him to reach Elya's bedside before he dies. Time has run out for Elya and for Sammler who has missed the opportunity to speak to Elya. Life does not always offer a second chance. By his concern with essentials, with large utterances and intellectual debate, Sammler has lost the chance to say something, however imperfect, in time.

In its final violent scene the novel circles back to its starting point, the black pickpocket, but this time Sammler is determined to act in the present, to intervene, rather than remaining at a safe distance. Feffer, associated with technology and "new" ideas, is helpless in the pickpocket's grip. Physically powerless himself, Sammler turns to Eisen. Eisen, Sammler's wife-beating son-in-law, is clearly a Yeatsian barbarian, a rough beast whose second coming is a horror. Shambling on his mutilated feet, his long curls fusing head and neck, Eisen prepares to save the day. In New York he carries with him his crude medallions, inscribed with Jewish symbols, stars of David, rams' horns, scrolls, candelabra, even a Sherman tank. To restrain the violence before him Sammler has to turn to Eisen who wields the symbols of atavistic patriotism, clubbing the thief with his bag of medallions. Orwell's analysis of the motives which restore civilized order — patriotism, love of violence, leader worship — is horrifically realized in this scene as Eisen acts on Sammler's dictates. Once unleashed, however, Eisen is quite unable to stop, and prepares to beat the Negro to death. Sammler's comment in his monologue, on the prophets of violence, unable to restrain the revolutions their words initiate, finds its correlative in the action. Sammler recognizes that he has his existence in time, that the present is before him in all its horrors and its obligations, and that he must act. Action, however, is not once and for all, but continuous. Feffer acts to restrain the pickpocket. His action leads to Eisen's intervention. Sammler then has to intervene to restrain Eisen. Eisen sees events in simplistic terms, arguing that he must hit the black hard if he is not himself to be killed. He tells Sammler: "'You know. We both fought in the war. You were a Partisan. You had a gun. So don't you know? . . . If in — in. No? If out — out. Yes? No? So answer.' It was the reasoning that sank Sammler's heart completely" (234).

Human decisions are not so simple as Eisen implies. Sammler has been "in" the world, and has killed. He has also been "out" of the world, distant, yet morally no better. Sammler "knows" that there is at times a need for violence. He also knows the need for its restraint. In this the role of time is important. Man is neither "in" nor "out," doomed by the finite world, nor perfectible beyond it, but has to make the best of his existence in time. Moral decisions have a temporal dimension, and cannot be taken in a spirit of calm discussion or simplistic logic. The complex logic of the events of *Mr. Sammler's Planet* belies simplistic thinking, constructing a novel which, while it asserts the importance of intellectual discrimination, based on the awareness of history, also responds to the pressures of the present. The art of Wells, with its enthronement of the future, the art of Eisen, with its symbols of the past, are deployed in the service of an altogether more complex, morally active novel. The worlds of past, present and future are inextricably interwoven, and amidst them the best that man can do is to maintain moral vigilance.

The novel closes with Sammler's recognition of the ambiguity of human action and of human knowledge. Contemplating the face of criminal Elya, he says: "He did meet the terms of his contract. The terms which, in his inmost heart, each man knows. As I know mine. As all know. For that is the truth of it — that we all know, God, that we know, that we know, we know, we know" (252). For Bellow — unlike his critics — the relation of ideas, what we know, to action is not merely a literary, formal problem but a moral one. Mr. Sammler, exponent of Valéry, Burckhardt, Ortega, Wells, Orwell, Arendt, and Kierkegaard, finally learns their lessons in action. While the complex logic of events demonstrates the importance of careful intellectual discrimination, the repetitions and recurrences of the plot subject each idea to moral criticism, founded upon the demands for action in time. Long-distance views of human history, whether optimistic or pessimistic, give way to present ethical imperatives. The opposition of moon and earth, variously figured as between infinite and finite, eternal and temporal, Utopia and apocalypse, vision and nightmare, is not finally encircled in ironic detachment. Rather, the novel argues that amidst the change and contingency of the sublunary sphere there is only one fixed pole: the moral imperative. By a sense of longer perspectives, by an understanding of what is owed to the past, the individual may be able to maintain his precarious knowledge and carry it forward into a civilized future. He can only do so by neither abdicating the demands of the present, nor by surrendering totally to its standards. Unsubmerged by the sea of ideas, the novel emerges as a profoundly moral construction, carrying both aesthetic and intellectual conviction, a statement which is a restatement of important, if not original, human truths.

Notes

1. David Galloway, "*Mr. Sammler's Planet*: Bellow's Failure of Nerve," *Modern Fiction Studies* 19.1 (1973): 17-28; Jennifer M. Bailey, "The Qualified Affirmation of Saul Bellow's Recent Work," *Journal of American Studies* 7.1 (1973): 63-73; Mas'ud Zavarzadeh, "The Apocalyptic Fact and the Eclipse of Fiction in Recent Prose Narratives," *Journal of American Studies* 9.1 (1975): 69-83.
2. Edward Alexander, "Imagining the Holocaust: *Mr. Sammler's Planet* and Others," *Judaism* 22 (1972): 288-300.
3. Saul Bellow, *Mr. Sammler's Planet* (Harmondsworth: Penguin, 1971), 5. Subsequent references in the text from this edition.
4. George Orwell, "Wells, Hitler and the World State," *Collected Essays* (London: Routlege & Kegan Paul, 1961), 162. Subsequent references in the text from this edition.
5. "Literature and Culture: An Interview with Saul Bellow," *Salmagundi* 30 (1975): 16-17.
6. Saul Bellow, "A Comment on Form and Despair," *Location* 1 (1964): 10-12.
7. See Karl Popper, *The Poverty of Historicism* (London: Routlege & Kegan Paul, 1961), 17.
8. José Ortega y Gasset, *The Revolt of the Masses* (London: Allen & Unwin, 1932), 26. Subsequent references in the text from this edition.
9. Søren Kierkegaard, *Fear and Trembling* (Princeton: UPP, 1941), 52.
10. Notably in Alfred Rosenberg, *Der Mythos des 20. Jahrhunderts* (München: Hoheneichen, 1930). For a complete analysis of Rosenberg's misinterpretation of Eckhardt, see Albert R. Chandler, *Rosenberg's Nazi Myth* (Ithaca, N.Y.: Cornell UP, 1945).
11. Published in Britain as *Reflections on History* (London: Allen & Unwin, 1943).
12. Paul Valéry, *Reflections on the World Today*, trans. Francis Scarfe (London: Thames & Hudson, 1951), 150. Subsequent references in the text from this edition.
13. See William J. Scheick, "Circle Sailing in Bellow's *Mr. Sammler's Planet*," *Essays in Literature* 5.1 (1979): 95-101.

* * *

Humboldt's Gift (1975)

A Higher Selfishness?
Roger Shattuck

Saul Bellow has written repeatedly about overextended family men who fancy themselves solitaries and cranks. His first novel starts out like one by Kafka or Beckett with a man alone in his room, warding off doubts about his own existence. Ten pages later he is surrounded by a large cast of in-laws, relatives, and partying friends. Moses Herzog appears on the first page of Bellow's sixth novel, living alone in a big house in the Berkshires, eating "Silvercup bread from the paper package, beans from the can." Herzog's elected solitude can hold out for barely a dozen pages before he is navigating dizzily among ex-wives, old friends, loyal family, and a new girlfriend toward a realignment of his social life. Even *Seize the Day* and *Mr. Sammler's Planet*, two of his finest books, conform after their fashion to this pattern. Now comes Bellow's eighth novel — ambitious, sardonic, vulnerable. In his first "big book" since *The Adventures of Augie March* the solitude is becoming very real and leans toward self-absorption.

Humboldt's Gift is immediately recognizable as a novel by Bellow. No other contemporary novelist writes with his careful mixture of control and abandon. Yet compared to previous works it shows striking differences that cannot be described as developments of earlier tendencies. The changes occur at all levels. The characters' names have a jocose eighteenth-century flavor: Charlie Citrine, Von Humboldt Fleisher, Rinaldo Cantabile. Citrine, the floundering family man here, appears to confront solitude more fatefully than Bellow's other protagonists. The tone of the narrative has shifted markedly toward irony. Yet the currents of philosophizing reach a more urgent pitch than ever before. It is necessary to read *Humboldt's Gift* with great care — with caution even.

From *New York Review of Books* (18 Sep. 1975): 21-25.

The elements of Bellow's story are as variegated as anything in Dickens or Dostoevsky. The time is the early seventies. About fifty-five, Citrine enjoys the substance and the trappings of success as a playwright and biographer. Broadway, Hollywood, and President Kennedy have welcomed him. He has returned to live in Chicago where he grew up, and now a painful court settlement with his divorced wife (she has their two young daughters) is sapping his resources and his attention. A beautiful young girlfriend, Renata, is remodeling his life according to her plans for marriage and life in heavy syrup. In the midst of this decline, vividly yet somehow unfeelingly narrated by Citrine himself in the first person, a series of mysterious events awakens him from his long slumber of money, success, and bourgeois values. An imperious, small-time gangster type with a rasping intelligence forces his way into Citrine's life. This character, Rinaldo Cantabile, obliges Citrine to plunge back into his memories of Humboldt, a great boisterous figure of the artist as a young dog, whose reputation as a poet in the thirties lured Citrine out of the Midwest. For fifteen years they were inseparable, blood brothers, until Citrine's success led to bitter estrangement.

Now, five years after Humboldt's death in shoddy obscurity, Citrine flies out of Chicago with Renata and stops off in New York to pick up Humboldt's legacy to him. It consists of a long fond letter of reconciliation and an apparently worthless film treatment. Reaching Spain, Citrine finds himself deserted by Renata, near broke, and pursued into the depths of his middle-aged desperation by Cantabile. The endlessly agitated gangster has a scheme for making big money out of Humboldt's film scripts. Wary yet fascinated, Citrine retreats deeper and deeper into theosophy and meditation. He resolves to reorganize his life when things calm down. Perhaps he will. At the end of the novel Citrine is reinterring Humboldt in proper style thanks to money made, against all expectations, from the scripts. An old friend of the family calls Citrine's attention to a strange sight in the New Jersey cemetery: crocuses.

In the foreground of the story lie two well-tried themes. Bellow's touch is sure in depicting the comedy of a vain man's attempt to age gracefully or even honorably. A kind of embittered absorption clings to the second theme: the perils of worldly success and its lurking connections with money, sex, power, and crime. The setting is Chicago — not a mere background but a vibrant city of people and places laden with associations. New York, Corpus Christi, Madrid, and Paris drift by like painted flats for the characters in transit. Chicago represents a personage of its own, with an exciting physical existence and, if not a mind, at least a character. Cantabile belongs to its entrails, almost literally as one scene insists.

After bullying Citrine and in effect beating him up in the middle of a busy street, Cantabile is suddenly gripped by the need to empty his bowels. He forces Citrine to precede him down into the lower regions of an old Russian Bath, described like an allegorical sequence out of Dante. Held at gun point, Citrine witnesses Cantabile's defecation.

> . . . thinking improving thoughts, I waited with good poise while he crouched there with his hardened dagger brows. He was a handsome slender man whose hair had a natural curl. It was cropped so close that you could see the roots of his curls and I observed the strong contraction of his scalp in this moment of stress. He wanted to inflict a punishment on me but the result was only to make us more intimate.

The timing and texture of this moment strongly recall the scene of the pickpocket who exhibits himself to Mr. Sammler in the apartment lobby. Both scenes establish an emphatically physical base for the action and certify the authenticity of the works that contain them. All the details of the infernal scene in the new novel are also designed to tell us that it could happen only in Chicago, the teeming environment that produced both the gangster and his intellectual victim. To his own city Bellow applies his full powers.

Partly for this reason I find that the outrageous Cantabile comes close to overshadowing Humboldt, a more orthodox portrait of hounded genius in New York. Cantabile become Citrine's nemesis, the male fury who pummels him awake to his own predicament as no woman has been able to do. Citrine cannot miss what is happening. "But it was just possible that Cantabile's death-dealing fantasy, his imaginary role as Death's highest-ranking deputy, was intended also to wake me up — '*Brutus, thou sleep'st*,' etcetera. This had occurred to me in the squad car."

The whole second half of the novel is curiously suffused with images of sleep, at times confusing because many of them refer to a state of higher consciousness rather than to Citrine's bemused worldliness. But no ambivalence mars Cantabile's role as the demon who goads Citrine to react to himself.

Through all these events there is an elementary test on which Bellow performs superbly. His prose frequently makes you want to read it aloud — to someone else or to yourself. I can do no better than to quote. Citrine is watching the opposing lawyers in his divorce case.

> Tomchek and Srole entered the courtroom, and from the other side came Cannibal Pinsker in a bright yellow double-knit jazzy suit and a large yellow cravat that lay on his shirt like a cheese omelette, and tan shoes in two tones. His head was brutally hairy. He was grizzled and he carried himself like an old prizefighter. What might he have been in an earlier incarnation, I wondered. I wondered about us all.

A hundred pages later Citrine flees from these ordeals of the mind in an airplane with his girlfriend beside him.

> My head lay on the bib and bosom of the seat and when the Jack Daniel's came I strained it through my irregular multi-colored teeth, curling my forefinger over the top of the glass to hold back the big perforated ice

cubes — they always put in too many. The thread of whisky burned pleasantly in the gullet and then my stomach, like the sun outside, began to glow, and the delight of freedom also began to expand within me. Renata was right, I was away! Once in a while, I get shocked into upper wakefulness, I turn a corner, see the ocean, and my heart tips over with happiness — it feels so free! Then I have the idea that, as well as beholding, I can also be beheld from yonder and am not a discrete object but incorporated with the rest, with universal sapphire, purplish blue. For what is this sea, this atmosphere, doing within the eight-inch diameter of your skull? (I say nothing of the sun and the galaxy which are also there.) At the center of the beholder there must be space for the whole, and this nothing-space is not an empty nothing but a nothing reserved for everything. You can feel this nothing-everything capacity with ecstasy and this was what I actually felt in the jet. Sipping whisky, feeling the radiant heat that rose inside, I experienced a bliss that I knew perfectly well was not mad. They hadn't done me in back there, Tomchek, Pinsker, Denise, Urbanovich. I had gotten away from them. I couldn't say that I knew really what I was doing, but did it matter so much? I felt clear in the head nevertheless. I could find no shadow of wistful yearning, no remorse, no anxiety. I was with a beautiful bim. She was as full of schemes and secrets as the Court of Byzantium. Was that so bad? I was a goofy old chaser. But what of it?

There are moments of excess in these two passages.[1] But both surpass their momentary weaknesses, and the second displays Bellow's remarkable capacity to create an "air of reality" and then to move convincingly beyond it. Adopting a deliberately archaic style, he carries us through delicate filterings of sensation to poetic recognition crinkled slightly by irony, yet sustained by unabashed philosophical reflexion — and then down again. The rhetorical effects, like "bib and bosom" linking up with "beautiful bim," go by effortlessly.

Bellow found his style and his voice with *Augie March*, his third novel. Since then he has alternated regularly between first and third person narrative. Yet that alternation does not seem to modify the controlling sensibility in his novels any more than does the varied series of central characters he creates. A Jewish intellectual from Chicago speaks in a voice indistinguishable from that of an eccentric ivy-league millionaire crashing around the African landscape. These modern picaros talk to us from inside deeply disjointed worlds, with a ready supply of funny stories and off-beat culture, stumbling occasionally into a moment of illumination.

However, there is something beyond the prose that makes *Humboldt's Gift* read well, aloud and in the mind. Divided into loose unnumbered sections of varying length, the book gives the impression of recording Citrine's voice wherever he goes. Everything is included. We read long digressions on pet subjects, overblown descriptions, and remarks implying that no accumulation of detail will suffice to portray a character. Some of the throwaway lines, comic and critical, bring things to a standstill. "I don't want to interfere in your marriage, but I notice that you've stopped breathing." "It made me think what a tremendous force the desire to be interesting has in the democratic USA." The book is studded with trinkets and oddities. But unlike what is going on in much contemporary French and American fiction, Bellow's irregularities grow not out of doubts about the value of continuous narrative but out of a calm confidence that he has a story to tell. That story can carry with it many excrescences. Robbe-Grillet and Burroughs, though very different from each other in other respects, go to great lengths to fit one sentence to the next according to aural and visual patterns that evade linear narrative. In contrast, Bellow's faith in the shapely existence of a tellable story unites and lends significance to the miscellaneous elements of Citrine's world.

Out of all these aspects of Bellow's fiction grows its most characteristic quality: the sense of plenitude. The world is full to overflowing, and it all connects even though the ultimate enigma will never be dissipated. It is not just that Bellow tells us in scrupulous detail how everyone's breath smells and what they wear and the way they move — and sometimes overdoes it, as I have pointed out. His filling in of the parts outruns mere naturalism and represents a desire to direct the base act of attention to everything that confronts us — that means to everything there is. This sensuous and spiritual plenitude furnishes both the subject of Citrine's epiphany in the jet and the narrative technique by which it is conveyed. Bellow has had to earn the right to use totem-taboo phrases like "universal sapphire" and "everything-nothing capacity."

This full-bodied novel will reward readers of all types, for it successfully blends forward motion with reflection. I must also point out some things I see as flaws or problems deep within it. Bellow does not hesitate to make transitions and to introduce flashbacks and new characters in a casually episodic way. Yet he is writing the consecutive story of one man's five-month crisis. Though part-picaro, Citrine concerns us to the extent that we follow the Aristotelian action he lives through. Such a story imposes a basic narrative economy. Two characters (Naomi's hippie son and Cantabile's PhD wife) severely strain that economy. I would even question the contribution of Citrine's visit to his brother in Texas. And is it necessary to have two film treatments rather than one? They begin to interfere with each other in such a way as to detract from the play-within-a-play effect.

I also found myself wondering why Citrine has two alter egos — Humboldt for his earlier days of budding talent, and Cantabile for his present vulnerability. That complex arrangement would work effectively if Humboldt came through more convincingly. "I saw Humboldt in the days of his youth, covered with rainbows, uttering inspired words, affectionate, intelligent." The poet animates several magnificent scenes during his long decline. But something unassimilated about this larger-than-life character intimates that he is based too closely on a real person or persons. Overabundance in this case has extramural sources.

Thus Humboldt brings us to the second problem, the fictional quality, a more delicate matter than economy. *Humboldt's Gift* is not a *roman à clef*, yet it toys repeatedly with that possibility. The process goes on both at the outer edges of the story, where "real people" (Stevenson and Kennedy, literary types like Philip Rahv and Lionel Abel) prowl in the shadows, and at the center where Citrine is endowed, more or less, with Bellow's age, profession, background, success, place of residence, and much more. Since before Rousseau and Sterne the novel has embraced autobiography without shame. No form of self-revelation through fiction need upset us. What troubles me here, however, is the tone of the book, audible yet less insistent in Bellow's recent novels. It is a tone of self-irony, which seems to increase in direct proportion to the autobiographical content, and in compensation for it. The more closely Bellow projects himself into Citrine, the more mocking his voice seems to become. The risks involved here will emerge better if we look not directly at Citrine, whose nearly nonfictional voice we never stop hearing, but at another person, this one historical, who figures in the story through his writings.

More than either Humboldt or Cantabile, Rudolf Steiner is Citrine's guide to the promised land. Steiner (1861-1925) was a German literary scholar and philosopher who invented anthroposophy (his brand of theosophy) and wrote books like *Knowledge of the Higher Worlds and Its Attainment*, *The Philosophy of Spiritual Activity*, *Between Death and Rebirth*, and *The Occult Significance of Blood*. He also founded theaters, schools, and study centers, some of which still exist. Citrine has been reading Steiner, reflecting at length on his doctrines of metempsychosis and spiritual communication during sleep, and consulting a Chicago anthroposophist, Dr. Scheldt. Much of his theory and imagery of upper wakefulness comes out of Steiner. One of the few things about which Citrine feels certain at the end of the novel is that he will go to live for a spell at the Goetheanum, or Rudolf Steiner Institute, near Basel. I find over twenty passages in which Steiner and his ideas are discussed seriously.[2] Yet at several points Citrine resorts to irony. "All the way to Texas I read occult books. There were many stirring passages in them, to which I shall come back later."

Twentieth-century artists like Kandinsky have looked to Steiner for a new content in art. Swedenborg played a parallel and more powerful role for an earlier generation. To Citrine, however, Steiner's doctrines seem to lead out of art.

Of course I was just a beginner, in the theosophical kindergarten.

But I was serious about it. I meant to make a strange jump and plunge into the truth. I had had it with most contemporary ways of philosophizing. Once and for all I was going to find out whether there was anything behind the incessant hints of immortality that kept dropping on me. . . . I had the strange hunch that nature was not out there . . . but that everything external corresponded vividly with something internal . . . and that nature was my own unconscious being.

What are we to make of the anthroposophist Steiner haunting Bellow's astringent pages? In seeking an answer I came upon Bellow's 1963 essay, "Some Notes on Recent American Fiction." In the crucial passage he berates middle-class writers who are brought up on a mixed diet of affluence and radical ideas.

> They are taught that they can have it both ways. In fact they are taught to expect to enjoy everything that life can offer. They can live dangerously while managing somehow to remain safe. They can be both bureaucrats and bohemians. . . . They are both conservative and radical. *They are not taught to care genuinely for any man or any cause.* [Italics added.]

Bellow could be our Jeremiah; the denunciation has not lost its sting. *Humboldt's Gift* might be read as a fictional treatment of that lamentation, especially of the last sentence. The passage also brings out an important overlap in the book's construction. Citrine nourishes a fierce devotion to Humboldt. In this respect he has lifted himself out of middle-class security. But Humboldt is five years dead and survives for Citrine by proxy in his literary legacy and his widow. Gradually Humboldt takes on the appearance less of a man than a cause — posthumous justice for a mistreated talent.

At the same time, the nearest approach to a cause that Citrine sees himself as espousing is Steiner's spiritualist doctrines. I am not prepared to call Steiner a quack, for his concern with humanity and education partially redeemed his tendencies to superficial cultism. But Citrine is primarily attracted to Steiner's ideas about transcendence and immortality of the self — a highly egotistic cause.

Bellow seems to want to reconcile these two elements when he has Humboldt end his legacy with the admonition, ". . . remember: we are not natural beings but supernatural beings." But every detail in the book tells us that Citrine cares "genuinely" about Humboldt (or Humboldt's memory) and speculates with only half-committed conviction about Steiner's anthroposophy. The fact that Humboldt is not fully convincing as a character contributes to these confusions about man and cause.

I believe that Bellow uses Steiner as a kind of clue to tell us that part at least of what he is writing here is the "Intellectual Comedy of the Modern Mind," the subject Citrine has reserved for his uglier and more intelligent daughter to write about one day. But the reader is left floundering in his attempts to fit together the presumed integrity of Citrine's feelings toward Humboldt and the ironies that undercut his reflections on Steiner's doctrines. This split contributes to the uneasiness of Citrine's narrative voice and the jocularity with which the text sometimes addresses the reader as "you" or "Dear Friends." And the uncertain tone stems also from the original dilemma of fictionality — are we listening to Citrine or to Bellow? Irony, however subtle, will not resolve these conflicts, only confirm their presence.

There is another split or disparity in the book. Bellow displays it convincingly at the seat of Citrine's character. Despite his loyalties to his family and his past, Citrine is driven by a deep need to escape his Midwestern middle-class origins. *Middle* is precisely the word; he was born like Houdini the escape artist (so he reminds us several times) in Appleton, Wisconsin. His aspiration to a larger life takes on two contrasting forms: high intellect and the underworld. He covets both. The story turns on this axis. While he reads Steiner, he lets himself be morally kidnaped by a hoodlum. He seeks spirituality and finds himself examining watches in an elegant apartment belonging to a Mafia type. "These may or may not have been stolen. . . . I was excited, I admit, by these currents of criminality." Citrine sums himself up succinctly as "a lover of beauty who insisted on living in Chicago."

An ancient theme lodges in these divided circumstances. For it has been argued many times that the stature and dignity of humanity reside in the capacity of certain individuals to range wide, to accept no limit on their freedom of experience and of moral movement. Bellow treats the theme with increasing ambivalence in the novel. First of all he shows Citrine being deprived one by one of the presences in his life that could mediate between the extremes. Humboldt was the major one. Earlier there was his boyhood sweetheart. "When I loved Naomi Lutz I was safely *within life*."

Institutions also fail to hold Citrine's life together. His marriage died years ago of early blight. Money lasts much longer. It functions, we are told at first, as a "vital substance" representing "freedom." Humboldt conceives the metaphor of money as blood in a bond of friendship sealed by exchanging blank checks. But the power of money backfires when Humboldt cashes Citrine's check for a whopping sum, and it explodes when the divorce settlement cleans out Citrine. When Humboldt's film treatments turn out to be marketable after all for considerable sums, it is too late. By then Citrine, in his search for a higher selfishness, has lost interest in money. And by then his last two supports have collapsed also: sex, for which Citrine imagines himself well-preserved, and his writing. Renata leaves him flat in Madrid and marries a mortician. Though he juggles a few fond projects, Citrine never sets pen to paper. At the end he is a solitary in earnest, and an institutionless man. No element remains to reconcile his soaring and his slumming selves.

The theme of irreconcilables in man contains potential grandeur. It runs intensely through St. Augustine and Faust, through Baudelaire and Dostoevsky and Melville. But instead of power and passion Bellow again chooses irony for his treatment. Citrine does not really register the presence of evil; he keeps seeing it as a mockery. Cantabile half-hypnotizes him into playing the part of a hired gun in a borrowed hat, "a dummy impersonating a murderer." But nothing seems to be at stake. The whole mood that surrounds Citrine is desultory and sardonic, even when he is thrust up against evil, or attains spiritual release. And why not? Isn't the dandy the hero of modernity? He walks invulnerable inside his all-encompassing aesthetic of detached intensity in living.

Bellow himself provides an answer when he has Mr. Sammler reprove Hannah Arendt for accepting the expression "the banality of evil." In the earlier novel he writes, "The idea of making the century's great crime look dull is not banal." The idea of making Cantabile look comic, harmlessly attractive, is not banal either. Citrine may be a dummy, but the gun Cantabile carries, as a Chicago cop finds, is deadly, a Magnum. Bellow wants no part of Dostoevsky's heavy dramatics, but what he does write sounds occasionally like spoof resorted to as a means of evading the large questions he cannot help raising.

And then there's the ending, the crocuses Citrine sees in the cemetery. At the end of *The Adventures of Augie March* it was a French peasant woman walking off across the fields; in *Henderson the Rain King* it was the Persian boy carried in Henderson's arms; in *Herzog*, the freshly picked flowers. In the final burial scene of *Humboldt's Gift* I find no hint at parody, nothing to cloud the implication that a kind of redemption is beginning. Somehow, we are to understand, Citrine will place himself back within life.

Can it be so? I read unconvinced. The previous pages have set the stage for comic catastrophe. The celebrity-writer who has hobnobbed with Kennedys is now so deeply wounded that he must settle for a rest cure at the Swiss Steiner Center. As his life comes apart, Citrine talks to himself constantly about significant changes for the better taking place within him. But I detect no shift in mental metabolism, no climacteric, only a stronger concern with survival of the self. The well-rounded sensibility responding to the plenitude of life, the voice itself, does not change. For it is Bellow's, masked by the irony that provokes our caution.

Humboldt's Gift shows no flagging of Bellow's intelligence and stylistic powers. He writes like a bird planing, sure of his height, sure of his wings, sure of the language there beneath him, sustaining his flight and as transparent as air. Alert to all his ancestors and rivals from Diderot to Joyce to Pynchon, Bellow has chosen to write an autobiographical novel in the realist tradition. By sheer command of words, he succeeds in animating the busy, smug, self-deprecating *I* of the narrator. But, as my earlier remarks should suggest, the fictional impulse is out of adjustment. The spark is unsteady. Charlie Citrine is too close to Bellow to fill out a fully extruded novel. He is not close enough to impose the dark change of confession. Bellow, of course, plays across that gap — whence his arch and often apologetic tone. He knows there are no rules. But in the characters of Augie March, Henderson, Herzog, and Sammler, all in some degree projections of himself, he employed devices to create an adequate distance from himself. In *Humboldt's Gift* Bellow gets in his own way.

He must have foreseen the risks and decided to take them. He sounds like an ironic ventriloquist, a nearly impossible feat. I was absorbed by the book because Bellow cannot write a dull page. But his awaited masterpiece of exuberant intelligent fiction is still to come. One can hear it muttering through the sardonic treasures of *Humboldt's Gift*.

Notes

1. In the first passage, "jazzy" overloads the picture; the shoes aren't needed. The fussiness about ice cubes in the second passage has only sham documentary interest, like the brand names that keep cropping up. "Bim" strikes my ear as an inappropriate British usage.
2. We might have seen it coming. In *Augie March* Einhorn is on the mailing list of "the Rudolf Steiner Foundation in London."

⁕ ⁕ ⁕

Humboldt's Gift: A New Bellow?
Edmond Schraepen

Even after a superficial reading of *Humboldt's Gift* two features of the novel immediately stand out: first, the world of distraction is more overpowering, wilder and more hectic than ever; then, the mystical strain which had always been more or less subdued in Bellow's fiction now surfaces outspokenly and even programmatically, and takes on a new dimension. A closer look at the novel reveals thematic antitheses which are related to a basic opposition between the distracting world and the transcendental. Actually, this opposition is part of the central conflict between the private and public spheres, which is a familiar pattern in Bellow, but made more complex here by the new turn in Citrine's openly mystical experiences. I wish to examine mainly how Bellow integrates these experiences into his comic form and see how successful he is.

 Humboldt's Gift makes us feel, almost physically, that "the world is too much with us"; never before had Bellow rendered the world of distraction with such excessive particularity. Charlie Citrine is burdened with and entangled in the material world; at times, he wishes to get away from it all and wonders when he will "rise at last above all this stuff, the accidental, the merely phenomenal, the wastefully and randomly human, and be fit to enter higher worlds."[1] The protagonist's attitude towards this world actually oscillates between the two contradictory impulses of fascination and repulsion. The same ambivalence

---

From *English Studies* 62.2 (1981): 164-170.

inhabited Mr. Sammler's mind, but the difference between the two novels is one of mode, satirical in *Mr. Sammler's Planet,* comic in *Humboldt's Gift.* On the one hand, Citrine is powerfully attracted to the "rich, baffling, diverse reality" of contemporary America; he has a "craving for high stimuli, for incongruities and extremes" (99). He even feels attached to the "noisy, bumptious types" (173) who fill much of his life because of their vividness, their striking actuality. As he remarks: "The reason why the Ulicks of this world (and also the Cantabiles) had such sway over me was that they knew their desires clearly. These desires might be low but they were pursued in full wakefulness" (396). These more or less grotesque types are shown as representative of the mad whirling world in which Citrine is caught: they heighten his predicament and enhance the novel's comedy.

Contrary to what Kerry McSweeney asserts,[2] the interruptions and intrusions by "noisy, bumptious types" as well as "the silly and delusive objects, actions and phenomena . . . in the foreground" are necessary to feed the tension between fascination and repulsion. McSweeney objects to "superfluous" detail, but I think that Bellow needs to show an excess of distractions in order to suggest a measure of the mad agitation that Citrine has to cope with, to suggest how insistently the world presses on him and how hard it is to get away from it. Further, the noisy types are part and parcel of one of Bellow's major structuring devices: character contrasts and similarities, a complex set of doubles and mirrors. For instance, the Cantabile-Citrine relationship echoes, on the parodic mode, the Humboldt-Citrine relationship. Thaxter is a lower grade version of Humboldt. Ulick, Swiebel and Szathmar are all reality instructors who act as advisers and protectors to Citrine. The three of them mediate, in some way, between the corrupt world and Citrine. True, Bellow uses these characters somewhat systematically and there is something contrived in their occasionally starting Citrine on "mini-lectures," but they *are* necessary. And Citrine has a way of compounding with them and with their world which is in keeping with the comic mode of the novel. Indeed, there is a kind of ironic dialectic between them and Citrine in that, while they often try to use and even exploit him by drawing him into their schemes, he in turn uses them for his own special, speculative purposes. It could be said that Citrine uses the vividness and the shock value of the distracting world as a spur to an exploration of his higher spiritual purpose, as a way of waking from his spiritual sleep. It may be argued that Citrine "redeems" ludicrous occasions by extracting insights — metaphysical or other — out of them; as striking examples we have the scene in which Cantabile compels Citrine to follow him into the toilet, or when the latter is forced into the role of "hit man," or again when Citrine is taken to the top of a skyscraper frame.

Actually, Citrine also uses his own oddities — for instance, his American fondness for the sensational — to gain something in the spiritual realm. Pursuing one's own eccentricities to see what one can get out of them is a movement familiar to Bellow's protagonists. Citrine is indeed a typical hero of comedy in that he is always open to new experiences as long as he can gain some kind of knowledge from them. For instance, he thinks that Steiner's theories may be lunacy, but he also looks into anthroposophy seriously for whatever knowledge it might yield concerning the transcendental. Citrine is very much like Henderson going along with Dahfu's lion-therapy course, thinking that he "might pick up a small gain here and there in the attempt." This is akin to Herzog's stumbling forward to see whether he could not recover his balance in that way; it also belongs to the impulses of a comic character. In this respect, throughout the novel, Citrine blames himself for being a "goofy old chaser," but this goofy old chaser also earnestly attempts to bridge the gap between this world and the next.[3] In view of Citrine's comical aspects, and of the specifically laughable sides of his metaphysical explorations, this endeavor is somewhat ambiguous, and he might indeed be charged with trying "to kid his way to Jesus"; it is as though he wants to have his metaphysical cake and comically eat it too, thus displaying a familiar Bellovian ambivalence.

The question can thus be legitimately raised whether Bellow's comic mode can do justice both to comic incident and to the seriousness of Citrine's concerns. On the one hand, Bellow wants us to take seriously Citrine's belief in the immortality of souls and in the possibility of establishing contact with the dead. Hence the repeated use of such rhetorical devices as the narrator's direct addresses to the reader, his calling attention to special states of consciousness, and the "mini-lectures" he delivers about these. Indeed the many interpersonal features — addressing the readers, questions, recapitulations, switching from the past to the present tense — used by the confessional narrator give the novel's discourse a strong communicative focus, emphasizing Citrine's urge to convey to his readers his strong sense of mission. Obviously, Citrine wishes to convince us that he has something important to impart. Now what makes us attend with sympathy to this voice, is, on the one hand, the sharp, witty, untiring intellectual drive of Citrine's narrative — the exhilarating, bracing activity of a powerful mind ready to broach *any* topic — and Citrine's self-humorous way of confessing his mistakes and of making amends, on the other.

It should be pointed out that Citrine's strong tendency to give us straight lecturing, almost slipping into the essayistic novel at times, and his lengthy ruminations about the transcendental, do not point to some new crank in Bellow: on the contrary, they reflect some of his familiar basic concerns. Indeed, Bellow believes that the realm of the unconscious presents the novelist with a large field to be explored, and he sees this reconnoitering of a largely uncharted territory as part of a resistance movement against the colonization of the "private sphere" by the "public sphere"; in other words, investigating the unconscious is bound up with a defense of the self against stifling, destructive forces. Further, to Bellow the unconscious — which encompasses the soul[4] — is actually a new frontier where a sense of what binds all men together might be rediscovered, and so restore alienated man to a "common life" again, the ultimate goal of all Bellow heroes.

On the other hand, it should also be noted that the narrator's own suspicions about Steiner, his own deflating self-irony, and the mockery of other characters, qualify Citrine's metaphysical meditations and venture into the anthroposophic new frontier. By placing Citrine's visionary states and insistent intimations of immortality within the mold of his comic mode Bellow "naturalizes" them, i.e., he brings them down to a more accessible level of communication, he assimilates them to the everyday, matter-of-fact, "common-sensical" world of comedy where exalted states tend to become the butt of jokes. But this is part of Bellow's comic strategy: Citrine makes us laugh at him the better to gain our sympathy and attention for his serious concerns. Actually, at the heart of Bellow's seriocomic stance is the doubleness of vision typical of high comedy: Citrine may be seen as a lonely prophet, a guru, a schlemiel, an eccentric, etc., but the value of his spiritual explorations is upheld.

Further, the novel seems to suggest emphatically that the weight and pressure of the distracting world is such that otherworldly aspirations can only be treated comically; our modern sophisticated way of life makes no allowances for, say, intimations of immortality, it provides no "room" for metaphysical promptings. Citrine is a sort of metaphysical romantic quester faced with an overpowering reality — specifically American reality — which cannot afford the individual his full spiritual expression. In this respect, it is worth noting that the discrepancy between reality and aspiration has always been a source of comedy (Bellow's great comic fiction has often been concerned with the area of wish). Bellow, who has long thought that "the world is too much with us," strives to create distance from the overwhelming external world by having his protagonist engage in a probing of his "innermost" world, in an exploration of his "metaphysical field." Thus there is an expanding inward movement in the novel, an inner broadening of its scope, which counters the pervasively encroaching force of the outside world. But it is also precisely on this point that Bellow may be found fault with. For Citrine's consciousness, while it resists the pressure of the distracting world, of History, is also invaded by distractions and historical influences. In other words, Citrine is too often like a filter open to the pressures of the world. Further, even if we grant that the clash between the wised-up, sophisticated, dislocating, violent world and a somewhat helpless Citrine can only be treated comically, we may wonder whether Citrine need be humiliated the way he is, whether his humiliation or "Victimization" need take such extreme forms. Need Citrine be, for instance, such a willing and ludicrous victim, as when he is turned into a "hit man" by Cantabile?[5]

The concept of "reclaiming" or "redeeming," which is germane to comedy, consistently operates throughout *Humboldt's Gift*. Indeed, the novel is to a great extent Citrine's way of compensating for his failure to face the dying Humboldt through a loving and compassionate evocation of his friend's life and eventually through an actual reburial of the dead poet. Actually, this tender recreation of the past is a loving message, a gift from the living to the dead which parallels Humboldt's posthumous gift of a movie scenario to Citrine, with the accompanying explanatory letter as a friendly message of reconciliation from the dead to the living. This "exchange" of gifts supports Citrine's assertion that the dead and the living are a community and epitomizes his efforts at establishing lines of communication between the two worlds. Humor keeps this reaching towards the dead from slipping into sentimentality or morbidity, as when Citrine is told by Denise that "the deceased were [his] bread and butter" (116), since he writes biographies, or later when he remarks that the dead owed him a living.

Establishing some contact with a transcendental realm, communicating with the world of the dead, is presented as being of the utmost importance for the survival of the self and even of democracy.[6] This is bound up with the main theme of the novel, i.e., the opposition between the distracting material world, the public sphere, and the spiritual, transcendental world, the private sphere. Among the antitheses which support the thematic structure of the novel the most recurrent is undoubtedly the waking vs. sleeping motif. Sleep is seen as a desire to evade impending revelation; Citrine is presented time and again as a "sleeper," trying "to burst the spirit's sleep," to borrow Henderson's — and Shelley's — phrase; America itself is pictured as sleeping and as spiritually anesthetized by material affluence. By waking Bellow means spiritual alertness, defense of the inner self. To achieve these Citrine advocates a specific strategy which he makes explicit in two passages, both of which I take to be central to the novel. In the first Citrine tells his childhood sweetheart that

> the old philosophy distinguished between knowledge achieved by effort (*ratio*) and knowledge received (*intellectus*) by the listening soul that can hear the essence of things and comes to understand the marvelous. But this calls for unusual strength of soul. The more so since society claims more and more and more of your inner self and infects you with its restlessness. It trains you in distraction, colonizes consciousness as fast as consciousness advances. The true poise, that of contemplation or imagination, sits right on the border of sleep and dreaming. (306)

In the second passage Citrine tells an indifferent and bored Renata that

> the world has power, and interest follows power. Where are the poets' power and interest? They originate in dream states. These come because the poet is what he is in himself, because a voice sounds in his soul which has a power equal to the power of societies, states and regimes. You don't make yourself interesting through madness, eccentricity, or anything of the sort but because you have the power to cancel the world's distraction, activity, noise, and become fit to hear the essence of things. (312)

Citrine sounds like something of a *lonely prophet* here, meeting with incomprehension on Naomi's part and with Renata's bored indifference. He is actually quite aware of the comic potential of such a role. Earlier in the novel Cantabile had suggested that Citrine might be booked into a night club to hold forth on any topic, preferably of the high-minded sort. Renata at one point sees him as kind of guru, and Citrine even calls himself "a higher-thought clown." Still, even though Citrine realizes the comical aspects of his position, he is in real earnest about his "message." And with regard to this, the point he wishes to make here is that poetic imagination, which to Citrine is bound up with contemplation and originates in dream states, is the instrument needed to purge consciousness and to achieve that "higher consciousness" where one can gain a sense of personal connection with the universe, and where the childhood "home-world," dear to Humboldt, can be recovered. To effect this leap into higher consciousness, one must counter the stifling pressures of distraction and gain new perspectives on death, death seen as part of a life-death continuum. Once one is free from the overwhelming distracting world, from constricting thoughts of death and from the limitations of the self-conscious ego, there occurs an expansion of the inner self, in other words an expansion of the private sphere and a welcome contraction of the public sphere. The waking vs. sleeping motif is thus related to the main theme in an essential way. What Citrine is striving for in the *spiritual realm* is the single-mindedness, the clarity of purpose of the "positive sinners" of the *material realm*.

Expansion of the private sphere with the attendant provision of spiritual nourishment, such is Citrine's goal, the sense of his mission. In this Citrine is the worthy successor of Herzog, who had also been appalled by the spiritual emptiness prevailing in America, and by the deadening all-embracing "reification" process generated by an object-centered, object-consuming America. Time and again the novel shows us characters exaggerating "their subjective style," as Mr. Sammler would say, playing "the bad social game" (125), in other words, projecting themselves into the external world to compensate for their sense of inner void, thus yielding to the demands of the public sphere and sacrificing their inner lives, the private sphere, in the process.

Humboldt's life may be read as a kind of cautionary tale: he wanted to "drape the world in radiance," he wished to pit poetic imagination against the prevalent materialism of the U.S., he longed to be an Orpheus leading America away from the swamps of a stifling affluence, but he failed because he himself yielded to the American cultural values, preferring "ideas" to "poetry" (269). In other words, Humboldt gave up fighting for "higher consciousness." Citrine is determined to pick up the challenge where Humboldt had left off: "I had business on behalf of the entire human race — a responsibility not only to fulfill my own destiny but to carry on for certain failed friends like Von Humboldt Fleisher who had never been able to struggle through into higher wakefulness" (396). Citrine finds it hard to achieve this in the midst of all the distractions which assail him. Entangled in the over-powering American reality, increasingly harassed by Denise and her lawyer, "Cannibal" Pinsker, by the judge Urbanovich, by the I.R.S., and in a way by his mistress Renata, running out of money and badly in need of a breathing spell, Citrine "flees" to Spain. It is as though he were caught in an inextricable net of relationships with all sorts of people making demands on him. Most relationships actually reinforce the theme, with Citrine trying to get away from an "invading," encroaching character. So we are not too surprised when Citrine takes refuge in Spain. The trouble is that, while withdrawing from the dis-tracting world may be the right thing for Citrine's soul, it certainly does not do any good to the novel, which gets bogged down and whose texture becomes significantly thinner. The spiritual just doesn't have the appeal, nor the convincing concreteness — which we expect in a realistic novel — that the distracting world has to offer. Bellow himself seems to have felt this, for he reintroduces Cantabile towards the end of the novel, presumably to inject some excitement into a novel which was fading into the mystical. By removing Citrine from the distractions of American reality, Bellow has also removed one pole of the tension on which the novel is built.

Notes

1. Saul Bellow, *Humboldt's Gift* (New York: Viking, 1975), 291. Sub-sequent references in the text from this edition.
2. Kerry McSweeney, "Saul Bellow and the Life to Come," *Critical Quar-terly* 18.1 (1976): 70.
3. Incidentally, not only is Citrine cast as something of a goofy old chaser, but he also evinces some of the features of the schlemiel: he is gulled, taken advantage of, manipulated and "knocked" — sometimes with a wry acceptance and willingness on his part — but retains his essential resilience. These reverberations from comic types enhance Citrine's comic status and stature.
4. In an article published at just about the same time *Humboldt's Gift* came out ("A World Too Much With Us," *Critical Inquiry* 2.1 [1975]: 9) Bel-low writes: "Why, since the unconscious is by definition what we do not know, should we not expect to find in it traces of the soul as well as of aggression? In any case, the unconscious is today the sole source of impulse and freedom that one branch of science has reserved for art."
5. The forced quality of the dialogues between Citrine and Cantabile just before and during the scene clearly show the strain in credibility.
6. The terrible, stark oppressiveness of the last scene — the reburial of Hum-boldt — does not indicate that death should be accepted as the ultimate, overriding reality, as the crocus symbolism makes clear. What Bellow seems to suggest is that death and burial do remain terrible, oppressive facts, for all the well-oiled machinery of our death-denying sophisticated modern society, but that these facts have to be faced and acknowledged if one wishes to remain human.

* * *

Gender and Self-Deception in *Humboldt's Gift*
David L. Cowles

Human nature requires that each of us create a stable worldview (or language) — a way of describing, limiting, and interpreting the vast jumble of life around us.[1] As a rule we prefer worldviews that make us feel comfortable, connected, and self-justified. Hence the conflict: the modern world, with its future-shock changes, its fragmentation, and its unsettling uncertainties, insistently resists our psychological need for order, certainty, comfort, importance, and connection. Things happen that seem to violate our necessarily reductive ways of seeing the world. Or we may desperately *want* to see the world or ourselves a certain way. At such times we may twist our very perceptions to make them fit our wishes or our preconceived notions. No one can fully escape such self-deception; it's part of our ancestral heritage, a defense mechanism that helps us maintain stability and self-image. But it can also cause problems. First, living in a world in which we perceive inaccurately can be dangerous. Further, self-deception involves an inherent paradox, for in order to deceive myself, I must know, in some way, the very thing I am hiding from myself. Such an irresolvable contradiction can obviously cause inner conflict.

In the real world, where truth is uncertain and where we can only evaluate someone else's limited perspective from our own equally suspect position, it is often difficult to distinguish self-deception from mere error. But in a work of fiction, where the author *creates* a world, the truth is, in some sense, whatever the author says it is. The novelistic worldview becomes a sort of transcendental signifier in its own closed language system, which enables us to evaluate the languages of its characters from an apparently stable, centered perspective. A novelist can portray a self-deceiver by showing that on some level a character recognizes but denies a novelistic "truth."

Self-deception takes many forms in *Humboldt's Gift*: rationalization, evasion, displacement regarding motives, repression, and so on. But two particular aspects dominate: collusion and inauthenticity. First, because it is much easier to maintain an indefensible position if we can get someone else to go along, self-deceivers often collude in their falsified worldviews. Sufficiently empowered groups may impose their ways of seeing not only on their own members, but on outsiders as well. We see such collusive self-deceit throughout *Humboldt's Gift*. In particular for this discussion, the relegation of both men and women to gender-based roles epitomizes the self-deceptive collusion and imposition at the novel's center.

From *Saul Bellow Journal* 8.2 (1989): 14-23.

Second, as Lionel Trilling shows in *Sincerity and Authenticity*,[2] a person can be perfectly sincere — that is, not consciously hypocritical — without being authentic, or true to one's real feelings and nature. Self-deceptive inauthenticity is, according to Amelie Rorty, a deception *of* the self, *by* the self, and *about* the self.[3] And we may be perfectly *sincere* in doing so; indeed, sincerity is the hallmark of self-deceit. Traditionally (as in Rousseau, Kierkegaard, Sartre, etc.) authenticity's great enemy is society. Our culture teaches us through socialization to see the world in certain ways. The more crucial a matter is to social power structures, the less autonomy our culture gives us to see for ourselves. At its most successful, culture keeps us from even recognizing that other ways of seeing exist; its preferred languages seem entirely natural. When we blindly accept such socially mandated worldviews, we risk losing our own identity. As John Stuart Mill describes such people, "By dint of not following their own nature, they have no nature to follow."[4] As we shall see, breaking out of these societal molds entails the nearly impossible task of seeing the world from a perspective other than one's own.

These issues of self-deceptive collusion, imposition, and inauthenticity are central for Bellow's Charlie Citrine. Citrine tells his story as a man in his late fifties who has only recently managed to escape socially mandated, sexually based roles and has finally achieved a limited authenticity. As Bellow sets the situation, Citrine writes to deconstruct his own false past self and to reconstruct a better, more honest one in its place. His concern throughout is with his authentic self — with what it is and what it should be. To find satisfactory answers, Citrine must learn to jettison his socialized masculine roles, to abandon his sincere but inauthentic beliefs and behaviors, and to listen to the inner voice of his own deepest, most real self. It is this authentic self that provides the key to the satisfactory worldview Citrine has sought, ironically, through the very social forms that have prevented him from finding it.

Citrine, a Pulitzer Prize-winning biographer and playwright, seeks transcendence. Obsessed with the problem of death, anxious to leave a legacy of truth to humanity, Citrine longs for a higher spiritual life and consciousness. He believes such a state is possible because he has felt from his youth a certain "lifelong intimation" that he believes "must be either a tenacious illusion or else the truth deeply buried."[5] In the world of *Humboldt's Gift* as Bellow has created it, this intimation constitutes a sort of base truth. Citrine deceives himself when he ignores it to interpret his universe in more worldly ways. Then, like all self-deceivers, Citrine finds himself torn by conflict and self-contradiction.

Citrine is surrounded by characters who represent various socially approved options — all of which are in some way unsatisfactory. The most important of these characters is Von Humboldt Fleisher, whose poetry provides Citrine with a traditional means of transcendence through the imagination. But America dislikes true poets; they don't fit neatly into the roles it provides. America destroys Humboldt, driving him to madness in its own defense: "It was not Humboldt, it was the USA that was making its point: 'Fellow Americans, listen. If you abandon materialism and the normal pursuits of life you wind up at Bellevue like this poor kook'" (156).

Indeed, Humboldt cannot sustain his poetic gift because he succumbs to the roles offered by his culture — all of which are clearly male-specific. For example, he adopts the myth of the poet. "Instead of being a poet," Citrine says, "he was merely the figure of a poet. He was enacting 'The Agony of the American Artist'" (156). "The noble idea of being an American poet" makes Humboldt expend his energies in game, pranks, drinking, and especially sex — all the traditional behavior of a bohemian "Poet." As Fredrica Bartz shows, Bellow does not glorify this version of the poet; rather, he shows its inadequacy as a limiting social role. It is a debilitating male myth.[6]

Humboldt tries to play both sides of this myth. He sees himself as a specifically American poet. He adopts the traditional roles stipulated by the male American dream and tries to incorporate them into his poetic outlook. "He maintained his normal American interests" (15), Citrine says, in things like cars and women. He adopts rationality as the principal means of discovering truth — an approach both Citrine and Bellow clearly reject. Even more important, Humboldt becomes obsessed with money. He tells Citrine, "If I'm obsessed by money, as a poet shouldn't be, there's a reason for it. . . . The reason is that we're Americans after all. What kind of American would I be if I were innocent about money, I ask you? Things have to be combined" (159).

Indeed, combined with this, Humboldt sees himself — as mythical poet — as somehow above others. He develops a monumental case of egoism — seeing himself at the center of the world — a staple of self-deceit. He comes to believe that whatever he does or wants is somehow good simply because he is the great American Poet. "Humboldt had the conviction that there was wealth in the world — not his — to which he had a sovereign claim and that he was bound to get it. . . . 'With a million bucks,' he said, 'I'll be free to think of nothing but poetry'" (159). Receiving good news, Humboldt rushes to celebrate sexually with an unwilling woman named Ginny — wanting, he says, only to do her good, but she won't hold still for it. He treats everyone this way, including his wife, Kathleen. In a moment of insight Citrine says: "I saw the position into which Humboldt had placed Kathleen . . . : Lie there. Hold still. Don't wiggle. My happiness may be peculiar, but once happy I will make you happy, happier than you ever dreamed. When I am satisfied the blessings of fulfillment will flow to all mankind" (22-23).

Trying to graft these self-deceptive masculine roles into his poetic vision causes Humboldt to experience serious inner contradiction. But instead of abandoning the real cause of his problems and seeking his authentic self, he tries another self-deceptive standard: he invents ways to keep from thinking about his problems. He distracts himself with pills, alcohol, and sex. He also turns attention from himself to others. He wildly projects his own faults onto Citrine. He madly blames Kathleen for imagined sexual encounters even worse than his own. All these things constitute one aspect of sleep, an important motif in this novel. Humboldt needs to wake up; instead he acquires earplugs and a mask to keep his authentic self snoozing.

Citrine's problems parallel Humboldt's. Citrine, a different sort of poet, also finds himself trying to choose from among a limited number of socially approved masculine roles, each of which violates the vague but powerful intuitions he feels. Ultimately, Citrine partially succeeds where Humboldt has failed, but only after first trying Humboldt's approach, and only when circumstances force him to abandon his self-deceit.

Citrine, like Humboldt, develops his own myth of the poet — or playwright and historian. "I had," he says, "or assumed that I had, needs and perceptions of a Shakespearian order. But they were only too sporadically of that high order" (186). He sees himself as a sort of modern knight errant. He takes great pride in his French Legion of Honor medal (which turns out to be a very minor, unpoetic order possibly associated with farming). Citrine's play, *Von Trenck*, follows the Humboldt masculine formula, with its hero "fighting duels, escaping from prison, seducing women, lying and bragging, trying to set fire to his brother-in-law's villa" (174). Citrine also uses his knight/poet status, as Humboldt does, to attract women.

Citrine adopts several of America's other required roles and beliefs, too. He embraces rationality as the only way to truth. "I believed that being an intellectual assured me of a higher life," he says. "In this Humboldt and I were exactly alike" (186). Like Humboldt, Citrine has been caught up in materialism. He has the finest of everything, from women to imported toothpicks. Money provides comforts and a comfortable self-image. Citrine tries to deny his own mortality through sports and physical fitness. He dreams about great racquetball victories. He brags to Renata about his low blood pressure, his good health, and his escaping a mugger. Renata herself functions for Citrine largely as further proof to himself that he is not aging. He enjoys association with gangsters; their machismo invigorates him. And he, too, becomes egoistic, seeing the world as revolving around himself.

The women in Citrine's life demonstrate his egoistic, socially approved male perspective. Citrine sees his many female associates only as they relate to him. They offer *him* choices. And he chooses only women who reflect a selection of America's acceptable female roles. Renata, for example, clearly represents male-fantasized sex. "You don't understand real women," she tells Citrine. "*I've* kept your sex powers alive. I know how. Marry me and you'll still be balling me at eighty" (328). Renata's "ideal" (327) amounts to marriage to a distinguished man capable of maintaining her in style. Significantly, she has learned her "tactics" from her mother, the phony "Señora." Yet ironically, though Citrine uses the young Renata as evidence against his own aging, images of death surround her. Certainly Renata and her sexual identity represent spiritual death for Citrine, and only after she has left him can he discover his real self.

Citrine's ex-wife, Denise, represents another traditional feminine role: the exotic bitch. Denise, too, has learned to be a woman by imitating her mother, who turned Denise's son-of-a-gangster father into a federal judge — apparently through a heavy course of browbeating. Denise works in the same way to shape Citrine into a cultured, highbrow gentleman. Even years after their divorce, Denise wants Citrine to remarry her so she can get back to work on him. Nearly breastless, sexually "impatient but dutiful" (115), nagging, sharp-minded and sharp-tongued, Denise is repeatedly identified with castration, a standard part of her stereotyped role identification. Denise and Renata are opposites, but both represent traditional male views of female roles, and both have similar deadening effects on Citrine.

Feminine role identifications also infect Citrine's other women. Kathleen Humboldt, because of some "secret feminine reason" (23), colludes in Humboldt's imposing self-deceit. "Wonderful things are done by women for their husbands," Citrine says of Kathleen. "She loved a poet-king and allowed him to hold her captive" (25). As with Humboldt and Citrine, Kathleen's acquiescence in her culturally assigned sexual role deadens her to her real self: "Kathleen was a somnambulist," Citrine says. "She went to sleep. What else could she do? I understand these decades of sleep" (28).

Citrine sees all women (even his daughters) in sexual terms — as things to be used. And they in turn seek to use him in some masculine role. Naomi Lutz is the single exception. Naomi certainly fits into certain role patterns, but she also maintains her own individuality. She rejects Citrine principally *because* he puts himself into roles that she, from her authentic self, cannot comprehend. Yet only with Naomi does Citrine feel natural, not foreign. "When I loved Naomi Lutz I was safely *within life*," Citrine says. "Its phenomena added up, they made sense. . . . What a blessed life I might have led with Naomi Lutz. . . . I would have smiled at the solitude and boredom of the grave. I would have needed no bibliography, no stock portfolios, no medal from the Legion of Honor" (76-77). Naomi may be a bit goofy, but only when defined by narrow, culturally mandated values. She is Citrine's great lost opportunity — a symbol of the authenticity he has exchanged for male roles. Yet even thinking of Naomi, Citrine reverts to sexual descriptions and sees her principally as a tool, a reified thing that would have had an effect on him.

So Citrine adopts the same masculine roles Humboldt has. But Citrine is even less comfortable at playing them. "Ah!" Humboldt laments to Citrine. "You're not a real American" (124). Indeed, Citrine often feels like a "foreigner." For one thing, he can't accept the finality of death — a requirement of American culture. Moreover, he finds little to interest him in actually making money. Finally, Citrine's inner promptings — his intimations — keep telling him that there is something false about America's materialist mentality. He too feels the inner conflict inherent in self-deception. Also like Humboldt, Citrine uses the masculine roles he plays to distract himself from having to deal with this conflict. For example, when he feels anxiety about death, he distances himself through rationalism: "For relief, I tried to convert this into serious intellectual subject matter. I believe I did this kind of thing rather well" (197). This is self-deception in a pure form. Again, such self-deceptive distraction is a form of sleep. "I often said 'Wake up!' to myself," Citrine explains. "As if I had a dozen eyes, and stubbornly kept them sealed. 'Ye have eyes and see not.' This, of course, was absolutely true" (46).

To escape his problems, Citrine must abandon the masculine roles his society demands he adopt. Born in the same town as Houdini, Citrine must similarly become an escape artist. In doing so, he must essentially forsake the socially constructed self he has developed. As I have said, overcoming any form of self-deception is immensely difficult. Because we can only perceive from a well-established perspective — a language whose words both give us ways of describing reality and limit the ways we can — we don't see first and then interpret. We interpret in the very act of perceiving. This is why it is so difficult to get outside oneself and see the world from a new perspective. It is trying to see one's own eyes without a mirror.

To escape the confines of his own socially imposed worldview, Citrine must abandon his self. He must learn to see the world from a position in which his self plays the smallest possible part. Only in this way can he overcome the kind of egoism Humboldt exemplifies. By at least partially achieving this negative status, Citrine can become not an intellectual, not a poet-biographer, not a sexual being, but a comparatively neutral soul.

Citrine does this in two ways. First, he uses tools he learns from Rudolf Steiner and anthroposophy. He wants to be the clairvoyant who "can see the circumscribed self from without. . . . Dearest God, . . . you see this as you see an external object" (393-94). "The job, once and for all," Citrine explains, "was to burst from the fatal self-sufficiency of consciousness and put my remaining strength over into the Imaginative Soul. As Humboldt too should have done" (417). Citrine begins learning "to stand apart from my own frailties and the absurdities of my character" (439). By achieving such detachment, Citrine escapes self-deception in the only way possible. By relinquishing the self, he has reduced egoism and gained a comparatively unbiased perspective. He has eliminated (or at least diminished) his prime motive for self-deceit.

Second, Citrine reduces the distractions imposed by his culture. Ironically, he can achieve a degree of authenticity only when he abandons part of his self — the ideological, socialized roles. In doing so, he hears more clearly the whispers of his own deepest self beneath the distracting shouts of social and egoistic voices. This is another variation of losing one's self in order to find it. In the process Citrine also loses his fear of death and discovers unity, connection, peace. In a further irony, only by abandoning his self-deceived perspective can Citrine achieve the status his self-deceit was supposed to provide. He no longer plays a specifically masculine role. He now adopts a sort of mothering stance toward Renata's young son, Roger, who is left in his care. Citrine easily rejects the sexual advances of his neighbor, worries more about the kidnapped Thaxter than about his finances, and turns away Cantabile and his offers of sex, power, fame, and money. Though Citrine must continue to deal intermittently with the outer world, Humboldt's legacy allows him to concentrate on spiritual, nonmaterial endeavors. Roger's presence also suggests another identity for Citrine: having rediscovered his authentic self, lost in his childhood, he has again become a child himself — a novitiate in a monkish order of the selfless self.

Ironically, Citrine does all this with a new system — complete with a manual. Neither Citrine nor Bellow fully accepts Steiner or anthroposophy. As Citrine says, "There were passages in Steiner that set my teeth on edge. I said to myself, this is lunacy. Then I said, this is poetry, a great vision" (439). Bellow does not suggest that we all rush to our offices, lock our doors, and read Steiner to the dead. Citrine's system is metaphorical — a new myth. At the end of *Humboldt's Gift*, Citrine hasn't been able to discover his truest self in complete, easily discernible form. It doesn't work that way. But he has changed — and for the better. He no longer deceives himself in his old ways, he has largely relinquished his egotistic perspective, and he no longer defines himself according to masculine social roles.

All this may be self-deceptive on Bellow's part. Indeed, his depiction of Citrine's problems depends on the very socially bound concepts of gender and inauthenticity Citrine seeks to elude. And Citrine's substitution of one system for another may show the impossibility of ever escaping the limitations of language and worldview. But Bellow does not merely identify and lament our subjection to self-deceptive collusion, imposition, egoism, and inauthenticity, as many contemporary writers would. Though culturally approved in academic circles, that sort of fatalism, Bellow seems to believe, is just another form of self-deceptive evasion based on its own socially determined vocabulary. Instead of surrendering to the abyss of deconstructive fatalism, Bellow has suggested symbolically a general method for rising above the bonds of American gender-based self-deception and inauthenticity — a far more rare and difficult task.

Notes

1. Psychologists refer to *schemas* as a rough equivalent to what I call "worldview." Deconstructionists and other language theorists use *language* to make a similar point.
2. Lionel Trilling, *Sincerity and Authenticity* (Cambridge: Harvard UP, 1972).
3. Amelie Oksenberg Rorty, "Belief and Self-Deception," *Inquiry* 15 (1972): 393.
4. John Stuart Mill, *On Liberty* (New York: Norton, 1975), 58.
5. Saul Bellow, *Humboldt's Gift* (New York: Viking, 1975), 439. Subsequent references in the text from this edition.
6. Fredrica Bartz, "*Humboldt's Gift* and the Myth of the Artist in America," *South Carolina Review* 15.1 (1982): 79-83.

* * *

To Jerusalem and Back (1976)

Unsentimental Journey
Edward Grossman

After Saigon disappeared as a byline from American papers, Jerusalem became the place where most front-page foreign news is filed, with Beirut second. Aside from the reporters living in Israel and telexing stories daily, there are the stars of journalism — talented ex-reporters who no longer need to slip their opinions in between the lines — who visit for a week or two, maybe a month, and write up their experience. Many choose the diary form, since that seems to be the easiest, most natural way of listing a whirlwind series of encounters, interviews, sights, ideas, responses. The Israeli diary has become a genre. Though most of the writing produced so far hasn't been able to convey more than surface impressions (often marked by hilarious mistakes due to ignorance or simplemindedly good intentions), it is clear that these are meant to be thoughtful pieces, supplying what is missing in regular news and TV "stories." The implicit claim is that the reader might profit something from following the tourist-writer through Israel, that overwritten country.

In his short new book in diary form, Saul Bellow demonstrates the possibility of making good on such a promise. Admittedly, Bellow is not a journalist, if journalism is defined as writing that is published in newspapers and magazines, or any writing that will be less interesting tomorrow than it is today. Bellow has not often published anything other than novels and stories; but he has occasionally written short pieces of reporting and reflection combined — such as a magazine essay fifteen years ago on Khrushchev, which still stands up tolerably today. *To Jerusalem and Back*, while recognizably Bellow's work, is something of a departure. It handles the stuff of the daily headlines without the tools of metaphor, and it is obviously meant, among other things,

From *Commentary* 62.5 (1976): 80, 82-84.

to affect, directly and quickly, what is called public opinion. From one aspect, *To Jerusalem and Back* is in the tradition of political pamphlets, which have their ground in the moment they are written, and which act to educate and rally sentiment, the sooner the better. From another angle, this book should be read as a continuation of Bellow's life-long meditation on the themes of good-heartedness and private longing in an age of commercial, cultural, and political racketeering.

"Probably the trade I have followed for so many years has made me naive." Is it disingenuous for Bellow to note this? For years he has been an open-eyed specialist in American urban paranoia and the slugging rise of ex-slum boys. But confronted by the Israelis, their past and present and their prospects, Bellow thinks that he has been spared harsh, truthful blows in comparison, thanks to being a writer, an academic, and, especially, an American. Bellow — who once had his fictional creature Henderson declare, "The truth comes in blows" — believes that Americans continue to be sheltered from some of the deadlier rackets operating on a mass scale in the world. If this is temporarily comfortable for his countrymen, it is downright dangerous for those dependent on American support and understanding, like the Israelis. So continually in *To Jerusalem and Back* Bellow, worried by this innocence, enacts the role of one of those reality instructors who hold forth in his novels, about whom he evidently has mixed feelings. Here the object of the teaching is at once the reader and Bellow himself. There is no pretense that Bellow is about to pick up something new about human nature at his age, but he can learn how it has revealed itself in arrangements and crimes, and in the particulars of the look and history of a region — the Middle East — with which he was previously not very familiar.

Like his other books, this is bookish and down to earth. Bellow gets much of his Middle Eastern education from an excellent reading list, and quotes from it generously for the reader's benefit. Elie Kedourie, Malcolm Kerr, Bernard Lewis, Theodore Draper, Walter Laqueur, Yehoshafat Harkabi — these writers are usually unencumbered by the jargon and mythology propagated by area experts and transformed into hopeful media clichés. With all their different emphases and styles, Kedourie and the others studied by Bellow agree that Zionism was not the region's Original Sin; that non-Muslim minorities in the Middle East have a precarious hold on their communal independence and civil rights, if not their very lives; that Arab socialism is more rhetoric than substance; that the Palestinian refugee question has always been incidental to the Muslim Arabs' refusal to have a Jewish state in their midst; and that Israeli territorial concessions alone will never cause peace to break out. Such views, based more or less explicitly on evidence of recurring blood lust exploitable but not controllable by political gangsters, of which the Lebanese slaughter is the latest expression, are unpopular for obvious reasons in America, Europe, and also Israel.

They sort badly with neo-Marxist and corporate think-tank projections of what should happen in the so-called Third World. To accept them, even seriously to consider them, is presumed by some to be equivalent to closing off the mind or giving in to despair. Although Bellow doesn't swallow his reading list uncritically, *To Jerusalem and Back* is certainly not an optimistic book; however, it is not despairing, either. So far as Bellow undermines the conventional wisdom for himself and for a far larger audience than his authorities can command, his book has a liberating effect.

Bellow could have done his homework in Chicago but he did most of it in Jerusalem, between listening to people talk and walking around the city for three months. There is a constant tension and reverberation between his readings and his observations:

> Here in Jerusalem, when you shut your apartment door behind you, you fall into a gale of conversation — exposition, argument, harangue, analysis, theory, expostulation, threat, and prophecy. From diplomats you hear cagey explanations; from responsible persons, cautious and grudging statements rephrasing and amending your own questions; from parents and children, deadly divisions; from friends who let themselves go, passionate speeches, raging denunciations of Western Europe, of Russia, of America. I listen carefully, closely, more closely than I've ever listened in my life, utterly attentive, but I often feel that I have been dropped into a shoreless sea.

Attempting to achieve "clarity," Bellow notices first that the Israelis are less confident than when he visited last, before the Yom Kippur War, and that the role of Israel's failings and offenses that is publicized abroad is also given wide currency inside Israel:

> The New Left sees it as a reactionary little place. Its detractors tell you how it abuses its Arab population and, to a lesser extent, Jewish immigrants from North Africa and the Orient. It is occasionally denounced by some Israelis as corrupt, "Levantine," theocratic. Gossip traces the worst of the Israeli financial swindles to the most observant of Orthodox Jews. I am often told that the old Ashkenazi leaders were unimaginative, that the new Rabin group lacks stature, that Ben Gurion was a terrible old guy but a true leader, that the younger generation is hostile to North African and Asian Jews. The North African and Oriental immigrants are blamed for bringing a baksheesh mentality to Israel; the intellectuals are blamed for letting the quality of life (a deplorable phrase) deteriorate.

The extremely typical epitome of this self-criticism comes in the words of an Israeli novelist who informs Bellow that "Israel has sinned too much . . . lost its moral capital and has nothing to fight with." That was before the Entebbe mission, yet Bellow understood that this writer was wrong, that his words were not to be taken literally. Bellow does not downplay Israel's woes and shortcomings, he has an inkling of the mediocrity and cant here and there, high and low, but he is good enough — and this is unusual these days — to get behind the words and see that the incessant weighing of the national soul on the scales of moral beauty is actually proof that the Israelis are faithfully carrying out their peculiar and unhappy assignment. American and European radicals, Bellow says with bitterness, "appear to believe that the Jews, with their precious and refining record of suffering, have a unique obligation to hold up moral burdens everyone else has dumped." Like it or not, the Israelis, being Jews after all, seem to be doing their duty, acting perforce not so much in their own interest as in the interest of those for whom they are surrogates.

Bellow manages to state this perception without giving the impression of smugness, complacency, or satisfaction; that is because, with rare breaks, the dominant mood of *To Jerusalem and Back* is one of uneasiness, an emotion that the not-so-private diarist urgently wishes to communicate to his readers. His fear is that Americans and other people in the West will focus on Israel's "multitude of faults" and acquiesce in the imposition of stillborn solutions on the Middle East, in order to obscure what is really at stake. For if Western radicals, consciously or unconsciously, expect Israel to be their better half, too many others prefer to blink the whole issue, which for Bellow comes down to nothing less than the survival of virtue: "The 'civilized world,' or the twentieth-century ruins of that world to which so many Jews gave their admiration and devotion between, say, 1789 and 1933 . . . has grown sick of the ideals Israel asks it to respect." Israel is, indeed, a terrible bother to the "humanistic civilized moral imagination," which Bellow says is sunk in "lethargy and sleep."

However, his own imagination is humanistic, civilized, moral. Calling it "inadequate," he can propose nothing better, not even cynicism, though the temptations of cynicism have never been stronger, and though, from time to time, Bellow gives in to them, only to draw back before the barrenness and false comfort. Here Bellow is incorrigible. Disappointed, educated, he remains a humanist, a liberal. If he acts the reality instructor, demanding of readers that they forswear illusion, it is not so he can give them the low-down, and rub their noses in that other lie, which holds that humans today are universally mean and worthless. Nor does Bellow, in contrast with the colorful gallery of steam-bath philosophers who inhabit his novels, appear to relish the task he has taken on. To inform himself and think about the "butcher problems" — the Sixth Fleet, the terrorist bomb that explodes in a restaurant in Jaffa Road — is unpleasant. He would rather be enjoying literature, or sitting in one of Jerusalem's quiet places, being moved mystically:

> I enter a flagstoned court in the Greek quarter and see that it is covered by grapevine. . . . Light shimmers through the leaf cover. I want to go no farther that day. . . . I am tempted to sit down and stay put for an aeon in the consummate mildness. . . . The origin of this desire is obvious — it comes from the contrast between politics and peace. The slightest return of beauty makes you aware how deep your social wounds

are, how painful it is to think continually of nothing but aggression and defense, superpowers, diplomacy, war.

What is real, the "consummate mildness" of personal, poetic experience, or the "butcher problems"? Which one prevails? Bellow's debate with himself on this throughout *To Jerusalem and Back*, continuing when he is home again in Chicago, provides the book with a dimension beyond polemic. Bellow is not blind to the fact that these Israelis — to whom he feels so close, as an American and as a Jew — have lost something in their inescapable preoccupation with war, become split or hypertrophied. Their beleaguered land is "both a garrison state and a cultivated society, both Spartan and Athenian." And, for all his concern about the dreaminess of Americans, he knows we too "have mechanisms operating within, answering to more remote stimuli, phantoms of crisis that set off endless circuits of anxious calculation." He honors, maybe envies, those writers who refused "to submit to what societies and governments consider to be important" (Stendhal, E. E. Cummings, Mandelstam, Sinyavsky), and wonders, more than half-convinced, whether "to remain a poet . . . is also to reach the heart of politics." Nevertheless, that is not the route he has taken, and by reason of temperament and circumstances he probably had no choice. *To Jerusalem and Back* is in "the public realm":

> What drives the soul into the public realm is, first, the reality of the threat to civilization and to our own existence; second, our duty to struggle and resist (as we conceive this); third, the influence of public discussion in the press, on television, in books, in lecture halls, or at dinner tables, in offices; and fourth, perhaps, is our own deep desire to send the soul into society.

This last motive, for fame, should not be misunderstood. Actually, it took courage for Bellow to publish this book. Lately it may seem that everybody is writing first-hand about Israel; in fact, these are mostly journalists and glorified journalists. The writers who have reputations as masters of American culture, which they made with novels addressed to the entire literate public, yet who are identifiable in one way or another as Jews, have tended to shun the subject of Israel and may never have set foot there. Some are known for overt political engagements, going back to the Vietnam era or before, in the course of which they have done everything from signing petitions to abandoning fiction in favor of books on burning current issues. To be specific, these were some pages of caricature devoted to Israel in *Portnoy's Complaint*. The silence of Norman Mailer is more typical, however. It would be nice to give the benefit of the doubt, to credit such writers with an unwillingness to add to the pile of superficialities and pieties already written concerning Israel — not unintelligent, they must realize how little they know when it comes to this subject. That is possible. But one's stronger suspicion is that to delve into the Jewish state and its relations with America would mean raising in public questions of the writer's identity that are frightening and would best be left alone; rather than go into this, the tacit excuse for silence is that Israel is of interest and importance only to Jews, and to write about it, let alone rally support, would betray parochialism. Against this background, Bellow's achievement is more impressive still.

* * *

In Defiance of Reason:
Saul Bellow's *To Jerusalem and Back*
Steven David Lavine

As a work of political and social analysis, Saul Bellow's *To Jerusalem and Back: A Personal Account* is more than a little disappointing. In Israel, Bellow consults with a great many experts, politicians, and interested parties, and he reads widely in books related to the Arab-Israeli conflict, but the resulting book reveals little effort to synthesize his findings. The loose journal form allows Bellow to move from one subject to the next without sustaining an argument. Thus, in one five-page section, he moves from a consideration of the age of Jerusalem to Elie Kedourie's *Arabic Political Memoirs* (where he learns that Egypt employed an American public relations firm in formulating its revolutionary program) to "America's two-hundred year record of liberal democracy" versus Israel's difficulties in establishing a "just society" to the "inordinate demands Jews make on themselves and others."[1] While even this sketchy outline will reveal that Bellow does more than merely ramble, there is still a want of hard thought, of ideas engaged, analyzed, and judged. Occasionally opinions are arranged so as to create the possibility of debate — a Russian view of American political naiveté versus an American view of Russian foreign policy failure (18-20). Andrei Sinyavsky's vision of art as a meeting place versus an Amnesty International report on the condition of Russian "prisoners of conscience" (33-34) — but seldom is the debate actually joined. Instead, Bellow seems to stand to one side, looking on in bemused silence, suggesting perhaps, in the words of his friend David Shahar, that "where there is no paradox there is no life" (15).

All this is not to say that there is a complete want of social and political thought. Certain themes do recur. On the social level, Bellow does manage to depict a society living with the constant threat of annihilation — talking, talking, talking its way to a solution. Politically, it is not difficult to deduce Bellow's opinions that there is some justice on both sides in the Arab-Israeli debate, that the democratic West has lost its sense of purpose and cannot be counted on to support Israel indefin-

From *Judaism* 28.1 (1979): 42-50.

itely, that America, the best intentioned of the Western powers, is too politically naive to cope with the Soviet Union, and that as things now stand one cannot be very hopeful about the possibility of any peaceful solution. Further, it seems likely that the dovish view presented by a friend after Bellow's return to Chicago approximates Bellow's own political position. But that is about it, and, with the possible exception of Bellow's musings on the decline of the West, there is little here that will surprise or inform even the most desultory newspaper reader. As Irving Howe put it in *The New York Times Book Review*, "a reader may find it frustrating, if only because one expects from a writer like Bellow more sustained argument, deeper probing. We don't get it."[2]

In a book composed almost entirely of theories about the Arab-Israeli situation, written by a novelist known for his concern with the power of ideas, this absence of "deeper probing" becomes, in itself, a prominent feature. Every page evinces Bellow's passionate concern for the survival of Israel and certainly no reader of Bellow's novels or of his public pronouncements about the role of the artist can doubt the seriousness with which Bellow approaches his calling as a writer. One must conclude then either that in moving from the novel to non-fiction Bellow has gotten in over his head or that he has something in mind besides direct social and political analysis. The book itself seems at times to support the first of these alternatives. Thus, midway through, Bellow writes, "I know Auschwitz and the Gulag, Biafra and Bangladesh, Buenos Aires and Beirut, but when I come back to facts anew I find myself losing focus" (84); and, less than ten pages from the end of the book, he expands upon this problem:

> Trying to put it all together, "to come to clarity," as one of my professors used to say. What a nice thing to come to. But this subject resists clarification. Matters like Islamic history, Israeli politics, Russian ambitions, and American problems — foreign and domestic — interpose themselves, to say nothing of Third World upheavals and the crisis of Western civilization. Instead of coming to clarity, one is infected with disorder. (175)

These disclaimers, combined with the unanswered questions, the juxtaposed irreconcilable political opinions, and the occasional comments such as "we are informed about everything. We know nothing," suggest that confronted with the actualities of the Israeli situation, Bellow has been overwhelmed. Indeed, he has come to sound like his own characters — most notably Herzog, Sammler, and Von Humboldt Fleisher — who are defeated in their attempts to find a rational vision which will bring coherence to the apparent chaos of modern life.

However, when one recognizes the similarity between Bellow in *To Jerusalem and Back* and the heroes in his earlier works, a new perspective opens up. Perhaps Bellow has never really intended social and political analysis as the primary objective of *To Jerusalem and Back*, but rather has attempted to dramatize in a non-fictional context the concerns that have occupied him in his fiction: most notably, the forces in contemporary life which either deny the existence of the soul or drive it into hiding and, to go all the way back to Joseph in *Dangling Man*, the feeling that our minds are our essential selves — "It is our humanity that we are responsible for it, our dignity, our freedom" — and the opposite sense that it is all too much for us — "That human might is too small to pit against the unsolvables. Our nature, mind's nature, is weak, and only the heart can be relied on."[3] Perhaps Bellow is trying to do what he has always admired the great Russian novelists for doing, to present social life in a way which suggests that it cannot finally contain or limit what is best in the human spirit. This reading has the advantage of explaining Bellow's own sense that *To Jerusalem and Back* is a success: "In the book I recently did on Israel I discovered that it was as easy to write about great public matters as about private ones. All it required was more confidence and daring."[4] More important, it brings together a variety of comments and observations during the course of the book which would otherwise be irrelevant or simply unexplainable, and it prepares a way for the explanation of the place of *To Jerusalem and Back* in Bellow's career as a writer.

Early in the book, after a conversation with an Armenian Archbishop and the foreign-news editor of *Le Monde*, Bellow comments:

> I have been hearing conversations like this one for half a century. I well remember what intelligent, informed people were saying in the last days of the Weimar Republic, what they told one another in the first days after Hindenburg had brought in Hitler. . . . I remember what people said about the Italian adventure in Ethiopia and about the Spanish Civil War and the Battle of Britain. Such intelligent discussion hasn't *always* been wrong. What is wrong with it is that the discussants invariably impart their own intelligence to what they are discussing. Later, historical studies show that what actually happened was devoid of anything like such intelligence. (7-8)

If *To Jerusalem and Back* were intended as a work of social and political analysis, Bellow's readiness to admit defeat, to deny the possibility of a rational observer reaching a correct understanding of a contemporary event, would be remarkable indeed. However, if the general direction of the book is to suggest that in this century the complexity of human life, that is, public life, has reached such a pass that reason no longer seems adequate, then this historical account of reason's failures only supports his point. As Mr. Sammler had told Dr. Lal: "I am familiar with many explanations of things. To tell the truth, I am tired of most of them." And again, "I am extremely skeptical of explanations, rationalistic practices."[5] Of course, Sammler's statements of skepticism come during a thirty-page explanation of the course of Western civilization, but Sammler tries to abandon such practices and so does Bellow in *To Jerusalem and Back*, with just about equal success.

Sammler, you will recall, hopes to replace such explanations with a greater grasp of the immediate; as he puts it, quoting Sydney Smith: "Short views, for God's sake, short views" (106); and again, in other terms, "One had to learn to distinguish. To distinguish and distinguish and distinguish. It was distinguishing, not explanation, that mattered" (61). In a general way one might say that in *To Jerusalem and Back* Bellow has conducted an experiment in distinguishing and short views. Avoiding the mental turnings and twistings of Herzog, Humboldt, and Sammler himself, Bellow has attempted to immerse himself in Israeli life and to distinguish, to see what is happening at the immediate moment whether or not that tends to an overall explanation of the Arab-Israeli situation. Indeed, at several points in the book, Bellow speaks of his project in terms reminiscent of Sammler's. Explaining why he has not objected to a view expressed by Prime Minister Rabin, Bellow writes, "I have come to listen, not to differ" (113); and, more generally, he describes his task as one of observation rather than explanation, "I was here to observe, to sense a condition or absorb qualities" (111). While such an approach would be inadequate for a social or political analysis, it is, it seems, just what is required of the person interested in short views. It is possible that the most accurate social science analogy here would be with anthropology, and it is perhaps not totally by chance that Bellow, during the course of *To Jerusalem and Back*, chooses to remind the reader that he was once a graduate student in anthropology (130).

If Bellow's project is to "distinguish" and "observe" rather than to explain, we must ask what it is that he observes. Early in the book, Bellow himself suggests an answer. Discussing the "bravest of modern writers . . . the Mandelstams and the Sinyavskys," Bellow writes, "Perhaps to remain a poet in such circumstances is also to reach the heart of politics. Then human feelings, human experience, the human form and face, recover their proper place — the foreground" (22). Bellow suggests that the writer must go beyond the realm of opinion and theory, that he must attempt to observe the human reality — the personal, the emotional, perhaps even the spiritual — behind all the intellectualizations. What this might mean in the concrete can be seen from the very first pages of *To Jerusalem and Back*. There Bellow encounters a young Hasid who is willing to pay him to give up unkosher food. As the scene ends, Bellow observes: "In me he sees what deformities the modern age can produce in the seed of Abraham. In him I see a piece of history, an antiquity" (5). Bellow refuses to pass judgment on the relative merits of these positions. Instead, what he sees, and what he allows the reader to see, is the absolute relativity of judgment which is the result of each man seeing the world through the glass of his own emotional and spiritual convictions.

Here, with nothing earth-shaking immediately at stake, this relativity is accepted mildly enough. When Bellow becomes an observer in Israel, it will become more problematical; with a nation's future at stake, mere demonstration of the very human fact of the relativity of all judgments would hardly be adequate. Instead, Bellow will try to go beyond such relativity, to recapture those human facts which should be able to form a ground on which all judgments could be made. And, at the same time, in the continual dialectic between expressed opinion and human fact, the import of the "perhaps" in the quote above — "Perhaps to remain a poet in such circumstances is also to reach the heart of politics" — will become apparent. Bellow himself is not certain: perhaps some political solution still might be found through the application of reason, perhaps one must instead intuit the essential human facts behind the political situation. Once more Bellow is in the position of his heroes from Joseph to Charlie Citrine, torn between a trust in the intellect and a trust in the human heart.

Another example will clarify the book's continual movement between expressed opinion and human fact. The conversation with the Armenian Archbishop, to which we have already referred, is the first of what will be a long series of discussions of Israel's situation. Here what Bellow observes is not merely the actual opinions but also the whole process of discussion: "And the talk goes on. What is still being perpetuated in all civilized discussion is the ritual of civilized discussion itself" (8). After more talk of the Russians, and Communism, and the Vatican, Bellow observes, "Dessert is served." What Bellow sees is the enormous disparity between the threat at hand (which is, after all, the threat of the destruction of Israel) and the comfort and civility of the occasion. If there is to be explanation, perhaps it is this very disparity which most immediately requires comment, and in the casual phrase, "the ritual of civilized discussion," Bellow lays the groundwork for such an explanation. To this we shall return shortly.

Even more striking than this simple disparity is the disparity Bellow observes between the kind of ideas to which men commit themselves and the kind of men they actually seem to be. Shlomo Avineri, a political scientist at Hebrew University, argues that communism has been a boon to Eastern Europe and that in the democratization of communism is to be found the hope of the world. Bellow muses:

> How much more do intellectuals need to learn about the U.S.S.R.? Knowing something about life in Communist countries, I disagree completely with Avineri. In my judgment this is a frivolous analysis — heartless, too, if you think how little personal liberty there is in Eastern Europe. One has no business to give away the rights of others. (44)

But then comes the double take: "But I look at Professor Avineri and see that he is an engaging fellow, far from heartless" (44). Again and again in *To Jerusalem and Back* we will encounter this sort of mental action, as Bellow moves from intellectual formulation to seemingly contradictory human fact. And this action will occur at all levels, not only between discussions of the Israeli situation and the nature of the discussants, but also, for example, between Professor Werblowsky's rationalistic explanations of Joseph Karo's mysticism and of the Sabbath, and Werblowsky's own evident spirituality in his writings and in his conduct of the Sabbath meal (51-54), and between Meyer Weisgal's behavior as a devoted servant of Israel and his style as an old-time dandy (71ff.).

But if Bellow multiplies his examples, they are all finally reducible to the poles of "politics" and "poetry," or "politics" and "peace." By politics, Bellow means "everything in the public part of life" (95); by poetry and peace he means all the rest, all that might be subsumed in the phrase "the human form and face," all we mean when we refer to the individual, the personal, the emotional, the spiritual. In *To Jerusalem and Back*, Bellow presents, as he has in his novels, the intolerable pressures placed on the individual who attempts to operate at the public or political level, who attempts to apply reason to the problems of public life. Thus, as in his essay "Distractions of a Fiction Writer," Bellow considers "what the literary imagination faces in these political times."

> We can't avoid being politicized . . . because it is necessary after all to know what is going on. Worse yet, what is going on will not let us alone. Neither the facts nor the deformations, the insidious platitudes of the media (tormenting because the underlying realities are so huge and so terrible), can be screened out. (21)

One of Bellow's few moments of relief in Israel comes in the company of two poets, and of this event he writes: "They released me from weeks of preoccupation with the merciless problems — the butcher problems of politics"; and then, thinking of the full-time politicians he has met, Bellow wonders, "It is perhaps astonishing that they aren't demented by the butcher problems, by the insensate pressure of crisis" (80). Throughout *To Jerusalem and Back*, in the continual movement from opinion to opinion and from opinion to human fact, Bellow dramatizes the pressures placed on the writer — and ultimately on any intelligent man — who tries to survive in the world of politics.

When Bellow observes Israel, what he sees most prominently is, similarly, this "insensate pressure of crisis." Beneath every conversation is the constant worry about survival: "The subject of all this talk is, ultimately, survival — the survival of the decent society created in Israel within a few decades" (25). Whatever the apparent topic, the real worry is the immediate threat of destruction. Discuss the Arab-Israeli situation and "the nightmare of annihilation" is invoked: "This is what Israel lives with" (38). Talk with a cabbie and he tells you about a friend killed in a bomb explosion a few days before: "And this is how we live, mister! Okay? We live this way" (43). The fact can never be forgotten that "you cannot take your right to live for granted" (26). Thinking about these things, trying to make sense of life at the public level, Israelis become actual versions of Bellow's imaginary characters. Bellow has always written about characters *in extremis*; in Israel he finds an entire nation *in extremis*. Herzog is nearly destroyed "by the need to explain, to have it out, to justify, to put in perspective, to make amends"; Sammler muses about the "endless literal hours in which one is internally eaten up. Eaten up because coherence is lacking"; Humboldt's poetic efforts "to free and to bless humankind" end in madness.[6] And now, in Israel, Bellow writes of a Professor Talmon: "Would matters be easier for him if he didn't think so many things? Although he is the source of these speeding thoughts, he seems at times to be their target" (137). In his fiction, Bellow is always forced to consider the possibility that his characters are merely psychologically defective, that is, that their problems are individual and accidental rather than common and necessary; in Israel Bellow finds a nation whose exterior problems are absolutely undeniable. He suggests something of both the parallel and the difference when he writes, "One of the oddities of life in this country: when someone says 'the struggle for existence' he means that literally" (70).

The full extent to which Bellow sees Israel as embodying the crises he has depicted in his fiction may be seen by comparing a passage from *Humboldt's Gift* with one from *To Jerusalem and Back*. Charlie Citrine describes the typical Humboldt harangue:

> And this rained down on me, part privilege, part pain, with illustrations from the classics and the sayings of Einstein and Zsa Zsa Gabor, with references to Polish socialism and the football tactics of George Hallas and the secret motives of Arnold Toynbee, and (somehow) the used-car business. Rich boys, poor boys, jewboys, goyboys, chorus girls, prostitution and religion, old money, new money, gentlemen's clubs, Back Bay, Newport, Washington Square, Henry Adams, Henry James, Henry Ford, Saint John of the Cross, Dante, Ezra Pound. . . . (30)

Humboldt seeks the order which will contain and explain all the best and the worst of European culture and of American life. In *To Jerusalem and Back*, Bellow details the public facts forced upon the consciousness of the Israelis.

> In Israel, one has no such choice. There the violent total is added up every day. And nothing can be omitted. The Jerusalemite hooked by world politics cannot forget Gerald Ford and China, Ronald Reagan and California; he is obliged to know that Harold Wilson has just asserted in a speech that England is still a force to be reckoned with. He cannot afford to overlook the latest changes in the strategy of the French Communist Party nor the crises in Portugal and Angola; he must remember the mental character of the Muslim world, the Jews of the Diaspora. Israelis must, in fact, bear in mind four thousand years of Jewish history. The world has been thrown into their arms and they are required to perform an incredible balancing act. (46)

What may be only willfulness or insanity in a Humboldt or a Herzog is an absolute fact of life in Israel. For Bellow the pathos of the Israeli situation is that having sought "to lead Jewish lives in a Jewish state," they now "must reckon with the world, and with the madness of the world, and to a most grotesque extent" (163); the wonder is that in the face of these pressures they have accomplished so much: "It is both a garrison state and a cultivated society, both Spartan and Athenian. It tries to do everything, to understand everything, to make provision for everything. . . . I don't see how they can bear it" (46). At a time when "the civilized world seems tired of its civilization," the Israelis have taken up the burden: "Jews, yes, have a multitude of faults, but they have not given up on the old virtues" (57). Thus the problem of the continued existence of Israel becomes the problem of the continued existence of Western civilization, and the solution to one problem is likely to be solution to the other.

With this analysis in mind, we can return to Bellow's view of the disparity between intellectual opinion and human fact. What we are now in a position to see is that intellectual opinions, as they are presently formulated, are an offshoot of the whole crisis of Western culture. They are, above all, efforts to find some release from the pressure, to regain some peace of mind. Bellow writes, "The search for relief from the uneasiness is what is real in Israel" (26), and again, "A great deal of intelligence can be invested in ignorance when the need for illusion is deep" (127). The danger, of course, is that in terms of peace of mind one opinion is pretty much as good as the next. Again and again in *To Jerusalem and Back*, Bellow and the commentators he quotes insist that what is needed is a return to reality: "Professor Lamm calls for a return to political realism" (70); "I wonder about the effects of limitless expectation on the American sense of reality" (129); "I don't know how much reality there is in this — little, I suspect" (175). Alternatively, Bellow images forth the problem as a matter of waking up: "I am forced to consider whether Western Europe and the United States may not be under the influence of a great evil, whether we do not go about lightly chloroformed" (84); "And Israel's political leaders do not seem to me to be awake" (131). The danger Bellow identifies is that in the face of the pressure of crisis, thinking may become not a way of addressing reality, but rather a sort of ritual: "Such concentrated attention comes close to being a sort of magical activity to avert a disaster" (106). Herzog asks himself, "Did I really believe that I would die when thinking stopped?"; now Bellow considers that a similar mechanism may be at work in Israel and in the Western world generally: "You are at times seduced into thinking that anything that can be studied and written up is also susceptible to reasonable adjustment" (170). Bellow fears then that with thought becoming such a magical activity, a nation, like an individual, may well lose sight of its own best interests: "I'm not at all certain now that civilized minds are more flexible and capable [than "primitive" ones] of grasping reality or that they have livelier, more intelligent reactions to the threat of extinction" (130).

In light of this analysis of apparently rational, intellectual activity, it is not surprising that at the climax of *To Jerusalem and Back*, just before Bellow prepares to leave Jerusalem, a long section is devoted to

one of the West's "masterminds," Jean Paul Sartre. In a discussion
reminiscent of Mr. Sammler's treatment of the theories of Hannah
Arendt, Bellow takes exception to Sartre's views on the Middle East;
indeed, he asks, "Did this influential thinker and prominent revolution-
ist know what he was saying?" (121; *Sammler* 17-21). In describing
Sartre's ideas, Bellow comments, "A definition is a definition. Sartre is
not conspicuously flexible" (122), and he takes Sartre as an example of
the very particular proud myopia of French culture. He continues:

> Truth is timeless, certainly, and one doesn't have to be up to date to be
> right, but in taking positions or advocating actions that may cost people
> their lives one should be as clear as possible about historical facts. Here
> the danger that "thinkers" can constitute for the rest of humanity begins
> to be very plain. (123)

The question becomes how one can regain this desired flexibility, and
the answer, as is suggested by the whole course of *To Jerusalem and
Back*, particularly by the movement between intellectual opinion and
human fact, is that one must recover the "human form and face." If
thinkers were forced to test their ideas against immediate human fact, if
they were forced to recognize the personal, the emotional, the spiritual,
and even the fumblingly intellectual components of the individual
human life, a flexibility might be achieved which would, at least, discourage the sacrifice of human life in the name of political theory.

Lest this conclusion seem far-fetched, it is worth remembering
Bellow's recent essay, "A World Too Much with Us." There, considering the place of the writer in the twentieth century, Bellow takes
up the case of Sartre and, in particular, Sartre's assertion that "the
Third World finds manhood by its burning ever-present hatred and its
desire to kill us." Bellow suggests that if Sartre were forced to take up
this proposition imaginatively, he would have to abandon his theory:

> He is not a good novelist but the art itself would have obliged him to deal
> with the real, or approximately real, human beings, not the zombies of a
> pamphleteer. . . . It is not inconceivable that a man might find freedom
> and identity by killing his oppressor. But as a Chicagoan, I am rather
> skeptical about this. Murderers are not improved by murdering.[7]

Even if one is not so confident as Bellow about what the rediscovered
"human" might look like, one can see what he is getting at. Only by
recovering the "human form and face" can those ideas which make us
so willing to take life be defeated. The task is not an easy one. As Bellow writes in *To Jerusalem and Back*, "it is obvious that the humanistic
civilized moral imagination is inadequate. Confronted with such a
'metaphysical' demonstration [Bellow has been discussing the Holo-
caust], it despairs and declines from despair into lethargy and sleep"
(58). What is required is nothing less than the gathering of all our
intuitions about the "human form and face" into a new definition of
man. But it is the task that Bellow has always taken on as a novelist,
and it is his task, once more, in *To Jerusalem and Back*.

To Jerusalem and Back takes its place then in the whole progression of Bellow's work. It becomes yet another examination of the problem Bellow formulated so eloquently in his Nobel Prize Acceptance Speech: "Out of the struggle at the center has come an immense, painful longing for a broader, more flexible, fuller, more coherent, more comprehensive account of what we human beings are, who we are, and what this life is for."[8] And, whatever its limitations, *To Jerusalem and Back* is surely a significant step forward in Bellow's development. Since *Herzog*, it has been evident that Bellow is torn between the desire to plunge into the immediate, concrete world and the counter-desire to withdraw into mysticism. Herzog, you will recall, ends his progress resolving to enter the world of men and action but still sitting in his Ludeyville, Massachusetts, lawnchair, enjoying his new-found peace. In *Mr. Sammler's Planet*, with its evocation of the 1960s, Bellow attempts, with somewhat mixed success, to engage that concrete world. *Humboldt's Gift* weighs the alternatives of Humboldt's possibly self-destructive attempt to engage immediate social reality and Citrine's possibly self-destructive absorption in the mystic and the irrational, but no final decision is reached. In *To Jerusalem and Back*, there is a decisive movement toward the concrete world once again, but now in a fashion that preserves Bellow's sense of the private and the poetic while still addressing the public world.

Finally, in *To Jerusalem and Back*, Bellow works toward a solution to a problem apparent in all his earlier efforts. Bellow's novels are attempts to develop that further definition of "what we human beings are, who we are, and what this life is for"; he has even referred to these works as "piece(s) of research."[9] But in his novels Bellow has been far more successful in dramatizing the process by which characters overcome the liabilities implicit in older ideas of man than he has in showing what the new man, the good man, would be like. Novel after novel has ended with a character brought to a moment of epiphany: Tommy in tears before the body of the dead stranger, Henderson feeling that "it was my turn now to move," Herzog in his lawnchair. But Bellow has been unable to take his characters further. Bellow himself treats this as a limiting aspect in his work:

> I don't think that I've represented any really good men; no one is thoroughly admirable in any of my novels. Realism has restrained me too much for that. I should *like* to represent good men. I long to know who and what they are and what their condition might be. I often represent men who desire such qualities but seem unable to achieve them on any significant scale. I criticize this in myself. I find it a limitation.
>
> INTERVIEWER: I'm sorry; what exactly is this limitation?
>
> BELLOW: The fact that I have not discerned those qualities or that I have not shown them in action.[10]

Arguably, in *To Jerusalem and Back*, by eschewing the introverted psychological problems of a Herzog or a Humboldt and by looking instead at the conversation and actions of men such as Teddy Kollek and Meyer Weisgal, Bellow has come closer to presenting good men in action than in any of his earlier fiction. Paradox survives, and there is more to be said about "what their condition might be," but here, at last, Bellow is able to show men acting, and acting valuably, in the world of other men.

Notes

1. Saul Bellow, *To Jerusalem and Back: A Personal Account* (New York: Viking, 1976), 10-15. Subsequent references in the text from this edition.
2. "To Jerusalem and Back," *The New York Times Book Review* (17 Oct. 1976): 1.
3. Saul Bellow, *Dangling Man* (New York: Signet, 1965), 111, 90.
4. Joseph Epstein, "A Talk with Saul Bellow," *The New York Times Book Review* (5 Dec. 1976): 92-93.
5. Saul Bellow, *Mr. Sammler's Planet* (Greenwich, Conn.: Fawcett Crest, n.d.), 196, 206.
6. Saul Bellow, *Herzog* (Greenwich, Conn.: Fawcett Crest, n.d.), 8; *Mr. Sammler's Planet*, 86; *Humboldt's Gift* (New York: Avon, 1976), 115.
7. Saul Bellow, "A World Too Much with Us," *Critical Inquiry* 2.1 (1975): 4-5.
8. Qtd. in "A Time for Rethinking: Bellow's Challenge," *Newsweek* (27 Dec. 1976): 62.
9. Gordon Lloyd Harper, "Saul Bellow: An Interview," *Paris Review* 9.36 (1966): 67.
10. Harper, 67.

* * *

The Dean's December (1982)

An Interview with Saul Bellow
Matthew C. Roudané

The interview with Saul Bellow took place in two sessions. The first discussion, on December 26, 1982, occurred at the University of Chicago, while we held the second conversation, on March 5, 1983, in Bellow's apartment overlooking Lake Michigan. Over tea and with a marvelous view of the lake, Bellow clarified some key issues regarding his work. Reflective, articulate, often with a street-wise, wry smile, Bellow discussed openly his artistry.

Q.   As a writer, what keeps you in Chicago? Is there an alluring quality to this milieu here that engages you?

A.   I don't suppose I would have been living here if there had been a more attractive life for a writer elsewhere. But the idea of a great good place for writers and painters is a flop in America. There is no such thing. In the 1920s and '30s artists went to Paris and had a hell of a good time, as I tried to do in '48. I went there directly after the war because I was eager to see the action. But I found no great action when I got there. There were not many flowers of culture in 1947-48. Everybody concentrated on gluing the pieces together. For artists the great age had already been petering out before the war. By the great age I mean the international culture — the gathering in Paris of a group of great figures, few of them French: Stein, Hemingway, Joyce, Pound, Picasso, Brancusi, Modigliani, Diaghilev, Stravinski, and so on. It was an international culture that made Paris its headquarters. But it was French only in location. I think that politics had already been ruining this great movement in the arts even before the Second World War. Political ideologies in the '30s contributed to its ruin.

Q.   And so you have made Chicago home turf.

From *Contemporary Literature* 25.3 (1984): 265-280.

A.   When I say that Chicago *speaks* to me I don't mean that I treasure all of its utterances. What am I doing here? When that is asked I recall the title of a book of poems published many years ago by a poet from the Philippines. It was called "Have Come: Am Here." What is the use of pretending that any modern city is not inhabited principally by philistines? We must not forget, however, that these same philistines are our sisters and our brothers. And frank philistinism suits me better than bogus "culture." Other cities present themselves as "cultural centers." Where is their painting, their poetry, their philosophy? They have nothing to show us but press releases. Young executives are happy to be associated with a town which has a reputation for being where the action — every sort of action including the cultural — is. But what can New York or San Francisco give us except the *air* of having something?

Q.   Are you suggesting that the illusion is all these cities have?

A.   I add that Chicagoans have for the most part escaped contamination by pseudo-culture. I say "for the most part" because television and cultural journalism do great damage to the innocent vulgarity of Chicago. Still the "ethnic neighborhoods" resist with admirable stubbornness. You ask why I live here, and what I give in reply is a mini-sermon against the vanity of seeking "the great good place," the ideal situation. There is no such place.

Q.   Still in your case it is Chicago . . .

A.   Of course I'm part of the mixture. I am one version of its consciousness, a self-conscious reflection of the mixture.

Q.   These are the qualities that engage your imagination, the imagination of a novelist?

A.   The words I just used, "self-conscious reflection of the mixture," suggest a passive receptivity. It isn't that at all. After something like half a century in Chicago I think I may claim to have well-founded views on American commercial democracy. I know that art is not one of the stronger interests of American communities. That's not what the enterprise is about. The main enterprise was not to produce a "higher life" but stable prosperity, a middling condition, personal liberties guaranteed, a reasonable facsimile of justice. A state of decent dullness. That hasn't worked either. The decay of the city makes that clear to everybody.

Q.   Your concern with the condition of the human spirit seems germane to your artistry. You seem fixed on, if I may use the term, existentialist themes. True?

A.   You seem determined to make me explain how it is possible to combine art with Chicago. We have all been brought up to the view that art is associated with a favoring culture. This may be phrased as, "Tell me where you come from and I'll tell you what you are" — a simple standard which does not yield impressive results. Environments matter, but they do not determine being. Being towers over them. To cover oneself with labels or shut oneself up in pigeon holes is also one of our own deliberate choices. There are times when the genius of our species, for mysterious ends of its own, needs to create something like a nation of Chicagos. A surrender to desolation is not, however, acceptable to spirited people. One must rather try to decipher the necessarily obscure message concealed within the appearances. Perhaps this is what you meant by "existentialist." It's not one of my favorite terms. Some years ago I visited one of the heroes of the last days of the Warsaw ghetto, a Jewish cardiologist in the Polish city of Lodz, a place reminiscent of Chicago, a manufacturing town. I asked him why he had settled in such an unattractive spot. His answer was, "What difference do surroundings make?" My question struck him as simpleminded. If I had been thinking, I wouldn't have asked it. His answer referred me to Jewish history, to the ancient, the millennial Jewish power of accommodation to place. In a ghetto, a slum, a hole in the ground, a tenement, your spirit lived independently. You had no need of a supporting culture. Your soul made — no, burnt — its own clearing.

Q. I've heard that your mother was not pleased with moving from Eastern Europe to this side of the ocean, especially with four children.

A. With three. I was born on this side of the water. No, she hated it. She had already moved too much, she thought — from Latvia to Petrograd. Then to Lachine, an industrial village near Montreal. She found herself in a melting pot with French Canadians, Indians, the Scotch-Irish, the Sicilians, and Ukrainians. The mixture of languages and races was confusing to her, fascinating to me. I've never feared to speak foreign languages, always assuming that whatever others spoke I could speak, too. Why not? And I took it for granted — what else was I to do, in childhood? — that this was what life was. Junkyards are just as miraculous as orange groves. I was three years of age when we moved to Montreal. On St. Dominique Street, Orthodox Jews mingled with kilted Highlanders and nuns from the parish school. To Henry Adams it would have been a frightful comedown, for me it was all gold.

Q. Although you are an American writer, your interests seem very international in scope.

A. No way for me to have learnt of Mt. St. Michel. But the next development, like it or not, was international — cosmopolitan, planetary. I didn't make too much distinction between European and American. Chicago, when you examine it closely, turns out to be a collection of European communities — German, Polish, Italian, Greek, Irish, Jewish. And now there's a large Negro and Puerto Rican population, and a contingent from India and Thailand — thousands of Koreans; and as for Mexicans, since most of them are illegal immigrants there is no way to estimate their number.

Q. In your novels you are concerned with what Heidegger called a free-floating anxiety, *angst*? I ask because all your protagonists seem tormented by or are aware of its presence.

A.   Ah, yes. Well, Heidegger gets it from Nietzsche. I didn't read Heidegger until quite recently, and then discovered that he was Nietzsche's principal anatomist. The cause of this anxiety is (I speak with proper reticence for these philosophers) a slippage in the self-valuation of the individual. Nietzsche defines nihilism as the dislocation of the reigning values. For Nietzsche this is by no means an intellectual problem. He is describing an historical event, or rather a long chain of events — the triumph and decline of Christianity, if you come right down to it. Nihilism is not an idea, it is an event.

Q.   Could you give me an example from one of your novels that would fit what you are talking about: this sense of anxiety, slippage, dislocation?

A.   A book to illustrate what Nietzsche means by nihilism? I don't think of novels in that illustrative way. But I suppose it wouldn't be too hard for a Nietzschean adept to examine a book like *Herzog* as a case of slippage in self-valuation. I don't see why such a subject shouldn't be a source of high comedy. Perhaps Nietzsche would agree that to turn a comic light on a Herzog might be something of a victory for the Will to Power. Herzog is a comic portrait of the enfeeblement of the educated man, a person of good instincts and decent feelings who, in the crisis of his life, casts about for help from his "education" and finds that this "education" is little more than a joke. Herzog, then, reviews his life, reenacting the roles he has been taught. The learned Herzog is merely foolish. The pussycat husband, winning his wife's affections through "goodness," is ludicrous; she simply cuckolds him. As the "romantic hero" he is a goose, and as the betrayed and avenging husband he is what movie billboards used to call "a laff-riot!" In the roles of which his education consists there is little more than farce and burlesque, and so Herzog looks for repose in what he was before he had accumulated this mass of "learning." He returns to Square One. There he asks himself the essential question, What was it that I ought to have been doing? Or, What was my created soul? And, Where is it now? And finally, Why was it necessary to try to replace it with a synthetic soul? I was vastly surprised by the seriousness and solemnity of my readers. They were entranced uncomfortably by the March of Ideas, challenged by it most unpleasantly. For some the book was something like a six-hour comprehensive exam in the History of Modern Thought. When I was a kid at school we were often told by a teacher (a moment of charm) to put on our thinking-caps. My readers were oppressed by the thinking-cap, and blind to the whirlwind comedy. Too bad. I am largely to blame for that. W. H. Auden once remarked that I had written my book too well. I understood much later that he was trying to warn me against "fine writing." I think he was right.

Q.   Now about *Henderson the Rain King*, which is to my mind a remarkable achievement in blending the comic with the serious — "bursting the spirit's sleep"?

A.   "The spirit's sleep" comes from Shelley. It seemed good fun to
have a brute like Henderson quoting Percy Bysshe. I was inspired also
by the James-Lange theory. William James felt that you could change
your character by your behavior, by sending muscular impulses to the
brain. This would result in the formation of new brain centers. By
smiling you could create smiling-powers. These might become permanent. Do you remember the Coué method? You were to say to yourself, "Day by day in every way I'm getting better and better." And day
by day you were *sure* to improve. If you wished to be more leonine,
plausibly enough you behaved like a lion. My friend Meyer Schapiro
had brought to my attention a book by Professor Schindler, a neuro-
physiologist, *The Image and Idea of the Human Body*. That King
Dahfu had also read it was dead certain. Schindler too seemed to think
that the brain could be modified by motor activity.

Q.   Let's jump way up in your career: how does Albert Corde in
The Dean's December fit in with the Bellow vision? The novel is
stylistically different. The famous Bellow humor, for instance, is
largely missing. What are your thematic concerns in this novel?

A.   I wanted to write a book about Chicago, and I went out to look
at the town again. This new inspection didn't inspire humor. The facts
were dreadful. What were my thematic concerns, you ask? One of my
themes is the American denial of real reality, our devices for evading
it, our refusal to face what is all too obvious and palpable. The book is
filled with protest against this evasion, against the techniques of illusion and the submission to taboos by means of which this is
accomplished. Corde thinks that we are becoming wraiths, spooks. It
seems to him that we have lost all capacity for dealing with experience
— no capacity to think about it, no language for it, no real words.

Q.   At the Mount Palomar observatory during the closing scenes of
The Dean's December, there is, if I am reading it right, a real sense of
love between Albert and Minna, a real connection.

A.   It *is* real. Why shouldn't it be? It is real, and therefore it is an
achievement. The estrangement of human beings from one another is a
fact of life, no longer a hypothetical matter. The price you pay for the
development of consciousness is the withering of the heart. Therefore
one must *will* the recovery of feeling, and one must use one's intelligence, too; one must take private reckoning, at which we have become
very skillful, and turn it around, force its reversal. *How* is one to educate oneself to feeling? I treated the subject comically in *Henderson the
Rain King*. There I suggested that it might be done by imitating a noble
beast, or by imitating an African king who has himself come under the
influence of a noble beast. *Henderson* is probably the better book
because its argument is less direct. *The Dean* is more important
because it's closer to the actual truth as that truth is experienced by
intelligent human beings. Corde recognizes the necessity of ennobling
reckoning. He comes to understand that we carry about, within, an

iceberg which has to be melted. Intellect, itself a source of coldness, must become involved in the melting project. To have intellect devoid of feeling is to be crippled. To recover the power to walk — in feeling — we begin by calling on the will. The return of love begins with the *study* of love, with discipline. If you wish Eros to return you must prepare a suitable place for him. I think a terrible mess has been made of the E. M. Forster imperative "to connect" — or Auden's "we must love one another or . . ." — because writers have tried to do it by fiat. Under Forster's influence certain novelists have said, "I really do believe in connection, so I am going to order it to happen. So let there be. . . . Let there be love. Let there be connection." Most of us are aware how phony this has been. We know more, much more, about separateness, isolation, dislike, than we care to admit. But writers have tried to fetch in connection from every point of the compass — from Christianity, from political movements, from sex, fanaticism, or terrorism — from whatever you like. The louder the connection by fiat is proclaimed, the worse the results. So that you have tenderness and sympathy à la Forster, you have Laurentian sexuality, you have Hemingway with the earth "moving" under his sleeping bag, and so on, but you don't have very much truth. It may be better to take the *worst* case to be truer, and work back from acknowledged disconnection. This is what I did in *The Dean's December* — I didn't exceed my own speed limit anywhere; or the speed limits of those whom I know extremely well; or of emotional life as I've observed it. I took my bearings with my own sextant, and did my best to stay on course.

Q.   Perhaps the Bucharest setting, then, provided you with a necessary perspective for the Chicago events.

A.   Yes, because in Bucharest and Eastern Europe one can see a more old-fashioned sort of human attachment. I don't know whether it's true, either; I suspect that its historical moment also may be past. This is the Tolstoyan sentiment of relatedness, the Slavic mode of connection made famous by the geniuses of the nineteenth century. Nowadays the "Slavic mode" includes the concentration camps, the secret police, horrible wars, the mercilessness of the new — or perhaps also the old — Slavism. What is the emotional truth, then, for modern man? I don't know if you're familiar with a novel by Céline called *Journey to the End of the Night*. Consistently, to the very last page, you see in it a desperate resistance to sentimentalism, to bourgeois falsification of the emotions. It makes the ultimate resistance to what a modern truth-teller like Céline would consider to be the gummy falsehood of modern emotionalism. Céline is proud — perhaps too proud — of his freedom from illusion. It is very much the freedom of a mass man.

Q.   Is this similar to what you called in *To Jerusalem and Back* "the spiritual vacancy of America"?

A.   Not exactly. But one has to look these things in the face, and not fall prey to one's own "decent" upbringing, which insists on the triumph of the Good and the victory of Love. My own preferences are nice and liberal. I *tried*, myself, very hard to hold these beliefs. But that was when I was young. In the end one can only accept what has withstood the harshest of tests.

Q.   Reality?

A.   Yes. And truthfulness, utter truthfulness. I don't know whether Céline is telling the truth. He has a girl, carried away by what she thinks is love, murder her lover because he won't reciprocate her feeling. He — the victim — tells her that all love is carrion, and stinks, "I won't have any part of it." And she kills him. Out of what, love? Hate? Rage? The woman is demented. So I am very concerned with such issues; with the mess we have made of our effort to put "desirable" emotions upon an acceptable aesthetic and political footing; I think this has gone all sour. Cockeyed! On all sides. Nihilists and *bien pensants* are equally nutty.

Q.   And so you as a novelist are concerned with giving shape to a precarious reality by holding a mirror up to experience.

A.   Yes. I think it probably is the injunction to hold "the mirror up to nature." I come back to that.

Q.   You have noted, with respect to *The Dean's December*, that "it became clear to me that no imagination whatsoever had been applied to the problems of demoralized cities . . . no one has been able to take into account the sense of these lives." Especially in light of the works of, say, Dreiser, Zola, Sinclair, Wright, or Barthelme — and then yourself — could you elaborate on what you meant?

A.   We could start by asking ourselves what understanding of the modern scene we would have without Dostoevsky and Tolstoy, without Balzac, without Proust, without writers who gave a musical pitch, as it were, to the interpretation of the modern psyche and contemporary civilization. All that is changed. Americans today take their interpretations from psychologists, sociologists, economists (very strong on economists), and from journalists. These are mere technicians, devoid of musical or other feelings. The influence of literature is virtually nil. See the figures for what "educators" call "functional illiteracy." Try to talk to "educated" people. In browsing through the book of a friend, I came upon an epigraph from Dickens' *Little Dorrit*: "He disposed of an immense amount of solid food with the benignity of a good soul who was feeding someone else." Last time I visited an elementary school, I saw kids learning to read by punching the keys of electronic machines. What would these poor children have made of a good soul and its benignity? The technicians have been a disaster, humanly. They've done no better in higher education. Their definitions of equality and justice result in chaos. Dickens in *Hard Times* had a presentiment of this. A modern writer trying to describe what has happened in our

American Manchesters might call *his* book *The Great Noise*. We live within a Great Noise that destroys meaning. Public men speak of "compassion," "sharing," "caring," but the principal source of much of the noise is not "caring" or "sharing" but sheer rage.

Q.   Tying this in with your latest novel, then, was *The Dean's December* an effort to present the condition of the demoralized city, what you call the "inner slum"?

A.   What I meant was there is a correspondence between outer and inner, between the brutalized city and the psyche of its citizens. Given their human resources I don't see how people today can experience life at all. Politicians, public figures, professors address "modern problems" solely in terms of employment. They assume that unemployment causes incoherence, sexual disorders, the abandonment of children, robbery, rape, and murder. Plainly, they have no imagination of these evils. They don't even see them. And in *The Dean's December* what I did was to say, "Look!" The first step is to display the facts. But the facts, unless the imagination perceives them, are *not* facts. Perhaps I shouldn't say "perceives" — I should say "passionately takes hold." As an artist does. Mr. Corde, the Dean, passionately takes hold of Chicago and writes his articles like an artist rather than a journalist. He's an in-between type, perhaps like the Orwell who wrote *Down and Out*, or the *Wigan Pier* book.

Q.   Would you consider Hemingway here?

A.   Well, Hemingway was a sophisticated artist who started out as a journalist. He was the very special sort of highbrow who detests highbrows, a man whose simplicity was saturated with complexities.

Q.   *The Dean's December* could be read as a social protest novel, a novel concerned with the decaying moral landscape of the city, the jails, the bureaucracies, the Mitchell rape case. But on another level, couldn't it be read as a novel of consciousness, as in Joyce's *Ulysses* or Faulkner's *The Sound and the Fury*?

A.   The book is a protest, all right, but it's not a "protest novel." "Protest novel" makes me think of terms like "cookware" or "rumpus-room." It certainly is a "novel of consciousness," though. Its object is to draw one man's highly developed "consciousness" towards our disorders. The challenge is to make a close inspection of them. And what he sees wakes Corde up. He's been an artist — but an artist under wraps, so to speak, an artist privately. I assume that when you say "novel of consciousness" you refer to novels of *exquisite* consciousness, to Virginia Woolf, perhaps, or to Joyce or to Proust. Joyce carries his exquisite consciousness finally into the lowlife of Dublin's streets, and Proust turns his to wartime Paris — to society women flipping open the paper to read about the Battle of Verdun while they butter croissants and sip their morning coffee. But exquisite consciousness as a rule avoids dealing directly with the prisons, hospitals, or trenches. Novelists like Céline, nihilists whose specialty is rough stuff, have no use for the exquisite consciousness. Now what does the more developed sort of consciousness — not necessarily exquisite — make of the Chicago scene? The Dean learns that *every* kind of critical consciousness today *avoids* that scene. Nobody, nobody at all wants to see it because it looks to be the final collapse. But Corde's attention is turned towards it — half unwillingly at first.

Q.   *The Dean's December* seems to be stylistically in contrast to your previous novels. The humorous-serious style of *Seize the Day*, *The Adventures of Augie March*, and *Henderson the Rain King* seemed to give way to a more somber tone, and to a nonfiction novelistic style. Is this accurate?

A.   Perhaps. Yes, I see what you mean. But I wasn't thinking "novel" when I wrote the book. I was dealing with a sort of mind rather than with a literary form. Let me try to explain this: Corde is a man who has had an "aesthetic" upbringing and who has never found a life appropriate to such an upbringing. After all, to have been brought up on Baudelaire, on the French novelists from Stendhal to Proust, on Joyce, etc., is not only to have read books but to have received a kind of spiritual training. And what does one do with such a training, with the tastes, the outlook, the demands, the passions that have been created by years of immersion in poems, novels, paintings? Such an outlook, such passions are not hoarded, they demand use. They have combined to form a kind of person; and what does that kind of person *do*? All of this happens in the barbarous boondocks of far-away Chicago, and it happens not only to a reader like Corde, who has never found a life appropriate to his upbringing, but also to writers whose native heath happens to be in the barbarous boondocks, Carl Sandburg's "city of the broad shoulders." The Russian Communist Establishment would refer to such writers as "rootless cosmopolitans." Well, cosmopolitan is what the best of us have to be in these times. It does those rare romantic and Symbolist plants that nourished us much good to be transplanted. Chicago kids, fifty years ago, were devouring the masterpieces of modernism — what Wyndham Lewis in his autobiography, *Rude Assignment*, called "small-public art." Lewis isn't much read now, except by reactionaries and hatchet-men. I read him, too. He's a bit cracked but he's a wonderful writer. In *Rude Assignment*, which is a history of his own career, he distinguishes first of all between great-public and small-public artists. The novel of the mid-nineteenth century — Balzac, Dickens, etc. — was addressed to the great public. Ordinary literacy was all that was required of a reader. Then a more sophisticated public appeared. You needed patience, skill, you needed an ear to read *Madame Bovary*, you had to be something of a connoisseur. The new small-public writers bred their own readers. The great public went the way of philistinism; the small public preferred the shadows, the twilight. Then came a new development: education in the Western democracies familiarized a large student public with small-public art. Suddenly you had God knows how many B.A.s in the United States — millions of them — who had been educated in "twilight" arts, tacking up reproductions of Paul Klee on their walls. Wyndham Lewis didn't anticipate this yeastlike expansion.

Q.   Do you mean in terms of how one reaches that new reading public?

A.   In part. In fact I was thinking of the manner in which Mr. Corde, Dean Corde, wrote his articles on Chicago. I was trying, too, to answer your question about the "nonfiction novelistic" style you observe in *The Dean's December*. Corde's cast of mind would not endear him to the average Chicagoan. It's not that Corde is "precious" — one can read Corbière or E. E. Cummings or Wallace Stevens without disfiguring one's American character. But Corde's account of Chicago does not find favor either with the Chicago public or with academic colleagues. (Nobody yet has taken the measure of professorial vulgarity.) I can see your next question coming — Yes, I have disassociated myself from "academics." There was never a time when I did associate with them as a colleague, and I find the new English Department stars, the deconstructionists, singularly silly. If they were as interesting as they think themselves to be I should have no objection to them. Let them inherit everything. The "tradition," the whole works. But can they be legitimate heirs if they are dull? Boredom has become wonderfully prestigious among the highbrows. And the dullness of these people is infectious. Students are infected by it. Dullness makes them a great public — philistines.

Q.   In what ways is *The Dean's December*, to use your own words, "a personal risk"? Does this risk-taking relate to what you noted in your Nobel Award speech as "a time to move on"?

A.   I was inwardly close to chaos when I began the book. I wrote easily and quickly but I was in a painful state. I could not eat, I suffered from insomnia. But my personal discomfort is of no importance. The "personal risk" was simply that I feared that I would be unable to maintain order, that I would fall into incoherence.

Q.   Many reviewers wrote negatively of your "personal risk."

A.   Well, what can you do with people who refuse to open their feelings generously? They simply go on strike against a book. They won't have it. That's ostracism, not criticism.

Q.   Could you discuss what are some of the dominant intents or themes in your artistry?

A.   In almost everything I write there appears a primordial person. He is not made by his education, nor by cultural or historical circumstances. He precedes culture and history. In a recent story I cite the Spanish saying, "*Genio y figura hasta la sepultura.*" *Genio* means temper or will, "genius." So it's "genius and face enduring to the grave." This means that there is something invariable, ultimately unteachable, native to the soul. A variety of powers arrive whose aim is to alter, to educate, to condition us. If a man gives himself over to total alteration I consider him to have lost his soul. If he resists these worldly powers, forces of his own can come into play.

Q.   Carl Jung writes about this, it seems, in "Archetypes of the Collective Unconscious," where he discusses universal, primordial events that we all may experience.

A.   I don't know that we are speaking of the same thing. I don't describe myself as a Jungian. I am only speaking from my own feelings.

Q.   Then give me an example of characters from your novels who embody this primordial impulse to which you're alluding.

A.   Waking one morning, somewhere in the heart of Africa, Henderson the Rain King sees a pink light on the clay wall, and embraces it with his whole soul. The pink reminds him of something he knew before he knew anything at all. Or Moses Herzog, at the very end of the book, realizes that his education was utter nonsense, but that there had been an aboriginal Moses E. Herzog — who was by no means extinct. This is what I am talking about. In an essay called "Le Peintre de la vie Moderne" — "The Painter of Modern Life" — Baudelaire says that genius is a power to recover our childhood voluntarily. You can go back at will to the earliest years of your life, before "education" had enclosed you in its patterns and representations.

Q.   When you're speaking of your own creative process, you seem to go back to harnessing the passions, to melding these passions with experience.

A.   I just don't think that we can function without pictures.

Q.   Why?

A.   Because I think that truth does present itself to us in pictures.

Q.   Abstract or expressionistic art works, then, when there is some kind of emotional connection between the art object and the viewer.

A.   Pictures are not invariably representational. I suppose that I'm thinking of something that Goethe said — I can't remember it literally — but it's something like the following: that a man is happy when for everything inside him there is something outside to correspond. I am thinking of that kind of correspondence. I don't understand abstract or expressionistic art, but I often feel drawn to it.

Q.   That is, we don't apprehend the *dinglichkeit*, or the thing in and of itself, the concreteness of experience. Have you ever tried to paint?

A.   I have no gift for that. Music is more like it. I played the fiddle when I was a kid, and then for many years I played the recorder in amateur groups. I became quite a good recorder player. The two-octave limit ends by irritating you.

Q.   When I interviewed Edward Albee a few years ago, I asked about the influence of music in his theater, and he spoke of the sound

and sense and rhythm of the language, and how certain of his plays
were like pieces of music. Do you see any connection between your
music and your writing?

A.   Sometimes I feel that what I am writing has a musical quality.
There is, for me, a kind of music in "Him With His Foot in His
Mouth." Allow me to read a few sentences chosen at random:

> You will ask: With a wife willing to struggle mortally to preserve you
> from the vindictiveness of the injured parties, weren't you perversely
> tempted to make trouble, just to set the wheels rolling? The answer is no,
> and the reason is not only that I loved Gerda (love terribly confirmed by
> her death) but also when I said things I said them for art's sake, i.e.,
> without perversity or malice, not as if malice had an effect like alcohol
> and I got drunk on wickedness. I reject that. Yes, there has to be some
> provocation, but then what happens happens because the earth heaves up
> underfoot, and from opposite ends of the heavens I get a simultaneous
> shock to both ears. I am deafened, and I have to open my mouth.

Odd music, perhaps, but music nonetheless.

Q.   Did you really say that bad joke to Miss Rose years ago that
seems to shape Shawmut's reflections?

A.   Yes, I did. I also asked the lady if she was going to write her
memoirs on a typewriter or on an adding machine! And a few other
things of that sort. After all, Shawmut's a musician, a Pergolesi expert.
I don't mean to tell you how to read the story but it can be helpful to
hear a writer read a few sentences aloud. I loved writing "Him With
His Foot in His Mouth," and I wrote it without difficulty, just as if I
were speaking. Much of modern writing is essentially vocal. Among
nineteenth-century novelists, Trollope wrote for the eye, Dickens for
the voice. When you read Mark Twain you're hearing an American
voice. From Henry James you hear a very different sort of voice,
almost polyphonic in its effects. But it is a *single* voice, nevertheless.
If you don't follow its melody, its accents, its breathing and its
rhythms, then you have not read as you were intended to read.

Q.   Many commentators have noted that your voice is a voice for a
whole generation. Over the last four decades you've apparently captured something artistically valid and accurate about human experience.

A.   Well I suppose I *am* a sort of historian.

Q.   What is the function of a good novelist?

A.   To begin with, I agree with the description that Conrad gives
in the introduction to *Heart of Darkness* or *Lord Jim.* "To make you
feel, hear, to make you see. . . ." It's a kind of groping for the original
sense of being, a being that precedes social shaping. Perhaps that's the
difference between scientific writing and art. Art assumes that it faces
mysterious being. Science assumes that it deals with intrinsically knowable, ultimately knowable being.

Q.   Do you think that, as Hemingway would say, you "got it right"
with *Seize the Day*?

A.   Oh I got it right up to a point, but it was a limited point. I can sympathize with Wilhelm but I can't respect him. He is a sufferer by vocation. I'm a resister by vocation.

Q.   If you were to look back over your four decades of writing, what characters and novels delight you the most?

A.   I haven't much use for my earliest writing. *Dangling Man* and *The Victim* don't amuse me. It's true that I was stirred, moved, or as the young now say, turned on, in the writing of these books. They were real enough. But I was still sitting for my qualifying examinations. In *Augie March* I no longer cared about examinations. My attitude there was — to hell with it, here I come, ready or not. But there were two things wrong with *Augie March* as I see it now. It got away from me, for one thing. I had found a new way to write a book. It was my very own. But I had no control over it. I couldn't say no to any of the excesses. I didn't know how to check myself. Up to a point it was effective. Americans who read it felt liberated by its excesses, but I don't think *The Adventures of Augie March* is going to wear well. Its other fault was disingenuousness. I really knew much more about darkness than I let on. I knew perfectly well what nihilism was. I had no excuse for being such an ingenue. I felt like doing the ingenue, that's all. It genuinely corresponded to a kind of Americanism of the thirties — naive, easy-going, tolerant, all-accepting, youthfully affectionate. *Seize the Day*, my next book, was tougher. Wilhelm was like Augie, but Dr. Tamkin was a con man who gave his dupes psychological laughing gas.

Q.   Tamkin struck me as a classic illusion manufacturer.

A.   Yes. He was going to do people good, he was going to take them in hand and cure them. He was a shabby Aunt Sally. He was going to adjust them, not civilize them. If they didn't light out for the territory ahead, they were done for. I suppose that this was the first book that really described the mental confusions of the Americans, people in dire need of "orientation." I don't think anybody before me had examined the vulnerability of the new American to the new impostor. O. Henry's con men were ordinary shell-game operators. *Seize the Day* was a brand new shell game. The object was not just to cheat a farmer of his bankroll, but to work over the sensitive nice American, born for "happiness." I am also very fond of Lily in *Henderson the Rain King*. I have a special affection for her. Because there, too, you know, is an American type — the large-hearted, big broad, shining with enthusiasm, absolutely sold on love. But at the same time Lily is a social climber. Because she's in such a glow she's not even aware of it. She's one of my favorites. Henderson himself is another.

Q.   Your writing style has changed in the last decade. How would you describe this change?

A.   Yes, I think it has. I think it's more condensed. I think it hits harder than it used to. I think I have a much greater desire to strike sharp blows, to find more exact formulations. I greatly dislike books that waste my time. I detest superfluous sentences, unwanted paragraphs, needless pages.

Q.   If you're referring to Albert Corde, he is perhaps too aware, too sensitive — has incurred what both you and Camus call a "penalty" for perception.

A.   Corde was educated in Lincoln Park together with Dewey Spangler. They read poetry together. Corde took poetry seriously, whereas Spangler did not. Corde makes real demands upon language. To Spangler, the columnist, words do not matter. Now how does a Corde survive? Remember that he reads *The Chicago Tribune* every day. It is Corde's conviction that without art, it is impossible to interpret reality, and that the degeneration of art and language leads to the decay of judgment.

*   *   *

A Winter's Tale
Greg Johnson

Saul Bellow has long been our foremost novelist of ideas: after his earlier quiet, comparatively modest books, *Dangling Man* (1944) and *The Victim* (1947), his fiction has been characterized by a startling plenitude of intellectual vitality, his themes given through the voices of engaging, beleaguered, larger-than-life personae, whose private struggles have mirrored brilliantly the major concerns of the age. "In his finest passages," Joyce Carol Oates has written, "he is concerned with nothing less than the fate of civilization itself," and Bellow has generally managed to enliven his seriousness through shrewd and particularized characterization, an eschewing of the aesthetic curtailments of modernism (as well as those of its bloodless offspring, "postmodernism"), and an inimitable blend of vitality, humor, and moral passion. How surprising, then, that his first novel in seven years, *The Dean's December*, should be a relatively spare and quiet book, melancholy and occasionally even drab in mood and style, quite modest in its claims for the central character's "moral vision" and even, at times, for character itself. Some readers have reacted unfavorably to the novel, considering it a falling-off, disappointed by its relentless, brooding interiority and by the painfully clear likeness of the protagonist to Bellow himself. Yet the novel seems, to this reviewer, deliberately intended as a winter's tale, an admirable risk by a writer who has chosen not to repeat himself but rather to offer us a somber, unassuming, quietly lyrical evocation of intellectual disappointment — as if "the fate of civilization" has begun to seem a foregone conclusion, and a theme appropriately handled in an elegiac rather than a celebratory manner.

From *Southwest Review* 67.3 (1982): 342-45.

The novel's "plot" is quite simple, even skeletal, its main purpose being to serve as a framework for Dean Albert Corde's musing upon the modern condition. (John Gardner's querulous remark that Bellow's novels are not novels at all, but "essays," has at least some justification here.) Corde and his wife Minna, an eminent astronomer, have come to Rumania for the death and funeral of Minna's mother, whose abandonment of her youthful Marxism has caused her a life of quiet suffering and disenfranchisement under the Soviet regime; back in Chicago, Corde had been involved in a politically explosive cause, having published a series of objurgatory articles in *Harper's* on the "underside" of life in Chicago, particularly as it affects the city's blacks, and, more recently, having advocated the prosecution of several black hoodlums involved in the murder of a graduate student at Corde's university. Though the situations in both Chicago and Bucharest are vividly particularized, this is done through the ruminative filter of Corde's consciousness, and he is led inevitably from present facts to the broadest generalizations and surmises. (The real action in this book *is* Corde's thinking; most of its scenes occur in his memory rather than "on-stage.") There are plentiful occasions for comparing East and West, and for examining the nature of political power, the problems of urban existence, relations between the races, and so on. Corde himself apprehends this pattern: "Were these (the personalities, articles, trials, etc.) his own portion of the big scale insanities of the twentieth century? Did these present thoughts occur because he had been shut up too long in Minna's old room?" Well, yes. But the haunting undersong of the novel is exactly the ineffectuality of thought and meditation, the peculiar helplessness of intellectual clarity, the frustration of perceiving that even the strongest mind cannot make sense of the "big-scale insanities" or of the processes of consciousness itself. As Corde is forced to recognize, despairingly, "The language of discourse had shut out experience altogether."

Yet Corde, like his ancestors in Bellow's canon, possesses a relentless idealism. Even toward the end of the novel, having experienced firsthand the spiritual bleakness of life in Rumania, and having acknowledged his powerlessness to change the anarchic state of events in his own country, he describes that exalted personal goal: "To recover the world that is buried under the debris of false description or nonexistence." This also describes, of course, Bellow's own aim in writing *The Dean's December*, and as an operant principle prevents his book from becoming a mere essay-as-novel, the muted observations of a tired, disaffected professor. Though the novel's tone is appropriately somber, Corde's mind is constantly active in its attempt to recover the world, and in this activity Bellow shows once again his typical strengths as a novelist. He renders movingly the bleakness, both natural and spiritual, of a Bucharest winter. He gives a deft and convincing portrayal of the relationship — loving, quirky, unshakable — between

Corde and his wife. Most important, he brings a variety of characters engagingly to life. Corde's skeptical, somewhat shady, yet "poetic" lifelong friend, Dewey Spangler, now a successful and complacent journalist; Minna's courageous mother, Valeria, and her noble, slightly pathetic aunt Gigi (the two of them a center, in the Bucharest underground, of "an extended feminine hierarchy"); Corde's rather coarse and unsympathetic relatives back in the states — all are vivid, memorable creations. Even for the most "minor" characters, Bellow imagines fully, compassionately, and often with indulgent humor. Consider this description (so rich it deserves full quotation) of Corde's secretary back in Chicago, the redoubtable Miss Porson:

> This Miss Porson of his, Fay Porson, was an old slob (he was at present inclined to call her that) of no little charm. She couldn't have been much younger than Tanti Gigi, but she boasted that she turned on lovers half her age. In her late sixties, she was fleshy, but her bearing was jaunty. Her plump face heavily made up was whitish pink, as if washed in calamine lotion, and on some days she painted a raccoon band across her face in blue eye shadow — the mask of a burglar or a Venetian reveler. She kept up her pants with heavy silver-and-turquoise belts. The permanent Miss Porson, the Miss Porson of the deeper strata, turned out to be a bridge-playing Westchester matron. She had come to Chicago with her midlevel executive husband. Here she was widowed and here she preferred to remain. She could swing in Chicago. She was going to "put the sex into sexagenarian," she said. Corde had become fond of her. She was not the supersecretary and faultless organizer she claimed to be; she was overpaid. His dislike of administrative detail had made a hostage of him. Her erotic confidences and boasts set his teeth on edge. But he would not have been able now to replace her.

Though the novel as a whole presents a dark, certainly depressing vision, it also gives us, as in this passage, an abundance of imaginative energy, a counter-ballast of freshly perceived life.

It should be stressed, however, that the novel seems to represent a new direction for Bellow, perhaps a deeper level of awareness. Despite its variety of character and invention, there is really nothing in this novel's central consciousness to replace the wry thoughtfulness of a Mr. Sammler, the bumptious energy of a Eugene Henderson, the anxious and lovable fervor of a Moses Herzog. Compared to previous Bellow heroes, Albert Corde *is* a quiet, highly ruminative, occasionally somewhat arrogant presence: the author's great challenge has been to make his protagonist's complex and far-reaching ideas into action (or into an illusion of action), and he has succeeded to a remarkable degree. If this book is less "entertaining" than earlier Bellow novels, it is certainly no less admirable. The reader may wonder what could lie beyond the wintry landscape presented in *The Dean's December*, but it is to be hoped that Bellow, like his hero, will continue his varied, brilliant, constantly surprising "recovery" of the world.

* * *

The Dean's December
William Harmon

This dean is Albert Corde, a dean of students who was a professor of journalism after having been a journalist. He is married to a distinguished Rumanian-born astronomer, and he accompanies her to Bucharest where her mother, also a distinguished person but out of favor, is dying. The novel made out of this promisingly complex situation impresses me as a distillation of almost all of Bellow's strengths and weaknesses.

Here Bellow's old device of dangling, dangling, dangling finds its fulcrum in the liminal passage from a dismal December in Rumania to an analeptic January in California; in the shakeup of connections following the death of a mother-in-law and the remarriage of a widowed sister; and in what turns out for Corde to be yet another change of occupation. (Maybe the sequel ought to be called *The Journeyman's January*.)

Bellow's simultaneous pursuit of involvement and detachment here takes a rather curious route that removes the novel from its own centers of greatest interest. Corde's name, like Sammler's, hints at binding, gathering, synthesis, and harmony; but the novel is so designed that, until the end, the prevalent emphasis falls on separation, removal, and exasperating indirectness. Corde as Dean is set apart from Corde as Professor, who was presumably even more distantly set apart from Corde the journalist. In Bucharest, distanced from Chicago in so many ways, the Cordes encounter many obstacles and have such a hard time getting permission to visit the dying mother that Corde spends much of the time in physical, linguistic, occupational, and ideological isolation. Back in the States a sensational trial is underway in which the Dean has a personal and professional interest. (Bellow has added some improbable and unnecessary family connections involving a nephew and a cousin who are on the side opposite the Dean's.) At the same time, *Harper's* is running the Dean's long piece on Chicago. This article is evidently supposed to be a balanced assessment, even though it is thoroughly subjective, and we hear something about the virtue of order and the long-standing association between Chicago and Aristotle. But most people have paid attention only to Corde's handling of Chicago's crudity and crookedness.

Now *that* is indirect. We do not get the crudity. We get a selection of responses to one witness's ambiguous article on the crudity and other topics. We are given reports, recollections, and rumors, filtered through thousands of intercontinental miles and colored by Corde's sensibility, which is indistinguishable from the narrator's. The novel

From *Southern Humanities Review* 17.3 (1983): 280-81.

projects a strong sense of decency and even of delicacy, but the vitia-
tions and removals finally become irritating. Relying on so many three-
cushion shots, the narrator has to go through some excessively elaborate maneuvers. Another American journalist who *just happens* to be in
Bucharest *just happens* to be a boyhood friend of Corde's. Meanwhile,
as if the narrator's skill were exhausted by complexities of design,
other responsibilities are scanted. I most regretted Bellow's failure to
render in more detail the character of Minna, Corde's beautiful-
brilliant-accomplished-naive wife. She remains undeveloped.

Rumania, rendered here in stale dim neutral tones, could have
furnished an ideally anomalous viewpoint. But Corde, preoccupied or
indifferent, knows almost nothing about Rumania and makes no effort
to learn the language or anything else, except the local custom of
lubricating balky bureaucratic machinery with cartons of Kents.

It may be that Corde devotes so much thought to his dear dirty
Chicago that we take the novel's word for the pervasive boringness of
Bucharest. Here, Corde is removed and isolated in yet another way,
because he finds himself among people whose lives and professions
center on medicine and science, about which he knows virtually
nothing. Bellow arouses the reader's curiosity about these things, as
about Minna and about a scientist who thinks lead poisoning is killing
the earth, but he frustrates the reader by falling back on the old Bellovian recourse of earnest philosophical chat.

In what may constitute yet another device of removal, Bellow
makes Corde some sort of Welsh-Huguenot Chicagoan, not exactly
Gerald R. Ford's species of Mainstream Midwesterner but also not a
Jew. There seem to be almost no Jews in *The Dean's December*, and
no Jewishness, either. As with *Henderson the Rain King*, we have here
a Bellow who does without the trappings and idioms of the Jewish
background, and the approach seems to work. No one can complain of
Bellow, as some complain of Arthur Miller, that he writes about Jews
but calls them gentiles. Even so, Bellow may be writing at one more
remove from his characters' planet.

As Bellow grows older — he is now sixty-eight — he grows more
important and more distinguished. Saul Bellow as such no longer has
any public existence: he is "Nobel Laureate Saul Bellow." It is enough
to make one realize why Sartre turned the Prize down, and also why
Bellow protects his privacy and his publicity in the devious ways that
an awestruck Mark Harris documents in that strange volume, *The
Drumlin Woodchuck*, an entertaining and rather embarrassing account
of how Harris came *not* to write a book about Bellow. In his recent fiction, however, if not in his public relations, the important and distinguished writer has had to come to grips with Importance and Distinction themselves. Such problems seem to mean a good deal less to Bellow than they did to his friend John Berryman, but they do matter in
Humboldt's Gift and *The Dean's December*. Very few good serious
novels have to do with big shots. As John O'Hara demonstrated in *Ten*

North Frederick and *From the Terrace*, very important persons are very different from you and me. Their options, more numerous and more interesting, eventually weaken the plot of a novel, which seems to rely on inevitable necessity. Endowed with an extraordinary measure of wealth, power, or fame, a character cannot enjoy the pleasures of ordinariness, cannot suffer routine setbacks and disappointments. These conditions require the creators of Ahab and Gatsby, say, to come up with an adversary or problematic dream as great as the great character, along with a dutiful bureaucratic narrator to leaven the overpowering charisma. What *The Dean's December* lacks is an exact sense of Corde's aptitudes and capacities, as well as a sense that what he is up against is anything more than a knot of nuisances. The result is that Corde and his dimly brilliant wife are all dressed up in the titles of achievement, honor, and power but have nowhere to go, finally, but Mount Palomar — she to pursue her astronomy, he just to tag along, relax in the observatory, and look at the complicated heavens. There is a touch of celestial symbolism here as Corde gains a new equilibrium, but the placing-in-sidereal-perspective seems too willed, merely added on, not justified or prepared for. This upbeat epilogue reads like a pale xerox of the moment in *Ulysses* when Bloom and Stephen look up at the stars — "humid nightblue fruit" — a scene that itself is a parodic replay of Dante's refrain of "stelle" at the end of each canticle of his *Comedy*. After the ennui of Bucharest, Mount Palomar makes a nicer and possibly more refreshing conclusion than would a squalid, sordid, January-paralyzed Chicago; but the sense of removal feels more like escape than triumph. Saluted by the Nobel committee "for the human understanding and subtle analysis of contemporary culture that are combined in his work," Bellow may have felt constrained to be optimistic in spite of his novel's failure to provide real grounds for optimism. Abstract astronomy as emblem seems, finally, nothing more than sentimental.

*   *   *

The Dean's December: "A Companion Piece to *Mr. Sammler's Planet*"
Liela H. Goldman

Much of the initial critical response to Bellow's latest novel has to do with the dissimilarity of *The Dean's December* to his earlier works.[1] Guided by Bellow's own comments,[2] critics have stressed the uniqueness of the novel and little attention was paid to its obvious similarity to at least one work, *Mr. Sammler's Planet*. This essay will indicate the extent to which *The Dean's December* bears an affinity to this earlier work.

From *Saul Bellow Journal* 5.2 (1986): 36-45.

Youth and age, science versus humanism, American culture versus European culture, the lunacy of urban America, the protagonist traveling to a distant land to learn something about himself, coming to terms with death — these are the issues we have previously encountered in Bellow's works and which have become the hallmark of his fiction. Bellow's newest novel, *The Dean's December*, is written in the familiar Bellovian spirit. Bellow suggests that his latest novel opens new vistas in that it is a "heightened focus on political and social issues," the purpose of which is the raising of moral questions, the ultimate aim of literature.[3] Yet this concentration is not new. *Mr. Sammler's Planet* is Bellow's first attempt to deal with issues other than personal ones. The very name of the work suggests that the concerns are global, consequently broader and more complex. Both works focus on crimes — political and social — death, and "the problems of demoralized cities."[4] Alfred Kazin, in reviewing *Mr. Sammler's Planet*, calls it "a normal political novel of our day, didactic to a fault."[5] Whereby *Mr. Sammler's Planet* is overshadowed by the devastation of World War II, the near extinction of the Jews during the Holocaust era and again in Israel during the Six-Day War and juxtaposes this decline of humanity to the deterioration of the quality of life in democracy's largest metropolis, New York, *The Dean's December* is eclipsed by the repression of humanism in the somber communist city of Bucharest, which is contrasted to the depressive plight of the Blacks in the vibrant, volatile, and free midwestern city of Chicago. Both works take place under the shadow of death. While the background of *Mr. Sammler's Planet* is the Holocaust, with its millions of corpses and its effect upon the survivors — Sammler, Shula, Eisen, Bruch, the Arkins — and the foreground is the imminent death of one man, Elya Gruner and the affect of his death upon those near him, *The Dean's December* concentrates on the deaths of two individuals, Valeria Raresh, a doctor, a disillusioned Party member, fallen from grace, in Bucharest, and the unfortunate college student, Ricki Lester, in Chicago, and the significance these deaths have upon certain individuals and society. Instead of the alien, East European, examining life in the West, America, and comparing that to his earlier experiences, this latest novel presents an American, a midwesterner, as alien, who examines life both in the United States and Rumania.[6] At the core of both novels is the "sacredness of life" and the value of the individual within his own society.

The mood and tone of both works are somber. *Mr. Sammler's Planet* employs a satiric approach and offsets the depressing flashbacks with the springtime frivolity of terrestrial lunacy. The bleak, cold spectral solemnity of *The Dean's December*, however, is only occasionally lightened with humor.

As a companion-piece to *Mr. Sammler's Planet*, *The Dean's December* is also imbued with the spirit of Solomonic wisdom.[7] Both protagonists derive their name from Ecclesiastes: Sammler or Zamm-

ler, means Koheleth — the Hebrew word for Ecclesiastes, a gatherer
(of information); Corde's name is derived from the passage in Ecclesiastes which states "a threefold cord is not quickly broken" (4:12).
The Dean's December is Bellow's "three-fold cord." It is his third
attempt at defining himself as a writer. The first was through *Dangling
Man* and *The Victim*. With those he paid his respects to Anglo-Saxon
tradition. *The Adventures of Augie March* represented a breakthrough
for him. He found his own voice and his own style, but he also found
antagonism within the literary community which "felt it was being
challenged by the Jews."[8] The writing of this work, Bellow says,
required "more confidence and daring" as it deals with issues that are
unpopular with fiction writers, especially with writers who have established a pattern and reputation for themselves. Yet, it would seem, in
Bellow's case, that it is not the subject matter that called for "confidence and daring." Political, social, and moral protest issues have
been dealt with before in literary form by others — perhaps even more
effectively — as well as by himself. What needed daring was Bellow's
incursion into the literary domain of the WASP world. It was indeed a
challenge for which he now felt he had proper credentials: the Nobel
Prize. In this novel, written after receiving the Nobel Prize, he both
proves to himself and declares to the world that he is an international
literary figure who can handle issues of world-wide significance, not
only the parochial ones that have marked his earlier works. For this
purpose, he chooses to use the non-Jewish protagonist and non-Jewish
setting to reflect once again upon the human condition and the progress
of civilization in terms of life, death, and crime.

Although non-Jewish, Albert Corde is a typical Bellow protagonist: an intellectual, a writer, a reporter, a reasoner, a reflector. He
shares with Sammler the characteristic of being intimately involved in
the affairs of society. Both protagonists are confronted with the
brutality of mankind. Both attempt to preserve their belief, despite this
brutality, that life is sacrosanct.

Artur Sammler, a septuagenarian, is a survivor of the Holocaust.
European born and bred, he grew up a product of the Enlightenment,
yet in the shadows of philosophers like Schopenhauer (for whom he
was named). Returning to Poland to "liquidate his father-in-law's
estate,"[9] he and his wife were caught in the maelstrom of the Holocaust. Their fate became the fate of the moribund European Jewish
community. Artur, more fortunate than his wife, managed to survive
this debasement and rape of humanity. Resurrected from the dead, he
and his daughter, Shula, are brought to the United States through the
efforts of his nephew, Elya Gruner. He lives out his life in the crime-
ridden streets of New York among his semi-sane relatives. It is a mad
world he inhabits, where culture and education seem unrelated to one's
way of life. The Germany which spawned some of the greatest thinkers
of all time, also propagated a "conspiracy against the sacredness of

life" (21). The Holocaust was a crime not only against the Jews but against civilization, culture, education, against the Romantic belief in the perfectibility of the individual and the religious belief in the nobility of man. The roots of societal existence were extirpated so that life was no longer inviolable and death was meaningless. Death was meaningless only because no one cared. Hannah Arendt, twenty years later, was able to view these murders and murderers as "banal," an expression or idea which infuriates Sammler. He is, likewise, irritated and saddened by the present-day intellectual, "arrested in the stage of toilet training" (45), who either wallows in excrement or sexual perversity.

Sammler's experiences, however, have not embittered him towards life. He still actively participates in the affairs of all those with whom he comes in contact. More importantly, he cares about them, listens to their problems, offers unsolicited, at times unwanted, advice, discourses about worldly matters as well, and if he is at times impatient, that is the prerogative of a senior citizen. He also reflects that one should live "with a civil heart. With disinterested charity. With a sense of the mystic potency of humankind. With an inclination to believe in archetypes of goodness" (125). He says, in a discussion with Dr. Lal, "mankind cannot be something else. It cannot get rid of itself except by an act of universal self-destruction. . . . The best, I have found, is to be disinterested. Not as misanthropes dissociate themselves, by judging, but by not judging. By willing as God wills" (215).

Sammler, of course, is not totally honest. He does judge; he judges everything. The university students who crudely terminated his lecture he calls "barbary apes" because they "acted without dignity. . . . They had no view of the nobility of being intellectuals and judges of the social order" (45). He judges Angela and her way of life; he judges Wallace, Shula, Eisen, the thief, the victim. All within his orbit are stung by his criticism. Yet his judgments are value-affirming convictions. He objects to the younger generation's degradation of life as self-effacing. He says: "A human being, valuing himself for the right reasons, has and restores order, authority" (45). Sammler, as most of Bellow's protagonists, believes that chaos cannot determine destiny. Chaos and madness may be all-pervasive, but ultimately each person must fulfill his life-contract, which is a humbling human experience.

The Holocaust, "the century's great crime" to which the world was largely apathetic, is juxtaposed to a lesser, urban crime, pickpocketing on a bus. Here too, the authorities are uninterested. Those who are interested, Sammler, who is intimidated into silence, and Feffer, the pseudo-intellectual university student, are fascinated with the audacity of the crime for some inexplicable reason. (Feffer, a con artist, intends to make a profit from the crime, but Sammler cannot explain his fascination.) No sympathy is expended on the victim. The nameless Black thief, who is a caricature of himself, dressed like a prince, "gorgeously garbed" in a camel's-hair coat, dark Dior glasses, a red silk tie, a single gold earring, and smelling from French perfume, who never speaks but only acts, represents, as Mariann Russell points out, "a convenient metaphor for the disturbing elements in white society and is, in the last analysis, not an image of black culture, but a mirror image of the prevailing white culture."[10] This Black prince not only picks pockets on the bus, but also exposes himself to Sammler in the hallway of his apartment as a form of intimidation. This becomes the image for the entire novel: "reason and decency confronting raw, lawless, primordial threat."[11]

Bellow's use of the Black, though obviously symbolic, is dissatisfying and even inappropriate in a novel written in the sixties. Besides being a period of student protests, the 1960s was also a period of Black unrest, culminating in civil rights marches and demonstrations throughout the country. It was a time of tremendous progress for Blacks in asserting their unalienable rights in the imperfect democracy which they helped build and in demanding a share of the American dream. To have presented them in the Western stereotypic image of evil was not only thoughtless but indecent. This indiscretion is not mitigated by the fact that all the characters are evildoers to some degree. It should be remembered that this is the first Black character in all of Bellow's novels (except for the African natives in *Henderson the Rain King*), and on the basis of this presentation he leaves himself open to being termed a racist. It was predictable that Bellow would rectify this injustice in a future work. *The Dean's December* does just that.

That Bellow is addressing this problem becomes obvious when Albert Corde, who shares some of his creator's experiences and characteristics and is, for the most part, his spokesman, says: "No serious American can allow himself to be suspected of prejudice."[12] *The Dean's December*, Bellow claims, is "a protest about the dehumanization of the blacks in big cities. I'm speaking for the black underclass and telling the whites they're not approaching the problem correctly"; and he believes that the plight of the Blacks "represents a complete failure of the imagination of the country. We are now in the fourth or fifth welfare generation, people who've never worked, people sealed out, set aside, and they look to me like a doomed population."[13]

While in *The Dean's December* Bellow presents a more even-handed picture of the Blacks — they are not all evil, murderers, and rapists; there are some do-gooders and even some ambassadors — black is still used symbolically. It does refer to the "niggerhood" of everyone, "slums we carry around inside of us. Everyman's *inner* inner city" (207). And this social protest, albeit, according to Bellow, one of the novel's main points, is perhaps its weakest: it never really comes to life. It is filtered through the lens of reflection, similar to Bellow's earlier novels, such as *The Adventures of Augie March* and *Herzog*. These, however, are not "social protest" novels. They are personal problem narratives, novels of character. As a "social protest" novel, *The Dean's December* needs the immediacy of first-hand experience in order to provide the reader with access to the ghetto world — its life, its sorrows, its problems. Bernard Malamud, for example, makes this point the subject of his novel *The Tenants*. The difficulty with Bellow's novel is that the flashbacks remain undeveloped glimpses into the past. Consequently, the reader grieves with Minna over her dying mother, shudders from the cold with Albert in the heatless flat in one of Bucharest's dull streets, and suffers the bleakness of life together with the Rumanians, who in spite of it all have learned how to cope with their drab existence, but the reader is not led to agonize with the Black man in a society that considers him expendable.

The Rumanian episode is very effective. Bellow blends time, mood, and setting eloquently. The tight grip of the communist fist which holds and at times strangles its citizenry is rendered compellingly. Corde accompanies his wife, Minna, on a humanitarian visit to Rumania to see her dying mother. However, what could and should have been a simple family matter turns out to be a difficult and harrowing political situation. The insensitivity and coldness of the hospital director to the anesthetized woman who founded the institution but no longer holds most-preferred status, and to her benumbed, sorrowful daughter, an internationally famous professor of astronomy who defected to the West twenty years ago, is reflected not only in the frosty December air but in the chilly hospital and frigid flat as well.

The depiction of this East European satellite is dehumanizing and mirrors the night of the concentration camp universe, the background of *Mr. Sammler's Planet*. Both works assert Bellow's views on totalitarian states which he contrasts to life in the politically free, but socially imperfect, United States. Sammler managed to extricate himself from the bloody corpses, the mausoleum, and the war and continue his life among the zany creatures of New York. Likewise, Corde's situation in Rumania is claustrophobic. He rarely leaves his room. He meets and speaks with very few of the local inhabitants. All are intimidated by the secret police, knowing their wires are tapped and their walls have ears. Corde feels similarly restricted. Actually, in Rumania he is preoccupied with issues in the United States that he has left behind: the trial of a Black man, Lucas Ebry, for the murder of a student (the apprehension of Ebry and his subsequent trial were brought about by Corde's influence) and the furor over his articles in *Harper's* concerning the plight of the "underclass" in Chicago. Being in Rumania gives him a chance to get a clearer perspective of these issues and to justify his own stand. He is impatient, however, to take his near-lifeless wife out of Rumania so that she may regain her health, and to return to a country where freedom of speech and freedom of movement are a way of life, authority may be questioned, and where the ability to choose affirms one's humanity.

Bellow's strength has always been in the characters he creates, and *The Dean's December* is not so much a social protest novel as a work about Albert Corde, his sense of himself and how he reacts to political, moral, and personal situations. Albert Corde, the dean of *The Dean's December*, differs from Bellow's usual protagonist. He is not the larky, carefree individual that Augie March is, and that Eugene Henderson is, or even Charlie Citrine. He is not the whining catastrophe that Tommy Wilhelm is, nor the schlemiel-schlimazel that Moses Herzog is. He is, however, a middle-aged Huguenot-Irish version of that minutely observant septuagenarian, Artur Sammler. As does Sammler, Corde notices everything. "What a man he was for noticing! Continually attentive to his surroundings. As if he had been sent down to *mind* the outer world, on a mission of observation and quotation" (210).

He, too, is the prop which supports the weaker element of his orbit. Students in his college look to him as dean for advice. His wife leans on him during the difficult time of her mother's illness and ultimate death and needs him to keep her "posted on sublunary matters" (260). Sam Beech, the scientist, needs him to explain to the public in layman's terms his scientific findings concerning the welfare of the world. Max Detillion, Corde's cousin, needs him to reinforce his waning legal reputation. Dewey Spangler, a childhood friend, now a syndicated columnist, needs him to bolster his ego. Albert Corde also moves in a world of lunacy and tries to make sense of a world ruled by madness. Like Sammler, he is the humanist discursing the perennial problems facing man, knowing that the answers are not as simple as settling on the moon or taking lead out of a diet. Like Sammler, he too has a confrontation with a university student, a college drop-out, his nephew Mason Zaehner, who argues with him about Blacks.

Albert Corde is a Protestant. All Bellow's protagonists, except for Eugene Henderson, are Jewish. They are burdened with problems, and many of those are related to their Jewishness — assimilating into the Gentile community while not being able to fully divest themselves of their heritage. Albert Corde also has problems. They are not the monumental difficulties that interfere with life but rather the minor disturbances of everyday living. They call for an inner strength that comes with self-acceptance and social acceptance, i.e., with being a WASP in America. Corde does not have the problem of proving himself. He does not wrestle with angels or alter-egos. Unlike his Jewish fictional forebears, he exudes self-assurance. He is essentially a strong individual with a moral mission to right the wrongs of the world or at least to disseminate information concerning troubled mankind. As Joseph Cohen says: "Albert Corde, Bellow's dean, seemingly devoid of heroic propensities, may turn out to be his best balanced hero, which is to say, his most human and, therefore, most appealing character."[14]

This strength of character is applied by Albert Corde to all phases of his life. He changes careers in his middle age, but he does not have a mid-life crisis. Decision-making comes easily to him. When Minna wants to know what to do, Corde never wavers. He has suggestions. He has answers. When he has his confrontation with Alec Witt, the Provost, concerning Spangler's article, he knows what he has to do, and he tenders his resignation. Even at that point, his life doesn't fall apart. He will go back to journalism. He is high-minded and a man of principle. He feels strongly about the problems of his city, the West, and democracy in general, and he writes about them. To him, Chicago is not a location but a condition, as was Africa to Eugene Henderson. Corde is the moral humanist and a good man who not only leads his own life along axial lines, but is not afraid to tell others to do likewise. The characterization of the dean in *The Dean's December* provides the response to the question raised in all of Bellow's works: How should a good man live? The answer is like Albert Corde.

The fact that this work is not essentially different from Bellow's other works does not diminish its value to twentieth-century literature. It indicates, however, the point Bellow makes about his work: that he feels like the opera singer who sings his aria over and over again to the adulating applause of his audience. Exhausted, the singer asks: "How many times must I sing this aria?" He is told, "Until you get it right." Bellow will keep on writing and rewriting his aria until he feels he has "gotten it quite right."[15]

Notes

1. See Allan Chavkin's "Recovering 'The World That is Buried Under the Debris of False Description'," *Saul Bellow Journal* 1.2 (1982): 47-57.
2. See, among others, the Bellow-interviews by Michiko Kakutani, "A Talk With Saul Bellow: On His Work and Himself," *New York Times Book Review* (13 Dec. 1981): 1, 28-30; William Kennedy, "If Saul Bellow Doesn't Have a True Word to Say, He Keeps His Mouth Shut," *Esquire* (Feb. 1982): 49-54; and Cathleen Medwick, "A Cry of Strength: The Unfashionably Uncynical Saul Bellow," *Vogue* (Mar. 1982): 368-89, 426-27.
3. Kakutani, 28.
4. Kakutani, 28.
5. Alfred Kazin, "Though He Slay Me. . . ." *New York Review of Books* (3 Dec. 1970): 4. [See pp. 174-177 of this volume.]
6. Edward Grossman, "The Bitterness of Saul Bellow." *Midstream* 16 (Sep. 1970): 5
7. See L. H. Goldman, "Afterword," *Saul Bellow's Moral Vision: A Critical Study of the Jewish Experience* (New York: Irvington, 1983).
8. Kakutani, 28.
9. Saul Bellow, *Mr. Sammler's Planet* (Harmondsworth: Penguin, 1977), 18. Subsequent references in the text from this edition.
10. Mariann Russell, "White Man's Black Man: Three Views." *CLA Journal* 17 (1973): 93.
11. Beverly Gross, "Dark Side of the Moon," *The Nation* (9 Feb. 1970): 154.

12. Saul Bellow, *The Dean's December* (New York: Harper, 1982), 204. Subsequent references in the text from this edition.
13. Kennedy, 50.
14. Joseph Cohen, "Saul Bellow's Heroes in an Unheroic Age," *Saul Bellow Journal* 3.1 (1983): 53.
15. Kakutani, 1.

*   *   *

Saul Bellow's "Visionary Project"
Allan Chavkin and Nancy Feyl Chavkin

The Dean's December, a tale of two cities, Chicago and Bucharest, explores the quality of the modern individual's life and suggests that his freedom has been crushed in the East and is being threatened in the West. The Rumania depicted in the novel is actually a composite of several Eastern European countries and represents the penitentiary society of the Communist bloc in which Bellow sees no hope. In fact, Bellow's fear is that this penitentiary society may represent "our own future" when "we've worn ourselves out with our soft nihilism."[1] America is "a pleasure society which likes to think of itself as a tenderness society" (275) and thus will not admit the harsh realities of competition, suffering, and death that are endemic to the functioning of the twentieth-century American capitalistic system. Unable to see its situation clearly, America is moving toward spiritual bankruptcy and social anarchy. Just how desperate the situation has become is made clear in a passage in an early draft of the novel in which a public defender, Sam Varennes, paraphrases and ponders Albert Corde's dire analysis and prophecy. "'We're in dreamland?' said [Sam] Varennes. 'I seem to remember — wasn't there a book called *Capitalism Commits Suicide*?'" (MS 7.4, Deposit 63, p. 104).[2]

This complex novel is a retrospective crisis meditation in which Albert Corde, Bellow's protagonist and spokesman, attempts "to recover the world that is buried under the debris of false description or nonexperience" and to see clearly the reality of the everyday world (243). A twentieth-century heir to the romantic tradition who quotes from Blake, Shelley, and other nineteenth- and twentieth-century romantics, Corde believes in the power of the imagination to see without the beclouded lens of customary perception dulled by prejudice, by elaborate theories, and by a myriad of irrelevant facts.[3] Corde's description of his controversial two-part article that he published in *Harper's* reveals what Bellow intends to accomplish in his novel. Corde explains that in this "visionary project" he tries to make

First published in slightly different form as "Bellow's Dire Prophecy," in *Centennial Review* 33.2 (1989): 93-107.

himself the "moralist of seeing" who wakes up the conscience of the United States by "speaking up for the noble ideas of the West in their American form" (123-24). He stresses the need for "poetry" (the imagination) to uncover a reality which has become buried in the debris of the contemporary dump heap. "The first act of morality was to disinter the reality, retrieve reality, dig it out from the trash, represent it anew as art would represent it" (123).

Bellow has indicated that the genesis of his novel was in an abandoned non-fiction book on Chicago.[4] The remnants of the abandoned book surface in Corde's articles for *Harper's*, which typically Bellow summarizes for the reader and occasionally presents actual excerpts. In any case, while the *Harper's* articles consider at least briefly many issues, their preoccupations are with urban decay and the black underclass in Chicago, which is, according to Bellow, the representative American city. Bellow himself has stated that one of his primary intentions in the writing of this novel was to protest against "the dehumanization of blacks in the big cities. I'm speaking up for the black underclass and telling the whites they're not approaching the problem correctly."[5] Although the novel includes Bellow's delineation and indictment of a variety of social evils including the nihilistic totalitarianism of the Communist world, his attack upon racism and its concomitant evils is the most vociferous one in the work. The social deterioration of American society is a complex problem with a number of causes, but the primary one, Bellow implies, is inequality between the races. Although a major subplot of the novel focuses on Bucharest, the core of the novel consists of Bellow's evocation of Chicago.

Bellow's decision to abandon his non-fiction work on Chicago for his fictional tale of two cities is a complex issue itself. We believe that the primary reason Bellow chose the fictional form over the non-fictional one is that the former allowed him greater freedom in exploring the subject of the black underclass. While the so-called experts have failed to solve the problems of the urban poor or even properly articulate them, he believes that he at least can delineate this crisis because of his unique role as a novelist, "an imaginative historian, who is able to get closer to contemporary facts than social scientists possibly can."[6] The objective approach of non-fiction was inadequate because it could not convey the reality of the lives of the urban poor — their emotional, spiritual, and imaginative lives. The so-called "objective" approach of the experts was not able to deal with such an intangible subject. Explaining his choice of writing a novel on public issues, Bellow comments: "It became clear to me that no imagination whatever had been applied to the problems of demoralized cities. All the approaches have been technical, financial, and bureaucratic, and no one has been able to take into account the sense of these lives."[7]

Through Albert Corde, Bellow analyzes both the powerful and powerless. His view of the residents of the inner cities and their masters is not framed in "conventional pieties," and he refuses to play the role of liberal appealing to our guilt. Corde acknowledges that his breaking of taboos in his articles in *Harper's* has brought down condemnation on all sides: "Liberals found him reactionary. Conservatives called him crazy" (187). In these negative responses to the articles in *Harper's*, Bellow may have been anticipating reactions to the radical views that he expresses in his disconcerting novel.

The novel did generate some negative criticism when it was published in 1982. Even a fair-minded and sensitive reviewer such as John Updike criticized Bellow's spokesman Albert Corde for "fastidiousness." Updike writes: "But one wonders if to, say, Henry James the ethnic neighborhoods of Chicago so engagingly particularized by Bellow in *Augie March* might not have seemed as much a hopeless wasteland as black Chicago appears to Albert Corde."[8] It is exactly this kind of complacency that Bellow seeks to expose, for this assumption that the American city has always been "ugly and terrifying" prevents the possibility of accurately seeing the extent of the problem and correcting it (187). The ethnic neighborhoods that repulsed Henry James are not comparable to the slums of the black underclass that Corde sees. As some sociologists have pointed out, the term "underclass" refers to a new development; it refers, in fact, to what Douglas Glasgow calls a "relatively new population in industrial society."[9] Sociologists use the word "underclass" to distinguish this group of the most severely poverty-stricken people from the lower-class. Alphonso Pinkney argues that "two of the major defining characteristics of the black underclass are their poverty and the social decay in which they are forced to survive."[10] As Glasgow suggests, the lower class at least has the dream of upward mobility (G 8), but the social decay of the underclass is so severe that its members, to use Pinkney's language, "have been abandoned to a life of hopelessness" (P 117). In short, the underclass is almost completely isolated from mainstream society; and this isolation both prompts and reinforces deviant social behavior, the norm in underclass neighborhoods.

The term underclass does not suggest moral or ethical unworthiness but is used to define a group of society that lacks the possibility of upward mobility (G 8). In the 1960s the failures of the lower class were seen as forming "pockets of poverty" that would soon be eliminated in the Great Society, but actually these "pockets" were not "small isolated groups in a temporary condition of want, as the phrase suggests, but the permanent nucleus of a swiftly growing underclass" (G 8). Although the underclass that would soon consume the cores of nearly every major American city is not made up of exclusively black or other ethnic minorities, a disproportionately large number are young black men. In fact, one of the most depressing aspects of the crisis is that the black underclass seems to be becoming younger and increasingly violent. Many blacks in their early and middle teen years have already been written off as failures, without any hope of gaining access to mainstream life.

Certainly the problem continues to worsen. Recent research indicates that the rate of growth of the American poor is being surpassed by the rate of growth of America's most severely disadvantaged, the underclass. The number of Americans who live below the poverty line has increased to twenty-nine million, a growth of about five percent from 1970 to 1980. According to the Urban Institute, a research organization in Washington, during this same time period the rate of growth of the underclass has grown five-fold, from approximately 100,000 to half-a-million. And social scientists at the Urban Institute define the underclass more narrowly than others. According to the Urban Institute, the underclass consists of people who are chronically unemployed or on welfare and who live in areas with extremely high concentrations of high school dropouts, families headed by women, and unemployed working-age men. In contrast, other social scientists define the underclass less narrowly, and in their studies the underclass population is seen as numbering in the millions; in some of these studies the underclass numbers as high as eight or ten million. In any case, all recent studies, despite their differing definitions of the underclass, see a frightening growth in its population. A particularly disturbing recent development is the spread of the underclass neighborhood to adjacent areas. As working-class residents leave neighborhoods, the socially deviant gain control now that they are no longer held in check by the predominance of working-class people. The socially deviant behavior of the underclass now becomes the norm, and the healthy parts of the community soon become diseased. Anti-social behavior becomes the standard and then spreads to adjacent neighborhoods, corrupting them in time. In short, like a cancer, the underclass grows and consumes increasing amounts of the body politic.[11]

Although certainly there are many who are in agreement with Updike's view that Corde is "fastidious" and that Bellow is a false prophet of doom, social scientists are providing convincing evidence to undermine such a complacent view when they argue that the growing black underclass is a phenomenon that is fundamentally different from the ethnic poor who have always resided in American cities. The young of the black underclass are becoming increasingly angry, frustrated, and self-destructive. Treated as animals by society, "they frequently respond in kind" (P 117). In Bellow's view, American capitalism is committing a kind of gradual suicide; in fact, the situation has become desperate and we need "catastrophe premises" (MS 7.4, Deposit 63, p. 104).

America is facing a great "moral crisis" which the dean speaks of at times in eschatological tones. The situation is an "apocalyptic" one, to use Corde's language. The great compacts of the human race are no longer acknowledged by many in the East and the West. "The sacred solemnity of religion, marriage, and burial was what the old man [Corde's father-in-law] took as the foundation of foundations," but these are desecrated (MS 7.3, Deposit 63, p. 179). While the East has embraced a "hard nihilism" for some time, the humanist values upon which the West is based are being cynically abandoned by all classes of society. In fact, Corde argues, a spiritual sickness is poisoning the body politic, and the effects of "the slum of innermost being" are painfully manifested in the disillusionment and alienation of the underclass and the young. "America no more knew what to do with this black underclass than it knew what to do with its children. It was impossible for it to educate either, or to bind either to life. It was not itself securely attached to life just now" (201).

The implications of the spiritual corruption that Bellow calls "the slum of innermost being" become clear if one examines the two interracial murder cases and the violent death of the ghetto black Gene Lewis in the Chicago section of the novel. These three episodes reveal the extent of the spiritual sickness that Corde sees at the heart of American society.

The details of the Lester murder case are in dispute, but Corde's reconstruction and interpretation of the case are plausible and no doubt closer to the truth than his militant nephew's version. Corde suggests that the white graduate student Rickie Lester, driven by the culture's "sex compulsion," one hot night picked up two black hustlers and brought them back to his apartment, perhaps for kinky sex; in the process of robbing him, they gagged him and threw him out the window to his death. The whole sordid episode is a result of "the slums we carry around inside us" (207). A spiritual malady and a reduced consciousness pervade society. Death in this civilization in which no one is attached to life simply does not matter; in fact, the murderers of Lester are arrested only because of the dean's pressure on the authorities. Corde feels "unreasonable indignation," "upswimming rage," and "pity" (MS 7.3, Deposit 63, p. 53), but everyone else, including the provost of Corde's university, is ready to ignore this "tragedy," which is seen as merely an ineluctable item of the twentieth-century urban landscape.

The dean's zealous pursuit of justice angers both the college administration, which does not like the publicity that the dean attracts, and the radical student militants, who call him a racist and raise the issues of black housing in the neighborhood, South African investments, and Affirmative Action. Corde refuses to allow either of the two groups to deflect him from his pursuit of justice. "A campus radical forty years ago," Corde realizes "how little things had changed" (30). He is no longer sympathetic to the fanaticism and pressure methods that the radicals use. Like Blake, whom he quotes, Corde has abandoned belief in an apocalyptic transformation of society by violent revolution for a belief that a prerequisite for the radical alteration of society must be a fundamentally new perception of reality and a spiritual rebirth in which our inner slums are discarded.

Bellow reveals his views of the racial problem in Corde's recollection of his conversation with his nephew, Mason Zaehner, Jr., who is a friend and an advocate of Lucas Ebry, one of the murderers of Rickie Lester. Cynical about Lester's murder, Mason suggests to his uncle that the killing of the white student was an accident and argues that in any case, the man was looking for trouble when he picked up a black prostitute and her pimp; in short, he got what he deserved. As "a representative of the street people," Mason intends "to teach his ignorant uncle some lessons about Chicago's social reality" (35). He implies that his uncle is not only naive about the sordid everyday occurrences of his native city but also that he is a racist who is instinctively disgusted with the black underclass because as a man of routine he is repelled by the structureless lives of drink, drugs, scrounging, hanging out, shooting, and dying in the confined space of the ghetto. According to Mason, instead of his uncle's "quixotic" humanism, cynical realism is necessary to survive in Chicago: "he was saying, Let's not fuck around with all these high sentiments and humane teachings and pieties and poetry" (41). Corde concludes that his nephew is "the true voice of Chicago — the spirit of the age speaking from its lowest register; the very bottom" (42).

Embodying the spirit of a different age, that of nineteenth-century romantic humanism, Corde can agree with much of Mason's criticism of society for its treatment of blacks but not his conclusions; he refuses to accept the cynical and brutal realism that is pervasive in the modern world. This ubiquitous realism is shared by a Rumanian communist colonel in the secret police, a wealthy conservative Chicago lawyer, a militant street person, and a black hustler; the brutal murder of a young graduate student or the death of an old woman means nothing to these callous "realists." Like other of Bellow's protagonists, such as Moses Herzog and Kenneth Trachtenberg, Corde cannot accept this brutal "hardboiled-dom," which he considers fraudulent. Corde suggests that while Lester was naive and perhaps also lecherous, he didn't deserve to be murdered. His life is important: if his death does not matter, then how do the deaths of those in the black underclass matter?

As he has done so poignantly in such novels as *Herzog* (1964) and *More Die of Heartbreak* (1987), Bellow is clearly condemning here the rejection of basic humanist values and their replacement with a cynical realism. It is significant that the rich conservative Mason Zaehner, Sr. has the same basic outlook as his radical son. Corde suggests their basic philosophical similarity, despite their different places on the political spectrum, when he notes the resemblance between father and son; both have "the identical bullying lusterless put-down stare" (37). Moreover, both reveal their disdain for "poetry" and humanist values, which they consider escapist. Neither of these two is receptive to the dean's broader outlook. Corde finds that Mason Zaehner, Sr. will not even listen to his ideas. In his discussion with Mason Zaehner, Jr. about the Lester murder case the dean "would have liked to tell his nephew that men and women were shadows, and shadows within shadows, to one another," but doesn't because scornful Mason, Jr., like his father, would have ridiculed such cryptic "poetry" (32).

Yet it is this cryptic poetry, Corde suggests, that enables one to understand what is happening in the modern world. This particular remark on people as "shadows" that the dean had considered imparting to his nephew receives clarification in the tenth chapter of the novel, where the dean examines the Sathers's murder case and evokes a Dantesque vision of damned "whirling souls" in "the moronic inferno" of the modern city. The case involves a black man named Spofford Mitchell who kidnapped a young white housewife, Sally Sathers. Over a period of several days, he repeatedly raped her, locking her in his trunk between attacks; finally he shot her in the head and then "covered her body with trash" (194). Corde sees this murder and indecent discarding of the corpse under trash in a vacant lot as emblematic of the bestial degeneration of civilization in the modern American metropolis. "The old guy [Vico] wrote if the dead aren't buried and none of the compacts of the human race are respected we will be rooting among the corpses like swine" (MS 7.3, Deposit 63, p. 179).[12] As "a moralist of seeing" who wants to "retrieve reality, dig it out from the trash," the dean strives unsuccessfully to force Sam Varennes, the liberal white public defender of Mitchell, to see this barbarous degeneration (123). He wants Varennes to recognize that an evil has been perpetrated, that a human being has been brutally raped and murdered. Varennes's adversary relationship with the prosecutors, his defensiveness provoked by Corde's questioning, and his complacent acceptance of liberal platitudes undermine any real possibility of his imagining the torture that Sally Sathers endured at the hands of his client Spofford Mitchell. The novel implies that it is well-intentioned liberals such as Varennes who should bear partial responsibility for the abominable crimes of the underclass. "Liberal friends speak of the blacks as those to whom evil has been done. Certainly it has been done, but this [attitude] put the ignored black into the object-class. It sharpens his entirely human desire to be a *doer*" (MS 7.3, Deposit 63, p. 180). It is this natural longing to be "a doer" and not a passive victim that explains the reason for the content of the inner city's "black exploitation films" which "are fantasies of super-doing, kung fu, shooting, explosion, wild, daring sex" (MS 7.3, Deposit 63, p. 180).

Albert Corde suggests that "the doer" Spofford Mitchell perceives only with "genital literalness"; this black man sees "the forced momentary connections of his body with that of another (any other?) — as the only means of expression available to him" in an inhuman, unintelligible universe.[13] In fact, American society, "a pleasure society," conveys the wrong message to the underclass with the result that in extreme cases a man such as the emotionally and spiritually destitute Spofford Mitchell becomes a wild animal who can "relate" to another living being only in a physical, invariably violent, way. "Our pleasure society has suggested to the black that he has singular physical talents, and these in a world that lives by the body, a sort of animal worship, are valuable, and flattering. And why be a tame animal? Wild is better. And it's what everybody really wants" (MS 7.3, Deposit 63, pp. 180-81).

Another doomed wild animal who can relate to the world only with a violent "literalness" is Gene Lewis. Although his story takes up only a small portion of the novel, his grim fate becomes emblematic of that of the underclass. When Lewis's guards take him to the Criminal Courts Building for sentencing, they allow his girlfriend to give him a copy of *Ivanhoe* to read during the lengthy legal proceedings. Lewis's girlfriend has hollowed out the book and inserted a magnum revolver as well as a key to unlock Lewis's handcuffs. Once inside the courtroom, Lewis frees himself with the key and then forces his five guards against the wall and disarms them. In a bravado act of defiance, he shows Judge Makowski "that the magnum was not a toy" by firing a "shot into the floor" (162). Then he dashes out of the courtroom into an elevator which, to his surprise, goes up instead of down. On the next floor when he races out to change elevators, a group of detectives shoot him in the head ten times.

Like Mitchell, Lewis can serve as a symbol of the self-destructive inclination of the black underclass. Impulsive violence and premature death are as much a part of their urban jungle as the dreary streets. Implicit in Corde's description of the violent demise of Lewis is the notion that his dramatic and suicidal attempt to escape should be regarded as a kind of protest by a desperate but inarticulate man who knows that he has been written off by a society of which he is, to use Pinkney's language in the dedication of his book, a citizen "but not a part of it." In a manuscript draft of the novel, Dewey Spangler succinctly paraphrases Corde's explanation of the implicit meaning of Lewis's self-destructive performance in the Criminal Courts Building. "They [people such as Lewis] wanted to proclaim something to the world. I think you said that people for whom the rest of the world had no use were sometimes inspired to make a symbolic or interpretive gesture" (MS 7.3, Deposit 63, p. 177).

As the two murder cases and Lewis's self-destructive act reveal, society accepts murder and violent death associated with the underclass as inevitable. In the social and spiritual anarchy that has enveloped the inner cities, we no longer see each other as human beings. Echoing his earlier reference to men and women as shadows within shadows, Corde suggests that "whirling souls" of the inner city attempt to break through their sense of unreality by a violence that is perversely associated with sex. In this society, sex, savagery, and criminality have become closely connected. Pleasure has become "death saturated," and many "whirling souls" are "on the fast track for death" (196-97). Modern consciousness is a "reduced consciousness" that is "basically murderous" (193). Unfortunately, as Gerhard Bach observes, the public is "unable to apprehend its own predicament"[14] — it is in a stupor, unable to retrieve reality buried under the garbage heap created by the media, the city authorities, and the educational establishment.

What is the solution to the problem, then, of the ghettos of the decaying cities and the inner slums that threaten to destroy American society? Corde searches for "moral initiative" throughout society but finds it in only two people — two black men, Rufus Ridpath, the ex-director of the County Jail who is fired because of alleged corruption, and Toby Winthrop, an ex-hit man and ex-heroin-addict, who directs a detoxification center in the ghetto. Rejecting the narcissistic "realism" of the age, both of these men believe in "a moral life," and both strive for justice, despite the hostility to change and the prevailing cynicism. Neither of these men fits the heroic models admired by the young of the underclass — "black princes" whose wealth and power derive from criminal activities, such as controlling the drug trade or ruling the prisons.

Ridpath refuses to involve himself in the corruption around him, and as a result is persecuted. Those in power are suspicious of the warden because he saves millions of dollars for the County when he refuses to become involved in the graft with suppliers and contractors. Moreover, he reduces the number of murders and suicides in the prison and improves conditions for the incarcerated. Because he refuses to be a hustler living off the black crisis, Ridpath is regarded as politically dangerous, and therefore those in power set out to destroy his reputation. Although five grand jury investigations find nothing incriminating, no one remembers that Ridpath was found innocent, and thus his reputation and career are destroyed.

It is Ridpath who sends Corde to Toby Winthrop, who not only teaches Corde about the realities of Chicago but also embodies the kind of moral initiative necessary for a regeneration of society. Winthrop's account of his life as a heroin addict, his eventual rehabilitation, and his setting up of a detoxification center provide a vivid sense of life in the inner city and an example of the self-sacrifice necessary to revitalize a dying culture. A cold-blooded junkie-hitman for the powerful in Chicago, he is able to repudiate his past and re-attach himself to humanity by self-abnegating action. A casual reference by Corde to Dostoevsky's classic delineation of spiritual loneliness helps explain Winthrop's problem and his character; he reveals, to borrow the dean's description of the nineteenth-century Russian writer, "Dostoevsky's apathy-with-intensity, and the rage for goodness so near to vileness and murderousness" (161). In fact, Corde calls him a "murderer-savior" type, and while he does not specifically link him to Dostoevsky's characters, he is reminiscent of some of the convicts in *The House of the Dead*, who can commit execrable crimes, including brutal murders, and then after immense suffering and degradation be reborn as good, even saintly, people. In short, he symbolizes for Corde man's potential for regeneration and moral action after sinking to the abyss of degradation.

From Winthrop, Corde learns another lesson, too. The ex-heroin addict makes clear that his detoxification center should not be construed as a panacea for the racial crisis. While a few are saved, many hundreds of thousands are not — "they're marked out to be destroyed. Those are people meant to die, sir" (192). It is this grim conclusion that Corde also reaches after pondering the mounting evidence. It is a conclusion that a pleasure society does not want to face. Bellow in his novel insists, however, that his readers admit this truth because it is a prerequisite for any real solution to the problem of the doomed underclass.

By the end of *The Dean's December*, it should be apparent that at the heart of the problem is the reduced modern consciousness; "every man's inner inner city" is responsible for the external slums, and conversely, the urban ghettos are a concrete embodiment of our internal slums. This reduced modern consciousness that has generated the squalid slums of the underclass pervades the civilizations of East and West and severs the bonds of humanity. Overcome by apathy and extreme skepticism, modern man has lost his sense of enchantment with reality and his connection with his spiritual roots, "the deeper life"; most important, he no longer feels attached to humanity. Corde suggests that America must repudiate the social Darwinian metaphor, for civilization has become not so much a jungle as a "garbage dump" (264). The novel urges us to realize that it's not really the inner city ghettos that threaten us but "the slum of innermost being"; this realization is the first step that must be taken if we are to save ourselves as well as the underclass that is lost in a wilderness of despair and crime, "consigned to destruction" (206).

Notes

1. Saul Bellow, *The Dean's December* (New York: Harper, 1982), 20, 276. Subsequent references in the text from this edition.
2. This quotation is from unpublished drafts of the novel that are part of the Special Collections at the University of Chicago Library, where most of Bellow's manuscript material is held. Occasionally, unpublished passages from the manuscripts of *The Dean's December* make explicit what is subtly suggested in the novel. As we do here, when we refer to these manuscripts we shall use the abbreviation MS and the identifying numbers used by the Special Collections Staff. 7.4 refers to Box #7, Folder #4. In this

article the quotations from Bellow's early unpublished manuscripts of *The Dean's December* are from 7.3 (inscribed "1st version, Jan./Feb. 1980") or 7.4, Deposit 63.

3. Michael G. Yetman, "Toward a Language Irresistible: Saul Bellow and the Romance of Poetry." *Papers on Language and Literature* 22 (1986): 431, argues that like the English romantics, Bellow believes that "words reflect and at the same time interpret, humanize, even 'save' through imagination the stuff of literal experience." For a detailed analysis of Bellow's debt to English romanticism, see Allan Chavkin, "Humboldt's Gift and the Romantic Imagination," *Philological Quarterly* 62 (1983): 1-19.

4. Eugene Kennedy, "A Different Saul Bellow," *Boston Globe Magazine* (10 Jan. 1982): 16.

5. William Kennedy, "If Saul Bellow Doesn't Have a True Word to Say, He Keeps His Mouth Shut," *Esquire* (Feb. 1982): 50.

6. Michiko Kakutani, "A Talk with Saul Bellow: On His Work and Himself," *New York Times Book Review* (13 Dec. 1981): 28.

7. Kakutani, 28.

8. John Updike, "Toppling Towers Seen by a Whirling Soul," *New Yorker* (22 Feb. 1982): 8. Other reviewers too rejected Bellow's apocalyptic view of the current crisis and complained that we learn nothing new about the deterioration of life in America's cities. See Hugh Kenner, "From Lower Bellowvia," *Harper's* (Feb. 1982): 62-65, and Sheldon Frank, "Boring Bellow," *The Detroit News* (14 Feb. 1982): 2H.

9. Douglas C. Glasgow, *The Black Underclass: Poverty, Unemployment and Entrapment of Ghetto Youth* (San Francisco: Jossey-Bass Publications, 1980), 9. Subsequent references in the text from this edition, abbreviated G. Social scientists use different criteria to define the new phenomenon of "the underclass," but there does seem to be a consensus that the term refers to the most severely disadvantaged who live in poverty areas of the inner city and who account for a large share of social pathology.

10. Alphonso Pinkney, *The Myth of Black Progress* (Cambridge: Cambridge UP, 1984), 117. Subsequent references in the text from this edition, abbreviated P.

11. Isabel Wilkerson, "Growth of the Very Poor Is Focus of New Studies," *New York Times* (20 Dec. 1987): 15. Information in this paragraph is from Wilkerson's article.

12. In the novel there is a similar passage: "Nobody teaching the young language, human usages or religion, they will go back to the great ancient forest and be like the wild beasts of Orpheus. None of the great compacts of the human race respected. Bestial venery, feral wanderings, incest, and the dead left unburied" (251).

13. Yetman, 437.

14. Gerhard Bach, "The Dean Who Came In from the Cold: Saul Bellow's America of the 1980's," *Saul Bellow in the 1980's: A Collection of Critical Essays*, ed. Gloria Cronin and L. H. Goldman (East Lansing: U of Michigan P, 1989), 309.

*   *   *

Short Fiction
Mosby's Memoirs and Other Stories (1968)
Him with His Foot in His Mouth and Other Stories (1984)

The Rhetoric of Bellow's Short Fiction
Philip Stevick

In an uncommonly self-deprecatory passage introducing his own short fiction, Norman Mailer compares the art of the short story writer to that of the jeweler. "He stays in his shop, he polishes those jewels, he collects craft, lore, confirms gossip, assays jeweler's rouge, looks to steal the tricks of the arcane, and generally disports like a medieval alchemist who's got a little furnace, a small retort, a cave, a handful of fool's gold, and a mad monk's will. With such qualifications, one in a hundred becomes an extraordinary writer, but on the other hand, the worst of this guild makes a life from kissing spiders."[1] It is a descriptive act, with its ironic and begrudging admiration for a talent which Mailer has in short measure, which might easily seem to suggest Bellow. Everybody knows that Bellow is no polisher of jewels. Everybody who cares about Bellow knows that *Seize the Day* and *Dangling Man* are comparatively small and tight but that, in general, Bellow's talent needs space, consequently producing a series of expansive books for which the jeweler's metaphor is quite inappropriate.

Yet Bellow's short fiction carries an uncommon power and integrity. One who has read "Looking for Mr. Green" never forgets it. And I, for one, testify that even so minor a fiction as "A Sermon by Dr. Pep," never collected, never re-printed, hardly noticed by Bellow's critics, hangs in the mind with a curious kind of tenacity. The authority of the short fiction has something to do, of course, with the way in which it extends, in small, the characteristic thematic interests of Bellow, with his customary intensity and his customary intelligence. But the authority of the short fiction has something to do, also, with the highly individual way in which it is made. Not classic modernist stories, not "experimental" in any recognizable sense, they are, moreover, not like anybody else's.

From *Critical Essays on Saul Bellow*, ed. Stanley Trachtenberg (Boston: Hall, 1979), 73-82.

The classic modernist short fiction concentrates time, image, mind, and sensibility in the interests of evoking plateaus of insight, states of self-knowledge, epiphanic moments. Short fiction since the great modernists has tended to emphasize the ludic, the fabulous, and the linguistic, making reflective inventions, aware of their own artifice. Bellow's short fictions, unlike either, concentrate rhetoric. Not exploitations of the possibilities latent in language qua language, certainly not explorations of the limits of language and the claims of silence, they are exploitations of speech used for effect, or, just as often, speech intended for effect which is ineffectual. That is why their structures are often perplexing, or unconventional: because those structures often turn not upon event, or revelation, or insight, but upon social utterance. And that is why their import is sometimes elusive: because the center of that import is in the interaction of speaker and listener.

Only a portion of Bellow's short fiction has seemed to him worthy of reprinting. Undoubtedly some of it is apprentice work. But those early fictions, several not available in collected form, indicate the nature of the whole body of his short fiction. A remarkable number the stories in the years 1941 to the publication of *Mosby's Memoirs and Other Stories* in 1968 are monologues. Some of them, "Two Morning Monologues," "A Sermon by Dr. Pep," and the "Address by Gooley MacDowell to the Hasbeens Club of Chicago" are pure, sustained monologue, not dramatic monologues in the Browning sense, for there is little sense of audience, no drama, no ironic invitation to see through the speakers. Neither are they first-person stories, in which a "speaker" is imaged to tell his own story. There is no sequence of events. There is only the voice. Even certain early stories, such as "The Trip to Galena," which are not monologues, still tend toward that form, easily two thirds of that story, for example, being a spoken explanation, occasionally interrupted by the listener, of the central character's dilemma. Clearly, from the start, Bellow indicates a fascination with voice, virtually a wish to define man in terms of talk, *homo loquens*.

Of the later fictions that sustain the primacy of voice without allowing it the exclusivity of those early monologues, "Looking for Mr. Green" is an example. Its structure is not built upon images heavy with symbolic import, nor upon interior states of mind; its structure is built upon questions, basically the same question, and the answers, lies, and evasions which they evoke:

"Are you the janitor?"

"What do you want?" "I'm looking for a man who's supposed to be living here. Green."

"What Green?". . .

"Does anybody here know how I can deliver a check to Mr. Tulliver Green?"

"Green?". . .

"Does Tulliver Green live here? I'm from the relief."

The man narrowed the opening and spoke to someone at his back.

"Does he live here?"

"Uh-uh. No." . . .

"Is this where Mr. Green lives?"

But she was still talking to herself and did not hear him.

"Is this Mr. Green's house?"

At last she turned her furious drunken glance on him. "What do you want?"[2]

The story is a wonderfully evocative rendering of the underside of Chicago, a brilliant parable of urban anonymity, class and racial hostility, the interaction of institution and individual, the shared paranoia of the contemporary world. But the central, irreducible element which is the means to this larger significance is Grebe asking, asking.

"A Sermon by Dr. Pep" shares almost nothing with "Looking for Mr. Green," except that both are Chicago stories and both structure themselves upon rhetorical acts. Dr. Pep's audience is addressed as "dear friends,"[3] but there is no sense of whether the audience exists. It is entirely possible that no one is listening. Yet Dr. Pep is relentlessly rhetorical, modulating between his philosophy of food and animal life, disease and health on the one hand and confidential anecdotes of his personal life on the other, hectoring, pleading, asking questions which he is about to answer, guessing aloud what some of his audience is thinking, dropping names, authorities, old friends, asking for more time, working for the single tear of pathos, anticipating disagreement, seeking assent, clarifying the seriousness of his address, imploring his audience to remember, choosing sides, naming enemies, wondering aloud, seeking a shared admiration. He confounds his audience with allusions they could not possibly recognize and a philosophy which he may or may not recognize as crankish and recondite; he also makes love to his audience with his words. But there is no audience, or if there is, Bellow prefers not to show it. Which is to say that "Looking for Mr. Green" and "A Sermon by Dr. Pep" present a paradigmatic display of Bellow's rhetorical technique. The appeals to the audience, in both of these quite different stories, are the very center of the fiction. The characteristic action, that is, is someone seeking to speak in such a way as to elicit the desired response. Yet in both, the response is elusive, or evasive, or mendacious, or altogether absent. And that, in the most radical and irreducible sense, is what Bellow's short fiction is "about": the wish to persuade, the act of attempting to persuade, and the sense that that persuasive attempt is, at least, problematic, at most, utterly ineffectual. It goes without saying that large questions, social, cultural, and metaphysical, are implicit in that basic impasse.

I suggest a third example of the principle I am attempting to articulate. "A Father to Be" is a small, unpretentious story, most memorable for Bellow's insights into the small humiliations, ritual castrations, if one likes, of a modern husband, more precisely husband-to-be. The low-grade domestic tensions and the urban, upper-middle-class world of the story make it seem not much different from countless art stories of the post-war period. So does its most potent moment of illumination in which Rogin sees a thoroughly uninteresting fellow passenger on the subway and fancies him to be the image of his future son grown middle-aged. What makes the story seem unusual is its structure, since it moves from point to point by a route that is not, like the conventional epiphany story, intelligible after the fact in terms of the nature of the epiphany. Some of the events of the story, in fact, seem to have little to do with the interior progress of Rogin: Rogin overhearing a conversation between two friends, one of whom confesses himself to be a considerable alcoholic, Rogin being shampooed by his fiancee as the story closes. The trouble is that the reader is likely to look for a system either of events or illuminations that provide the structural spine of the story. And what Bellow provides, instead, is a system of rhetoric, a curious chain of socio-linguistic interchanges (or pseudo-sociolinguistic interchanges, since Rogin is fond of addressing himself with questions and exclamations, the full range of rhetoric, so that what Bellow reveals of Rogin's inner life reads very like an animated conversation between two people).

Anterior to the action of the story, Rogin has had a telephone conversation with his fiancee, which he recalls and reports, a problematic conversation in which, although she has bought some roast beef at a delicatessen, she asks Rogin to buy some more and although he has given her spending money, she has given it to her cousin, who is "extremely wealthy,"[4] to pay the cleaning woman. No classic account of the principles of rhetoric can describe that opening interchange because what Bellow does is to catch, with extraordinary economy, the difficulty of responding to slightly unreasonable requests that come from somebody one cannot see but whose voice one can hear. Rogin moves into a reflection on Joan's extravagance, in which the emphasis falls upon his failure to complain, and from there to a larger level of reflection, which takes the form, typically, not of interior monologue but of highly animated speech. "Superimposition is the universal law. Who is free? No one is free. Who has no burdens? Everyone is under pressure" (145). *His* answers to *his* questions change his mood; his own inner rhetoric has persuaded him to be happy, observant, at one with the world of the delicatessen. The storekeeper speaks sharply to a Puerto Rican employee, and it is that exchange that draws Rogin into their world. Even choosing food at the counter becomes a rhetorical exercise, with Rogin's typical inner dialogue and a missed irony in his exchange with the clerk. The overheard conversation in the subway is less significant for what it tells Rogin than for the mode of its rhetoric — two shapeless men, one confessing an intimacy that is obvious before its revelation, with Rogin as accidental listener over the noise of the subway, at once feeling and understanding, also detached and uncaring.

So it goes. His epiphanic encounter with his imagined son grown old is, once again, not rendered as revery but as inner dialogue. And when he finally arrives at Joan's apartment, she addresses him with her own special rhetorical appeal. "'Oh, my baby. You're covered with snow. Why didn't you wear your hat? It's all over its little head' — her favorite third-person endearment" (153). Finally, shampooed — humbled, emasculated, baptized — Rogin responds with the verbal gestures that end the story. "You always have such wonderful ideas, Joan. You know? You have a kind of instinct, a regular gift" (155). "About" many things, the story is centrally about talking: conversing on the telephone, listening to strangers on the subway, ordering gherkins at a delicatessen counter, greeting a fiancee, asserting oneself and abasing oneself with words.

Finally, I suggest "The Gonzaga Manuscripts" as another example of the self delineated by social speech. The story attempts a subject which James once did with such authority and insight that comparison is inevitable. In *The Aspern Papers*, the quest of an American for the manuscripts of a poet whom he adores involves some typically Jamesian conflicts of class, style, and nationality. But what James's story finally asks is what such a quest ought to cost, in terms of the searcher's moral character. No such interest engages Bellow. The passion of Charles Feiler, the scholar in quest of the Gonzaga Manuscripts, is convincing enough but quite unambiguous and nonproblematic. The work of Gonzaga represents, for him, poetic excellence and clarity of vision, more than that, a kind of positive force in a negativistic culture. What the story turns upon is not at all the compromises he is willing to make to see the manuscripts; no compromises are suggested. It turns rather upon the responses that people who knew the poet make to his requests. It is, again, a story about asking questions and getting answers, bad answers, misleading answers, banal answers, answers that defile the memory of the poet. Characteristically, before he asks anyone else about the whereabouts of the manuscripts, Feiler asks himself if his quest matters. It is the one question he asks which receives a brisk, satisfying, wholly humane answer. It does matter. To recover the manuscripts is to bring that much of Gonzaga to the world, which is, for Feiler, an act of salvation, the world being badly in need of the act of faith that the poems represent.

Feiler has an encounter with a particularly repulsive British woman who baits him for his American-ness. It is a curious diversion from his purpose, which, as he sees it, only strengthens his resolve. His next encounter is with a Miss Ungar, a literate, educated woman, whose function is to provide an exchange of dollars for pesetas, should the opportunity arise to buy the manuscripts. "Have you ever heard of a poet named Gonzaga?" he asks. "Gonzaga? I must have. But I don't think I ever read him," she replies.[5] He responds with a burst of naive confidence. Guzman del Nido, Gonzaga's friend, military comrade, and literary executor is his next encounter. And, once again, the exchange between the two is more important to the cumulative power of the story than Feiler's motives, more important than del Nido's state of mind, more important than the Gonzaga manuscripts. Del Nido, it turns out, is crass, vulgar, and uncomprehending. "It's natural," Feiler muses, after the encounter, "to suppose, because a man is great, that the people around him must have known how to respond to greatness, but when these people turn out to be no better than Guzman del Nido you wonder what response greatness really needs" (130). During the course of the interview with del Nido, by the way, questions of Feiler's American-ness similarly arise, with the customary impasse in communication, the usual condescension, the ritual offenses. Del Nido tells a joke, with an American punch line, which gets a small laugh; and Feiler tells another, which nobody laughs at. Feiler, by that time, has summed up the interview in rhetorical terms, knowing by now what question gets what answer. "Clarence at once sensed that del Nido would make him look foolish if he could, with his fine irony and his fine Spanish manners. Del Nido was the sort of man who cut every-one down to size" (125).

The Povlo family, whom Feiler interviews next, prove to be "a family of laughers. They laughed when they spoke and when you ans-wered" (131). It surely occurs to the reader at this point that indiscrim-inate laughter is as symptomatic of rhetorical impasse as those witless jokes of a few pages before at which nobody laughs. The international misunderstandings throughout the story develop into a riot of offenses, misconceptions, and linguistic tangles: Feiler mistaken for an English-man, a dog with a Scottish name, Luis attempting to speak a few idio-tic words of English, another character speaking a line of French, and a series of jocular references to the atomic bomb. From here the story works toward its conclusion, its culminating misunderstanding, and as that last failure to find the poems develops, Feiler has yet another ex-change that must remind the reader of those several parallel exchanges before it. Alvarez-Povlo has taken Feiler for a financier; Feiler replies that he has come in quest of Gonzaga's poems. And Alvarez-Povlo replies: "Manuel? The soldier? The little fellow? The one that was her lover in nineteen twenty-eight? He was killed in Morocco" (140).

Like those stories I have described before, the primary unit of "The Gonzaga Manuscripts" is not the event or the moment of con-sciousness but the speech act. In each of the four stories, elements are introduced which tend to make communication unusually difficult: in "A Sermon by Dr. Pep," the very presence of an audience is prob-lematic; in "Looking for Mr. Green," the respondents are uniformly hostile and evasive; in "A Father to Be," the subtle play of power which Rogin's fiancee exerts over him affects every communication between them; and in "The Gonzaga Manuscripts," the characters are prevented from responding satisfactorily to Feiler both because of national misunderstandings and because of their parochial obtuseness. Except for "A Sermon by Dr. Pep," which is entirely public, the main characters in the other three stories all display an inner life which is not meditative or associative but which is, rather, inner speech. And in all four of the stories, the act of speech carries with it an investment of self which is extraordinary.

The implications of so rhetorical a fiction seem to me three. First, such a fiction necessarily devises its own range of verbal effects, its own grammar, as it were, of rhetoric. To some extent, to be sure, this grammar is derivative of earlier writers, Chekhov for example, for whom the appeal to another's attention is significant, or others, Kafka for example, for whom the question badly answered is central, or still others, a long tradition from Cervantes, through Diderot, Richardson, Dostoevsky, Conrad, and a substantial group of Bellow's contemporaries, for whom a passage of unmediated monologue is the best means to the presentation of self. Still, to a considerable extent, Bellow's range of rhetorical appeals is his own.

Secondly, such a fiction implies the invention of a grammar of either response or resistance. Once again, both Chekhov and Kafka clearly imply the difficulties of being heard, being listened to, being understood, and being properly answered. And the reader of Dickens, Mann, countless others, understands the barriers to communication that age, class, profession, and temperament provide. But here, too, Bellow finds his own way of laying out the problematics of making connections by public speech.

Thirdly, such a fiction implies certain valuations of the human community. In one sense, reasoning from Bellow, man is most fully human when he is speaking for effect, his mind, craft, and sense of others most fully engaged. At the same time, it is as easy to argue that if the center of human affairs is rhetoric, then all the world's a stage and all of us are merely role players. The idea of rhetoric inevitably carries both a pejorative and an honorific sense. It is a duality that the characters themselves imply. Bellow's characters are rhetorical because that is their nature, and the situations in which they find themselves compel them to be rhetorical. Consequently there is an obsessive, compulsive, repetitive aspect to them that undermines their dignity and makes them appear, to varying degrees, slightly comic. Yet their rhetoric is, finally, in the service of anxieties and desires that are more nearly existential, or spiritual, than social and persuasive. Consequently their rhetoric ennobles them, allowing them to present themselves, as characters in short fiction rarely do, as being passionately involved with the deepest questions of their humanness.

I suggest the beginnings of a grammar.

1. The compulsive list: "Money owing, rent postponed, hole in your glove, one egg, cheap tobacco" ("Two Morning Monologues," 236).[6]

2. The series of rhetorical fragments, suggestive of urgency or anxiety: "Presently I understood. The black market. This was not then reprehensible. Postwar Europe was like that. Refugees, adventurers, G.I.s. Even the Comte de la M-C. Europe still shuddering from the blows it had received. Governments new, uncertain, infirm. No reason to respect their authority" ("Mosby's Memoirs," 163).[7]

3. Interior questions presented serially: "To whom should she leave it? Her brothers? Not they. Nephews? One was a submarine commander. The other was a bachelor in the State Department. Then began the roll call of cousins. Merton? He owned an estate in Connecticut. Anna? She had a face like a hot-water bottle" ("Leaving the Yellow House," 39).[8]

4. The fragmentary afterthought: "They dug and saved. Mrs. Isaac Braun wore no cosmetics. Except a touch of lipstick when going out in public. No mink coats. A comfortable Hudson seal, yes" ("The Old System," 64).[9]

5. The summary epithet: "And she vetoed all the young women, her judgments severe without limit. 'A false dog.' 'Candied Poison.' 'An open ditch. A sewer. A born whore!'" . . . "Aunt Rose said he was a minor hoodlum, a slugger. . . . This hired killer, this second Lepke of Murder, Inc." ("The Old System," 52, 53).

6. The summary epithet used ironically: "that friend of liberty Franklin Delano Roosevelt . . . that *genius* of diplomacy, Mr. Cordell Hull" ("Mosby's Memoirs," 165).

7. The arch circumlocution: "She's a very handsome woman and my guess would be she has plenty of other opportunities even if Felipe does play the oldest bull with her." "The oldest bull; that's good!" ("The Mexican General," 187).[10]

8. The demonstrably bad joke at which nobody laughs: "Two dogs meet in the street. Old friends. One says, 'Hello.' The other answers, 'Cock-a-doodle-do.' 'What does that mean? What's this cock-a-doodle-do stuff?' 'Oh,' says he, 'I've been studying foreign languages.' Dead silence. No one laughed" ("The Gonzaga Manuscripts," 127).

9. The self-conscious shift of dictional levels: "It was supposed to be preliminary to worthwhile, in expectation of the important. If that's too high-flown, I was bored" ("The Trip to Galena," 791).[11]

10. The rhetorical question whose answer is implicit: "Is that something to surprise us?" ("Address by Gooley MacDowell," 225).[12]

11. The rhetorical question for which no answer is implicit or appropriate: "Or also what things happened, seeming neither intrinsic nor even called-for: what have these done to you, what have they made of you?" ("Address by Gooley MacDowell," 227).

12. Miming: "'Do as I tell you,' he said. 'That's exactly how he would say it. You imitate him marvelously,' said Paco" ("The Mexican General," 191).

13. The imputed response: "Now, friends, some of you will be thinking of the rule of nature and will ask my opinion, for instance, of the tame cat eating her way wag-headed into a mackerel with her nice needles" ("A Sermon by Dr. Pep," 459).
14. The self-address: "*I was never one single thing anyway*, she thought. *Never my own. I was only loaned to myself*" ("Leaving the Yellow House," 33).
15. The inner address that analyzes somebody else's rhetoric: "The girls called Pop Dick Tracy, but Dick Tracy was a good guy. Whom could Pop convince?" ("A Silver Dish," 49).[13]
16. The compulsive insult, non-specific in its address: "They send me out college workers in silk pants to talk me out of what I got comin'. Are they better'n me? Who told them? Fire them. Let 'em go and get married, and then you won't have to cut electric from people's budget!" ("Looking for Mr. Green," 99).
17. The formulaic appeal to conventional wisdom: "You're a teacher, aren't you. Five years in college. The best. Alright, you can't get a teacher job? The market is flooded? Go get another job for a while" ("Two Morning Monologues," 231).

Not much is gained by extending such a grammar since there is a kind of infinite plenitude in Bellow's rhetorical modes. Another area of Bellow's rhetorical virtuosity, however, is almost unanalyzable but needs to be noticed, and that is the way in which some of his narrative diction and some of his speakers display a subtle sense of their orientation which is sometimes merely American urban, sometimes Jewish, but is almost never the "Yinglish" of more deliberately Jewish writers. It is, of course, the word order that makes the difference in this sentence from "The Old System": "A vision of mankind Braun was having as he sat over his coffee Saturday afternoon" (47). With this, from "A Silver Dish," on the other hand, it is less easy to say where, exactly, its special rhythm comes from: "How, against a contemporary background, do you mourn an octogenarian father, nearly blind, his heart enlarged, his lungs filling with fluid, who creeps, stumbles, gives off the odors, the moldiness or gassiness of old men. I *mean*! As Woody put it, be realistic" (40). The point, in any case, is obvious enough, that Bellow's rather modest body of short fiction contains its own range of technical forms, imitative of the full range of passionate, persuasive speech, and that, at times, those rhetorical forms carry with them, often with the very slightest variations from standard speech patterns, a rhythmic sense of who the speakers are.

I have suggested that, along with its rhetorical appeals, the short fiction also necessarily contains a range of either response or resistance. A response ordinarily derives from a perceived kinship. In "Looking for Mr. Green," Grebe and his supervisor Raynor achieve a kind of union at the point at which they confess themselves to be former students of Latin, now, incongruously, working for a relief agency, and exchange a few formulaic words of Latin. Scampi and

Weyl in "The Trip to Galena," Mosby and Lustgarten in "Mosby's Memoirs" grope for some common sensibility, doppelgängers, that image of which Bellow is so fond, polar opposites yet able, at moments, to listen and understand, even implicitly to confess themselves brothers. Kinship in the conventional sense, that is, family, helps to achieve a rhetorical union in Bellow. But in "A Silver Dish," "Leaving the Yellow House," and "The Old System," blood relatives understand each other all too well, so that the communication, once made, is inevitably discounted.

What prevents the rhetoric from taking its proper effect is the usual generational or stylistic gap, as it is with innumerable other writers from Dickens to the present time. Fathers do not understand sons; orthodox Jews do not understand liberal or nominal Jews. But, as with the rhetorical appeals, Bellow provides a quite remarkable spectrum of barriers to communication, so that the image one carries away from his short fiction is rather like the image one carries away from Dickens, of characters posturing, protesting, confessing, explaining, insulting, all to some space slightly beyond the face of the person they are addressing. Consider a naive and well-meaning American speaking to arch, condescending Spaniards. Consider an orator at Bug-house Square, Chicago, speaking to an audience, no audience, we do not know. Consider a fiancé speaking to his fiancée, he being confident and successful in the world, cowed and humiliated by her, neither of them finally knowing each other. Consider an official white, speaking to ghetto blacks.

Moreover, consider the range of mechanisms that interfere with speech. The lapses into other languages are numerous, and significant. There are moments of Spanish, French, German, Latin, and Yiddish. And there are allusions which the respondent of the speech could not possibly recognize, references to books, public personages of faded fame, direct quotations from eccentric sources, nodding recognitions of areas of learning which must seem, to the listener, to be strange and arcane. And there are the mechanisms that inhibit rhetorical union: the law, the telephone, the conventions of the stranger knocking at the door, the anonymity of mass transit, the interposition of medicine and organic failure, American cars. Finally, there are those unbridgeable gulfs of spirit, between those characters who are obsessively in quest of something, or driven to confession, or hysterically assertive of their own sense of the contours of experience and those others who are tied to their dailiness.

Finally, I suggest that the short fiction, taken together, presents its own image of the human condition. It is not exactly the image of the longer fiction. Critics of Bellow, for a long time now, have called attention to his "defense of man," the extent to which he takes the full measure of the despair and nihilism of the contemporary condition, the dualities of madness and sanity, sickness and health, darkness and light, and then erects against it possibilities of action and dignity. His

Nobel Prize acceptance speech asserts as much, a defense of that human spirit that lies beyond intellectual vogue, beyond things, and beyond illusion. Yet it is hard, in the short fictions, to find that assertion of human dignity, not, God knows, that the short fictions are some kind of Americanized Beckett, virtuoso versions of the end. It is that, given their time and space, they are prevented from "working out." Mosby doesn't get his memoirs written, although he understands what he lacks; Feiler doesn't get his manuscripts, although he knows why he can't. It is rather more knowledge of the impediments than assertion of self that comes to the protagonists of the short fiction. Which is to say, truistically, that the short fiction presents the short view of experience, the long fiction the long. Any given chapter of *The Victim* shows Leventhal asserting, lamenting, explaining, caring, and suffering. But it does not show Leventhal finally discovering his wholeness. That is something that takes two hundred fifty pages. Not twenty.

There is an old Jewish joke in which a speaker asks, "Do you know something peculiar about you Jews? That if somebody asks you a question, you answer with another question?" The other speaker replies, "We do?" It is a slight and mildly amusing joke, but it somehow carries with it the sense of Bellow's short fiction which I have described: its feeling for the problematics of intrapersonal speech, its attempt to define large areas of human nature by displaying modes of discourse, and its assertion that there is a way of looking at the world in which every question, whether it is merely a request for information or a metaphysical lament, has implicit in it another question.

Notes

1. Norman Mailer, "Introduction," *The Short Fiction of Norman Mailer* (New York: Dell, 1967), 9.
2. Saul Bellow, "Looking for Mr. Green," *Mosby's Memoirs and Other Stories* (New York: Viking, 1968), 85-109. Subsequent references in the text to this story and other stories in the collection are from this edition.
3. "A Sermon by Dr. Pep," *Partisan Review* 16.5 (1949): 455-62.
4. "A Father to Be," *Mosby's Memoirs*, 143-55.
5. "The Gonzaga Manuscripts," *Mosby's Memoirs*, 111-42.
6. "Two Morning Monologues," *Partisan Review* 8.3 (1941): 230-36.
7. "Mosby's Memoirs," *Mosby's Memoirs*, 157-84.
8. "Leaving the Yellow House," *Mosby's Memoirs*, 3-42.
9. "The Old System," *Mosby's Memoirs*, 43-83.
10. "The Mexican General," *Partisan Review* 9.3 (1942): 178-94.
11. "The Trip to Galena," *Partisan Review* 17.8 (1950): 779-94.
12. "Address by Gooley MacDowell to the Hasbeens Club of Chicago," *Hudson Review* 4.2 (1951): 222-27.
13. "A Silver Dish," *New Yorker* (25 Sep. 1978): 40-62.

* * *

On *Him with His Foot in His Mouth and Other Stories*
Daniel Fuchs

Four of the five works in *Him with His Foot in His Mouth and Other Stories* are recent and deal with aging. The fifth, "Zetland: By a Character Witness," is not a story but a fragment of a projected novel about Isaac Rosenfeld; written about a dozen years ago, it does not fit in with the *eheu fugaces* coloration of the rest of the collection. The most ambitious and best fiction is "What Kind of Day Did You Have?" — a novella which reaches a level near that of Bellow's best short fiction. Of the new pieces, Bellow is most deeply involved with this work and with the problematic "Cousins." "A Silver Dish" is a lovely story and the most formally polished, even meeting *New Yorker* standards! — something which even the post-Nobel Bellow is too idiosyncratic a taleteller to always do. The title story is great fun but, once past its original impulse, too reliant on Bellow mannerisms. All in all, this collection is Bellow in fine form. He dramatizes here, with varying degrees of success, a sense of the transcendent value of character. In doing so he is mining his richest vein.

"What Kind of Day Did You Have?" is about a distinguished old man who nearly dies. Given a new lease on life, he pursues familiar eros in the face of thanatos. Though he does this in an imperative way, he even more conspicuously pursues habitual sublimated eros, the life of the mind, against death. For Victor Wulpy is a Marxist intellectual of an imperious stamp whose apparent confidence is matched only by his air of contempt. He is compared to a sultan, a king, a captain, and, more ominously, "a tyrant in thought."[1] The wonder is that he should have an affair with a rather ordinary, upper-middle class, divorced hausfrau. What kind of affair did they have? To answer the question, one must first consider the cast of mind of this particular intellectual, for "What Kind of Day Did You Have?" is one of those dense Bellow works in which idea is made flesh and flesh idea.

Victor Wulpy (modeled on Harold Rosenberg) appears to have imbibed Marxism from infancy rather than mother's milk. As a result, everything about the decadence of bourgeois culture seems crystal clear to him and witheringly cold. Wulpy speaks of the "animal human average" (122) (like Marx, he is a corrosive wit), the sellout of the intellectuals, and *The Eighteenth Brumaire* which "had America's present number" (103). He sees social classes prevented from acting politically, with clowns and ham actors filling the void. There is some question as to how to reconcile this partly justified cynicism with

From *Saul Bellow Journal* 5.1 (1986): 3-15.

proletarian utopianism, but it is never articulated. Focusing on the far-cical parody of revolution in the absence of true proletarian struggle (as in the late sixties in America), *The Eighteenth Brumaire of Louis Bona-parte* is a work, as Rosenberg points out,[2] which could be used to refute Marxism in its millenarian aspect. To this indictment Wulpy adds a contemporary twist: fictional personages take over when professional groups con the public with "standards" that conceal cheating.

Wulpy's icy clairvoyance carries into his personal life. "He could discuss a daughter," says the narrator, "like any other subject submitted to his concentrated, radiant consideration — with the same generalizing detachment" (107). True, his daughter is one of Bellow's wacked-out younger types, a violinist and rabbi-to-be, who offers her hapless mother a homosexual sex manual so that the old gal can compete for Wulpy's affections. Yet with parents like hers, what chance did the kid have? There was sure to be some outlandish retribution for her mother's humiliating status as her father's sexual secretary and factotum. The situation is somewhat reminiscent to me, though perhaps not to the author, of Mady, the philandering Pontritter, and the victimized Tennie of *Herzog*. But the religiously inclined narrator sees mainly the idiocy of the child, never thinking that marriage might be a sacrament (or a social contract) and not a joke. Hence, the more abuse Wulpy's wife can absorb the more noble we are to judge her to be.

More than this, Wulpy's coldness carries over into his actual love life. With a condescension the narrator does not seem to penetrate, Wulpy thinks of his middle-aged divorcée as a "girl" (74). He values her for the "*caresse qui fait revivre les morts*" (155), yet he cannot help thinking that the affair is "not serious. . . . Such old stuff — *not* serious" (156). Is love, then, a bourgeois illusion, tied up with property rights? Katrina's claim on him is minimal enough. "It wasn't just another adultery," she thinks. "She wasn't one of his casual women" (153). Are we to take this absence of negatives for a presence of positives?

The climax of the story has to do not with the sexual gratification they snatch from the jaws of time but with the meaning of the affair. Wulpy had given Katrina *Journey to the End of Night* to read, Céline's novel in which a central character refuses to tell his lover that he loves her and is shot dead as a result. Rather than with the woman of feeling, however, Céline's modernist sympathy is with the nihilist, a murderer whose honor resides in refusing false ideals. Katrina is not so much shocked by the novel as by Wulpy's commending it, thereby degrading what she wants to value most. While it occurs to her that his aim in doing so was "to desensitize her feelings" (154) so she would feel his loss less, her insight may well err on the side of generosity. Is Wulpy, then, simply a high-powered cynic? Despite his political stance, Wulpy often concedes "that the obscurest and most powerful question, deeper than politics, was that of an understanding between man and woman.

. . . Katrina, as a subject for thought, was the least trivial of all" (156).
We are so told, but it is not easy to see how Wulpy actually feels such
emotion. His affection is very muted, the object of it rather dull, and
the whole affair more than a bit tacky. So while we are supposed to
concur with Wulpy that "of all that might be omitted in thinking, the
worst was to omit your own being" (156), his emotional neutrality all
but does just this. Indeed, this relationship has as much to do with the
psychodynamics of master/slave as with illumination of thought. Affec-
tionately sadistic to his pathetic wife, Wulpy makes demands on his
mistress to which only a masochist would respond. Perhaps it is maso-
chism that compels her when, in the climactic moment of the story, she
asks him to say "I love you." (The private plane from Buffalo to
Chicago seems to be falling in a winter storm — more love and death.)
Surely the icy integrity of Wulpy could not brook such a cliché.
"Why," the sympathetic narrator asks, "should Victor declare, 'I love
you'? For her sake, he went on the road" (161). False intimacy she can
never get from Wulpy. Does she get true intimacy?

Again a personal issue is inextricably bound to the ideational
development of the story. Wulpy is pursued by Wrangel, a successful
sci-fi Hollywood producer, who had been Wulpy's student thirty years
ago. As Wrangel's name indicates, he is persistent in argument. He
mounts a critique of a man whose ideas he respects, which, with certain differences noted, we may assume is Bellow's critique of Rosenberg. If sci-fi paranoia and serious intellection seem incompatible, we
should recall that his next movie deals with the long reign of quantifi-
cation, the divine mind overthrown by the technocratic mind — a serious subject in grotesque form. Of course, whether he does the movie
or not depends first on financial considerations. In any case, the
opulently clothed Wrangel is an unlikely groupie, but he does put
Wulpy to the test. Familiar with Wulpy's ideas (including his essay on
The Eighteenth Brumaire), he rightly sees him as an apostle of the
new. The avant-garde is free of "this death grip of tradition." Wulpy
admires art which creates "a world of its own, owing nothing to the
old humanism" (112), a view with which the humanist Bellow would
have to feel uneasy. Also, Wrangel rightly objects to Wulpy's seeing
things in terms of class struggle, imposing thereby European concep-
tions of class on Americans. "I have a friend," (114) says Wrangel, a
friend who supplies a viable alternative. The "friend" is Bellow.

Wrangel opts for a Steinerian "created soul," which has been
temporarily replaced by "an artificial one." Religious humanism seems
more relevant to our moral predicament than does Marxism. Now,
Wrangel's friend holds, men live "mainly by *rationales* . . . made-up
guidance systems," what Bellow usually calls ideologies. In a typical
comic undercutting of his spiritual concerns, Bellow has Wulpy retort,
"Is this friend of yours a California friend? Is he a guru?" (114). But
Wrangel holds his ground.

Although he has come East to see Wulpy, Wrangel agrees with Sidney Hook that the problem of Wulpy's group is that they are merely talking radicals (a point which activist Marxists also make). Yet Wrangel thinks of Wulpy in a way that preserves him from himself. Wrangel sees past the usual categories to Wulpy's uniqueness: "A subtle mind. Completely independent. Not really a Marxist, either" (132). This is surely Bellow's view of Rosenberg as well. Improbably, the sci-fi producer agrees that "without art we can't judge what life is." Subtly (and this is even more improbable), though, he turns back on himself to say, "but even Victor's real interest is politics" (134), and, one should add, radical politics. Wrangel recalls that during the French student crisis Wulpy "agreed with Sartre that we were on the verge of an inspiring and true revolution" (134-35). This is a crucial mistake, which Wrangel does not or cannot make enough of. All he can say is that "he got carried away" (135). He rightly judges — and again, the judgment is surely Bellow's judgment of Rosenberg — that "in politics Victor is still something of a sentimentalist" (135) about Marx, about revolution. He notes Wulpy's limitations of vision. Yet Wulpy believes that it is precisely his imagination of power that gives him the edge over other intellectuals.

Surprisingly, Wulpy admits that old age has given him the "dispassionate view [he] always preferred" (146). But Wulpy confuses metaphysical and aesthetic passion, on the one hand, with political passion, on the other, under the ambiguous rubric of "a powerful reading of the truth of existence" (146-47). The ideational confusion is personally fruitful, though, in that he is for the first time having "lucid impressions — like dreams, visions — instead of lucid ideas" (147). This is what Bellow meant when, in an interview conducted by D. J. R. Bruckner, he said, "I think Victor was sustained by something he did not know."[3] Wulpy speaks, in Bellovian fashion, of a "shared knowledge that we don't talk about," rising to a positively spiritualist view: "Cryptic persistent suggestions: the dead are not really *dead*. Or, we don't create thoughts. . . . A thought *is* real, already created, and a real thought can pay you a visit" (148). In this context he reluctantly admits that Wrangel supplied "a California parody of things that I had been thinking myself" (147). Wulpy, after all, has had a life in the arts.

Wulpy's reluctant progress, then, under the aspect of mortality, is from tough to tender-minded, cold to lukewarm. But it is an inhibited progress, if it can be considered a progress at all. Sex, apparently, is the last lucidity — a fleeting one. Sexual affection is sexual affection, and love (whatever that is) is love; and he owes it to his self-respect as a mind not to confuse the two. Isn't either motive sufficient? Yes, for Katrina's sake he went on the road. Tenderness will have to do, man-and-womanness. Wulpy, if not Katrina, is sustained by an oblique intimacy. In the haunting climax of the story, the relatively simple, sensuous, middle-class Katrina knows what it is to be intimate with disillusioned truth.

"Cousins" is narrated by a familiar Bellow type — the urban *isolato* — divorced, distinguished, filial. The story is lyrical, our interest being not so much in what happens but in the contemplative consciousness of the central character. Everything depends on Ijah Brodsky's temperament, and an intriguing one it is. This is hardly new, but story as poem in Bellow has rarely been so obvious. The narrative "I" allows for greatest elaboration of intimate detail, retrospection and, above all, sentiment. The protagonist thinks of a series of cousins who are set in something of a dramatic pattern, but it is what Ijah feels about them that counts. Bellow has always been a novelist of "character," and what we essentially get here is a return to his earliest form — pure character sketch. The difference is that where the early sketches were monologues by the characters, here we get a monologue about character — not character as such, but a special version of the *amor fati*, the pull of relation, the mysterious attraction of cousins. I suspect that, generally speaking, Bellow's generation was the last of the earlier immigrant Jewish milieu to feel this kind of intimate involvement — as opposed to the nuclear family involvement, which is still very deep, and which, as his ex-wife points out to him, Ijah does not have — and it is a bit hard to see where sentiment lets off and sentimentality begins. Ijah, an intellectual sort of investment banker (research department), calls his cousins "the elect of my memory" (242), but one may wonder why.

The story begins with a vivid description of Tanky Metzger, a rackets type who could get fifteen years for his activities. The respectable Ijah is asked to write a mitigating letter; he does so because of the special status cousins have for him. Tanky associates with gangsters, but so do aldermen, city officials, journalists, big builders, fundraisers for charitable institutions — "the mob gives generously" (227). While this is not yet the familiar they-all-do-it cynicism, Ijah soon crosses the line. The foundations of political stability, of democracy, are "swindle and fraud," he holds, with the top executives and lawyers "spreaders of the most fatal nets" (244). If so, why not revolution or anarchy or, at least, reform, rather than being part of the establishment? The problem is that in Ijah we have another instance of the creeping sentimentality/cynicism that has infringed on Bellow's late work. Ijah sees part of the problem when, thinking of why he wrote a letter for Tanky, he says, "I had no space to work out whether this was a moral or a sentimental decision" (240).

His mind echoing with Hegel and Heidegger, with, in his own description, disintegration and antarctic frigidity, Ijah clings to cousins like an ocean survivor to a life raft. With Tanky, a certain balance between moral and sentimental is achieved. With Tanky's sister, Eunice, whom Ijah doesn't so much contemplate as encounter along the way, American madness takes over. Cynicism finds an objective correlative. Living with a husband who spends what he earns on himself,

Eunice pays for her children's tuition with her inheritance. Totally in the money culture, she explains her involvement in a med-school admittance payoff: "You can guess what a medical degree is worth, the income it guarantees" (250). She welches on half the payoff, negating her bond of "integrity." It is hard to judge whether her base or noble motive is worse. Why does she stay with her husband? Because "I'm covered by his Blue Cross-Blue Shield" (252). Marriage has often been a metaphorical insurance policy in bourgeois culture; here it is a literal one. No wonder our investment banker reads anthropological studies of Siberia, where the "powers of darkness surrounded you" and you are confronted by "demanding spirits whose mouths were always gaping. The people cringed and gave ransom, buying protection from these ravaging ghosts" (253). It is the same world as the rackets and the medical schools gone corrupt — and, as Ijah sees it, the world of investment banking, which shores up its Brazils and Irans by the protection of government guarantees, leaving the public to bear the risk. Can feeling be anything but sentimental when reality is so cynical? The "careerists" in his building seem no less bizarre than Siberians. "Human beings, by definition, [are] half the time mad" (254), thinks Ijah, thereby undercutting an earlier Bellow balance. For example, there is Charley Citrine's attack on the Freudian Philip Rieff for suggesting that life is a hospital.

In all this darkness Cousin Motty just does not stand up as representative of what life ought to be, as Bellow's defensive rhetoric all but implies: Motty is "the head of the family, insofar as there is a family, and insofar as it has a head" (258). The tentativeness of the story's movement is partly accounted for by Bellow's admission to Bruckner that "I began to think I was wrong and Nietzsche was right about the disappearance of the gods" (56). This does not literally figure in the story except as resultant mood, the fruits of reading Heidegger on Nietzsche and others. Is the ice broken by such filial-to-the-n[th] displays as observing old Motty's birthday? Maintaining that "the very masses are turning their backs on family," Ijah clings nonetheless to his admittedly "imperfect love" (261) of the old man. He links this affection to the disintegration he sees in the life process and the social order. But even Ijah wonders about the connection: "What do I want with Motty anyway, and why have I made a trip from the Loop to molest him?" (265). Yet he feels that the old man silently consulting with himself is in touch with the original person, the soul, the perspective of the Blakean divine eye. In the dissolution of mortality and history, "the untenability of existence" releases this original self, which is now "free to look for real being under the debris of modern ideas" (268). The man on the dump, the rose on the dungheap, the crocus in concrete — such minimal images of renewal (the last from *Humboldt's Gift*) occur to me as descriptive of the thinning air of late Bellow. "Getting on top of the collapsed pile" (262) is the way Ijah puts it.

If Tanky, Eunice, and Motty are instances of social and natural disintegration beyond which some form of soul exists, Cousin Scholem represents a putative triumph of spirit over circumstance. But Scholem does not quite come off as a character, being a dubious amalgam of the Isaac Rosenfeld prodigy type and an actual World War II veteran and cabbie whose quest for Soviet-American accord received national media attention. Scholem thinks he has out-Darwined Darwin and has made the first major philosophical breakthrough since the *Critique of Pure Reason*. All this was cut short by the Japanese attack on Pearl Harbor. Volunteering, Scholem comes to the defense of democracy and his theories, culminating in the grand meeting of Americans and Russians at the city of Torgau. His great work postponed, he is presently a taxi driver. The spectacular comedown works for Bellow in a comic context (for example, Wallace Gruner), but it jars in an elegiac one. The elderly Scholem has had cancer surgery, and the doctors say he will soon be dead. He wishes to be buried in Torgau. Bellow is stirred by the positive impulse in the man, which he thinks of as typically Jewish. Amid decadence, Scholem upholds the "moral law," purity of thought, patriotism; he "wanted to affirm that all would be well, to make a distinguished gift [like Humboldt, like the novelist himself], to bless mankind. In all this Scholem fitted the classical norm for Jews of the diaspora" (276). Bellow attributes Scholem's cancer to his effort to be pure in decadent Chicago, adding that driving ten hours a day in traffic also had something to do with it.

A relative with money will get specialists to read Scholem's great work (totally unbelievable at the point), even though he thinks of Scholem as a megalomaniac. Ijah, in typical Bellow fashion, regards such psychological terms as "a menace," thinking that "they should all be shoveled into trucks and taken to the dump" (281). More cultural garbage. In the muted anticlimax of an ending, Ijah barely sees the ailing Scholem in Paris at a convention of taxi drivers, which confirms the basically sentimental quality of the connection. Yet there is a metaphysical perspective. Time wastes us; relation is a kind of immortality or an expression of the *amor fati*. At the story's end, we see Ijah, movingly, in his frailty, like the cousins he observes, an instance of time's depredations. Bellow anticipates the charge of sentimentality by having Ijah's ex-wife express it. He turned to cousins, she says, because of the lack of real connection with nuclear family. Further, when nuclear families are breaking up, collateral relatives enable him to indulge his "taste for the easier affects." He "lacked the true modern severity" (288). More power to him. Wulpy had that, almost. But one need not embrace the true modern severity to feel uneasy about Ijah's expression of emotion. Nothing here is dramatized. Character sketch does the work of plot. Bellow claims that the story is "metaphysical, not sentimental" (Bruckner 56), but it is clear that the two are not mutually exclusive.

There is, I believe, a more deeply felt character sketch in "Zetland: By a Character Witness." Here we get Isaac Rosenfeld without complications, and the prose moves with a greater fluency than in "Cousins." There is much more to the Rosenfeld portrait than is given in this fragment,[4] including the most brilliant writing Bellow has not published. But he gave up on the projected novel about Rosenfeld because he did not want to portray him as "a kind of Dostoyevskian clown" (Bruckner 60), as a victim, and that is the way the book was turning out.

Though it is less central to Bellow's own patterns of feeling — and was perhaps for this reason easier to mount in terms of dramatic disposition — "A Silver Dish," next to "What Kind of Day Did You Have?" is the best story in the collection. Once again, a central question is "What do you do about death?" (191). Morris Selbst is the sort of man only a daughter could love — or a tender-minded son. A ne'er-do-well and petty con artist, this immigrant "became an American, and America never knew it. He voted without papers, he drove without a license, he paid no taxes, he cut every corner. Horses, cards, billiards, and women were his life interest, in ascending order" (198). This fugitive from a picaresque novel is set in a religious domestic context of Christian proselytizers and Jewish converts so straightlaced as to almost forgive his mendacities. The crisis comes when he steals a silver dish from the kind, paternalistic Mrs. Skogland, to whom, in this Depression story, he had come to borrow money. "Kind has a price tag," says cynical Pop years later to his long-tried son. The story exists in two time frames, that of the embarrassed boy and that of the mellow man in his sixties thinking of the recent death of his ancient father; this contrast is its point. The story is a Sunday morning rumination in which all is retrospective in the son's central intelligence.

Woody Selbst, the son, is his father's opposite. Unbidden, he believes even as a youth that "God's idea was that this world should be a love world, that it should eventually recover and be entirely a world of love." Typically, Bellow must undercut such traditional tender-minded assumptions. "He wouldn't have said this to a soul, for he could see himself how stupid it was — personal and stupid. Nevertheless, there it was at the center of his feelings" (199-200). These feelings serve him well years later in coming to terms with Pop, hospitalized, feeble, rebellious in his deathbed. That's what you do about death; you mitigate its effect by transformations of feeling. Pop dies as Woody holds him, thereby preventing the old man from removing the intravenous needles. "You could never pin down that self-willed man," Woody says admiringly of Pop's perversely resolute spirit (222).

In the hallowed haze of sexagenarian retrospection, the question of sentimentality once again arises. Pop is really a narrow, bastardly sort of guy who, as Woody thinks, "never suffered." Is he so different from Eunice's husband, a contemptible egotist who spends everything on himself? Selfless Woody loves Pop for his selfishness. Sentimentality is much less an issue here than in "Cousins." How can you forget a father — particularly one whose inflexible will helped you escape as a youth the clutches of rather oppressive spiritualism? To this extent Woody shared his desire for freedom. This desire in Woody sometimes takes the form of travel to exotic places. An image from a recent safari haunts him. A buffalo calf disappears into the White Nile, snatched by a crocodile. But Woody's vision of love persists, a moral, perhaps Jewish world, beyond the victimization of Darwinian nature.

The title story is a bright *jeu d'esprit*, comical in some ways already familiar to the Bellow reader. After the gloom of *The Dean's December*, it is good to see Bellow operating in the boisterous mode. Harry Shawmut is an academic musician whose romantic nature is indicated by the transcendent way he conducts Pergolesi. Music is freedom, but so, alas, is wit; the first, Auden once wrote, is "pure contraption . . . an absolute gift"; the second, like poetry, "fetches / The images out that hurt and connect."[5] The story pivots around an insulting remark Shawmut made thirty years back to an innocent spinster librarian, Miss Rose. The crack, presumably unlike the many others which the story gives us, was unprovoked. Shawmut, in true Bellovian fashion, wishes to absolve himself of gratuitous offense. The incident brings to mind the episode of the pink ribbon from Rousseau's *Confessions*. Rousseau was asking to be absolved by his awareness — the purity of honest consciousness. So is Shawmut. But where Rousseau was solemn, Bellow, in contemporary fashion, makes comedy of a neurotic quirk. The story is cast as one long letter of indirect apology to the wronged Miss Rose. Look, cries Shawmut, look how this aggression in me has messed up my life. But what we see becomes so involuted in plot and often moves so far from Shawmut's weakness that we barely remember that the librarian was the cause of this confession, or that she would want to hear all this. Would she derive gratification, so many years later, from Shawmut's being torpedoed by his shameless brother? And what does this betrayal have to do with Shawmut's famous weakness? Silent people are also betrayed. For her to derive satisfaction from his tribulations, she would not be Miss Rose but Lucretia Borgia.

Shawmut, in his sixties, the quirky, ingratiating "I" of the story, is the only elderly character in this collection not concerned with death. (He does see his ancient mother in a nursing home, but to comic effect — she remembers the terrible brother and has no recollection of Shawmut.) Shawmut is involved in the long perspective, though, as his confession to Miss Rose shows. He is also on the receiving end of abuse, having been written a long, scathing letter on his character by an apparent friend of thirty years — this is the vaguely Gersbachian Walish. But the story is unconvincing here. Walish's rancor is attributed to the success of Shawmut's TV program, to the envious betrayal by friends, and to the plot complications: a felon brother businessman who does him in and a not particularly competent brother-in-law lawyer, who, in order to save Shawmut what money he has left, devises a crafty scheme which leaves Shawmut in exile in Vancouver fearing extradition. We have a familiar scenario: the idealist *putz* ground up in the businessman/lawyer double whammy.

If all this seems mannered, it may be because it is so far from the real-life event on which, in part, it seems to be based. Lionel Trilling informed me in conversation that he wrote such a letter to Bellow (perhaps echoed in Shawmut's fragmentary recollection of Walish's) in response to what he took to be Bellow's misconceived attack on him in a *Harper's* piece the year before.[6] And Bellow wrote the widowed Diana Trilling a letter, which she informed me of, expressing regret that he had caused Trilling any pain.[7] If my assumption is correct, the story is, in part, a larky reworking of a theme that could have been treated very differently — and a remarkable insight into the comic imagination. Of course, Shawmut's trait can produce the comedy we have here and, by Bellow's own account, literally did on two occasions. But the Walish letter seems a bit disconnected in the story. There is a passing allusion to a Trilling work of that period, *Sincerity and Authenticity*, when Shawmut is thinking about the appeal of Allen Ginsberg, who is putting his queer shoulder to the wheel: "this bottom-line materialistic eroticism is most attractive to Americans, proof of sincerity and authenticity" (22). If this means that there are dangers to accepting authenticity as a moral standard, he is reading Trilling rightly; if it means Trilling sets authenticity up as a standard, he is not. I would speculate that an ironic, problematic remark Trilling made in that book[8] to the effect that *Herzog* may be open to "the terrible charge of philistinism" for realigning our attitudes toward modernism vis-a-vis traditional values may have had to do with the flare-up. The incident was unfortunate since, in the cultural wars, both are fighting on essentially the same side — civilization — Bellow as religious humanist, Trilling as Freudian humanist.

Bellow's religious humanism figures in this story as well, again in the comically defensive position. Shawmut is stranded in Vancouver with his landlady, old Miss Gracewell, who reads Swedenborg and the occult, and thinks about poetic justice and the life to come. She is one of the spacey characters the Bellow protagonist feels a secret affinity for. Appearing near the beginning of the story and near the end, she serves to surround the mad events of the normal world in a fragile frame of spirit. Her strangeness — related to Shawmut's passion for religious music — is preferable to the strangeness of the workaday world. "The Divine Spirit, she tells me, has withdrawn in our time from the outer, visible world" (58), notes Shawmut sympathetically. She too posits an "awakened age of the spirit" (59). So we too come full circle in the thematic unity of these works.

Notes

1. Saul Bellow, *Him with His Foot in His Mouth and Other Stories* (New York: Harper and Row, 1984), 96. Subsequent references in the text to this story and other stories in the collection are from this edition.
2. Harold Rosenberg, "The Politics of Illusion," *Liberations*, ed. Ihab Hassan (Middletown, CT: Wesleyan UP, 1969), 122.
3. D. J. R. Bruckner, "A Candid Talk with Saul Bellow," *New York Times Magazine* (15 April 1984): 62.
4. See Daniel Fuchs, *Saul Bellow: Vision and Revision* (Durham, NC: Duke UP, 1984), 257-64.
5. W. H. Auden, *Collected Shorter Poems* (London: Faber, 1966), 125.
6. Lionel Trilling in conversation with the author, Spring 1975.
7. Diana Trilling in conversation with the author, Fall 1976.
8. Lionel Trilling, *Sincerity and Authenticity* (Cambridge: Harvard UP, 1972), 42.

* * *

More Die of Heartbreak (1987)

More Die of Heartbreak
Leonard Michaels

More Die of Heartbreak is less like a novel than an anatomy of love in the post-modern age; a loquacious, brilliant, entertaining book, mixing long flights of ideas with comic scenes that say a lot about the "entanglements" of "serious" men and calculating, ditsy, depraved, physically disgusting, and piteously needy women. I would guess that Saul Bellow himself, given his emotional and intellectual investment, really likes women rather in the way a preacher really likes sin.

The story mainly concerns two men — Crader and Trachtenberg — who talk about sex, love, marriage, and work while their lives grow increasingly chaotic and further apart. Trachtenberg, the narrator, does most of the talking and keeps promising a story of Crader's disastrous marriage, but doesn't really begin it for more than a hundred pages. Before and after, he tells about himself and often disrupts narrative momentum for the sake of his thoughts and talky paragraphs like eruptions of an awesome incontinence.

Trachtenberg erupts, but it is Crader whose name suggests "crater," as in a volcano. Presumably, Trachtenberg and Crader are aspects of each other, or essentially one man torn in half, his heart and mind going different ways. Trachtenberg says, when "a serious man" asks an "attractive woman" to marry him, it is a "preface to self-injury." He describes marriage as "two psychotics under one quilt." About sex, he says, "Whatever troubles people run into, they look for the sexual remedy . . . they turn to sex as the analgesic." Furthermore, people "do the act by which love would be transmitted if there were any," but, since there isn't, marriage, sex, and love are species of contemporary desperation. This is what Trachtenberg thinks. What does he think about thinking, his compulsion to generalize?

From *Los Angeles Times Book Review* (14 June 1987): 1, 12.

Of course, we all have these thoughts today instead of prayers. And we think these thoughts are serious and we take pride in our ability to think, to elaborate ideas, so we go round in consciousness like this. However, our speculations don't get us anywhere; they are like a stationary bicycle.

We think. Therefore, we think, think, think. None of it leads to a place of rest, but the process spins off occasionally into action. A major action occurs when Crader, who is a famous botanist with mystical seeing power, discovers that he loathes, rather than loves, his beautiful wife. This happens while they watch Hitchcock's thriller, "Psycho," and Crader detects a resemblance between his wife's shoulders, high and wide, and those of Anthony Perkins, a murderous lunatic in a repulsive movie. Crader has better reasons to loathe his wife — she likes the movie! — but the shoulders crystallize a truth; not merely in his feelings, but a truth about her.

It's very funny. Also very sad, because even the most beautiful people are subject to the grotesquely critical disgust of others. If this weren't true, the huge profits of the cosmetics and fashion industries would dwindle to nothing overnight, since they are drawn mainly from our fear of criticism. The book implies, most generally, that love is always based on some variety of glamorous illusion, and this holds even for one's ability to love oneself.

Bellow doesn't put it like this. He isn't a modern St. Augustine, but the idea is implicit even in the way Bellow makes characters live. He concentrates on the affective minutiae of their physical being. Few writers seize a person's essence as powerfully and absolutely as Bellow, in the twist and hang of lips, or the weight and light of eyes, or more largely the gestalt of torso, head and legs. Being seen by Bellow is like having a spiritual X-ray taken through one's cheeks or lips or any body part toward which he aims the fantastic instrument of his glance. The effect is often mercilessly reductive. Perhaps only saints could survive such seeing, for they lack usual human density and accessibility.

It is maybe a little excessive to say this book argues that to see, really to see, is to not love, except insofar as one loves to see. But there are several scenes where this is suggested. In one, a gang of sophisticated, accomplished men in a Japanese sex palace, gape at women who squat and exhibit their red, dilated interiorities. Between these men and the women's thing (or women generally), there is no common human ground. Look, guys, see where you pour your lives. The more "literal," says Trachtenberg, the more it is "mysterious." Yeats made some great poems of this paradox.

Finally, Crader flees his wife and everyone else to do research in the North Pole where he can't suffer humiliations of relationships, sex, love, marriage, etc. He can be true to himself, to his magical gift for seeing, restricting it to a harmless innocent application. The study of specialized plants in cold, pure, lonely, northern darkness, high above the human world.

* * *

The Headache of Explanation
Sanford Pinsker

As Artur Sammler, possibly Bellow's crankiest, least accommodating protagonist, puts it in *Mr. Sammler's Planet* (1970): "Intellectual man has become an explaining creature. Fathers to children, wives to husbands, lecturers to listeners, experts to laymen, colleagues to colleagues, doctors to patients, man to his own soul, explained." Nearly twenty years later Bellow's protagonists are still explaining, still disrupting fiction's delicate mechanism to deliver stump speeches drawn from the History of Ideas and the individual wounded heart. Kenneth Trachtenberg, the protagonist-narrator of Bellow's latest novel, "explains" the phenomenon — and, by extension, Bellow's working method — this way:

> If you venture to think in America, you also feel an obligation to provide a historical sketch to go with it, to authenticate or legitimize your thoughts. So it's one moment of flashing insight and then a quarter of an hour of pedantry and tiresome elaboration — academic gabble. Locke to Freud with stops at local stations like Bentham and Kierkegaard. One has to feel sorry for people in such an explanatory bind. Or else (a better alternative) one can develop an eye for the comical side of this.

Bellow's richest fictions — *Herzog* (1964), *Humboldt's Gift* (1975) — do, indeed, explore this "better alternative" — namely, the "comical side" of dreamy intellectuals with lives in great disorder. In short, urban comedians like Moses Herzog or Charlie Citrine are better architects of moral vision than accountants of hard fact. Bellow leaves it to others, drawn from the growing melange of wacky but memorable minor characters, to set these eggheads straight. What results are those zigzagging alterations of diction and detail, of the high-flown and the low-life — all forced to share space in the same thickly textured paragraph — that is a mark of Bellow at his best.

More Die of Heartbreak is filled with indications that Bellow remains, square inch per square inch, our most accomplished American writer. Consider, for example, the following paragraph in which the narrator finds himself shuffling through the broken pieces of his heart:

> I was a man weighed down with sexual infatuations and life aims . . . too hard to interpret. What should she care — and *why* should she? — for the imaginations, the sexual pictures I carried in my head of her female wealth, the fallopian tubes like the twin serpents of the caduceus; or like the ornate clips for sheet music springing up on the trombones and cornets of marching bands. I'm afraid that such preoccupations identify a genuinely modern individual. (Can you say worse of anybody?) And the more guileless such an individual is, the more kinky the women who will attract him.

From *Midstream* (Oct. 1987): 56-58.

Bellow's prose has been with us for so long that we greet such passages with recognition and delight; his characters may be in a bad way at the moment, but we feel certain that they will solve their problems and, more important, that they have the sheer brain power to solve *ours*. When the storm clouds pass, Herzog will finish his Big Book, as will Charlie Citrine, Artur Sammler, and Albert Corde.

With that said, let me hasten to add that in *More Die of Heartbreak* there are not so many Big Projects to complete as there are overriding questions to answer — namely, what do women want, and why have a special class of women selected me for special, heartbreaking attention? The first query, of course, is Freud's; the second is Kenneth Trachtenberg's. To be sure, dangerously unsuitable women are as much a staple of Bellow's fiction as con men with wacky get-rich schemes or conniving lawyers with subpoenas. What is new, however, is the wide, uninterrupted space that Trachtenberg gets to pontificate about all three.

Presumably, Trachtenberg is on a mission of mercy. His Uncle Benn, a world-renowned botanist, needs massive doses of handholding — as the disastrous consequences of a recent marriage become increasingly clear — but uncle and nephew are so nearly identical (which is to say, each sounds suspiciously like Mr. Bellow) it is hard to keep them straight. As Trachtenberg, an assistant professor of Russian, freely admits:

> Uncle was forever proposing to hold heavyweight conversations, and you had to be careful with him. He would only increase his unhappiness by confused speculations. I had to be vigilant with myself too, for I have a similar weakness for setting things straight and I know how futile it is to work at it continually. . . . We were doubly, multiply, interlinked. Neither of us by now had other real friends, and I couldn't afford to lose him.

Not since *The Victim* (1947) has Bellow given himself over to such an extended exercise in secret-sharing. Indeed, Trachtenberg can match his uncle heartbreak for heartbreak, kinky affair for kinky affair. Both subscribe to the dream of living peacefully — "Two human beings bound together in love and kindness" — and both are shocked, and then plunged into confusion, when their respective women give them such drubbings.

To the rest of the family Benn is a *schlemiel*, pure and simple. And though Trachtenberg might demur, he is cut from the same cloth. This doubling of perspective and situation not only accounts for a good deal of the repetition, the sheer tediousness, of the novel, but also for the lack of a dramatically realized tension. All too often Trachtenberg tells what Bellow does not show. The following paragraph, though brilliantly crafted, is, alas, all too representative of what ultimately turns sour in *More Die of Heartbreak*:

My work was cut out for me: I was to help my dear uncle to defend himself. I didn't suppose that the Layamons [Benn's in-laws] meant him great harm; only they weren't likely to respect his magics or to have the notion of preserving him for the sake of his gifts. There was quite a lot at stake here. I can't continually be spelling it out. As: the curse of human impoverishment as revealed to Admiral Byrd in Antarctica; the sleep of love in human beings as referred to by Philip Larkin; the search for sexual enchantments as the universal nostrum; the making of one's soul as the only project genuinely worth undertaking; and my personal rejection of existentialism, which led me to emigrate and which makes me so severe in my analysis of motives. That has been indicated.

It is a safe bet that Bellow's critics will explore what Trachtenberg, despite his denials, keeps spelling out in these bursts. After all, a novel brimming with allusions — to Poe, Balzac, Larkin, Admiral Byrd, Hitchcock's *Psycho* — and spiced with themes that run the gamut from plant mysticism to the glaciers of the heart, is the stuff that makes academics race to their typewriters.

But for all the novel's intricate embroidery, for all of Trachtenberg's wide-ranging and, yes, let me admit it, often fascinating speculations about sexuality and the posthistorical consciousness, the bald fact is that Bellow is rather like those Englishmen Trachtenberg describes as being "so often pleased with a striking beginning that they stop right there. The next requirement [he insists] is to carry your thought forward, to take it out of the category of bright sayings." *More Die of Heartbreak* is filled with "bright sayings" (including its title), but about the mysteries of love the best Bellow seems able to come up with is a declaration that we must come to know that we *cannot* know:

Of course, we all have these thoughts today instead of prayers. And we think these thoughts are serious and we take pride in our ability to think, to elaborate ideas, so we go round and round in consciousness like this. However, they don't get us anywhere; our speculations are like a stationary bicycle.

Granted, some eggheads are more interesting than others, and Bellow's take front seat. Meanwhile, those who keep their eyes fixed on the Main Chance and the Big Bucks — in this case, Benn's corrupt uncle and those who are out to redress old (legal) grievances — ride off into the sunset in their limos.

Ironically, this is the power turf that Mailer — in a novel like, say, *An American Dream* — can explore with a darker, genuinely mythological vision. As Bellow's narrator admits at one point: "At any time of day she was gotten up elaborately, and she looked and smelled like a collection of attractions from the finest shops, from Bonwit's, Gucci's, Tiffany's (sophisticated people will know more fashionable names and smile at my ignorance)."

On the other hand, when it comes to sharpers, to con men, to sheer *characters*, Bellow is on very solid ground indeed. As Trachtenberg puts it: "Say what you like about America, but few countries have welcomed originality more warmly. . . ." In *Seize the Day* (1956), this spirit is exemplified by Dr. Tamkin who initiates a drowning Tommy Wilhelm into the mysteries of the commodities market; in *More Die of Heartbreak*, the comic mantle passes to Fishl Vilitzer:

> Not very long ago he had conceived of a combined yoga-style and commercial venture. Describing himself as the local representative of a West Coast maharishi, he put out an investors' manual and mailed it to a substantial number of subscribers. The general idea was to play the market from a spiritual base. Meditation, by reducing the oscillations of consciousness, made you a more capable investor.

Had there been more of Fishl's antics, and less of Trachtenberg's droning voice, *More Die of Heartbreak* would have been a better book. But, then again, it would not have had either the obsessive energy or the quirky appeal that make us turn to Bellow again and again.

* * *

A Contemporary Fall: *More Die of Heartbreak*
Ellen Pifer

Contemplating flowers appears to have become a serious occupation for Bellow's later protagonists. In *Humboldt's Gift* (1975) it is a more serious occupation for Charlie Citrine than the customary business of America; in *More Die of Heartbreak* (1987), contemplating plant life receives even more prominent attention: Benn Crader is an internationally renowned botanist who, in the words of his nephew, the novel's narrator, is both a research scientist and a "plant clairvoyant."[1] Working "like a contemplative, concentrating without effort," Uncle Benn, a university professor, not only studies plant anatomy but appears to see "behind the appearances" (253). "Studying leaves, bark, roots, heartwood, sapwood, flowers, for their own sake," Uncle Benn, says his nephew, "contemplated them" — that is, "he saw into or looked through plants. He took them as his arcana. An arcanum is more than a mere secret; it's what you have to know in order to be fertile in a creative pursuit, to make discoveries, to prepare for the communication of a spiritual mystery" (27).

This visionary enterprise, "contemplating flowers," delineates only one of the numerous thematic and structural affinities between *Humboldt's Gift* and Bellow's most recent novel. Charlie Citrine, the narrator of *Humboldt's Gift*, reviews the tragic history of his old friend, the poet Von Humboldt Fleisher, as he tells his own story. In *More Die of Heartbreak*, Benn Crader's nephew, Kenneth Trachten-

---

From *Saul Bellow Against the Grain* (Philadelphia: University of Pennsylvania Press, 1990), 152-163.

berg, is compelled by a similar bond of love to recount the story of a man he reveres. By reviewing the life of his uncle, whom he regards as his spiritual father, Ken attempts to put that life as well as his own in perspective. Citrine, furthermore, attributes the demise of Humboldt's personal life and artistic vocation to the poet's loss of faith in his visionary imagination. Similarly, Ken Trachtenberg pays tribute to his uncle's gift of seeing, as a "plant clairvoyant," and attributes Benn's recent "fall" to loss of confidence in that visionary power.

The author of many "books and articles," Uncle Benn enjoys a "big reputation" in the field of botany (32). Yet despite Crader's eminence as a scientist, says his nephew, "not even the 'laws' of physics or biology were permitted to inhibit him" (15). "Uncle was sure," Ken later explains, "that nature had an *inside*" (128). In his research on plants, Benn Crader has worked "like a contemplative, concentrating without effort, as naturally as he breathes, no oscillations of desire or memory" (253). To his own, characteristically modern "oscillations of consciousness," Ken contrasts his uncle's mode of contemplation — one that, in Ken's description, bears a definite resemblance to Rudolf Steiner's account of "inward" vision: Benn "really *knew* the vegetable kingdom. He practiced the scrutiny of secret things — total absorption in their hidden design." "There were times," Ken also notes, "when you felt [Benn's] power of *looking* turned on you. . . . This is the faculty of seeing; of seeing *itself*; what eyes are actually for" (317, 14).[2] In the end, however, Uncle Benn fails to "make the psychic transfer to human relations" (106); the complexity and deviousness of personal relationships disturb and ultimately foil his powers of insight.

Born and raised in Paris, Ken accepts a teaching post at his uncle's midwestern university in order to be near his mentor. It is from Benn that his nephew, a man in his middle thirties, hopes to learn something of the "higher spheres" of existence, knowledge to which Ken's natural father, Rudi Trachtenberg, is wholly indifferent. An American expatriate who remained in Paris after the Second World War, Ken's father is a cosmopolitan whose many accomplishments belong strictly to the sexual and social spheres of life. In "tennis, [his] war record, . . . in sex, in conversation, in looks," Rudi Trachtenberg is, according to Kenneth, an unqualified success. In an era that celebrates physical fitness and erotic invention, Rudi is a paragon — a "Hegelian . . . Master Spirit" (65). "The historical thing which millions of sex-intoxicated men were trying to do and botching, he did with the ease of a natural winner" (37).

The very type or product of those "conditioning forces" against which Augie March seeks to defend the "primordial person," Rudi Trachtenberg is indifferent to the "fundamentals" his son urgently seeks to discover (10-12). Like Herzog, Ken Trachtenberg admits that he "used to be sold on" theories and ideas but "discovered that they were nothing but trouble if you entertained them indiscriminately."

There are some "matters" — including the "matter" of Uncle Benn's "fall" — "for which theorizing brings no remedy" (19).[3] Ken's "partial deafness," moreover, directly links him to Artur Sammler, whose partial blindness emblemizes the Bellovian hero's divided consciousness, oscillating between the "superstructures of explanation" and the soul's "natural knowledge" (47). "Modern life, if you take it to heart, wears you out," Ken reflects. "Even my hearing aid was off, and when I fiddled my finger under my long hair and tapped on it, something like a sonic boom went off in my skull" (118). Turning on his hearing aid, Ken tunes into "modern life"; like a "sonic boom" in the "skull," the impact of his re-entry is shattering.

With his uncle, a widower, Ken shares a propensity for ineffectual and "confused relations with women"; he cannot even persuade Treckie, the "childlike" but willful young woman he adores, to marry him. Instead, Treckie has removed herself, along with their little girl, Nancy, thousands of miles away from Ken — to live in Seattle with another man. Aware that he lacks his father's sexual talent, Ken tries "to right the balance" by giving himself "more mental weight." Yet this attempt to compensate mentally for lack of physical or sexual authority only goes to show, In Ken's view, "how far we've fallen below the classical Greek standard. We've split things in two, dividing the physique from the mind" (39-40). Searching for a way to mend this "split," Ken wants to realize his "soul in the making" (37).

Looking to his uncle for guidance, Ken finds, instead, that Benn Crader is also prey to divided consciousness. As Ken says, "I had come to America to complete my education, to absorb certain essential powers from Uncle, and I learned presently that he was looking to *me* for assistance" (92). What happens to Benn in the human sphere, Ken discovers, is partly due to his special nature as "a man of feeling"; for Benn, a middle-aged widower, proves acutely susceptible to "*love* longings" and their peculiarly modern distortions (278). When, in his mid-fifties, Benn suffers an onslaught of erotic longing — impulses that Rudi Trachtenberg is much more adept at handling — he impulsively sets out to achieve conjugal bliss. Believing himself to have fallen in love with a "perfect" beauty, a woman much younger than he, Benn peremptorily marries Matilda Layamon. Unfortunately, the marriage brings him neither peace nor love. It is a disaster — one that could have been averted if he had paid heed to the warning signals emitted by his "prophetic soul" (326). Distracted by desire, failing to trust in his intuitive powers because they strike him as "irrational," Benn becomes prey to those "oscillations of consciousness" Ken has sought, under his uncle's influence, to quell.

When Ken initially sets out to absorb his uncle's influence, he is not sure whether Benn's gift for "contemplating flowers" may be carried over into the human sphere. Eventually, he discovers that Benn's insight into plants does "overlap," to a considerable degree, with the sphere of "human relations" (106). Alarmed, however, by what he sees, Benn decides, like Von Humboldt Fleisher, not to credit his visionary powers. As a poet Humboldt "wanted to drape the world in radiance" but lacked "enough material."[4] The "short supply" of "material," which Citrine attributes to the poet's failure to trust in his visionary imagination, similarly plagues Uncle Benn. As his nephew observes, "the whole vegetable kingdom was [Benn's] garment — his robe, his coat. . . . Still Uncle's garment was incomplete. It didn't quite button" (119). This tragic incompleteness is partly due, of course, to the fact that human beings make far more complex demands on one's powers of insight than members of the "vegetable kingdom." But as Benn and his nephew both come to realize, Benn's failure also derives from his refusal to heed the promptings of his inmost self.

Characterized as a mysterious "daemon or inner spirit," Benn's inmost self — which he also calls "that second person of mine" — has guided him at crucial moments in his life. (This "daemon" is the polar opposite of Herzog's "demon" of "modern ideas," whose insistent demand for theories and explanations must be silenced before Herzog can commune with *his* inner spirit.) It was "that second person inside" him that prompted Benn to "become a botanist" in the first place (58,84). By the same clairvoyant power that allows him to see into plants, he detects something repellent in the "hidden design" beneath Matilda's lovely outward appearance. Not liking what he sees, he attempts to dismiss these "visions" as mere "irrational reactions" (263). Exposed to his uncanny insight, which he cannot explain, certain features of his fiancee, despite her "classic face" and form, appear malign (124). Whether Matilda's "sharp teeth" or wide, mannish shoulders *objectively* reveal her true nature is a moot question (143). For Benn they have disturbing significance, provoking a troubling response that he ought not to ignore. By this time, however, the wedding has been planned, the invitations engraved; thus he chooses to "go against [his] deeper instinct" and marry Matilda (326). Weakly attempting to justify that decision to his nephew, from hindsight, Benn tells Kenneth, "I was warned . . . not to marry. It was a sin to disobey the warning. But a man like me, trained in science, can't go by revelation. You can't be rational and also hold with sin" (298).

By marrying the wrong woman Benn also entangles himself in her family — becoming the pawn of her father's elaborate financial schemes. A rich and prominent physician, Dr. Layamon is far more dedicated to empire-building than to the art of healing. Embroiling his son-in-law in a financial maneuver designed to yield millions of dollars, Dr. Layamon tells Benn, "If you're going to share the bed of this delicious girl of high breeding and wallow in it, you'll have to find the money it takes." By urging Benn to regain several million dollars he has been "screwed out of," Dr. Layamon proposes to help his son-in-law earn the right to "wallow" in Matilda's bed. (Dr. Layamon is obviously heir to the "pigdom" that Henderson summarily abandons.) Years earlier, Benn's Uncle Vilitzer had purchased from Benn and his sister, for a modest sum, a piece of family property that Vilitzer secretly knew would soon be worth millions. Shortly after the purchase, Uncle Vilitzer was able to resell the Craders' family property, for no less than fifteen million dollars, to a multinational corporation as the prospective site of the Electronic Tower, a monstrous skyscraper that presently dominates the skyline of the midwestern metropolis where Benn and the Layamons reside. By threatening to reopen a lawsuit against Uncle Vilitzer at this time, Benn will, according to Dr. Layamon, force his uncle to pay him several million dollars. In this way, Layamon tells his son-in-law, "you can be made whole" (171).

The ironic effect of Dr. Layamon's pledge is not lost on the reader, who later observes how the purported goal, to make Benn financially sound or "whole," shatters his psychic well-being. Instead of making the "psychic transfer" from the plant kingdom to the human sphere, as his nephew had hoped, Benn's vision is severely impaired by his entry into the Layamon family and his descent into the maelstrom of American greed, ambition, desire. His remarkable "marine blue, ultramarine" eyes — eyes that, before his ordeal with the Layamons, seemed to embody "the power of seeing itself, created by the light itself" — are soon beclouded by "sorrow" and guilt, "sin and punishment" (14, 234, 240). The Layamons thus serve "to bring Benn in, that is, to bring him back" into the world of property and power, "down from the sublime regions" of lofty contemplation. They are not, however, entirely to blame. "Benn," says his nephew, "had *wanted* to come down, he had a special wish to enter into prevailing states of mind and even, perhaps, into the peculiar sexuality associated with such states" (165-66). By insisting that his fascination with Matilda's alluring beauty *is* love, Benn undergoes his version of the West's current "ordeal of desire" — implicating him in the "fallen state" in which, says Ken, "our species finds itself" (100, 19). Dwelling in "the absence of love" and attempting to compensate for "inner poverty" with "sexual enchantments," contemporary humanity is in dire straits (241, 118, 155). Whether conscious or not of their "human impoverishment," plenty of people are, as Citrine already notes in *Humboldt's Gift*, "oppressed to the point of heartbreak" (350).

Even before Benn Crader's disastrous marriage to Matilda Layamon and his subsequent "fall," he has gone on record affirming the universal need for love and the "heartbreak" brought on by its absence. To a journalist who interviews him about the "dangers of radioactivity from Three Mile Island and Chernobyl," Benn makes the unexpected reply that serves as the novel's title and suggests its central theme: "It's terribly serious, of course, but I think more people die of heartbreak than of radiation" (197, 87). Implicit in Benn's unorthodox statement is his perception of two invisible yet deadly forces. While science has made the first one clear to us — warning of the terrible dangers produced by extreme levels of radiation — the lethal condition of "heartbreak" cannot be detected by instruments. As invisible to the naked eye as radiation, the misery of "human impoverishment" is registered, Bellow makes clear, not by scientific instruments but within the human heart.

Nothing less than a new vision of human life — one that breaks through the current "claustrophobia of consciousness" and places love squarely at the center — must be found, Benn's nephew is convinced, if more people are not to "die of heartbreak" (33). Just as Ken traces his uncle's unique visionary powers to an extraordinary "heart" and the love it generates, so he is able, under Benn's influence, to perceive how "an overflow of feeling" transforms the very nature of a person moved by love. When, for example, Ken tells Uncle Vilitzer's son Fishl of the schemes being laid by the Layamons against his father, Fishl's filial piety is profoundly aroused. Right before Ken's eyes, Fishl metamorphoses from a vulgar "entrepreneur and seed-money man" to a dignified and devoted son:

> He didn't even look like the double-chinned suave man who had received me. . . . The eyes, the nose, not a single particular of his appearance remained the same. I thought, You don't even begin to know a person until you've seen the features transformed in an overflow of feeling. A totally different Fishl came before me as soon as he saw that he might be in a position to defend his father, save him from his enemies. (182)

The impact of this transformation becomes even more pronounced when one considers that Fishl has been cut off, financially as well as emotionally, by his father. Heartless and, by all reasonable standards, utterly *un*deserving of affection, Harold Vilitzer continues, up to the moment of his death, to be loved unrequitedly by both his son Fishl and his nephew Benn. Thus Uncle Vilitzer occupies the unusual, and paradoxical, position of denying the reality of love while being its recipient.

Although Ken's revelation of the power of love centers upon Fishl rather than his father, a brief digression on the character of Harold Vilitzer helps to clarify the reality old Vilitzer would deny. Annoyed by Fishl's many bizarre, and failed, business ventures, Harold Vilitzer has refused, for fifteen years, even to see his son. Nor does he appear, in extreme old age, to have any regrets about his behavior — anymore than he regrets having cheated Benn by turning a fifteen-million-dollar profit on the Craders' family property. "Where money is concerned," Uncle Vilitzer declares, "the operational word is *merciless*" (282). From Vilitzer's "message" of mercilessness, Ken traces the logic of unalloyed materialism:

> Death is merciless, and therefore the ground rules of conduct have to include an equal and opposite hardness. From this it follows that kinship is bullshit. You can see how this would reflect on my attachment to

> Uncle [Benn], on Uncle's attachment to me. Against us there stood Vilitzer's exclusion of his son Fishl. . . . Fishl's emotions towards his father were further evidence [in his father's eyes] of his unfitness, his ignorance of the conditions of existence. (282)

When Benn and his nephew visit Uncle Vilitzer in order to talk about his swindling of the Craders, the old man gets angry and even tries to "take a sock" at one of them. Catching the octogenarian in his arms, Ken notes that Vilitzer "felt as light as an empty plastic egg carton. . . . He was scarcely even a tenement of clay; he was wickerwork, porous plastic. Only the pacemaker unit under his shirt had any weight" (286-88). Ken's impression is of a man whose heart has been virtually replaced by the tiny machine fitted to his breast. Nearly a corpse, Vilitzer is not so much a skeleton as a hollow shell. A mere semblance of humanity, he honors no human bond that would hamper his grip on his hundred-million-dollar financial kingdom. Nor can this desiccated creature acknowledge the final irony of his existence: that death, to which Vilitzer has opposed his "equal and opposite" code of "mercilessness," will soon arrive to sever his (death)grip on his money. Uncle Vilitzer has built his kingdom not in opposition to death, but under its yoke.

Through Ken's bond with his uncle — the warmth of an "attachment" deemed worthless by Vilitzer — he has become more "receptive" to phenomena and "the power behind" them (299). Gazing at Fishl, who now looks "totally different," Ken recalls Benn's "second person inside"; there may be, he suspects, "such a person also in Fishl" (182-83). Almost immediately, he has the extraordinary "impression" of *seeing* this "second Fishl": "As I watched closely, the singularity of this seemingly comical fatty seemed to detach itself from him and, with a tremor, move away. I give my impression of this just as it came to me. Another Fishl was sitting there in the fully buttoned vest. . . . Intimations, maybe, of a second Fishl." If, at this instant, "the real Kenneth" is perceiving the "real Fishl" — if Ken's "inner spirit" is making contact with Fishl's — then the border between "inner" and "outer" reality has, at least momentarily, been dissolved (186). Under the influence of his uncle, Ken transcends, at least momentarily, the mind-body "split" and penetrates, in Citrine's phrase, "behind the appearances."

The theme of idolatry, although less pronounced in *More Die of Heartbreak* than in *Humboldt's Gift*, permeates the later novel as well. To begin with, Benn's early praise of Matilda's external "perfection" — her "classic face" and "hyacinth hair" — suggests his tendency to idolize her beauty (53, 124). As Ken says, "It wasn't [Matilda's] beauty that I questioned, it was the Edgar Allan Poe stuff [Benn] was giving me about her. . . . Too much of the marble statue in the stained-glass niche" (121). Underscoring the connection, Ken comments on Matilda's silence, "Edgar Allan Poe's Helen standing in her niche had nothing to say. The representative of beauty was dumb, a terrific advantage for a sensitive devotee of classic figures" (139). Like Renata Koffritz's exquisitely preserved beauty, moreover, Matilda Layamon's marble "perfection" is suggestively associated with death. An "extravagant, luxuriant sleeper," Matilda, Benn observes upon marrying her, abandons herself to sleep like "Psyche embracing Eros in a blind darkness" (142). Here, as in the earlier novel, Bellow implies that when Eros is idolized, "the sex embrace was death-flavored" (69).

The gradual "disintegration" of Matilda's image in Benn's eyes — and his attempts, at the same time, to deny his troubling "visions" — ultimately precipitate his "fall" from "whole" vision into "critical consciousness" (265). Benn's "fallen state" is shockingly revealed to the "plant clairvoyant" one night at the Layamons' luxurious duplex. Temporarily staying with his wife at the home of her parents, Benn is awakened by a disturbing telephone call. Too restless, after the call, to return to bed, he wanders about the Layamon residence while the rest of the family are asleep; eventually he enters his mother-in-law's private study, customarily barred to outsiders, in order to "have plant contact" with a beautiful azalea he has admired from afar (299). To his shock and dismay, he finds that this exquisite plant is actually a fake.

Standing in the corner of Mrs. Layamon's study, the red azalea — from whose flowers Benn has, from outside in the hallway, repeatedly drawn inspiration — proves a cunning silk replica wrought by Oriental hands. The "plant clairvoyant" has been duped by a "damn near perfect imitation" that is thoroughly "false." In shock, Benn telephones his nephew in the middle of the night, to report the disastrous news:

> A stooge azalea — a stand-in, a ringer, an impostor, a dummy, a shill! I was drawing support for weeks and weeks from this manufactured product. Every time I needed a fix, a contact, a flow, I turned to it. Me, Kenneth! After all these years of unbroken rapport, to be taken in. . . . The one thing I could always count on. My occupation, my instinct, my connection . . . broken off. (300, latter ellipsis Bellow's)

To Benn this dismal error is much more than a "sign" of professional failure. He blames himself for having severed his "connection" not only to the plant kingdom but to that inner kingdom of his essential self. For straying his calling — the serious business of "contemplating flowers" — he has, he tells his nephew, been duly "punished": "I've been punished, Kenneth. For all the false things I did, a false object punished me" (300).[5] Gulled by desire, Benn has forfeited "wholeness" for idolatry. Like the "grumpy old man" in Menasha Klinger's story at the end of *Humboldt's Gift*, who takes the mere appearance of a flower for the real thing, Benn has been seduced by "the plastered idols of the Appearances" (*HG* 487).

When Benn reveals to his nephew the humiliating discovery — that he has "lost the privilege of vision, fallen into the opposite and brutal prevailing outlook" — Ken, registering the impact of that "fall," loses heart (328). "What had happened to [Benn] affected me as well," he says. "I could feel the perturbation widening and widening . . . and became aware that I had come to depend upon his spirit. Without its support, the buoyancy went out of me." That buoyancy gone, Ken feels more convinced than ever of the "inner poverty" of "modern life," which his new country, America, embodies in the extreme: "Your soul had its work cut out for you in this extraordinary country," he laments. "You got spiritual headaches. . . . There seems to be a huge force that advances, propels, and this propellant increases its power by drawing value away from personal life and fitting us for its colossal purpose. It demands the abolition of such things as love and art . . . of gifts like Uncle's" (301, latter ellipsis Bellow's). Fortunately, just at the moment Ken begins to formulate a general picture of doom, he recovers, if not his former "buoyancy," a more lucid state of mind:

> Of course, we all have these thoughts today instead of prayers. And we think these thoughts are serious and we take pride in our ability to think, to elaborate ideas, so we go round and round in consciousness like this. However, they don't get us anywhere; our speculations are like a stationary bicycle. And this, too, was dawning on me. These proliferating thoughts have more affinity to insomnia than to mental progress. Oscillations of the mental substance is what they are, ever-increasing jitters. (301)

With this revelation Ken breaks off his formulations, pondering his uncle's parting words. It is "time," Benn tells him before hanging up the telephone, "I took hold" (300). "When you've fallen from grace, what do you take hold of?" Ken wonders (301). Instead of sinking into misery, however, he recollects a story about "Whistler the painter," told to him by his Aunt Lena, Benn's first wife:

> It was Lena who introduced [Ken] to the valuable idea that modes of seeing were matters of destiny, that what is sent forth by the seer affects what is seen. She liked to give the example of Whistler the painter when he was taken to task by a woman who said [of his art], "I never see trees like that." He told her, "No, ma'am, but don't you wish you could?" This could be a variation on "Ye have eyes and see not." (305)

Whistler's retort offers a challenge to those who, like the woman in Aunt Lena's story, worship "the plastered idols of the Appearances."[6] Thus, Ken recalls the biblical passage, "Ye have eyes and see not," the judgment against idolatry that recurs throughout the Old and New Testaments. Entranced by appearances, Whistler's interlocutor "sees not"; the victim as well as the perpetrator of "inner poverty," she deprives herself of a rich and vital picture of the world.

Resolving to "take hold" of his own life, Ken decides to fly out to Seattle to visit Treckie and his daughter. On his way to the city, however, he experiences another setback. In a fit of vengeful fury that recalls Herzog's abortive plan to murder his rival, Gersbach, Ken imagines beating up Treckie's current lover, a ski instructor, and fighting him to the death. Arriving at Treckie's apartment, he finds that the "ski instructor," whom he has mentally stereotyped as thick and brutal, has "gone to Mass." Venting his jealousy and frustration, Ken heads for the bathroom, proceeding to "wreck it" by smashing everything in sight. But then, as in Herzog's case, "actuality" takes over, demonstrating the futility of his actions. Treckie's "settled intimacy" with another man, he notes, is manifested in every concrete detail — confirmed even by the household odors and mundane arrangement of objects (309-10).

His illusions shattered, Ken realizes that he has been guilty of that same "Edgar Allan Poe stuff" he has scoffed at in Benn (311, 121). Even his admiration for another woman, his friend Dita Schwartz, has not released him from this "ordeal of desire."[7] Now, however, face to face with Treckie, the "child-woman," he perceives not a work of "perfection," not a "marble statue" or idol, but a specific human being — a human being, furthermore, who wants no part of him. Although the revelation is "downright shocking" to his ego, Ken faces the fact that, as he puts it, "I failed to turn *her* on" (312). For her part, Treckie calmly accepts Ken's "tantrum," regarding his wreck of the bathroom as a "minor inconvenience" and their "mutual quitclaim" (319).

As Ken and Treckie "conclude the matter" of their failed relationship, Uncle Benn is present both in Ken's thoughts and in his conversation with Treckie. "He's a famous man in his field," Treckie says of Benn, "but he does make an awfully flaky impression when he sounds off." His statement, "quoted in the paper," that "more people died of heartbreak than of radiation poisoning," strikes her as "a crazy remark" (315). Meanwhile Treckie, aware that Ken looks down on her interest in trendy "California-type stuff" like "applied Zen" and "group psychotherapy," defends her "life-style." As their daughter watches television cartoons in the next room, she tells Ken, "We're a pluralistic society, after all. Multiple acculturation is what it's all about." To Ken, in search of "a desperately needed human turning point," Treckie's relativistic chatter is virtually indistinguishable from the "cartoon sound effects" coming from the television set: "the bangs, whistles, buzzings, blams and tooting" (314-16). He sees, nonetheless, that for Treckie he "didn't even exist. That was nothing to get excited about, as it was one of the commoner human experiences — neither to give a damn nor to be given a damn about. In practice it was accepted as a matter of course, though at heart nobody quite came to terms with it" (319).

What human beings know "at heart," this passage reminds us, is quite different from what they *appear* to accept. This is the meaning suggested by the novel's title, which draws attention to the "hidden design" behind the appearances of modern life. To say, as Benn does, that "more people die of heartbreak" is not to diminish the dangers of radiation or the threat of nuclear disaster. It is to say that other, less obvious but still urgent "matters" also threaten us. On the other hand, Benn's statement may have a still more radical implication for contemporary culture. Bellow may be suggesting that the widespread apprehension of material doom is itself symptomatic of a deeper crisis. In any case, Bellow's narrator reaffirms, in words that articulate the novelist's own search for a way out of the current state of "human impoverishment," his commitment to "Project Turning Point" (330). Ken remains convinced "that, really, conscious existence might be justified only if it was devoted to the quest for a revelation, a massive reversal, an inspired universal change, a new direction, a desperately needed human turning point" (315).

After saying goodbye to Treckie and flying back to the Midwest, Ken receives another telephone call from his uncle, one that signals a "turning point" or "new direction" in Benn's life. Taking hold of his fate in radical fashion, Benn has decided to abandon Matilda, her family and Dr. Layamon's schemes. Calling his nephew from a Miami airport, Benn is on his way to the North Pole, where "an international team of scientists" is conducting "special researches. And I signed on," says Benn, "to check out lichens from both poles . . . and work out certain morphological puzzles." Benn's timely escape from Matilda may indicate that he will never overcome his "confused relations with women"; yet his present determination to save himself is a marked departure from his former "evasive action" (233). In contrast to his tortuous attempts to quell his "visions" and to rationalize his alliance with Matilda, Benn's current decision, he tells his nephew, has been "carefully felt through. Rather than thought out. It's a survival measure" (334).

Like Henderson, who went "beyond geography" to save his soul, Benn must take extreme measures for his own "survival." "We're going to be based in northern Scandinavia," he tells Ken, "at the edge of Finland, actually. And beyond." There, at the edge of the world, "night and ice" will provide a "corrective" to internal disarray: "Ice for the rigor. And also because there'll be no plants to see, except the lichens. Because if there's no rapport," says Benn, "if the rapport is dead, I'm better off in plant-free surroundings" (334). Ken does not condemn his uncle's flight from the Layamons; though "mystified," he gives Benn's "expedition [his] blessing." For what his uncle must accomplish, he knows, even "Novaya Zemlya" may not be "remote enough" (335). In so chaotic a time, "when so many supports and stabilities are removing themselves from [the individual]," one must take radical steps to regain a sense of connection. Clearly, Benn must "remove himself" from the distractions of modern life — from the "magnetic attraction of anarchy" (330).

To the North Pole, where "magnetic attraction" does not exert its customary force, Benn Crader sets out to "preserve himself humanly" — and, if possible, to recover his "gift" of vision. Whether or not he will redeem his "fall from grace," Benn's gift for "contemplating flowers" still offers Ken a model for achieving "perfected insight." Minding Benn's apartment and his plants while his uncle is away, Ken will continue, as he says, to "retrieve from my memory bank those wonderful hours when, under [Benn's] influence, not only my lungs were breathing but my mind breathed too. Some of his powers of seeing *had* been transmitted to me. So I saw" (278). Having stilled "the oscillations of consciousness," Ken can "breathe" mentally as well as physically — the expansion of the "chest," Lewis's "seat" of feeling, effecting an expansion of the psyche and its powers.

At the end of *More Die of Heartbreak*, Ken Trachtenberg remains committed to his "Project Timing Point." His author, moreover, appears to be engaged in a similar project: the search for a "turning point," the "quest for a revelation." In the latter stages of this quest, the novels published since *Mr. Sammler's Planet*, Bellow has ventured more and more openly against the grain of contemporary formulations and cultural "orthodoxy." And while he continues to enlist the conventions of the realist novel, the impact or effect of his fiction is to overturn some of realism's time-honored traditions. In most realist fiction from Cervantes to Dreiser to Hemingway, "the conditioning forces" clearly hold sway over the tiny figure of the individual, who is caught in their force-field even as he seeks a "channel" to freedom. Yet the central preoccupation of Bellow's fiction appears to be moving further and further "beyond" that force-field and its "magnetic attraction." In his own rendering of reality the novelist seems headed, like Benn Crader, for "the edge" of the familiarly known world: "And beyond."

True, Bellow still honors the novelist's obligations to the historical moment and the geography of place; and he delights, perhaps more than ever, in rendering the significant details and particular absurdities of the contemporary urban scene. At the same time, however, his handling of these traditional materials tends, like Charlie Citrine's "upside-down" postures, to overturn the realist's ruling premises. What Ken Trachtenberg says of his "Project Turning Point" thus has special relevance for the direction that Bellow's fiction is taking: "The secret of our being still asks to be unfolded. Only now we understand that worrying at it and ragging it is of no use." Instead, the individual "must maneuver [him]self into a position in which metaphysical aid can approach" (330-31). Engaging in his own novelistic "maneuvers," Bellow has been working his way through the local coordinates of history and geography to regions of human experience as remote from Stendahl's "mirror carried along a highway" as "Novaya Zemlya." By effecting this "massive reversal" in the genre's traditional emphases and effects, he may have reached a "turning point" not only in his own career but in the development of the realist novel: a point at which the "primordial person," rather than his alteration by "the conditioning forces," is of crucial interest. In Bellow's own fiction, in any case, it is the "secret" of the human being, his "hidden design," that the novelist's art is increasingly dedicated to unfolding.

Notes

1. Saul Bellow, *More Die of Heartbreak* (New York: Morrow,1987), 234, 305. Subsequent references in the text from this edition.
2. In *Knowledge of the Higher Worlds and Its Attainment*, trans. George Metaxa (Spring Valley, N.Y.: Anthroposophic Press, 1947), Rudolf Steiner instructs a student of his philosophy "to place before himself the small seed of a plant" and to contemplate both its visible and "*invisible*" reality by picturing the "*plant of complex structure*" that will "*later be enticed from the seed by the forces of earth and light*" (60). In *An Outline of Occult Science* (4th ed., New York: Rand McNally, 1914), Steiner elucidates the relationship between the "force" of "light" and the human capacity to see. "There lies hidden in what is perceived by an organ the force by which that same organ was formed. The eye perceives light; but without light there would be no eye. Creatures spending their lives in darkness do not develop organs of sight" (86). Echoing Steiner's thought, Ken Trachtenberg says, "The light pries these organs out of us creatures to purposes of its own" (14).
3. While reviewers of *Herzog* tended, to Bellow's dismay, to overlook the novel's "comic portrait of the enfeeblement of the educated man" (Matthew Roudané, "An Interview With Saul Bellow," *Contemporary Literature* 25.3 (1984): 268-69 [see pp. 234-247 in this volume]), reviewers of *More Die of Heartbreak* were more alert. Even though Terrence Rafferty, "Hearts and Minds," *New Yorker* (20 July 1987): 89-91, found the novel "phenomenally dull," he noted the "comedy" created when the "characters' high-powered cerebral equipment . . . gets tangled up in the works" of everyday life. More favorably disposed toward the novel, Paul Gray, "Victims of Contemporary Life," *Time* (15 June 1987): 71, deemed *More Die of Heartbreak* "a consistently funny variation of the theme of intellectual haplessness."
4. Saul Bellow, *Humboldt's Gift* (New York: Viking, 1975), 107. Subsequent references in the text from this edition.
5. Earlier in the novel, Benn is described as perceiving, beneath the plastic dusting on a Christmas tree, that the tree, contrary to all appearances, is *real*. "You couldn't fool Uncle about a tree," Ken confidently asserts (127). Now that statement must be retracted; having "deviated" from his "original, given nature," Benn is duped by fate. Here too Steiner's influence seems to be operating. In *Knowledge of the Higher Worlds and Its Attainment*, Steiner distinguishes between a real plant seed and its "*artificial imitation*," which does not contain "*secretly enfolded within it*" the "*force of the whole plant. . . . And yet both* [the real and the imitation seeds] *appear alike to my eyes. The real seed, therefore, contains something invisible which is not present in the imitation*" (60-61). It is this "invisible something" or "hidden design" that Benn has lost the power to detect.
6. The incident concerning Whistler is also described by Owen Barfield in his study of idolatry, *Saving the Appearances: A Study in Idolatry* (1957; New York: Harcourt, Brace, 1965): "When a lady complained to Whistler that she did not see the world he painted, he is said to have replied: 'No ma'am, but don't you wish you could?'" Both Whistler and the lady,

Barfield points out, are referring to the activity — "which in Whistler's case was intenser than the lady's" — of "*figuration*": the process by which each individual perceives and represents to himself the phenomenal world. This activity consists, Barfield adds, of "two operations": "First, the sense-organs must be related to the particles [of light, waves, quanta, etc.] in such a way as to give rise to sensations; and secondly, those mere sensations must be combined and constructed by the percipient mind into the recognizable and nameable objects we call 'things'" (24). Barfield's account of "figuration" articulates in more philosophical terms Ken Trachtenberg's assertion about "modes of seeing": "that what is sent forth by the seer affects what is seen."

7. Though highly attracive in her own right, Dita Schwartz does not produce the illusion of "perfection." She has been marked, and marred, by existence. Her "scarred" face, the result of an "adolescent case of acne," takes on emblematic significance in the novel. In contrast to Treckie's smooth and "pink face," as well as Matilda's "classic face," Dita's blemished skin, though it causes her anguish, bespeaks her honest and straightforward nature (205, 189).

* * *

A Theft (1989)

Less Brains, Better Legs
George Packer

Saul Bellow describes his latest protagonist as "a raw-boned American woman. She had very good legs — who knows what you would have seen if pioneer women had worn shorter skirts. She bought her clothes in the best shops and was knowledgeable about cosmetics. Nevertheless the backcountry look never left her. She came from the sticks; there could be no mistake about that. Her people? Indiana and Illinois farmers and small-town businessmen who were very religious."

In fact, it would be easy to mistake Clara Velde of *A Theft* for one of Bellow's male, Jewish, city-bred heroes, possessed of the unmistakable voice that Gabriel Josipovici has described as the utmost formality mixed with the utmost desperation. Clara seems less a high-fashion executive or Bible-fed hick — Bellow claims she is both — than an Augie March or Moses Herzog or Charlie Citrine with slightly less brains but better legs. She plays the questing, self-analyzing, mouth-flapping role that stands at the center of nearly all Bellow's work, without which there would be no story at all. But it does not seem accidental that she is a woman.

Clara's energetic, discontented Park Avenue life comes undone when an engagement ring is stolen. The emerald was given to her years ago, under duress, by Ithiel Regler, a "big, *big* picture" type in Washington who has penetrated the depths of the twentieth century but proved incapable of marrying the woman who loves him most. After four bad marriages, Clara still hasn't gotten over him. When the ring disappears, neither a private detective, her psychiatrist, her confidante Laura Wong, her work, nor Regler himself (with whom she maintains a close friendship) can save Clara. The source of the novella's quick-paced tension is not the mystery of the ring's theft and return but of

From *Nation* (15 May 1989): 674-75.

Clara's frantic reaction and ultimate self-discovery. For the ring "was involved with her very grip on existence." It represents not just her undying passion for Regler but her vision of herself as a coherent individual; and at the center of the vision is love.

Clara Velde has a less sophisticated predecessor in another recent Bellow heroine, Katrina Goliger, from his extraordinary novella "What Kind of Day Did You Have?", found in the collection *Him With His Foot in His Mouth*. Both women, in middle age, are under the kind of pressure that is always constricting the chests of Bellow's male protagonists. For the women, though, the pressure comes from loving the sort of men these have become.

Much-scolded as a misogynist, Bellow has typically drawn his female characters as either man-eating ex-wives or "potato-love" sexpots. The shift toward a sympathetic female point of view answers the spiritual and sexual defeats of his intellectually muscular males, last represented by Uncle Benn in *More Die of Heartbreak*, who fled marital and Western decline to the far tundra — "Even that was not remote enough." In eternal pursuit of the problem of the individual in the modern world, Clara's Ithiel Regler and Katrina's Victor Wulpy have no interest left in real personal life; great thinkers, they are on the road out of existence as individuals. At one point Clara puts this to herself with true clarity: "You couldn't separate love from being. You could Be, even though you were alone. But in that case, you loved only yourself. If so, everybody else was a phantom, and then world politics was a shadow play. Therefore she, Clara, was the only key to politics that Ithiel was likely to find."

It's up to a woman, then — this woman — to continue the Bellovian struggle of worrying about being human and rescuing oneself from the swarming threats to humanness, which in Clara's case are cynicism, despair, psychoanalytic abstraction and the menace of New York City in the form of an offstage Haitian thief. Clara doesn't buy "the collapsing culture bit" that preoccupies Ithiel Regler and has preoccupied the novels of Bellow at least since *Mr. Sammler's Planet*: "I'm beginning to see it instead as the conduct of life without input from your soul. Essential parts of people getting mislaid or crowded out — don't ask me for specifics; I can't give them."

The problem with *A Theft* is the specifics. Characteristically, most of it is talk, but the world outside the talk seems sketchy at best, the story is in a peculiar hurry to end. This lack of a material medium deprives Bellow of his brilliant way with figurative language, lessens the tension inherent in each scene and disembodies his characters, leaving sheer voice. Clara's Austrian *au pair*, who secures the return of the ring from her boyfriend, the Haitian thief, is indistinguishable from the story's New Yorkers, saying things like, "The day of the fashion show we had lunch, and you made a remark like 'Nobody is anybody.' You were just muttering, talking about your psychiatrist. But when you started to talk about the man in Washington just now, there was no nobody-anybody problem." The *au pair* has come to New York to perfect her English. Obviously, landing in a Bellow novella is the right method.

In the end, this girl, impulsive, deep-feeling and wise like Clara, returns Clara to herself, and in an unexpected twist gives Clara reason to have hope for her troubled daughter as well. The epiphany of the last page ("The main source of tears came open. . . . I do seem to have an idea who it is that's at the middle of me") depends on all of these connections and losses and finds making emotional sense. They don't, but in Bellow's case that never destroys a book. He is still up to so much along the way — more, in his seventies, than nearly anyone else, and against every trend away from ideas in fiction — that even a lesser work like *A Theft* is worth a slow, careful read.

* * *

It Doesn't Ring True
Andrew Gordon

In his review in *Saul Bellow Journal*, Allan Chavkin calls *A Theft* "a marvelous short work that reveals Bellow's genius has lost nothing with age. . . . Bellow is now at the height of his creative power."[1] I beg to differ with him and with other reviewers who have either lavished praise on *A Theft* or hedged and waffled about the novella's flaws for fear of desecrating a national monument. *A Theft* left me cold; I could neither believe in the central character, Clara Velde, nor care much about the theft of her beloved ring. We read Bellow because he makes us smile, he makes us feel, and he makes us think. But *A Theft* is neither as funny, as moving, nor as wise as the best of Bellow, and judged against his finest novella, *Seize the Day*, it is a minor work and a major disappointment. *A Theft* is weak fiction because it lacks dramatic tension, relies too much on telling rather than showing, and suffers from bland or unrealized characters and stilted, unbelievable dialogue.

Let me first admit the positive qualities of the work. Ithiel Regler deserves a place in Bellow's rogue's gallery of memorable tough guys, eloquent wheeler-dealers, and vulnerable men of the world; he most resembles Victor Wulpy, the womanizing "world-class intellectual" of "What Kind of Day Did You Have?". And there are the barbed one-liners and pungent passages we have come to expect from Bellow. On one of Clara's ex-husbands, Mike Spontini: "He would rather be an

From *Saul Bellow Journal* 9.1 (1990): 79-83.

imbecile on the Grand Canal than a husband on Fifth Avenue."[2] On psychiatry: "If a millipede came into the office, he'd leave with an infinitesimal crutch for each leg" (42-43). And on another ex-husband: "This marriage was like a Thanksgiving turkey. After a month the bird is drying out and you're still eating breast of turkey. It needs more and more Russian dressing, and pretty soon the sharpest knife in the city won't slice it" (36).

Given the pleasures of some of his characterization and the occasional tang of his style, the story nevertheless falls flat because there is not enough at stake, insufficient dramatic tension. Tommy Wilhelm in *Seize the Day* is trapped from the outset in a day of judgment, sinking ever deeper into a sea of troubles. Tommy has problems to spare, crises wherever he turns. By contrast, Clara Velde is a wealthy Park Avenue matron, a successful career woman and mother who has had decades to grow accustomed to her failure to wed Ithiel, the man she most loved, and to her string of disappointing husbands. Her crisis — the theft of a ring and trouble with an *au pair* girl — comes late in the action and is quickly resolved. Granted, the ring is supposed to be symbolic, central to her identity, but compared to Wilhelm's crippling woes, Clara's troubles seem small potatoes.

When Wilhelm breaks down sobbing at the end of *Seize the Day* ("The source of all tears had suddenly sprung open within him"), one feels as if something enormous has been released; when Clara does the same thing at the end of *A Theft* ("The main source of tears came open" [109]), one wonders what in the world she's crying about.

Perhaps a more apt comparison of the crisis in *A Theft* would be to the theft of Dr. Lal's manuscript in *Mr. Sammler's Planet* — another crime that eventually brings characters together and leads the protagonist to self-realization. But the obstacles to the return of the manuscript are more convoluted and comic than those involving the return of the ring, so that the long-delayed meeting of Sammler and Lal is far more gratifying than the brief reunion of Clara and Gina.

There is also an absence of dramatic tension in Clara's relationship with her confidante Laura Wong. Ms. Wong allows Clara to talk at great length, just as Dr. Tamkin draws out Tommy Wilhelm. But far too much of this novel is *told* to Laura Wong, not *shown* to the reader. And Wilhelm's dialogues with Tamkin are constantly charged with the tension of the unspoken: how far can he trust this questionable Doctor? In contrast, there's no tension in Clara's monologues with Ms. Wong; Wong is patently a narrative convenience, never characterized as much more than a stereotyped "inscrutable Oriental." When Clara at the end comes to the paranoid conclusion that Wong craves Ithiel for herself, I wondered how Clara could possibly be jealous of a cipher.

For us to believe in Clara and in Clara's responses, she must be surrounded by believable characters. The minor characters in *Seize the Day* — Rubin, Perls, Maurice Venice, Rappaport — are all as grotesque and unforgettable as Dr. Tamkin and sketched with quick, vivid strokes. By contrast, most of the minor characters in A *Theft* — Dr. Gladstone, Steinsalz Gottschalk, Marta Elvia — scarcely exist. A week after you've read the novel, I defy you to remember their names or anything about them. The only exceptions are a few comic characters: Wilder Velde, a passive, stolid loser who is Clara's present husband, and two Italians — Clara's third husband, Spontini, and Spontini's friend, "the billionaire leftist and terrorist Giangiacomo F., who blew himself up in the seventies" (2-3). Yet even there Bellow could be accused of ethnic stereotyping: Why do all the Italians have to be adulterous or explosive? (Gina's split character is also ascribed to her being part Viennese and part Italian). And why does he give us yet another black thief (shades of *Sammler*)?

There is also unrealized dramatic potential in the relationship between Clara and her ten-year-old daughter Lucy, who is a kind of double for Clara and plays a key role in the denouement. Lucy is alluded to or reported on but never *shown* interacting with her mother or in any action at all. Compare, for example, how skillfully Bellow handles the relationship between Leventhal and his nephew Phil in *The Victim* or between Herzog and his little daughter Junie in *Herzog* to see what he can do at his best with adult-child interactions.

More crucially, Clara's relationship with Gina Wegman, young Austrian *au pair*, also falls flat and leaves a dramatic vacuum at the center of the novel. Gina is supposed to serve as another double or alter ego for Clara: both have reckless affairs with dirty, criminal, French-speaking men before settling for safe marriages (why Bellow consistently links sex with *theft*, as in *Mr. Sammler's Planet* and here, is something for critics to ponder further). But Gina is kept at such a distance, reported on but rarely seen acting, that she never comes to life. For a supposedly passionate woman, her few lines of dialogue are bland. She doesn't even speak like a convincing foreigner. To Clara, Gina seems mysterious, but to the reader, merely nebulous. For comparison's sake, consider the vivid, unforgettable sense we get of the mysterious Dr. Tamkin, who is at the heart of *Seize the Day*.

Aside from the lack of dramatic tension and of fully realized characters, A *Theft* also suffers from some stilted dialogue. We expect Bellow characters to speak in his idiosyncratic, hyper-charged blend of slang and intellectual rhetoric. But how could Bellow let Clara talk with such clinkers as these:"A sexy woman who couldn't find the place to put her emotionality" (3), "He's the overweening overlord" (3), "A sexy woman may delude herself about the gratification of a mental life" (3), and "The whole scene was like a mirage to me, how they were haberdashed" (60). Because Clara's voice is unconvincing, she becomes that much more difficult to believe in.

Clara seems to be an older, less appealing version of Demmie Vonghel from *Humboldt's Gift*. There are so many similarities between the two characters that it is possible they have the same real life model, a woman Bellow loved. Both are bighearted, generous, big blonde WASPs. Both are long-legged, knock-kneed, and clumsy. Both are all-American and combine the look of a pioneer woman with the Eastern sophistication of a Seven Sisters graduate. Both come from very religious families and teach Latin in a private school. Both want to get married and pressure a man to buy them a ring. Both have a good-girl/bad-girl split. Both like to walk around naked at home when their lover is around. And finally, both get hysterical late at night. Bellow seems to have recycled Demmie into Clara, making her older and more disappointed and giving her an unconvincing and undeveloped career as "the czarina of fashion writing" (2). Clara is also given a reckless sexual past but a rather dull, repressed present (Bellow made the same narrative mistake in *The Dean's December*). Ultimately, Demmie is a more poignant character than Clara because we see her through the eyes of Charlie, who loved her and lost her when she died in a plane crash. Nobody loves Clara passionately; Ithiel Regler respects her, but he keeps her at a distance. So does Bellow.

In sum, Bellow has done much better elsewhere. He is not working at the top of his form in *A Theft* because there is not enough at stake: not enough dramatic interest and not enough emotion. Perhaps Clara's life is too remote from Bellow's; he becomes clumsy and starts making false moves. This "ring cycle" just doesn't ring true.

Is *A Theft* a misstep due to Bellow's age? I doubt it; a single lapse doesn't necessarily mean that the master has lost his touch. Bellow has bounced back before, following up the flat and dispiriting *The Dean's December* with the lively stories of *Him with His Foot in His Mouth* and the comic energy of *More Die of Heartbreak*. He has been prolific in the 1980s and has just brought out another novella, concentrating on short works now, perhaps recognizing that he may be running out of time. We should be grateful, if not for *A Theft* then for this final burst of energy, this late efflorescence from a great storyteller; one thinks of Melville and *Billy Budd*.

Notes

1. Allan Chavkin, "Bellow's *A Theft*," *Saul Bellow Journal* 8.1 (1989): 70.
2. Saul Bellow, *A Theft* (Harmondsworth: Penguin, 1989), 3. Subsequent references in the text from this edition.

* * *

Bellow's *A Theft*:
The Human Pair in "Gogmagogsville"
Gloria L. Cronin

Reviewers of Bellow's recent novella, *A Theft* (1989), seem at best mildly interested and at worst singularly unmoved by this puzzling new fiction. At a loss to place it in context with the author's previous work, many provided a muted critical response and excessive commentary on the unprecedented act of a paperback first printing. Most were largely unconvinced by the belated appearance of Bellow's first major female protagonist, and furthermore, they seem unable to distinguish a central thrust or any genuine large-scale significance in the text. While most praise the book for its language, neatness, and control, nearly all find it lacking in focus and energy. David Denby comments that *A Theft* "nearly founders under the weight of Bellow's heaped-up encomiums of his heroine Clara Velde"; he also describes Teddy Regler as "a bit of a hyped article."[1] John Seelye comments on the "peculiarly flat quality that extends to characterization," its "wallpaper thinness," and "inadequate backdrop."[2] Robert Boyers notes that "in *A Theft* [Bellow's] heart is just not in it," and wonders if it is a work of "deliberate self-limitation."[3] Robert Towers remarks: "What charm this somewhat undernourished little book possesses lies in its language," but "such verbal exuberance is not enough to make *A Theft* seem more than skimpy"; he concludes that this book "suggests only the armature for an uncompleted and weightier work based upon the relationship of Clara and Ithiel."[4] Anita Brookner, one of the few female reviewers, notes that "as a vignette of an exhausted love affair it is neat but no more."[5] Tim Appelo complains simply: "We wuz robbed."[6] Richard Eder complains of unanchored episodes, pointless, undeveloped characters, scrappiness, and narrow thematic spaces.[7] Mark Feeney expresses outright anger as he condemns Bellow for the "ugly moral undercurrent . . . impolite people might call racism — with its picture of the city as a dark, threatening jungle."[8] Joyce Carol Oates finds the book "strangely lacking in the richly textured and sharply observed ground base of reality that has always been the strength of Mr. Bellow's fiction,"[9] while John Updike finds the book "jumpy and skimpy . . . like a set of signals to someone offstage."[10]

Scholars, like the reviewers, have also been largely negative in their responses. Liela Goldman roundly chastises Bellow for his stereotypically sexist portrayal of Clara Velde as flighty fashion maven.[11] Elaine Safer points out comic irony in Bellow's use of the obtuse first-person narrator who fails, she argues, to "penetrate any of the ironies . . . involving the main character, Clara Velde."[12] The most positive responses by far are those of Marianne Friedrich and Allan Chavkin.

Friedrich performs a creative manipulation of Jungian individuation theory by bringing together the twin romance paradigms embodied in the Hera and Tristan-and-Isolde myths in an attempt to valorize Clara Velde.[13] Chavkin goes so far as to argue enthusiastically that *A Theft* "is a marvelous short work that reveals Bellow's genius has lost nothing with age. . . . Bellow is now at the height of his creative power."[14] Andrew Gordon complains in response to Chavkin's and other critics' positive assessments that "*A Theft* left me cold; I could neither believe in the central character, Clara Velde, nor care much about the theft of her beloved ring. . . . *A Theft* is weak fiction because it lacks dramatic tension, relies too much on telling rather than showing, and suffers from bland or unrealized characters and stilted, unbelievable dialogue."[15] Even Bellow himself has added to the debate: "[This story] gives an independent view of human reality different from the prevailing contemporary view. . . . And I can tell from the early reception of a story like this by my contemporaries that I have given a new view."[16] But just exactly what is new here?

This text enacts the latest permutation in Bellow's comic opera on the dynamics of the heterosexual human pair. Not surprisingly, its situations parallel those of earlier novels as Clara and Ithiel alternately embrace and flee, seek higher consciousness, and become mired in temporal mundanities. Bellow's demythologization of romantic love in "Gogmagogsville" once again hinges on the ironic portrayal of a male protagonist who can never resolve the dichotomy between desire for ultimate union with the female and the pursuit of the rational. Then there is the continuing Bellovian conversation about the failure of marriage, as in *Henderson the Rain King* and *Humboldt's Gift*; the failure of divorce, as in *Herzog*; and the failure of heterosexual relations, as in *Mr. Sammler's Planet* and *More Die of Heartbreak*. Also familiar is the appearance of a protagonist, albeit a female one, who idealizes ultimate union with the exotic, all-powerful member of the opposite sex. Clara just happens to be the female quester who falls for the mythicized all-powerful male, Ithiel Regler, who, as the object of such romance ideology, cannot bear the weight of her expectations. Most significantly, both characters have antecedents in all the previous novels in that whatever higher intuitions they attain have relatively little to do with the success or failure of "the human pair."[17]

Smaller in scale, more muted in tone, and done in reversed gender, *A Theft* deals with some very old Bellow themes related to the failures of heterosexual love. There is the Hawthornian theft of the human heart; the lure of the intellect; the classic evasions of the male lover; the overweening romantic aspirations of just one partner (this time a female); the social chaos of "Gogmagogsville"; the seeming impossibility of higher synthesis; the human comedy of sexual desire; the failure of psychiatry; the decreasing significance of the personal factor; the quest for the essential, unified self; power politics; the loss of human qualities; the issues of boredom, stewardship, and the human contract; the increasing absence of civilized spaces; the proliferation of ethnic others as confusing and lower types of the human; the diminished status of the individual; and the problematic relation of love to being. The clues to Clara and Ithiel's particular failure to form the human pair can also be found in this typically Bellovian thematic matrix.

Clara, like the male protagonists before her, never really sees through the specific failure of her romantic quest: "We have this total, delicious connection, which is also a disaster" (9), she explains, not really understanding the disaster. The disaster is of both their makings. For Ithiel's part, the only time he has ever found for this love affair is between jobs. And though Clara admits she has pressured Ithiel into buying the emerald engagement ring in the first place, she never really admits fully that while the diamond is "the real thing, conspicuously clear, color perfect, top of its class" (16), Ithiel is unable to match his gift in the giving of his love. He has traded their love for a career because, Clara tells us, he is "flying high as a wunderkind in nuclear strategy, and he might have gone all the way to the top, to the negotiating table in Geneva, facing the Russians, if he had been less quirky" (17). She calls him analytically deep, comments on his breadth of knowledge, his fantastic reports, and his reputation for dependability (19), while the text steadily reveals him as a preoccupied Washington analyst and an abandoning lover. Ironically, the one moment she feels they have achieved the status of the perfectly synchronized human pair is the moment they are geographically separated and can only communicate on a transatlantic telephone, while she — student-wife fashion — types, organizes, and edits his notes "in a style resembling his own. . . . She could do any amount of labor — long dizzy days at the tinny lightweight Olivetti — to link herself to him" (20). This is matched by the equally ironic account of Clara naked in the kitchen, preparing Ithiel's food wearing only clogs, while Ithiel, seemingly oblivious, is stretched on the bed "studying his dangerous documents (all those forbidden facts) . . . not that the deadly information affected Ithiel enough to change the expression of his straight profile" (23).

Despite the gift of the emerald ring it seems "Ithiel was not inclined to move forward" (25). While Clara contemplates their child and imagines possible Old Testament names for him or her we are told: "He didn't want to make any happy plans. He was glum with her when she said that there was a lovely country cemetery back in Indiana with big horse chestnuts all around" (26). He is also indifferent to Clara's affair with Jean-Claude and has had an affair or two of his own. What emerges in Ithiel's character is the "insignificance of the personal factor" (30). While Ithiel is lying in bed describing the weakening of the status of the individual, which he says is "probably in irreversible decline" (30), his own behavior ironically shows why. As Clara comments in a rare moment of clarity:

> He could be as remote about such judgments as if his soul were one of a dozen similar souls in a jury box, hearing evidence: to find us innocent would be nice, but guilty couldn't shock him much. She decided he was in a dangerous moral state and that it was up to her to rescue him from it. . . . You couldn't separate love from being. You could Be, even though you were alone. But in that case, you loved only yourself. If so, everybody else was a phantom, and then world politics was a shadow play. Therefore she, Clara, was the only key to politics that Ithiel was likely to find. Otherwise he might as well stop bothering his head about his grotesque game theories, ideology, treaties, and the rest of it. (30-31)

At every turn the text undercuts Clara's generous views on Ithiel's geopolitical and interpersonal skills. In fact it reveals her as a rather stereotypical racist, classist, WASP snob attracted sexually to the politically powerful man of geopolitical affairs. The very qualities she admires in him — masculine rationality and restraint — are the very qualities which prevent Ithiel from forming the human pair. Overvaluing these qualities in him and undervaluing her own feminine emotional range, Clara fails to confront the classic contradiction inherent in her own version of the male mystique. Yet she does finally accuse him of being "as frozen as his pledge" (43) and of crawling off "to [his] office hideaway" to do his "thing about Russia or Iran" (55) when he cannot face human relationships. However, as the implied author comments: "She might as well have been talking to one of those Minoans dug up by Evans or Schliemann or whoever, characters like those in the silent films, painted with eye-lengthening makeup" (55). Later, though she admits to having been somewhat deceived about the myth of the human pair, she makes him her last offer. The implied narrator reports: "Teddy was stirred, and looked aside. He wasn't ready, and perhaps never would be ready, to go farther. No, they never would be man and wife. When they stood up to go, they kissed like friends" (80).

After the apotheosis of tears, Clara still mistakenly believes that Ithiel and their love have given her the clue to her authentic self. "When he decribed me to myself in Washington, I should have taken Ithiel's word for it. . . . He knows what the big picture is — the big, *big* picture; he doesn't flatter, he's realistic and he's truthful. I do seem to have an idea who it is that's at the middle of me" (109). In fact, the reader by now severely doubts that Ithiel Regler has the big picture on anything and realizes that sans Ithiel, utility husbands, and anyone else, Clara has come to this knowledge herself. In fact it is Gina Wegman who provides the confirmation of Clara's, not Ithiel's, ability to deal with the chaos of "Gogmagogsville." Clara cannot acknowledge that through his denial of her, Ithiel has forced her to find and trust her own vision of the big picture.

Clara also contributes her share to the weakening of the personal factor in "Gogmagogsville." Though her world is rich in ethnic types, Ithiel (and she) exist in her hierarchy as the preferred type — the classic, superior Greek rationalist, white, Anglo, male, heterosexual, and empowered. Ranked beneath him are the Spontinis and Veldes, then the Gladstones, followed by the sleazy Gottschalks of the world. Gina Wegman, a European banker's daughter, can slide down and back up the scale unscathed. Oriental Mrs. Laura Wong seems to defy even Clara's categorizing, being designated simply as a New York lady. However, far beneath the WASP world of people like her and Ithiel exists a whole teeming underworld of blacks and Hispanics. Reliable domestics like Peralta and Elvia exist at the top of this subgroup, while beneath them the Caribbean Frederic exists as the highly suspect new immigrant — poor, black, sexually predatory, and dishonest. He becomes the character upon whom all Clara's worst racial suspicions center. He is the "other" to Ithiel Regler, who remains for Clara the measure of masculine intelligence, integrity, and racial superiority.

Clara is never forced to reevaluate her dishonesty in her racist hierarchizing or in not returning the insurance claim on the ring and all that these acts symbolize. Empowered as a white, protestant, executive-level professional woman raised on old-time religion and a white middle-class work ethic, Clara is immersed in the values of her class and type. Furthermore, she stubbornly clings to ancient romantic ideals embodied in the mythology of the ring, despite evidence of a shifting world. Bellow clearly intends us to see her as a "type" when he describes her as having an "ancestrally North Sea nose," being "big boned," "from the sticks," from "Indiana and Illinois farmers and small town businessmen who were very religious," and raised on "old-time religion" (1). "In her you might see suddenly a girl from a remote town, from the vestigial America of one-room schoolhouses, constables, covered-dish suppers, one of those communities bypassed by technology and urban development" (39-40). He concludes, she is a "daughter of Albion" (23). From this advantaged position, she can afford to "slum" with Clifford, now in Attica jail, while designating Hamilton, the jeweler, as one who "might have been an Armenian, passing" (17). This is the same woman who has had intimate associations with both Spontini and Giangiacomo, mafia crooks and billionaire revolutionists, and who, all by herself, has stolen a considerable sum from the insurance company. In her peculiar accounting, these colorful, global, master thieves fare better than a petty thief like Frederic, a thief of the human heart like Ithiel, or her own thieving and "utilizing" self which makes a mockery of her romantic aspirations and her ideology of the human pair.

Falsely idealizing herself and Ithiel, Clara describes him as having the "eyes of Hera in my Greek grammar" (17), as "concentrating like Jascha Heifetz" (23), as possessing "a classic level look" (17), and as possessing the power and secrecy of an operator (19). He is a classical Greek to her tenth-century Roman Catholic soul forged in the middle ages. For her "what a man is seems to be defined by Ithiel" (74-5). Clara sees them both as the "human pair" of higher types who rise above "Gogmagogsville" and its profusion of "lower" types.

Unselfconscious about her own social caste privileges and Ithiel's, she ironically identifies Wilder as a decadent, arrogant WASP. She tells Laura Wong he is "big and handsome, indolent, defiantly incompetent" (3). Correctly identifying the chauvinistic mentality that lies behind this condition, she adds,

> He's *there*, isn't he? What else do I want? In all the turbulence, he's the point of calm. . . . He's the overweening overlord, and for no other reason than sexual performance. It's stud power that makes him so confident. He's not the type to think it out. . . . But what really settles everything, according to him, is masculine bulk. (4-5)

She imagines him as "sitting in the middle of his female household like a Sioux Indian in his wickiup. Like Sitting Bull" (45). But the reader wonders what makes Wilder so very different from Ithiel or Clara in any of these respects. According to her, "Gogmagogsville" is a condition which destroys the formation of the human pair by jeopardizing the personal factor and hence preventing the proper formation of the human heart. It is full of false, unusable, dubious "Others" (usually wild and socially unintelligible ethnic types) and makes the achievement of an authentic self very hard. It requires lovers, psychiatrists, detectives like Gottschalk, numerous utility husbands, and divorces to negotiate the confusion. The only people who really qualify for the "human pair" are types like she and Ithiel.

Yet Clara cannot be taken too seriously in these respects, or as a female protagonist. She has been a silly wayward teenager whose youth is full of such matters as inappropriate lovers, sexual misdemeanors, suicide attempts, and bad judgment. She has had four "utility" husbands and a "spotted" sexual career. Furthermore, she bears close resemblance to Bellow's male protagonists. She has a "big head" like protagonists from Joseph to Uncle Benn Crader and Kenneth Trachtenberg. She is "rawboned" and big like Augie, Humboldt, and Henderson. She is an idealist and seeker of higher states of consciousness like Joseph, Artur Sammler, Charlie Citrine, Dean Corde, and Uncle Benn. And like them all, she has never given up the quest for romantic fulfillment.

However, the real problem with Clara as a credible female character is that her quest is somewhat gender unintelligible in the context of a burgeoning body of other late twentieth-century female quest texts. If we have learned anything at all about authentic female quest patterns in contemporary literature, it is that they begin in rebellion against such patriarchal mythologies and traditional styles of masculinity. Hélène Cixous notes:

> Things are starting to be written, things that will constitute a feminine Imaginary, the site, that is, of identifications of an ego no longer given over to an image defined by the masculine . . . but rather inventing forms for women on the march, or as I prefer to fantasize, "in flight," so that instead of lying down, women will go forward by leaps in search of themselves.[18]

Describing women's quest patterns in contemporary American literature, Carol Christ,[19] Rachel Blau DuPlessis,[20] Carol Pearson,[21] and many other critics outline the shape of the new female hero's transformation of the traditional male journey archetype. They note that the journey nearly always begins in rebellion against patriarchal designations of female roles and proceeds to rejecting the image of oneself as passive, negotiating the tension between autonomy and attachment, descending into the past, experiencing nothingness, going through a phase of awakening, arriving at transforming insight, and finally attaining empowerment. Along the way, self-naming rituals are common to the pattern, and the rewriting of personal history takes place. The final action is often centered around "lighting out." Hence culture, language, and uniquely female human experience are reimagined, necessitating the formation of new cultural paradigms and myths of female experience. The new territory of being that has been conquered and occupied by the newly emergent female hero is usually named and made clear to the reader. Clara is not quite recognizable within this developmental economy because she is really another of Bellow's male questers. As a male-identified rather than a self-identified person, Clara actually reifies such an ancient heterosexual mythology.

Bellow's premises for female development clearly run counter to those of many contemporary women readers and writers who expect to see women at least problematize the myth of heterosexual romance and the human pair as neither essential to, nor as the only point of, the female quest. Bellow seems to believe that faith in the human pair is the most important drive toward human love, bonding, and devotion, because on these characteristics, developed within the emotional economy of this pair, hinge the development and survival of crucial human qualities. In his relational economy, as farcical and unattainable as the myth of romance and "the human pair" is, its loss as a driving force in the human psyche results ultimately in moral collapse — the triumph of "Gogmagogsville" over what is left of a tenth-century soul and a courtly tradition of romance, i.e., civilization as we know it. For Bellow, the failure of the human pair equates with the loss of an important key to higher consciousness, albeit one his protagonists have never found. Clara's is a triumphant soul in his accounting precisely because she preserves this romantic *ethos* almost whole *despite* her failures and her Bible-belt origins. "Gogmagogsville" has not made her cynical about the type of love she has for Ithiel. Despite suicide attempts, a childhood among Indiana farmers, and "old-time" protestant American religion, not to mention the business world and four utility marriages, she is more whole in this respect than her rather pathetic male counterpart, Teddy Regler, who has recognized these profound qualities in Clara but cannot summon sufficient energy for this romantic expression of the "individual factor" because he is lured by Washington geopolitics and consulting with great men on secret documents. His, according to Bellow, is probably the worse theft because it is the theft of a potentially remarkable human heart and of the potentially remarkable "human pair."

However, even given the above concessions to Bellow's noble, if misplaced, authorial faith in the masculine romantic myth of the heterosexual pair symbolized by the emerald ring, the book fails for most readers. Clara's female development and achievements are not clear enough, her character not exceptional enough, her life too fogged over by Ithiel for too long, the achievement of an authentic sense of self too slenderly and unconvincingly bestowed, the generating circumstance of the theft of an emerald ring too ephemeral and too embedded in irony to generate mythic or metaphorical power. The depiction of lower consciousness and the failure of the human pair in "Gogmagogsville" is too thin and scattered for *A Theft* to really succeed.

Notes

1. David Denby, "Memory in America" (rev. of *The Bellarosa Connection* and *A Theft*), *New Republic* (1 Jan. 1990): 37-8. [See pp. 329-333 of this volume.]
2. John Seeyle, "The Ring and the Book" (rev. of *A Theft*), *Chicago* 38 (Apr. 1989): 101.
3. Robert Boyers, "Losing Grip on Specifics" (rev. of *A Theft*), *Times Literary Supplement* (24-30 Mar. 1989): 299-300.
4. Robert Towers, "Mystery Women" (rev. of *A Theft*), *New York Review* (27 Apr. 1989): 51.
5. Anita Brookner, "Ring of Falsehood" (rev. of *A Theft*), *The Spectator* (15 Apr. 1989): 29.
6. Tim Appelo, "Saul Bellow Turns Paperback Writer" (rev. of *A Theft*), *Savvy* (10 Apr. 1989): 24.
7. Richard Eder, "Love in Gogmagogsville" (rev. of *A Theft*), *Los Angeles Times* (19 Mar. 1989): 3.
8. Mark Feeney, "What Made Frederic Seize the Ring?" (rev. of *A Theft*), *Boston Globe* (5 Feb. 1989): 88.
9. Joyce Carol Oates, "Clara's Gift" (rev. of *A Theft*), *New York Times Book Review* (5 Mar. 1989): 3.
10. John Updike, "Books: Nice Tries" (rev. of *A Theft*), *New Yorker* (1 May 1989): 114.
11. Liela Goldman, "Revisioning Knowledge and the Curriculum: Feminist Perspectives." Conference at Michigan State University, East Lansing, May 1990.
12. Elaine Safer, "Degrees of Comic Irony in *A Theft* and *The Bellarosa Connection*," *Saul Bellow Journal* 9.2 (1990): 8.
13. Marianne Friedrich, "*A Theft*: Bellow's Clara between Anarchy and Utopia," *Saul Bellow at Seventy-five: A Collection of Critical Essays*, ed. Gerhard Bach (Tübingen: Narr, 1991), 177-88.
14. Allan Chavkin, "Bellow's *A Theft*" (rev. of *A Theft*), *Saul Bellow Journal* 8.1 (1989): 70.

15. Andrew Gordon, "It Doesn't Ring True" (rev. of *A Theft*), *Saul Bellow Journal* 9.1 (1990): 79. [See pp. 314-317 of this volume.]

16. Sybil Steinberg, "Story Behind the Book: A Conversation With Saul Bellow" (rev. of *A Theft*), *Publisher's Weekly* (3 Mar. 1989): 59-60.

17. Saul Bellow, *A Theft* (Harmondsworth: Penguin, 1989), 78. Subsequent references in the text from this edition. — In *Dangling Man*, Joseph cannot sustain higher awareness through his marriage or his desultory love affair. Asa Leventhal regains something of his marriage after his summer ordeal, but higher states of consciousness also elude him. Augie March loses Thea, eschews marriage, and is last seen committed to the impermanence of a life on the high seas. Tommy Wilhelm finds a generalized love of humanity deep in a New York subway, alone, and only when stripped of a carping offstage wife, his children, and his money. Henderson, after violence and brutality to wife, children, and housekeeper, plus an exotic sojourn in Africa, finally declares his desire to return to Lily and the kids purged of excessive wanting of higher states. But when we leave him clutching a foreign orphan self and dancing for joy on the polar ice cap, we wonder how realistic this desire is. Herzog, that much battered divorcé, is last seen dismissing a sexually interested woman and embracing the solitude of nature. Humboldt, unable to retain his beloved Kathleen and consumed by greed, ambition, and sexual jealousy, loses his bid for higher states. Charlie can only gain a brief glimpse of higher states of consciousness while standing on his head, alone, abandoned, and doing exercises in a hotel room in Spain. Sammler also misses out. He expresses hatred and mistrust for all the women in his life and embraces the monastic simplicity of bachelor's rooms, Meister Eckhardt's sermons, and the Bible. His only achievement with regard to participating in the human pair is the beginnings of social responsibility for his wavering-witted daughter and love for his dead male benefactor. Dean Corde is almost always seen alone — first in his bed in Rumania, covered by an ancient afghan, ruminating on geopolitics sans a preoccupied wife, last while driving alone along Lakeshore Drive as a minor epiphany reminds him of just how many removes from higher reality he really is. His wife also misses out. She seems much more capable of a scientific than a metaphysical reading of the night skies, and is also mired in interpersonal inadequacies. Uncle Benn Crader finds marriage contaminating and claustrophobic. Smitten with a latent misogyny, he escapes to the solace of the polar icecap among those less complicated life forms — his beloved lichens. Nephew Kenneth, the academic expert on the Russian mystics' views on love and higher states of human consciousness, cannot translate all this knowledge into the formation of a truly viable human pair either.

18. Hélène Cixous, "Castration or Decapitation?", trans. Annette Kuhn, *Signs* 7 (1981): 52.

19. Carol Christ, *Diving Deep and Surfacing: Women Writers on Spiritual Quest* (Boston: Beacon, 1980).

20. Rachel Blau DuPlessis, *Writing Beyond the Ending: Narrative Strategies of Twentieth-Century Women Writers* (Bloomington: Indiana UP, 1985).

21. Carol Pearson, *The Hero Within: Six Archetypes We Live By* (San Francisco: Harper & Row, 1986).

* * *

The Bellarosa Connection (1989)

Memory in America
David Denby

"In these democratic times, whether you are conscious of it or not, you are continually in quest of higher types." So says the narrator of Saul Bellow's new novella, *The Bellarosa Connection*. An elderly expert in memory training, a professional sorter of old impressions, the nameless narrator is at the point of taking stock of his life, his relations, his allegiances. He's engaged, therefore, in an activity close to the making of fiction, and in this business of "higher types" he probably speaks for Bellow. In his recent stories and novellas, Bellow seems eager to be impressed — to be bowled over, really — by the men and women he puts before us. He celebrates the quality that lasts — not breeding in the social sense, but what used to be called "character," something found equally in a Viennese *au pair* girl and a distant relative dying obscurely in New Jersey. Greatness in ordinary human form.

Like the gold coins once poured on the head of newly crowned czars, Bellow's praise now falls without irony on intellectuals making their way in our amiably philistine business civilization. One encounters such extraordinary examples of winged sapience as the aging, disabled, but eagle-proud art critic and aesthetic philosopher Victor Wulpy (clearly based on Harold Rosenberg), who dominates the novella "What Kind of Day Did You Have?" (included in Bellow's 1984 collection of short fiction, *Him with His Foot in His Mouth*). And in the same collection (it is one of Bellow's best books) appears the fierce young Chicago-born Zetland (a.k.a. Isaac Rosenfeld), writer and bohemian, devouring Melville in darkened, cavelike apartments. Unlike Henderson or Herzog or Citrine, these men are never foolish in their spiritual striving.

Generosity in brilliant old men is sufficiently rare that one wonders: Is this longing for human distinction in Bellow's late fiction a

From *New Republic* (1 Jan. 1990): 37-40.

needed comfort, an extra log on the fire as the day grows colder and turns into night? Has there been a softening of his gaze? And does his giving vein have any necessary connection with the form of these long stories? These fictions are not concise and fiercely organized, like *Seize the Day* or some of the shorter pieces in *Mosby's Memoirs*, but contemplative and digressive, spilling over with lists and categories and ideas, a sort of roiled Whitmanesque landscape of the American mind.

I hasten to add that women, highly intelligent though not exactly intellectuals, come in for their share of the tumbling gold. This is a new turn for Bellow, and sometimes he's not quite in control of the shower of praise. The novella *A Theft* nearly founders under the weight of Bellow's heaped-up encomiums of his heroine Clara Velde. A bustling, worldly figure, Clara works as a fashion-magazine executive and lives on Park Avenue with her fourth husband. For more than two decades, however, she has loved the fabulous Ithiel Regler — Teddy Regler, with his "eyes from Greek mythology," who serves as globe-trotting adviser to Presidents and Shahs, an original deep thinker who has the ability to put the big picture together. A bit of a hyped article, this Teddy. He comes off as half talk-show guest, half Richard Goodwin's fantasy for himself.

As for Clara, she is handsome and blond, and her big-boned body is topped with a capacious noggin — she "needed that [big] head; a mind like hers demanded space." Born back-country in the Midwest and raised on the Bible, she now exudes smarts and taste ("She bought her clothes in the best shops and was knowledgeable about cosmetics"). Yet somehow she's romantic and impulsive too, a woman driven by loyalty and honor. Bellow compares her to a medieval heroine, to a Renaissance heroine — he keeps upping the ante.

Clara recognizes a fellow woman of honor in her *au pair* girl Gina, an amazingly self-possessed Viennese slumming in New York. Gina's disreputable Haitian boyfriend steals a ring that Teddy Regler had given Clara years earlier, and Clara's nobility expands in many remarkable acts of trust. Despite much descriptive energy and charm, the tale strains one's patience. Bellow resorts to such awkward narrative devices as a Chinese-American dressmaker-confidante who gets to hear Clara's racy and intimate speculations. He displays an alarmingly smooth knowingness about the details of Park Avenue domestic management. The book might have been written by a social secretary of remarkable, and remarkably obsequious, observational powers; Bellow's eager new sophistication fits badly with the highfalutin, morally strenuous tone of the exchanges between Clara and Gina.

The restricted, even smug, social circumstances of the story, moreover, reveal the limits of his generosity, which is reserved for a small circle of cultivated whites, while servants and menacing outsiders of varying hues hover in the background. *A Theft* is a rare case of class boundaries limiting Bellow's consciousness. Though witty from one sentence to the next, the tale lacks humor and proportion, and suffers overall from an atmosphere of strained triviality. The irony of a noble character triumphing in such worldly and gilded circumstances doesn't come through with any force. Clara has clearly been oversold; we're in danger, much of the time, of not caring about her, big head and all.

But no such troubles should mar anyone's enjoyment of *The Bella-rosa Connection*, a seriously funny *jeu d'esprit* of Bellow's old age. The narrator is a masterful man — the millionaire founder of the Mnemosyne Institute of Philadelphia, which trains businessmen and statesmen in memory use. A retired widower, long cut off from his New Jersey roots, he roams around his 20-room Main Line mansion, both flattered and oppressed by his own powers. He may long to "forget about remembering," but he knows that the only retirement from memory is death. In himself, he is not a memorable or lovable Bellow character. Highly intelligent, he's neutral in temperament, disconnected from life, the practitioner of a hollow craft (brute memorization) that leaves him vulnerable to emotions drifting below the level of conscious recall. But this time Bellow is in control. He plants a small bomb beneath the surface of the narrator's suave self-sufficiency.

Plagued by a sense of isolation, the narrator recalls his strong-souled New Jersey relatives Harry and Sorella Fonstein, whom he hasn't seen in years. He has allowed this connection with the admirable but unfashionable Fonsteins to lapse in part because he can remember them so well; memory has substituted for experience. He also let it lapse because the Fonsteins were something of a threat. As a youth, the narrator's own father had compared him unfavorably to Fonstein, a "gimpy Galitzianer" — he has a bum foot and wears an orthopedic shoe — who had fled from Hitler, suffered, and survived. While the memory expert and nascent millionaire, then a languid American Jew, was living in bohemian indolence in Greenwich Village, Fonstein made his way to America and became a rich man himself, largely due to the entrepreneurial skill of his wife, Sorella.

It is Sorella in her lifelong struggle for her husband's dignity who receives Bellow's extraordinary appreciation — all the more extraordinary for being grounded so firmly in sexual disgust. The narrator's first impression of her borders on the ludicrous:

> Sorella Fonstein sometimes sat on the sofa, which had a transparent zippered plastic cover. Sorella was a New Jersey girl — correction: lady. She was very heavy and she wore makeup. Her cheeks were downy. Her hair was done up in a beehive. A pince-nez, highly unusual, a deliberate disguise, gave her a theatrical air. She was still a novice then, trying on these props. Her aim was to achieve an authoritative, declarative manner. However, she was no fool.

Bellow's short sentences, however tough and definitive, never turn into a form of appropriation. He's not omnivorous, like Updike; the surfaces of whatever he's describing remain hard, resistant, rooted in the world, sitting on zippered plastic. He comes at the object in a rush, slyly generous, so eager to be impressed, and makes a quick, darting pass. Then he comes back and makes another pass. The method is accumulative, the perceptions renewed, revised, restated, reaffirmed. The narrator fixes Sorella in his mind at different stages of her life, and she grows, in all her dismaying bulk and pretension, into an increasingly bold and dignified figure. Sorella "made you look twice at a doorway. When she came to it, she filled the space like a freighter in a canal lock." Yet this cargo vessel made a good marriage, converted humiliation into strength. Rather than being a "merely square fat lady from the dark night of petty-bourgeois New Jersey," she was, in fact, "a spirited woman, at home with ideas." So armed, Sorella goes into battle for her husband.

The central anecdote of the story, one of Bellow's funniest ideas, seems far-fetched at first, but its eccentricity yields a surprising richness of thematic association. Having fled from Poland to Italy at the outbreak of the war, Fonstein was arrested by the fascist police and was about to be turned over to the S.S.; whereupon he was freed from an Italian prison by none other than Billy Rose. Billy Rose, the producer? Yes, the very same: Broadway Billy, husband of Fanny Brice, stager of pageants and patriotic Aquacades, art collector, Jewish entrepreneur and sexual fool, with a talent for humiliation at the hands of giggling chorus girls. Billy Rose had used his money and his mob connections in Italy to save a number of Jews. Italians working for him announced that they were coming from "Bellarosa."

After spending the remainder of the war in Cuba, Fonstein entered the United States, married Sorella, and for years tried to express his gratitude to Billy. Rose, however, refused to see him or acknowledge him in any way. But Sorella, who talks of the Holocaust constantly (oppressing the narrator with her knowledge), will not accept Billy's decision. The drama of the story, and nothing less than the situation of the Jews in America, unfolds from Billy's inexplicable stubbornness.

Portraiture in Bellow's work is always witty, a natural exercise of the muscular vivacity of his mind. He cannot write a dull or humorless account of any human being, and his description of Billy — an up-from-the-gutter Jewish boy observed by another Jewish boy with unillusioned wonder — turns into a dramatic debate between disgust and amazement:

> There was a penny-arcade jingle about Billy, the popping of shooting galleries, the weak human cry of the Times Square geckos, the lizard gaze of sideshow freaks. To see him as he was, you have to place him against the whitewash glare of Broadway in the wee hours. But even such places have their grandees — people whose defects can be converted to seed money for enterprises. There's nothing in this country that you can't sell, nothing too weird to bring to market and found a fortune on. And once you got as much major real estate as Billy had, then it didn't matter that

you were one of the human deer that came uptown from the Lower East Side to graze on greasy sandwich papers. Billy? Well, Billy had bluffed out mad giants like Robert Moses. He bought the Ziegfeld building for peanuts. He installed Eleanor Holm in a mansion and hung the walls with masterpieces.

Only an American could have written this extraordinary passage, and perhaps only Americans can understand it. Bellow goes well past the amused distaste of a cultivated Jew who doesn't need to be awed by Billy Rose's money. Billy, as Bellow develops the character, may be nasty, self-justifying, greedy, vain, dishonest, status-obsessed — a worm. And yet, and yet . . . Big money and big success can never be entirely ludicrous. Or *merely* ludicrous. The passage expresses a rueful acceptance of the vitality and the power of vulgarity.

Like God leading Israel out of Egypt, Billy committed an act of rescue. But then, eager to escape the "Jewish blues," he turned away from the objects of his beneficence; he escapes into deals, publicity, an art collection, women. He's the assimilated American Jew as clown, a shrewd man nevertheless driven to humble himself before slender, Palmolive chorus girls who undress for him and then taunt his "unheroic privates." This man seeking humiliation wouldn't dream of sitting down for ten minutes with a fellow Jew. According to the celebrity caste system Billy lives by, Fonstein is an untouchable. Anyway, having received help once, Fonstein might ask for it again. He might think he had a claim to it.

The elements of the Billy Rose rescue operation are concocted, I assume, out of rumor and hearsay enlarged by ironic fantasy. In any case, the reality of these events is not at issue, only their value as American myth. What could Billy's decision mean? And why pursue him to change it? Of all possible failures of the spirit, the refusal to accept gratitude hardly seems one of the worst. Bellow doesn't spell out the significance of it, but Sorella's solemn persistence points the way. A man who refuses gratitude won't acknowledge a bond with another human being — as if having given someone something, you've soiled your hands on him, and he's become a lesser being forever. To a woman of such outsized pride, the slight is repellent in its implications.

At the peak of her audacity, Sorella threatens to blackmail Billy into meeting her husband by dangling before him some compromising journals that have fallen into her possession, journals that form a record of Billy's sexual activities and business dealings, his humiliations and defeats. This time his refusal attains the level of outraged principle. "Even a geek," he exclaims, "has his human rights." Thus speaks democratic man. But there's some grandeur in his stubbornness. What famous man would not lose heart at the thought of *that* kind of public exposure?

The comedy of *The Bellarosa Connection* is generated precisely by its improbability, the forced yoking of this extreme of American-Jewish shallowness with a woman so powerfully representing the moral sorrows of the ages. One wonders, however, if Bellow hasn't forced himself to suppress all criticism of his heroine. Blackmail, even blackmail of a worm, is a low and desperate act, a use of memory as vengeance. Yet Bellow speaks only of Sorella's courage and resourcefulness. In other ways, it is a familiar face-off, another of Bellow's confrontations between intellectuals and gangsters, between mind and will (with the latter usually gaining the advantage). In this case, each Jew is a negation of the other. The struggle, as the narrator remembers it, ends in victory for Billy. Refused again, the Fonsteins disappear into the rest of their lives.

In his recent short fiction, Bellow has perfected a method of narrative suspension in which an entire life is encompassed, through expansion and digression, in a day or two of time. He packs the richness and the jostling philosophical ambition of a novel into these stories. In "What Kind of Day Did You Have?" Victor Wulpy, shaken by loneliness, summons his lovable bourgeois mistress Katrina Wolliger, who lives in Chicago, to meet him in Buffalo, so that she can fly back with him to Chicago, where he has to give a lecture to some corporate executives. Together they endure a bruising, jangled American travel day, filled with odd encounters and fragmentary conversations in airplanes, hotels, bars, and restaurants. Arrogant Victor is nearing the end, but there's no dying fall here; his life, despite all its physical difficulties, continues at its long-sustained zenith. Victor suffers a spasm of loneliness, but not of weakness. The story overflows with an emotion scarcely imaginable in our clownishly self-deprecatory media society: true intellectual pride.

Bellow's habits of suspension almost enforce prolonged savoring of "higher types" (and higher lower types, like Billy). In *The Bellarosa Connection*, the narrator's pleasure in telling the strange story is part of the engaging sideways movement of the piece. He keeps coming back to the oddity of his material, recasting it, turning it this way and that. The failure of the Fonstein-Billy connection, it turns out, is an intensified version of the generally botched or broken connections among Jews in America. In "Cousins" (also from *Him with His Foot in His Mouth*), Bellow's narrator announces, "I absolutely agree with Hegel (lectures at Jena, 1806) that the whole mass of ideas that have been current until now, 'the very bonds of the world,' are dissolving and collapsing like a vision in a dream." Hegel undoubtedly meant the end of feudal and religious bonds, but Bellow stretches it to include the dissolution of sustained relations, the development in its place of the awful American isolation ("individualism"). More is at fault than inadequate sociability: America drives people apart and makes them trivial, too. "The pursuit of loneliness," as Philip Slater called it.

In *The Bellarosa Connection*, the Old World Jews (and Sorella, generically, is one of them), brought up in grief, can never give up their obsession with dignity and obligation, while the New World Jews are moving too fast to allow themselves to be hindered by any claims at all. The memory expert and his Philadelphia-socialite wife found the Fonsteins depressing; Sorella's harping on the details of the Holocaust implanted information that would remain in the narrator's memory for life. He doesn't want to hear this stuff, any more than does Billy Rose, whom Bellow associates with George Washington, the American Adam himself, advising against "entangling alliances." The narrator drops the Fonsteins, and when he tries to find them years later, he discovers that other mutual relatives have also lost track of them.

Depressed, he has a nightmare that reveals to him the tenuousness of civilized life. As a protected American, he could not understand, as the Fonsteins certainly did, the inescapable nature of merciless brutality. Yet he can't discuss this with anyone but *them*. A fitting punishment. He is not, it turns out, like a novelist. A professional of recall, he has developed methods of retrieving information in functional, neutral chains; he has divorced memory from meaning, never understanding (until it is too late) the purpose of memory. The end of his life is haunted by this woman whose memories never escape meaning.

The final pages are a little rushed; the ironies are jammed together too harshly. But this eccentric story has a surprising force. Earlier Sorella had said, "The Jews could survive everything that Europe threw at them. I mean the lucky remnant. But now comes the next test — America. Can they hold their ground, or will the U.S.A. be too much for them?" The answer, in this story at least, is yes, it's too much. Realizing too late the meaning of his recollections of the Fonsteins, the memory expert asks God to remember them.

Several critics have suggested that Bellow's last two novels, *The Dean's December* and *More Die of Heartbreak*, have marked a falling off in his old age. *The Bellarosa Connection*, however, is a classic Bellow story. The rush of short declarative sentences — thought-tormented yet exuberant — produces a familiar excitement. Reading Bellow, one feels that he is writing at peril, as if he were going so hard and so fast that he would fly off the curve of his own momentum. At times, I have stopped myself from reading, anxiously wondering if he can possibly sustain the breakneck tempo. His mind is utterly exposed — there's no syntactical padding, none of the gracious furniture, the turnings, pauses, strategically placed pit stops for rest and regeneration shrewdly planted in a beautifully written long sentence.

A long sentence connects the world. Short sentences, normally, break it up. But such is Bellow's power for consecutive and multifaceted representation that he gives us a greater sense that the world is still *there* than anyone writing fiction in America. My question about age softening Bellow's responses to character now seems demeaning. He is generous because he is naive enough to write stories as if the world had some solidity, as if the words used to describe it still had some reference to courage and betrayal and the inescapable burden of human obligation. He remains an unfashionable great writer, a maximalist.

*   *   *

Memory and the Holocaust:
Mr. Sammler's Planet and *The Bellarosa Connection*
Regine Rosenthal

In his 1964 novel *Herzog*, Saul Bellow has chosen a protagonist who, faced by a personal and professional crisis in mid-life, is finally able to overcome these difficulties by having recourse to the deeply ingrained memories of his early years. Moses Herzog, the esteemed intellectual of Russian Jewish immigrant descent, is saved by his passion for reminiscence — that is, by finding in his Jewish upbringing the stabilizing, affirmative force and the humanity he badly needs in order to survive as a *mensch* in the midst of personal chaos and against assimilationist tendencies. For this reason, some critics have labeled *Herzog* Bellow's "most Jewish novel."[1]

The same epithet, however, has also been applied to Bellow's subsequent novel, *Mr. Sammler's Planet* (1970) for very different reasons.[2] Here again, Bellow has chosen a Jewish intellectual protagonist for whom memory plays a crucial role, not so much for its redeeming and supportive qualities as for its darker and haunting aspects: Mr. Sammler is a survivor of the Holocaust, a Polish-Jewish refugee from Cracow who was brought by his nephew from a German DP camp to the United States some twenty years ago. So the questions that arise about Mr. Sammler are: in what way and to what degree has the experience he has gone through affected him and in what way does memory play a role in Sammler's perception of himself and the world around him?

Two decades later, in *The Bellarosa Connection* (1989), Bellow has again chosen a protagonist who is a victim of the Holocaust. But here the emphasis has shifted away from the European survivor, Harry Fonstein, towards American Jewry, towards the ambiguity of Fonstein's benefactor, Billy Rose, and that of the narrator, a successful businessman in contemporary America. Thus the questions that arise are: what role does memory play in the New World? What about those Jews who were not immediately exposed to the atrocities committed in Europe? While Mr. Sammler, though deeply troubled by his past, eventually learns to turn his experience into one that adds to his own humanity, the significance of memory in *The Bellarosa Connection* has changed. Under the influence of the New World, the life-giving force has been replaced by an escape from memory, by a refusal to lead a humanly meaningful life.

From *Saul Bellow at Seventy-five: A Collection of Critical Essays*, ed. Gerhard Bach (Tübingen: Narr, 1991), 81-92.

In Cynthia Ozick's 1983 story "Rosa," the female protagonist Rosa Lublin, survivor of a concentration camp and present-day citizen of Miami, Florida, has her own theory about the problem of surviving. She explains to a recent acquaintance:

> "My niece Stella . . . says that in America cats have nine lives, but we [the survivors] — we're less than cats, so we got three. The life before, the life during, the life after. . . . The life after is now. The life before is our *real* life, at home, where we was born." "And during?" "This was Hitler. . . . For me there's one time only; there's no after. . . . Before is a dream. After is a joke. Only during stays. And to call it a life is a lie."[3]

Obviously, Rosa has been so severely affected by what she has lived through that her ability to adjust to a "normal" life in the present is deeply disturbed.

Bruno Bettelheim, psychoanalyst, child psychologist, and a former concentration camp prisoner himself, has dealt in much of his research with the psychology of extreme situations. Based on his own observations he differentiates three reaction patterns to extreme traumatization in the survivors. Those in the first group allow themselves to be destroyed by their experience. Like Rosa Lublin, at least in the beginning of Ozick's story, these individuals have lost all hope to reintegrate their shattered personalities. Survivors of the second group refuse to acknowledge any lasting effect of the event on their lives; they are marked by repression and denial. Only survivors of the third group are willing to face in a life-long struggle the extreme situation they have lived through and to turn it, if possible, into a positive experience.[4] This level of experience can be achieved, however, only if memories are allowed to surface and to be worked through. Primo Levi, author and survivor of Auschwitz, states in his essay "The Memory of the Offense" that

> the memory of a trauma suffered or inflicted is itself traumatic because recalling it is painful or at least disturbing. A person who has been wounded tends to block out the memory so as not to renew the pain; the person who has inflicted the wound pushes the memory deep down, to be rid of it, to alleviate the feeling of guilt.[5]

Mr. Sammler, as a survivor of the Holocaust, is perfectly aware of the abnormality of his own experience. He does not trust his own judgments because his "lot has been extreme" and "one cannot come out intact."[6] But does he also try to protect himself from the assault of incriminating memories by not even acknowledging their existence? To which of Bettelheim's groups of survivors does he belong? How does he deal with this immediate past, the twenty-two years following the nightmare, and what exactly did happen to him during the war years?

The events of the novel unravel from Mr. Sammler's perspective. The present and the past are mirrored in him as a focal point and third-person reflector. Most of what the reader learns about Sammler's current life in New York and his former experience in Europe is filtered through Sammler as the center of consciousness; it is dominated by his vision. At the same time, however, seeing or the supposed inability to see, which is one of the controlling metaphors of the book, is focalized in Sammler himself. Already at the very beginning, the reader learns about Sammler's "vision": "He had only one good eye. The left distinguished only light and shade. But the good eye was dark-bright, full of observation" (4). And Sammler's nephew Wallace expands on the implications of this physical defect when asking: "Of course . . . the world looks different to you. Literally. Because of the eyes. How well do you see?" (187)

Mr. Sammler, alternately referred to as "half blind" (13) and "Mr. Minutely-Observant Artur Sammler" (16), is particularly revered by members of his family and friends for his vision, for his interpretation of the world based on his past and his unique experience of "the war. Holocaust. Suffering" (81). He is their guru and confessor, the detached observer whom they trust not to meddle in their affairs while giving competent advice and expert interpretation of present-day phenomena. Sammler knows that his American niece Angela "thought he was the most understanding, the most European-worldly-wise-nonprovincial-mentally-diversified-intelligent-young-in-heart of old refugees" (73). But he himself questions these very qualities: "To deserve this judgment had he perhaps extended himself a little? Hadn't he lent himself, played the game, *acted* the ripe old refugee?" (73; emphasis added).

What then does the reference to Sammler's eyes mean? Is Sammler the "one-eyed God in the land of the blind,"[7] as Gloria Cronin asserts, or is he "a seer whose perceptions are keener, more profound,"[8] as Alan Berger proposes, a notion confirmed by Alvin Rosenfeld?[9] As mentioned above, Sammler has one good eye, which he makes ample use of to observe and interpret his present-day surroundings, and one blind eye that looks inwards and backwards in time. Only by an intricate interplay of both roles — the blind wise seer and the acutely observant critic of modern society — can Sammler try to balance and overcome the limiting and limited perspective of each.

Mr. Sammler's Planet relates the events of three days in the life of the protagonist in the late 1960s in the city of New York. By way of associations and recollections, Sammler's past slowly unfolds; and only by peeling away the different layers of his memory do both Sammler and the reader gradually realize how past and present are subtly but inextricably interrelated. Similar to Rosa in Ozick's story, Sammler perceives his life to roughly fall into three distinct stages: the prewar years in Poland and England, the Holocaust in Poland, and the postwar years in the United States. In her study on the Holocaust in literature, Sidra deKoven Ezrahi recognizes these stages as typical for the literature of survival: the first she calls the collapse of the "Ancien Régime," the second is the "Descent into the 'Anus Mundi,'" and the third is "The Survivor: After Liberation."[10] How do these three layers unfold in the novel?

Sammler is fully aware that the Holocaust has been a turning point in his life, that it changed his judgments as much as it affected his eyesight. Born as a Jew in Cracow but brought up by an emancipated, almost freethinker mother who named her son Artur after the German philosopher Schopenhauer, Sammler realizes in retrospect that "the old, the original Cracow Sammler was never especially kind. . . . He and his mother had had a reputation for eccentricity, irritability in those days. Not compassionate people. Not easily pleased. Haughty" (64-65). In Cracow, as a means of freeing himself from the bonds of Jewishness of his family (80), Sammler had developed an Anglophilia, which he came to share with his later wife Antonia and which made him move to England. There in London, they took pride in their high connections; they enjoyed being accepted as Polish Jews into the intellectual circles of Bloomsbury. But the experience of the Holocaust caused Sammler to change his views, forcing him to discover that "till forty or so I was simply an Anglophile intellectual Polish Jew and person of culture — relatively useless" (306). Now, he is no longer interested in his "absurdly British" past (80) nor in writing a memoir about H. G. Wells, his one-time famous acquaintance. Instead, he now is preoccupied with recollections of the Holocaust. Reaching down deeply into the innermost core of his memory, Sammler finally lays bare the different fragments that constitute his haunting past.

One clear day in Poland in 1939, Sammler, together with his wife and scores of others, is shot and tumbles into a mass grave, after he has already been blinded in one eye by a gun butt. Miraculously, Sammler survives but has to literally dig himself out from under the corpses in order to escape. Then, towards the end of the war, Sammler has another devastating experience. Having barely escaped another massacre in Zamosht Forest, this time instigated by Polish partisans against their Jewish co-fighters, Sammler manages to keep alive by hiding in a tomb, helped along by the peacetime caretaker of the cemetery. What troubles Sammler in this situation is not so much that the caretaker is risking his life for *him* — the Jew, the living dead — as that they basically dislike each other. The ambiguity in the relationship of savior to saved, of benefactor to beneficiary, is even heightened several years later, after the war's end, when the dutifully grateful letters from Sammler meet with increasing anti-Semitism on the part of the one-time heroic helper. Having relaxed into old prejudices, the more-than-human benefactor shrinks back to petty human proportions.

The recollection of the third incidence is the most shattering one for Sammler, and also the one he suppresses the most. Relentlessly, however, it takes hold of him, triggered by bits of conversation or important events in the present. Sammler is obsessed with the memory that once, as a partisan, he shot a German at very close range despite the fact that the man was not armed and begged for his life for the sake of his children. Most haunting for Sammler in this incident is the knowledge that he did not kill the man in self-defense but for the sheer pleasure of doing it. Extreme deprivation and inhuman conditions had awakened animal instincts in him that made him dispense with pity and enjoy the ecstasy of taking a life. "He was then not entirely human" (143).

The ambiguity shown here in the relationship of victim to oppressor — the possibility that the victim turns into the opposite, into the victimizer of the former oppressor — is the most unsettling insight that stays with Sammler and keeps him preoccupied in the ensuing years. The incident uncovers another, a darker side in him, quite different from his hitherto practiced condescending British aloofness. This side craves for the intensity of being embodied both in the ecstasy of killing *and* in the deep caring and warmth of human existence.

For about ten years following the war, Sammler remains so stunned by the disturbing encounter with such unknown aspects of his being that he withdraws into himself, feels disaffected and cold, "his judgment almost blank" (121). But then, when creatureliness returns, he is overcome at times by a sudden urge to be part of extreme situations again, such as occur on his last trip to Israel as a war correspondent covering the Six-Day War. Again in retrospect, Sammler identifies his motives for going there on his "self-assigned" mission (256):

> He had gone back to 1939. He wanted to refer again to Zamosht Forest, to more basic human characteristics. When had things seemed real, true? In Poland when blinded, in Zamosht when freezing, in the tomb when hungry. So he had persuaded Elya to let him go . . . and he had renewed his familiarity with a certain sort of fact. (251)

But the impulse to face the brutal facts of life once more is counterbalanced by a need for "disinterested purity and unity" (122), by a need to forget the diverging impulses in the self and to be absorbed into a larger whole: as soon as Sammler returns from the war he goes back to "the Forty-second Street Library reading, as always, Meister Eckhardt" (256).

These contradictory forces in Sammler are clearly reflected in his relationship to two major figures in the novel. The first one, the black pickpocket, has fascinated Sammler from the very beginning. For various reasons he sees in him a mirror image of himself that comes close, as Jonathan Wilson suggests,[11] to being his double or alter ego. Sammler admires the black man for his princeliness, the animal majesty in his appearance, and the elegance of his outfit; and he assumes it is his earlier London and Cracow self that is so "foolishly eager to catch sight of a black criminal" (121). But there is a deeper reason, one he is reluctant to admit. Sammler follows the black man around craving for a repetition of the offense because the pickpocket represents Sammler's own perpetration of crime, the act of killing he once performed in Zamosht Forest as the ultimate demonstration of power that human beings exert over their fellow human beings, a power that for centuries kings have reserved as a privilege for themselves (148). Thus, the pickpocket's eventual sexual exposure also is the demonstration of power in a different guise. It, too, connects to Sammler's past and to the recollection of Schopenhauer's claim that the human will is seated and instrumentalized in the sex organs (212).

In the final showdown with the black criminal, when Eisen almost smashes the black man's skull, Sammler sympathizes with the victim because he is reminded of his own confrontation with death. But he also shrinks from the passively watching bystanders, their "ecstatic state" of waiting for gratification (292), because they call to mind his own craving for violence back in Zamosht Forest and the ambiguity of being both victimizer and victim. Thus, Sammler's encounter with the pickpocket offers indeed an enlarged, intensified vision (16, 47), not only of the world without, as Sammler assumes, but also of the life within, especially within himself.

The other side in Sammler, the craving for human warmth, is represented by his nephew Elya Gruner. The fact that Elya is dying not only reminds Sammler of his own near-death thirty years ago or of the other recollections previously mentioned, but also makes him face and eventually come to terms with his own deficiencies. While Sammler considers himself a "failure" (153), he admires Gruner for qualities he finds lacking in himself, such as "feeling, outgoingness, expressiveness, kindness, heart" (306). Elya, the East European Jew, who was looked down upon by his late German Jewish wife Hilda for these very qualities and his supposed lack of cultivation, had come to know his "assignment" or "contract," as Sammler puts it. Elya, emigrated from Europe at an early age, has never abandoned his European Jewish past. Retaining his strong family feelings, he loves to reminisce with Sammler, though Sammler is neither interested in nor very informed about their Old World relatives. Despite Elya's shady dealings with the Mafia, and despite the illegal abortions he performs, Sammler acknowledges him admiringly in his final prayer over the dead Elya: "At his best this man was much kinder than at my very best I have ever been or could ever be. . . . He did meet the terms of his contract" (316) — the contract of his humanity.

Thus, the shattering experience of the Holocaust, as much as it may have had a dehumanizing influence on Mr. Sammler, has at the same time heightened his sense of humanity in all its forms. Ready to face the haunting memories of the past, Sammler nevertheless has to do it on his own terms. Taking the stance of a detached observer, he assumes the task of the survivor who is "assigned to figure out certain things, to condense, in short views, some essence of experience" (277).

In *The Bellarosa Connection* (1989), the concept of memory is again central to structure and theme. But by choosing the literary form of a fictive autobiography, Bellow has abandoned the third-person reflector point of view in favor of a first-person narrator who, in his early seventies like Mr. Sammler, looks back on certain episodes in his life. Unlike Mr. Sammler, the nameless Jewish-American narrator is not a survivor of the Holocaust; nevertheless, he makes it his task to tell, in recollection, the remarkable story of his distant relative, Harry Fonstein, who managed to escape from wartime Poland via Italy to the United States with the help of the American Broadway celebrity Billy Rose. Embedded in this plot another major theme of the novella unfolds — a theme it again shares with *Mr. Sammler's Planet* — namely the juxtaposition and reevaluation of the European versus the American Jew in the United States today. But whereas *Mr. Sammler's Planet* is a work basically serious in tone with only occasional irony or hyperbolic characterization, *The Bellarosa Connection* is an ironic, at times ludicrous, "tall tale";[12] its tone is set by the voice of the first-person narrator.

Due to the very personal and limited perspective of the narrator, the question soon arises about how reliable he is. What does he choose to tell and how does he relate it? Does he represent the judgment of the implied author or, as in most satirical or comic novels, is he ultimately made the butt of irony himself? How extensive is the temporal and emotional distance between the events narrated and the act of writing? What are the motives that have induced the narrator to organize his memory in such a form?

Memory is the key to understanding the narrator; it is also the basic irony underlying his stance. For though by writing down his recollections he has chosen to deal with the raw material of memory, he starts his work by declaring that he, the now-retired founder of the Mnemosyne Institute, would like, at last, to "*forget* about remembering."[13] Memory has been the basis of his worldly success, but the recollections which are his source of income are just "so much useless information" (34). "Memory is life" (2), he used to tell his clients; but this motto stands in clear contrast to the second major tenet of the Mnemosyne System, namely, to teach the mind to go blank, to will oneself to think nothing. As a final irony it turns out that the narrator values memory even more highly than any *actual* human relationship. He claims that he no longer needs to see his "much-appreciated in-absentia friends" (72), the Fonsteins, because even after thirty years of separation he can remember them so well.

The narrator writes his account at the end of a profitable memory-based business career of some forty years' duration. His success has enabled him, the child of Russian Jewish immigrants from New Jersey, to escape from his humble beginnings and to move on to Philadelphia, a WASP wife, and a mansion with a thirty-foot ceiling. Now that he has arrived in mainstream America, he starts feeling overpowered by the paraphernalia of his success; and the writing of the record for him is, in a way, a retreat into "emotional memory" (3), into recollections that are quite different from the money-making memory which has permitted him to rise in the world. On the other hand, only the assurance of being integrated into mainstream America allows him to acknowledge at last his hitherto suppressed immigrant Jewish background, while the success of his business career, a career strictly oriented towards recording and recalling facts, sets him free to turn towards recollections of a more personal, affective nature.

It had been the power of emotional memory that first attracted him to Harry Fonstein. Early on in their acquaintance, the narrator had detected a "tenacious memory" (31) in Harry that stood out favorably against the rote, mechanical recollections of his Mnemosyne clients. It attested to Harry's emotional involvement in and preoccupation with his past, to his rootedness in personal and world history. But despite a certain admiration for Fonstein — the reserved, well-bred, intelligent, noble, but tough European Jew — the narrator has never been able to really relate to him. He feels much closer to Sorella, Fonstein's remarkable wife, not only due to her New Jersey upbringing but also for her admirable business skills and her dynamic commitment to her husband. The narrator comes to see her with growing appreciation as the link between the Europe Fonstein represents and the business America of Billy Rose. Even after Fonstein has given up on making contact with his benefactor Billy Rose, Sorella cannot and will not forget. She plunges into studies of the atrocities of European history and the Holocaust to better understand her husband and his recollections of the past. In allusion to her enormous body size, the narrator even stylizes her, in a ludicrously inappropriate notion, into a monument to and living incorporation of the suffering of the European Jews: "Maybe Sorella was trying to incorporate in fatty tissue some portion of what he [Harry] had lost — members of his family" (48).

Unlike *Mr. Sammler's Planet*, *The Bellarosa Connection* does not unmask haunting memories of the protagonist's past but focuses on another aspect of survival — namely, on the relationship between victim and benefactor. While this bond was already depicted as a very tenuous and ambiguous one in *Mr. Sammler's Planet*, it turns even more ambiguous and ironic in *The Bellarosa Connection*, in which Harry Fonstein, rescued from Mussolini's Italy by a certain Bellarosa, years later identifies that person as the "famous, indefatigably vulgar and flamboyant Broadway producer"[14] Billy Rose, who had organized and funded — Mafia- or rather "Hollywood-style" (28) — an underground network for saving European Jews in Italy from destruction. But this ambiguity in the relationship between Fonstein and Rose is largely lost on the narrator. For the past forty years, since he first met Harry, he has failed to understand the implications of Harry's story, and the realization of his basic shortcoming has come to him only two nights ago in a dream. He has failed to comprehend all these years, because he, as an American, though a Jew, could not relate to the suffering of the European Jews. Having been brought up in and exposed to a completely different experience, the narrator interprets Harry's story within his own frame of reference as a Hollywood script of adventure and escape. "I got it in episodes, like a Hollywood serial — the Saturday thriller, featuring Harry Fonstein and Billy Rose, or Bellarosa" (11). Thus the attempt of the narrator's father, an immigrant from Russia and still part of the European experience, to teach his son a lesson, has failed. He had intended to use Harry's story of suffering as a means for straightening out his immature American son, to use Harry and the Holocaust for educational purposes.

Even when Billy Rose's deficiencies as savior and benefactor of Harry Fonstein become more obvious the narrator does not grasp the underlying human problem. When Sorella explains to him that Harry, out of a sense of moral obligation, had tried innumerable times to personally convey his thanks to Billy Rose but was never granted access to him, the narrator's uncomprehending comment is: "I break my head trying to understand why it's so important for Fonstein. He's been turned down? So he's been turned down" (22). And his mental advice to Fonstein is: "Forget it. Go American. Work at your business" (29). Even ten years later when Billy Rose, the epitome of American qualities, continues to absolutely refuse any emotional involvement in or obligation towards the Jews rescued by him and consequently turns down, once and for all, Sorella's threatening entreaty for a meeting with Harry, the narrator sides with Billy Rose. For him it is obvious why Rose wants to be spared entanglements and relationships with his beneficiaries, and he cannot fathom why Sorella is still out for some "closure" in Harry's life and insists on this meeting. But the ultimate implication of Sorella's comments on the cataclysmic scene is revealed to the narrator in that fateful dream when it suddenly dawns on him what Sorella has known all along: there has always existed a basic similarity of character between business- and success-oriented Billy Rose and himself.

> Yes, she was talking of me and also of Billy Rose. For Fonstein was Fonstein — he was Mitteleuropa. I, on the other hand, was from the Eastern Seaboard — born in New Jersey, educated at Washington Square College, a big mnemonic success in Philadelphia. I was a Jew of an entirely different breed. And therefore (yes, go on, you can't avoid it now) closer to Billy Rose and his rescue operation, the personal underground inspired by . . . the Hollywood of Leslie Howard. . . . There was no way, therefore, in which I could grasp the real facts in the case of Fonstein. I hadn't understood *Fonstein v. Rose*, and I badly wanted to say this to Harry and Sorella. You pay a price for being a child of the New World. (89)

Despite this momentous insight, the narrator proves unable to face the consequences. Refusing to confront any unfamiliar demands on himself, his immediate reaction to the revelation is to apply the amnesiac technique of the Mnemosyne System — namely, to shut out all unpleasant thoughts and unbearable imaginations. Thus, quite ironically, his recognition of a basic failing in himself does not induce him to change but to get wrapped up in it even more.

Linked to the recognition of a similarity to Billy Rose is the realization that he had always shielded himself against any serious consideration of the Holocaust and human brutality. He "didn't want to think of the history and psychology of these abominations, death chambers and furnaces" (29) and even now he rejects all disagreeable awareness by willing himself to think nothing, to regain and maintain peace of mind by forgetting. The lack of human depth and understanding in the narrator is evidenced once more in the long telephone conversation with the Fonsteins' house-sitter. Here the narrator fails to grasp that the accusation leveled against Americans in general applies to him in particular — namely, that for thirty years he had worked up an *imaginary* affection for the Fonsteins that would not stand the test of a real encounter. He finally discloses his deficient humanity when he confesses the true motives for writing the memoir. Afraid of aging and thereby losing his memory — for so long the basis of his business life — he writes down, with the accustomed "Mnemosyne flourish" (102), the story of Harry Fonstein and Billy Rose, not so much, as he maintained before, as an exercise in emotional memory, but as a check on the vitality of his own mental powers: "So, too, my recollection of *Fonstein v. Rose* is in part a test of memory, and also a more general investigation of the same, for if you go back to the assertion that memory is life and forgetting death . . . , I have established at the very least that I am able to keep up my struggle for existence" (72).

When we consider *Mr. Sammler's Planet* and *The Bellarosa Connection* as companion pieces covering largely the same thematic ground, it is evident that, with the passage of almost twenty years, Bellow's emphasis has changed. Whereas the former novel focused, particularly in the person of Artur Sammler, on the subject of Jewish survivors of the Holocaust, their problems of reintegration into everyday life and, more specifically, their confrontation with American society and American Jewry in the late sixties, *The Bellarosa Connection* has shifted away from the immediate victims towards their benefactors, families, and descendants in present-day America.

Sorella's uneasy question of whether the Jews who survived the hardships of Europe will survive the test of America is full of foreboding. "You pay a price for being a child of the New World" (89), the narrator realizes, and this price seems to be inevitable and high. The "unfortunate thinness of purely human themes" (76), which he had observed in Billy Rose, is paralleled by Gilbert, Harry and Sorella's American offspring, a prodigy in mathematics who had developed into "one of those science freaks with minimal human motivation" (99). It is, after all, when rushing to the rescue of their American son that Harry and Sorella are killed in a car accident.

Addressing again in *The Bellarosa Connection* the question of memory and the need and obligation to remember, Bellow identifies both Billy Rose and the narrator as deficient in this respect. In their inability to relate to the demands of contemporary life, they represent two alternatives of escape: Billy Rose refuses to remember the only memorable act in his life, thus illustrating Bellow's intimation "that the modern variant of a death sentence is the option to forget";[15] and the narrator builds his existence around a kind of memory that ultimately proves to be empty, devoid of any human meaning. This is also a telling reason why he is denied the individuality of a defining name. He remains anonymous throughout the novella, a fate which suggests that he stands for innumerable other Americans of his own and the next generations who fail to connect for lack of any substantial tie to the past. Thus, the memory of suffering with its ultimately humanizing influence on the European survivors is increasingly threatened in contemporary America by a pervasive flight from memory. The refusal to accept the obligations of memory is a decision against a humanly meaningful life; it is to choose death.

Notes

1. Liela H. Goldman, *Saul Bellow's Moral Vision: A Critical Study of the Jewish Experience* (New York: Irvington, 1983), 115.
2. Hana Wirth-Nesher and Andrea Cohen Malamut, "Jewish and Human Survival on Bellow's Planet," *Modern Fiction Studies* 25 (1979): 59. See also Alan L. Berger, *Crisis and Covenant: The Holocaust in American Jewish Fiction* (Albany: SUNY P, 1985), 96.
3. Cynthia Ozick, "Rosa," *The Shawl* (New York: Knopf, 1989), 57-58.
4. Bruno Bettelheim, "Trauma and Reintegration," *Surviving and Other Essays* (New York: Vintage, 1980), 19-37.
5. Primo Levi, "The Memory of the Offense," *The Drowned and the Saved*, trans. Raymond Rosenthal (New York: Vintage International, 1989), 24.
6. Saul Bellow, *Mr. Sammler's Planet* (New York: Viking, 1970), 233. Subsequent references in the text from this edition.
7. Gloria Cronin, "Holy War against the Moderns: Saul Bellow's Antimodernist Critique of Contemporary American Society," *Studies in American Jewish Literature* 8.1 (1989): 88.
8. Berger, 102.
9. Alvin Rosenfeld, *A Double Dying: Reflections on Holocaust Literature* (Bloomington: Indiana UP, 1980), 32-33.
10. Sidra deKoven Ezrahi, *By Words Alone: The Holocaust in Literature* (Chicago: U of Chicago P, 1980), 67-95.
11. Jonathan Wilson, *On Bellow's Planet: Readings from the Dark Side* (London: Associated University Presses, 1985), 148-149.
12. William H. Pritchard, "Blackmailing Billy Rose," *New York Times Book Review* (1 Oct. 1989): 11.
13. Saul Bellow, *The Bellarosa Connection* (New York: Viking Penguin, 1989), 2. Subsequent references in the text from this edition.
14. Paul Gray, "A Child of the New World," *Time* (2 Oct. 1989): 88.
15. Gerhard Bach, "Saul Bellow and the Dialectic of Being Contemporary," *Saul Bellow at Seventy-five: A Collection of Critical Essays*, ed. Gerhard Bach (Tübingen: Narr, 1991), 28.

*   *   *

"Something to Remember Me By" (1990)

Something to Remember Him By?
Peter Hyland

The lack of response by reviewers to the publication in 1991 of the volume *Something to Remember Me By: Three Tales* is understandable because on the face of it this appears to be the purely commercial recycling of a characteristic but not especially notable short story that had appeared in *Esquire* in the previous year, along with two novellas (*A Theft*, *The Bellarosa Connection*) that had already been published (and widely reviewed) in 1989 as individual volumes.[1] Yet there is something special about this publication. It is not unusual for a writer to collect together in book form stories previously published in the less accessible or more ephemeral periodical medium, whether literary review or mass-circulation magazine. Nor is it unusual to reissue out-of-print works, either because they are considered important enough, or simply to squeeze a little more revenue out of them. Bellow himself recycled stories in two earlier collections, and the success of *Herzog*, and later the award of the Nobel Prize, led to the re-issue of earlier novels. This collection is different, however, since the two novellas had only been in print for two years when the volume was published, and are still readily available.

The purpose of this publication appears to be to give special significance to the title story. The use of the phrase "Three Tales" in the title of the volume suggests an equality of weight amongst the three, despite the fact that the title story is not much more than a third the length of either of the other two; and the use of "Something to Remember Me By" as title of the volume itself inevitably promotes that story over the other two. The effect is to foreground both the monumental suggestion of the phrase and the implications of the story itself. This effect is amplified because Bellow has taken the unusual step (for him) of dignifying the volume with a Foreword.

Any story is in part given meaning by its context. In his Foreword, Bellow lists various of the forces that target the modern reader and that the writer has to compete against: "automobile and pharmaceutical giants, cable TV, politicians, entertainers, academics, opinion makers, porn videos, Ninja Turtles, et cetera" (x). This, of course, is precisely parallel to the jumble of communications amongst which "Something to Remember Me By" first appeared in *Esquire*: advertisements, letters to the editor, opinion pieces, articles by politicians, articles about entertainers, reviews, et cetera. In that context the story is a disposable object, read on a train or in a restaurant or during a TV commercial break: an object that belies its own title. Recontextualized as the title story in a volume published simultaneously in hardcover and paperback editions, however, the story is read in a different way; that is, its significance is at least in part derived from our expectations of it.

It appears, then, that Bellow was anxious to promote this particular story, and again the reason is to be found in his Foreword. Here, Bellow seems to be dismissing much of his own canon. In a rationalization of his return to short forms he writes of his urge to slim down his earlier "fat" books. For this he gives contradictory reasons. The first appears to be commercial: "to write short is felt by a growing public to be a very good thing — perhaps the best" (viii). This comes from a writer who has never been much concerned with the values of the wider public, however, and he follows it with an appeal to a more traditional critical authority when he approvingly quotes the opinion of F. L. Lucas that most books would be better if they were shorter, and that they can be "most effectively shortened, not by cutting out whole chapters but by purging their sentences of useless words and paragraphs of their useless sentences" (x). "Something to Remember Me By," I would suggest, is the fat Bellow novel stripped of its "useless" words and sentences, and as such it represents a kind of self-definition, a summary of the author's career.

The story is so fully constructed of characteristic Bellow elements that it may appear to be a cliche. Like most Bellow novels it is a story of memory. Its garrulous narrator believes in his own "special destiny" (213); idea-filled and air-filled he looks back over his life for a source of meaning. Memory is thus a structuring agency through which the narrator makes himself into the protagonist. The youthful Louie shares his background with Bellow protagonists from Joseph to Benn Crader and, of course, with Bellow himself: the child of Russian-Jewish immigrants, he is sensitive, intellectual, believing in his own power to "interpret" the life of Chicago (200). He is also thrown into the rougher places of life, and, forced into educating himself, he must learn what is taught by Reality Instructors. He is thus contrasted with an older brother who is doing well materially because he has embraced "reality" and who feels contempt for Louie: "You don't understand fuck-all. You never will" (203). His fractured relationship with his father (from whom he desperately desires love) is expressed in acts of paternal violence.

The story about his younger self that the narrator decides to pass on to his son is an unlikely choice: an embarrassing incident in which the youthful Louie, hoping for an erotic adventure with a beautiful girl, found himself stripped of his clothes and pushed into farcical humiliation. But this story encapsulates the central action of novels like *Herzog*, *Humboldt's Gift* and *More Die of Heartbreak*, in which the man of serious ideas is comically betrayed by sex. The girl is a version of the bitch-beauty of the novels who sometimes strips the protagonist materially, who always strips him of his dignity, and, most significantly, who makes him compromise his intellectual work, represented here by the loss of the book-fragment, which "may have been the most serious loss of all" (205). This story of farcical loss takes on greater resonance because it is also a story of the imminent loss of a loved one. Louie's preoccupation with his dying mother is countered by his own metaphysical attempts to deny the finality of death; like Citrine, he wants to be a Houdini.

Let us return to the question of the effect of the recontextualization of Bellovian elements in this volume. Although the story gives its title to the volume, it appears last, and as we approach it we should note the effect of the dedication. We first read the title, "Something to Remember Me By," and then on the following page the dedication of the story by the writer "To my children and grandchildren." On the next page begins the story told by a narrator who later identifies himself as "Grandfather Louie." This switching of the "me" between narrator and author inevitably blurs the distinction between the two, and the valedictory gesture of "something to remember me by" seems to belong as much to Bellow as to his narrator. Consequently, whether intentionally or not, the last words of the story (and the volume) sound like Bellow's own: "I haven't left a large estate, and this is why I have written this memoir, a sort of addition to your legacy" (222). They provide a "sense of an ending," and as such re-present this story not as Bellovian cliché, but as the quintessence of Bellow.

Note

1. The volume was published simultaneously in a hardcover Viking edition and a paperback Signet edition. References here are to the Signet edition.

* * *

Choosing to Read the Text:
Saul Bellow's "Something to Remember Me By"
Brigitte Scheer-Schaezler

> *My son, this is death.*
> I chose not to read this text.
> *Herzog*

The novella, first published separately[1] and then republished in the following year together with two other stories of similar length and form,
"The Bellarosa Connection" and "A Theft,"[2] is a compendium of Bellow's themes, characters and attitudes. It truly bears his signature especially in its stance of tragicomical balance. The author always was and
still is, in his own words, "a man trying to sign his name in the last
seat of a roller-coaster,"[3] and relishing it, too. Louie, the protagonist,
an old Chicagoan of Jewish descent is making preparations for his
death. He writes down for his grown son the story of how he as a boy
of seventeen, during his mother's final days, struggled to retain
decency and dignity under absurdly adverse circumstances that were
partly of his own making.

The novella bears Bellow's dedication "To My Children and
Grandchildren"; the protagonist of the story frequently addresses his
son, referring to himself as father and grandfather so that the identification between author and main character is closer than usual even
for Bellow, whose entire work has borrowed heavily from his life. Preparing for one's "second birth"[4] and the revelations of the life to come
(221) makes the upholding of many distinctions, among them the one
between fact and fiction, quite superfluous. Here again, as in *More Die
of Heartbreak*, "the mask and the face are no longer distinguishable."[5]
The writer is a "walking memory file";[6] life is becoming a memoir,
and "memory is life."[7]

Bellow's story might be read alongside John Updike's recently
published "A Sandstone Farmhouse"[8] which is also autobiography
thinly disguised as fiction. "A Sandstone Farmhouse" is a memoir as
well, a magnificent tribute to the memory of Updike's mother with
recollections from his childhood occasioned by her death. It is something to remember *her* by. This difference of purpose highlights Bellow's objectives as a writer and is a clue to his splendid achievements
as well as his rare but characteristic failures. In "Something to Remember Me By" the old protagonist has finally chosen to read the text that
he, like Herzog, avoided as a young man and to pass on as his gift and
legacy his own "reading" of it which is contained in his manner of
telling the story. But whereas the text — "My son, this is death"[9] —
is adequately established for full legibility, the reading remains
incomplete.

The scenic background, the major and minor characters and their predicaments and attitudes all fall into place in the mosaic of Bellow's fictional territory. The narrator remembers the time of his mother's final days in Chicago in February 1933 when he was a high-school senior.[10] Because his father insisted that he should not spend his free time in the library he had to work after school, delivering flowers. On one such trip which takes him way across the city to bring flowers for the wake of a girl he becomes entangled with a prostitute who steals his clothes, taking everything including the sheepskin coat that his mother recently bought for him and even the book in his pocket that he has been reading on his long streetcar trips, leaving him nothing but his shoes. In order to be able to get home in the freezing winter weather he has to put on the only clothes he can find, a woman's boudoir jacket and soiled dress. He makes it to the next speakeasy, looking for his brother-in-law, who has an office nearby, but cannot find him. In order to obtain streetcar fare and more suitable clothing he has to agree to take a drunken man back to his apartment, which happens to be in the prostitute's street, and to cook a pork dinner — he, the Jew! — for the man's two small daughters. When he reaches home late at night after a further futile search for his book, his father hits him, wordlessly. He is grateful for the blow because it means that his mother is still alive; if she had died during his absence, his father would have embraced him instead.

For Bellow readers wintery Chicago in the early thirties is a place of panoramic proportions and symbolic significance. We can see, feel and smell this world in black and white, its uneven distribution of darkness and light, snow and soot, as a backdrop to the theme of innocence and its loss, of guilt and shame versus the higher longings of one — by his own description — uncharacteristic inhabitant. We know it as a place of tremendous power (200) from *Augie March* and *Herzog*, from the marvelous "A Silver Dish"[11] as well as from numerous interviews and autobiographical pieces, especially the recently published "Memoirs of a Bootlegger's Son."[12] It is the place for the "starting out" of the protagonist[13] where the nature of his quest first manifests itself, his "lifelong absorption in or craze for further worlds" (193):

> I refused absolutely to believe for a moment that people here were doing what they thought they were doing. Beneath the apparent life of these streets was their real life, beneath each face the real face, beneath each voice and its words the true tone and the real message. . . . I couldn't have thought it then, but I now understand that my purpose was to interpret this place. (200)

The sense of place and the character's sense of mission are inextricably linked with each other. Raw and wild Chicago becomes the testing ground for the nature of reality. Its amorphousness demands interpretation, its chaos, clarity. It posits the dualism that is the lifelong enigmatic irritant of Bellow's protagonists.[14]

Reviewing all of Bellow's works, these protagonists now parade
before us in the four ages of man, or rather in the three, as Bellow is
not given to considering babies: the adolescent as in *Augie March*, the
grown-up as in *Henderson the Rain King*, *Herzog*, *Humboldt's Gift* and
The Dean's December, and the old man as in *Mr. Sammler's Planet*.
The old man remembering his adolescence in "Something to Remember
Me By" combines the early and the late manifestations that also appear
in the essential relational conflict of Bellow's male characters, the
struggle between father and son. The father wants a life for the son that
the son rejects. Again, autobiography and fiction become interchange-
able; we get the same family drama whether we read *Seize the Day* or
Herzog, where the father even threatens to shoot the son,[15] or "Zetland,"[16] or "Memoirs of a Bootlegger's Son":

> Pa, you see, thought that I was stupid and backward. He had a biased and
> low opinion of me and he was anxious for me to take shape, and quickly.
> . . . "Do you know what you are?" he'd say full of rage. "A junk of fat
> with two eyes staring from it. . . ." He kept his eye on the main business
> of life: to provide for us and teach us our duty.[17]

Even in such confrontations of great verbal and occasionally also
physical violence as in "Something to Remember Me By" the son never
questions the right of the father and his proper intentions but confirms
the position of the father as patriarch (207). The sons may reject the
fathers' prescriptions for their lives as Bellow's fictional sons —
beginning with the early characters like Joseph in *Dangling Man*[18] and
Tommy Wilhelm in *Seize the Day*[19] — do and as he himself obviously
did but they dare not reject the father. However, the only observably
expressed love as an overpowering emotion between Bellow's fathers
and sons flows from the grown son to the old and dying father. The
adolescents and the old men seem quite incapable of it. Although the
tone of the narrator in "Something to Remember Me By" has certainly
mellowed we suspect that in his emotional capacities he still belongs
more with Sammler — Louie, after all, also describes the present as
"these low, devious days" (222) — rather than with Herzog and all his
passion and overflow of feelings. Given the narrator's position at the
end of his life, it may be too late for him to abandon the pervasive substitution of "contemplation for emotional involvement."[20]

Many readers have regretted the emotional coldness of the old
men in Bellow. In this story with the young and the old narrator types
merging, the resemblance of their emotional detachment becomes all
the more striking. One reason for the protagonists' striving for a further, higher world may be their disgust with the actual world, with its
physical manifestations, particularly with the human body and its
decay. These people are acute observers of the physical features of
others, their attention always and, it seems, often involuntarily caught
by the peculiarities of looks, sounds, smells, manner of movement.
Passages such as young Louie's perception of the drunk he takes home

from the speakeasy abound in all works: "The parboiled face, the short nose pointed sharply, the life signs in the throat, the broken look of his neck, the black hair of his belly, the short cylinder between his legs ending in a spiral of loose skin, the white shine of his shins, the tragic expression of his feet" (219).

Since the plot might very well proceed without this, such passages are all the more surprising in a story that preaches brevity and sets out to be its demonstration piece (cf. Foreword vii-xii). The boy's cruelly sharp and unrelenting observations — "I saw and I saw and I saw" (192) — in what is, of course, a splendid descriptive passage, persist in the old narrators. More than occasionally they also look at people as if they saw them for the first time.

The reader begins to wonder whether all these minutely observant gatherers[21] of unrefreshing detail, all these compulsive registrars of the antics of human behavior and the human body, do not continue to regard the world with the eyes of the young and immature in whom such detachment might be excusable as a defensive measure. The boy-child as observer[22] who is himself not yet marked by life, who sees every wrinkle and dark spot on the other's skin because his skin is smooth and white, finds his elders grotesque. They may fascinate him but he sees himself as apart from them, confirmed in his belief in a separate, "independent" fate[23] — "to make something extraordinary of yourself" (200) — or "special destiny" (213). The more intently he watches, the more aloof he remains. Octogenarian Sammler on Angela Gruner or Margotte Arkin comes to mind — the perception, the stance, and the emotional distance are very nearly the same. Is it still true from this vantage point of the approaching end that "the conditions of life make the humanity of others difficult to discern"?[24]

However, it is in this very aspect that "Something to Remember Me By" may indicate a change in perspective in the main character. The essence of the story lies in the terrifying but ultimately redeeming destruction of the notion of apartness posited as necessity by the higher forces. This is the meaning of the "vortex" (187) whose depths abruptly swallow the protagonist bent on clinging to the one-dimensional reality of the "smooth, flat, and even" "turntable" (187) of his seemingly uneventful life. The tension is between seeing the others in their human form as grotesque and the view pronounced in the book in Louie's coatpocket: "*Ours* is the most perfect form to be found on earth" (193, italics mine). The change that occurs is not merely the exchange of the "realistic" for the idealistic position, but a change towards a more inclusive perspective, a possible "change of heart,"[25] acknowledging the need for communion. This old father turns toward his son, if not with love, then at least with gentleness and kindness, thus breaking the pattern that ruled the relationship between his own father and himself. The text that the protagonist has finally chosen to read — guided by such early proddings as the message of his book —

is that in the life of a good person there can be no such thing as apartness from the human condition. The events of the story demonstrate
this to him.

These events literally put him through various impersonations that
force him to be "the other." At the outset he wants to remain detached
from his surroundings. He does not "allow" himself to think about his
mother's death (187), very much like the boy Herzog, and it is to his
credit that he cannot really abide by this resolution. When pigeons are
shot right next to him, he intends to remain the cool observer: "This
had nothing to do with me. I mention it merely because it happened. I
stepped around the blood spots and crossed into the park" (188). There
is a third and most forceful denial of the common bonds of all beings
when he inadvertently comes across the dead girl at the wake: "I hadn't
expected to find myself looking down into a coffin . . . however, this
was no death of mine" (192f.). Being the voracious reader that he is
one wonders whether he might not have encountered one of the classic
anti-texts to this in Western literature, for instance John Donne's "any
man's death diminishes me" in his *Devotions Upon Emergent Occasions* of 1723.[26] However, the vortex has opened up and as he falls,
still unkowingly, his perspective begins to change: "As if to take
another reading of the girl's plain face, I looked again into the coffin
on my way out" (193). The face of death becomes his text, and he is
on his way to studying it. It is also then that he turns to his book and is
gripped by its demands for transcendence.

However, he is not by a long way ready for the application of all
this. The prostitute on the examining table is to him "an experimental
subject" (196). In no time their roles are reversed: *he* is lying naked on
her bed. He has to put on a woman's clothes; not only that, he has to
put on strangers' clothes three times — once for each denial? — before
he has experienced all the humiliation in store for him. He has to bear
the shame of being initially mistaken for a woman and prostitute in the
speakeasy and then being ridiculed: "Your behind is bare? Now you
know how it feels to go around like a woman" (215). He even has to
play the role of woman as he is forced to escort the drunken man home
as wives usually do, put him to bed, and cook dinner for the two little
girls. He has touched bottom: "I'm into it now, up to the ears" (219).
And a little later: "This was when the measured, reassuring, sleep-
inducing turntable of days became a whirlpool, a vortex darkening
toward the bottom. I had had only the anonymous pages in the pocket
of my lost sheepskin to interpret it to me" (221). As an old man he
understands that another text, the one that Herzog initially rejects, has
also been proffered to him in the chain of events.

The course that he learns to take is revealed in the one actual
event of the story, the act of sharing his memories and his insights. In
the face of the approaching end he desires to give a gift to his son to
whom, like the narrator in "Cousins," he wishes to "transmit my sense

of life."[27] It is an action not without a certain amount of egocentrism, since he renders his memories in order that he may be remembered, thus acting not only as the remembering subject but making himself simultaneously the remembered object, an unusual feat even for Bellow, expert Mr. Memory. His gift, like Humboldt's gift, is a text that contains the essence of the teller. It is the story of his many losses — the loss of money, of time, of clothes, the loss of dignity, of identity, of innocence, the loss of a book and even of its author as the title page has been lost, the impending loss of the mother — but more importantly it is a story that reaches out towards another human being through its painfully honest self-revelation.

He is breaking the chain of oppressive silence that was between his mother and him and even more between him and his father, who in the whole remembered part of the story does not speak a single word to his son and even beats him in silent rage (222). His self-revelation is a measure of his humility, the lifting of the veil that reclusive habit and age may have thrown over him in the eyes of his son. Now he allows himself to be seen as the all-too-human being who suffers because of his foolishness and is punished for blindly giving in to his sexual urges. The father is showing himself naked, making himself into a text for his son with a clear and ultimate message: there is no need to hide one's conduct in life, there is no need for all the habitual lies he has been prone to (194, 220, 221) because the world of desire and lust with its frustrations is merely the shadow world whose plots are surface plots that only dimly reflect the real action, the deep plot, that takes place in another world "from which matter takes its orders" (201). All his embarrassing tragicomical experiences serve him to show himself as what he truly is — a survivor of many kinds of shame, communicating to his son that one can overcome the indignities of the lower life as long as one keeps striving for the higher.

Will the son understand the meaning of this testament? We may doubt it since we learn that he was bored by his father's philosophical deliberations on other occasions and that he is, according to him, "too well educated, respectably rational, to take stock in such terms" (194). The gesture that has been made across the generations may remain a one-sided affair, in spite of all the gentleness and affection that lie in the repeated personal addresses. They are, after all, not spoken person to person but remain to be read after the father's death, denying mutuality of exchange. This is not entirely without an underlying subtle justification entailed in the narrative itself. The protagonist's "change of heart" may not be as complete and as comprehensive as one might wish. Allowing all the characters in the story to pass before one's inner eye, one cannot help noticing that men and women in the old man's rendering of the young man's experiences are still not accorded the same full measure of humanity. The world of significant thought and significant action is still reserved for the men. The women enter into it

only in momentary and often distracting appearances, their comings
and goings not truly affecting the life of the men. Wisdom is passed on
from father to son; self-revelation is between them. It is quite un-
imaginable that the story might be told to a daughter or granddaughter
— think of Sammler and Shula or Elya Gruner and Angela! — and not
just because of the sexual taboo but because in Louie's patriarchal
world, this kind of information-sharing and unabashed self-revelation
would hardly be permitted across sexual lines.

The relative importance of men and women is revealed in their
physical gestures: one might say that the men are remembered as
moving, even running, whereas all the women are prone: the dead girl
in the casket, the prostitute on the examining table, Louie's girlfriend
Stephanie in his arms on the snow-covered ground of the park behind
the bushes, even the mother on her deathbed. It is the men that literally
go about the business of life; the women merely react and are impeded
in their movements like the prostitute, who is fastened to the examining
table by wires, then pulls a muscle or at least pretends she did, limps,
and does what her pimp commands. It is true that young Louie is afraid
of "failing" his mother but not enough to prevent him from pursuing
his desires. The old man's confession is indicative of a change but this
change is incomplete. He writes instead of speaking; he gives no indication of a corrected perspective on the women that peopled his world,
for one by never once mentioning his wife, the son's mother, but especially by denying his son the chance to question him about his relationship with his mother, the grandmother, and the meaning of his having
failed her. He indicates that this is an aspect of utmost importance to
him, yet he already anticipates the son's non-comprehension: "That
may mean, will mean, nothing to you, my only child, reading this
document" (222). His appeal to "the power of non-pathos" (222) has a
helpless ring to it. Wanting to give and yet withholding, he has taken
"non-pathos" too far and his compassion not far enough. We fear that
he may discover like the narrator in *The Bellarosa Connection* that
"revelations in old age can shatter everything you've put in place from
the beginning."[28] Thus the piece is and remains truly Bellovian: a text
about a text dealing with "inward transactions,"[29] a stylistically brilliant yet tragicomically limited poetics of old age designed by our foremost connoisseur of human weaknesses and confusion.

Notes

1. *Esquire* 114 (July 1990): 64-75, 78-79.
2. Saul Bellow, *Something to Remember Me By: Three Tales* (New York: Signet, 1991). Subsequent references in the text from this edition.
3. Bellow as quoted in James Atlas, "Starting Out in Chicago," *Granta* 41 (Special Issue: Biography, 1992): 59.
4. Saul Bellow, *Herzog* (New York: Viking, 1964), 259.

5. Gloria L. Cronin and Blaine H. Hall, quoting Christopher Bigsby in a review of his article "E Pluribus Unisex? Gender and Identity in the US Novel" (*Encounter*, March 1988: 54-57), "Selected Annotated Critical Bibliography for 1988," *Saul Bellow Journal* 9.2 (1990): 84.
6. Saul Bellow, *The Bellarosa Connection* (New York: Penguin, 1989), 2.
7. *The Bellarosa Connection*, 2.
8. John Updike, "A Sandstone Farmhouse," *Prize Stories 1991: The O'Henry Awards*, William Abrahams, ed. (New York: Doubleday, 1991), 367-392. I do not pretend to know whether the main incident in Bellow's novella is autobiographical or not; what matters is the near-merging of the author and his concerns with the narrator as one in a long line of similar main figures.
9. *Herzog*, 244.
10. For an understanding of the emotional situation of the main protagonists it is highly instructive to compare the mother's death in *Herzog* (242-245) with the corresponding scene in this story; note that the scene in *Herzog* is also precisely dated as January of the year in which the protagonist turns seventeen so that the account in "Something to Remember Me By" is a kind of sequel to the one in *Herzog*.
11. "A Silver Dish," *Him With His Foot in His Mouth and Other Stories* (New York: Harper and Row, 1984), 191-222. Note that in this story the question raised in the first sentence, "What do you do about death — in this case, the death of an old father?" is also answered implicitly by reminiscing, "doing a life survey" (220).
12. "Memoirs of a Bootlegger's Son," *Granta* 41 (Special Issue: Biography, 1992): 10-35. This memoir was written in 1954 but published only recently due to the efforts of James Atlas. It portrays better than any other piece the relationship of Bellow's parents.
13. See Saul Bellow, "Starting Out in Chicago," *The American Scholar* 44.1 (Winter 1974-75): 71-77; and James Atlas, "Starting Out in Chicago." Atlas reprints some of Bellow's memoir and provides a commentary as well as biographical information based on other sources.
14. Compare these passages to the following one in Bellow's first published novel, *Dangling Man* (New York: Vanguard, 1944; my quotes from the Penguin edition, Harmondsworth 1966): "There could be no doubt that these billboards, streets, tracks, houses, ugly and blind, were related to interior life" (29). The consistency of concern over five decades is truly stunning. This is also evident in the very first sentence of *Dangling Man* that contains a near-summary of "Something to Remember Me By": "There was a time when people were in the habit of addressing themselves frequently and felt no shame at making a record of their inward transactions" (7).
15. See *Herzog*, 258.
16. Saul Bellow, "Zetland: By a Character Witness," *Him With His Foot in His Mouth and Other Stories*, 167-187. In this story considerable pleasure for Bellow's readers derives from the ironic reversal of the situation: "Pa will be upset when he hears I've dropped out of Columbia" (187). My point, however, is that the son is struggling against the father "who of course disapproved" (187).

17. "Memoirs of a Bootlegger's Son," 22.
18. See especially *Dangling Man*, 103.
19. New York: Viking, 1956.
20. Elaine B. Safer, "Degrees of Comic Irony in *A Theft* and *The Bellarosa Connection*," *Saul Bellow Journal* 9.2 (1990): 5.
21. See *Mr. Sammler's Planet* (New York: Viking, 1970), 16.
22. Bellow describes himself as such an acutely observant child: "I think that when I was a very small child it wasn't only what people said, the content of what they said, so much as the look of them and their gestures, which spoke to me. That is, a nose was also a speaking member, and so were a pair of eyes. And so was the way your hair grew and the set of your ears, the condition of your teeth, the emanations of the body. All of that. Of which I seemed to have a natural grasp. . . . I couldn't help but do the kind of observation that I've always done. It wasn't entirely voluntary. . . . Baudelaire's advice: in any difficulty, recall what you were at the age of ten." Saul Bellow, "A Half Life: An Autobiography in Ideas," *Bostonia* 6 (November/December 1990): 42f.
23. *The Adventures of Augie March* (New York: Viking, 1953), 455, 482.
24. Bellow as quoted in James Atlas, "Starting Out in Chicago," 60.
25. The "change of heart" is a phrase that recurs repeatedly in Bellow, most notably in *Herzog* (211). It is the change for which Herzog sighs from the bottom of *his* vortex: "The real and essential human question is one of our employment by other human beings and their employment by us" (283).
26. The sermon known as "The Bell" also contains the famous lines "No man is an Iland, intire of it selfe" as one of several illustrations of the idea. Sir Arthur Quiller-Couch, ed. *The Oxford Book of English Prose* (Oxford: Clarendon, 1952), 171f.
27. "Cousins," *Him With His Foot in His Mouth and Other Stories*, 240.
28. *The Bellarosa Connection* (New York: Penguin, 1989), 87.
29. *Dangling Man*, 7.

* * *

A Guide to Bibliographies

The body of Bellow scholarship is immense. As of 1995, the volume of criticism on Bellow — articles, reviews, and interviews — approaches four thousand items. The major source to facilitate initial research is Gloria L. Cronin and Blaine H. Hall, *Saul Bellow: An Annotated Bibliography* (New York: Garland, 1987; an updated edition is planned for 1997). This still is the most comprehensive guide to Bellow scholarship, with thoroughly annotated listings of reviews and articles on Bellow's oeuvre — novels, short stories, plays, essays, and travelogues. The authors have continuously updated their sourcebook in the annual "Selected Annotated Critical Bibliography" published in the *Saul Bellow Journal* from 1987 onwards. The *Saul Bellow Journal*, established in 1982, publishes critical essays, interviews and reviews twice a year, and has come to be a first-rate source on current Bellow scholarship. Earlier and still useful bibliographies and checklists are: David D. Galloway, "A Saul Bellow Checklist," *The Absurd Hero in American Fiction: Updike, Styron, Bellow, Salinger* (Austin: U of Texas P, rev. ed. 1970), 220-39; Francine Lercangee, *Saul Bellow: A Bibliography of Secondary Sources* (Brussels: Center for American Studies, 1977); Marianne Nault, *Saul Bellow — His Works and His Critics: An Annotated International Bibliography* (New York: Garland, 1977); Robert G. Noreen, *Saul Bellow: A Reference Guide* (Boston: Hall, 1978); Leslie Field and John Z. Guzlowski, "Criticism of Saul Bellow: a Selected Checklist," *Modern Fiction Studies* 25.1 (1979), 149-71; B. A. Sokoloff and Mark E. Posner, *Saul Bellow: A Comprehensive Bibliography* (Belfast, ME: Bern Porter, 1985 [updates earlier lists of 1971, 1974, and 1977]). Gloria L. Cronin and Liela H. Goldman's bibliography on "Saul Bellow" for *Contemporary Authors Bibliographical Series*, vol. 1: *American Novelists* (Detroit: Gale, 1986), 83-155, includes a valuable bibliographical essay outlining the several phases of Bellow criticism up to the mid-eighties. The collection of new critical essays on *Saul Bellow and the Struggle at the Center*, edited by Eugene Hollahan (New York: AMS Press, 1995), contains an updated "Selected Saul Bellow Bibliography" by Gloria L. Cronin and Blaine H. Hall.

Index

About the Editor

GERHARD BACH is Professor at the Paedagogische Hochschule Heidelberg in Germany and Honorary Adjunct Professor at Brigham Young University in Provo, Utah. He has edited several books, and his articles have appeared in such journals as *Studies in American Jewish Literature*, *The Saul Bellow Journal*, and *American Literary Realism, 1870–1910*.

ISBN 0-313-28370-2

90000>

EAN

9 780313 283703

HARDCOVER BAR CODE